Java I/O, NIO and NIO.2

■ ■ ■

Jeff Friesen

Apress®

Java I/O, NIO and NIO.2

ISBN-13 (pbk): 978-1-4842-1566-1

ISBN-13 (electronic): 978-1-4842-1565-4

Managing Director: Welmoed Spahr
Lead Editor: Steve Anglin
Technical Reviewers: Vinay Kumar and Wallace Jackson
Editorial Board: Steve Anglin, Louise Corrigan, James T. DeWolf, Jonathan Gennick, Robert Hutchinson, Michelle Lowman, James Markham, Susan McDermott, Matthew Moodie, Jeffrey Pepper, Douglas Pundick, Ben Renow-Clarke, Gwenan Spearing, Steve Weiss
Coordinating Editor: Mark Powers
Copy Editor: Kezia Endsley
Compositor: SPi Global
Indexer: SPi Global
Artist: SPi Global

Distributed to the book trade worldwide by Springer Science+Business Media New York, 233 Spring Street, 6th Floor, New York, NY 10013. Phone 1-800-SPRINGER, fax (201) 348-4505, e-mail orders-ny@springer-sbm.com, or visit www.springeronline.com. Apress Media, LLC is a California LLC and the sole member (owner) is Springer Science + Business Media Finance Inc (SSBM Finance Inc). SSBM Finance Inc is a Delaware corporation.

For information on translations, please e-mail rights@apress.com, or visit www.apress.com.

Apress and friends of ED books may be purchased in bulk for academic, corporate, or promotional use. eBook versions and licenses are also available for most titles. For more information, reference our Special Bulk Sales–eBook Licensing web page at www.apress.com/bulk-sales.

Any source code or other supplementary materials referenced by the author in this text is available to readers at www.apress.com/9781484215661. For detailed information about how to locate your book's source code, go to www.apress.com/source-code/. Readers can also access source code at SpringerLink in the Supplementary Material section for each chapter.

To my parents.

Contents at a Glance

Contents

About the Author

Jeff Friesen is a freelance tutor and software developer with an emphasis on Java. In addition to authoring *Learn Java for Android Development* and co-authoring *Android Recipes*, Jeff has written numerous articles on Java and other technologies for JavaWorld (JavaWorld.com), InformIT (InformIT.com), Java.net and DevSource (DevSource.com). Jeff can be contacted via his website at TutorTutor.ca.

About the Technical Reviewers

Vinay Kumar is a Technology Evangelist. He has extensive experience of 8+ years in designing and implementing large scale projects in Enterprise Technologies in various consulting and system Integration Companies. His passion helped him achieve certifications in Oracle ADF, Webcenter Portal and Java/JEE. Experience and in-depth knowledge has helped him evolve into a focused domain expert and a well-known technical blogger. He loves to spend his time in mentoring and writing technical blogs, publishing white papers and maintaining a dedicated education channel at YouTube for the ADF/ Webcenter. He has experience in Java, JEE and various open stack technologies as well. Vinay has been contributing to the Java/Oracle ADF/Webcenter community by publishing 300+ technical articles at his personal blog www.techartifact.com. He was awarded an Oracle ACE in June 2014. You can follow him at @vinaykuma201 or in.linkedin.com/in/vinaykumar2.

Wallace Jackson has been writing for leading multimedia publications about his work in new media content development since the advent of Multimedia Producer Magazine nearly two decades ago. He has authored a half-dozen Android book titles for Apress, including four titles in the popular Pro Android series. Wallace received his undergraduate degree in Business Economics from the University of California at Los Angeles (UCLA) and a graduate degree in MIS Design and Implementation from the University of Southern California (USC). He is currently the CEO of Mind Taffy Design, a new media content production and digital campaign design and development agency.

Acknowledgments

I have many people to thank for assisting me in the development of this book. I especially thank Steve Anglin for asking me to write it and Mark Powers for guiding me through the writing process.

Introduction

Input/output (I/O) is not a sexy subject, but it's an important part of non-trivial applications. This book introduces you to most of Java's I/O capabilities as of Java 8 update 51.

Chapter 1 presents a broad overview of I/O in terms of Java's classic I/O, New I/O (NIO), and NIO.2 categories. You learn what each category offers in terms of its capabilities, and you also learn about concepts such as paths and Direct Memory Access.

Chapters 2 through 5 cover classic I/O APIs. You learn about the File and RandomAccessFile classes along with streams (including object serialization and externalization) and writers/readers.

Chapters 6 through 11 focus on NIO. You explore buffers, channels, selectors, regular expressions, charsets, and formatters. (Formatters were not introduced with the other NIO types in Java 1.4 because they depend on the variable arguments capability that was introduced in Java 5.)

NIO is missing several features, which were subsequently provided by NIO.2. Chapters 12 through 14 cover NIO.2's improved file system interface, asynchronous I/O, and the completion of socket channel functionality.

Each chapter ends with assorted exercises that are designed to help you master its content. Along with long answers and true/false questions, you are often confronted with programming exercises. Appendix A provides the answers and solutions.

Appendix B provides a tutorial on sockets and network interfaces. Although not directly related to classic I/O, NIO, and NIO.2, they leverage I/O capabilities and are mentioned elsewhere in this book.

> **Note**   I briefly use Java 8's lambda expression and method reference
> language features and also use Java 8's Streams API in some examples,
> but don't provide a tutorial on them. You'll need to look elsewhere for that
> knowledge.

Thanks for purchasing this book. I hope you find it helpful in understanding classic I/O, NIO, and NIO.2.

—Jeff Friesen (September 2015)

> **Note**   You can download this book's source code by pointing your web
> browser to www.apress.com/9781484215661 and clicking the Source
> Code tab followed by the Download Now link.

Part I

Getting Started with I/O

I/O Basics and APIs

Input and output (I/O) facilities are fundamental parts of operating systems along with computer languages and their libraries. All but trivial computer programs perform some kind of input and/or output operations.

Java has always supported I/O. Its initial suite of I/O APIs and related architecture are known as classic I/O. Because modern operating systems feature newer I/O paradigms, which classic I/O doesn't support, new I/O (NIO) was introduced as part of JDK 1.4 to support them. Lack of time prevented some planned NIO features from being included in this release, which led to these other NIO features being deferred to JDK 5 and JDK 7.

This chapter introduces you to classic I/O, NIO, and more NIO (NIO.2). You learn about the basic I/O features they address. Also, you receive an overview of their APIs. Subsequent chapters dig deeper into these APIs.

Classic I/O

JDK 1.0 introduced rudimentary I/O facilities for accessing the file system (to create a directory, remove a file, or perform another task), accessing file content randomly (as opposed to sequentially), and streaming byte-oriented data between sources and destinations in a sequential manner.

File System Access and the File Class

A *file system* is an operating system component that manages data storage and subsequent retrieval. Operating systems on which a Java virtual machine (JVM) runs support at least one file system. For example, Unix or

Linux combines all *mounted* (attached and prepared) disks into one virtual file system. In contrast, Windows associates a separate file system with each active disk drive.

A file system stores data in *files*, which are stored in *directories*. Its file and directory objects are accessed by specifying *paths*, which are compact maps that locate and identify file system objects. Paths are either absolute or relative:

- An *absolute path* is a path relative to the file system's *root directory*. It's expressed as the root directory symbol followed by a delimited hierarchy of directory names that ends in the target directory or file name.

- A *relative path* is a path relative to some other directory. It's expressed similarly to an absolute path but without the initial root directory symbol. In contrast, it's often prefixed with one or more delimited "`..`" character sequences, where each sequence refers to a parent directory.

Paths are specified differently depending on the operating system. For example, Unix, Linux, and Unix-like operating systems identify the root directory and delimit path components with a forward slash (/), whereas Windows uses a backslash (\) for these purposes. Consider two examples:

```
/users/username/bin
\users\username\bin
```

Each absolute path accesses the `bin` subdirectory of the `username` subdirectory of the `users` subdirectory of the root directory. The path on the first line accesses `bin` in a Unix/Linux context, whereas the path on the second line accesses this subdirectory in a Windows context.

Windows and similar operating systems can manage multiple file systems. Each file system is identified with a drive specifier such as "C:". When specifying a path without a drive specifier, the path is relative to the current file system. Otherwise, it is relative to the specified file system:

```
\users\username\bin
C:\users\username\bin
```

The first line accesses the path relative to the current file system, whereas the second line accesses the path relative to the `C:` file system.

An instance of the java.io.File class abstracts a file or directory path. This instance provides access to the file system to perform tasks on this path such as removing the underlying file or directory. The following example demonstrates this class:

```
new File("temp").mkdir();
```

The example constructs a File object initialized to the file system object temp. It then calls mkdir() on this File object to make a new directory named temp.

Chapter 2 explores the File class.

Accessing File Content via RandomAccessFile

File content can be accessed sequentially or randomly. Random access can speed up searching and sorting capabilities. An instance of the java.io.RandomAccessFile class provides random access to a file. This capability is demonstrated in the following example:

```
RandomAccessFile raf = new RandomAccessFile("employees.dat", "r");
int empIndex = 10;
raf.seek(empIndex * EMP_REC_LEN);
// Read contents of employee record.
```

In this example, file employees.dat, which is divided into fixed-length employee records where each record is EMP_REC_LEN bytes long, is being accessed. The employee record at index 10 (the first record is located at index 0) is being sought. This task is accomplished by *seeking* (setting the file pointer) to the byte location of this record's first byte, which is located at the index multiplied by the record length. The record is then accessed.

Chapter 3 explores the RandomAccessFile class.

Streaming Data via Stream Classes

Classic I/O includes streams for performing I/O operations. A *stream* is an ordered sequence of bytes of arbitrary length. Bytes flow over an *output stream* from an application to a destination and flow over an *input stream* from a source to an application. Figure 1-1 illustrates these flows.

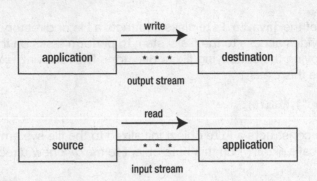

Figure 1-1. *Conceptualizing output and input streams as flows of bytes*

Java provides classes in the java.io package that identify various stream destinations for writing; for example, byte arrays and files. Java also provides classes in this package that identify various stream sources for reading. Examples include files and thread pipes.

For example, you would use FileInputStream to open an existing file and connect an input stream to it. You would then invoke various read() methods to read bytes from the file over the input stream. Lastly, you would invoke close() to close the stream and file. Consider the following example:

```
FileInputStream fis = null;
try
{
   fis = new FileInputStream("image.jpg");
   // Read bytes from file.
   int _byte;
   while ((_byte = fis.read()) != -1) // -1 signifies EOF
      ; // Process _byte in some way.
}
catch (IOException ioe)
{
   // Handle exception.
}
finally
{
   if (fis != null)
      try
      {
         fis.close();
      }
}
```

This example demonstrates the traditional way to open a file and create an input stream for reading bytes from the file. It then goes on to read the file's contents. An exception handler takes care of any thrown exceptions, which are represented by instances of the java.io.IOException class.

Whether or not an exception is thrown, the input stream and underlying file must be closed. This action takes place in the try statement's finally block. Because of the verbosity in closing the file, you can alternatively use JDK 7's try-with-resources statement to automatically close it, as follows:

```
try (FileInputStream fis = new FileInputStream("image.jpg"))
{
   // Read bytes from file.
   int _byte;
   while ((_byte = fis.read()) != -1) // -1 signifies EOF
      ; // Process _byte in some way.
}
catch (IOException ioe)
{
   // Handle exception.
}
```

I demonstrate both the traditional and try-with-resources approaches to closing files throughout subsequent chapters.

Some stream classes are used to filter other streams. For example, to improve performance, BufferedInputStream reads a block of bytes from another stream and returns bytes from its buffer until the buffer is empty, in which case it reads another block. Consider the following example:

```
try (FileInputStream fis = new FileInputStream("image.jpg");
     BufferedInputStream bis = new BufferedInputStream(fis))
{
   // Read bytes from file.
   int _byte;
   while ((_byte = bis.read()) != -1) // -1 signifies EOF
      ; // Process _byte in some way.
}
catch (IOException ioe)
{
   // Handle exception.
}
```

A file input stream that reads from the image.jpg file is created. This stream is passed to a buffered input stream constructor. Subsequent reads are performed on the buffered input stream, which calls file input stream read() methods when appropriate.

Chapter 4 explores the stream classes.

Stream Classes and Standard I/O

Many operating systems support *standard I/O*, which is preconnected input and output data streams between a computer program and its environment when it begins execution. The preconnected streams are known as *standard input*, *standard output*, and *standard error*.

Standard input defaults to reading its input from the keyboard. Also, standard output and standard error default to writing their output to the screen. However, these streams can be redirected to read input from a different source and write output to a different destination (such as a file).

JDK 1.0 introduced support for standard I/O by adding the in, out, and err objects of type InputStream and PrintStream to the java.lang.System class. You specify method calls on these objects to access standard input, standard output, and standard error, as follows:

```
int ch = System.in.read(); // Read single character from standard input.
System.out.println("Hello"); // Write string to standard output.
System.err.println("I/O error: " +
                ioe.getMessage()); // Write string to standard error.
```

As well as exploring InputStream and PrintStream, Chapter 4 also revisits standard I/O to show you how to programmatically redirect these streams.

JDK 1.1 and the Writer/Reader Classes

JDK 1.0's I/O capabilities are suitable for streaming bytes, but cannot properly stream characters because they don't account for *character encodings*. JDK 1.1 overcame this problem by introducing writer/reader classes that take character encodings into account. For example, the java.io package includes FileWriter and FileReader classes for writing and reading character streams.

Chapter 5 explores various writer and reader classes.

NIO

Modern operating systems offer sophisticated I/O services (such as readiness selection) for improving I/O performance and simplifying I/O. Java Specification Request (JSR) 51 (www.jcp.org/en/jsr/detail?id=51) was created to address these capabilities.

JSR 51's description indicates that it provides APIs for scalable I/O, fast buffered binary and character I/O, regular expressions, and charset conversion. Collectively, these APIs are known as NIO. JDK 1.4 implemented NIO in terms of the following APIs:

- Buffers
- Channels
- Selectors
- Regular expressions
- Charsets

The regular expression and charset APIs were provided to simplify common I/O-related tasks.

Buffers

Buffers are the foundation for NIO operations. Essentially, NIO is all about moving data into and out of buffers.

A process such as the JVM performs I/O by asking the operating system to drain a buffer's contents to storage via a write operation. Similarly, it asks the operating system to fill a buffer with data read from a storage device.

Consider a read operation involving a disk drive. The operating system issues a command to the disk controller to read a block of bytes from a disk into an operating system buffer. Once this operation completes, the operating system copies the buffer contents to the buffer specified by the process when it issued a read() operation. Check out Figure 1-2.

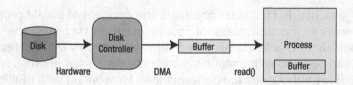

Figure 1-2. Filling a buffer at the operating system level

In Figure 1-2, a process has issued a read() call to the operating system. In turn, the operating system has requested to the disk controller to read a block of bytes from the disk. The disk controller (also known as a DMA controller) reads these bytes directly into an operating system buffer via *Direct Memory Access (DMA)*, a feature of computer systems that allows certain hardware subsystems to access main system (RAM) memory independently of the central processing unit (CPU). The operating system then copies these bytes to the process's buffer.

Copying bytes from the operating system buffer to the process buffer isn't very efficient. It would be more performant to have the DMA controller copy directly to the process buffer, but there are two problems with this approach:

- The DMA controller typically cannot communicate directly with the *user space* in which the JVM process runs. Instead, it communicates with the operating system's *kernel space*.

- Block-oriented devices such as a DMA controller work with fixed-size data blocks. In contrast, the JVM process might request a size of data that isn't a multiple of the block size or that is misaligned.

Because of these problems, the operating system acts as an intermediary, tearing apart and recombining data as it switches between the JVM process and the DMA controller.

The data assembly/disassembly tasks can be made more efficient by letting the JVM process pass a list of buffer addresses to the operating system in a single system call. The operating system then fills or drains these buffers in sequence, scattering data to multiple buffers during a read operation or gathering data from several buffers during a write operation. This *scatter/gather* activity reduces the number of (potentially expensive) system calls that the JVM process must make and lets the operating system optimize data handling because it knows the total amount of buffer space. Furthermore, when multiple processors or cores are available, the operating system may allow buffers to be filled or drained simultaneously.

JDK 1.4's java.nio.Buffer class abstracts the concept of a JVM process buffer. It serves as the superclass for java.nio.ByteBuffer and other buffer classes. Because I/O is fundamentally byte-oriented, only ByteBuffer instances can be used with channels (which are discussed shortly). Most of the other Buffer subclasses are conveniences for working with multibyte data (such as characters or integers).

Chapter 6 explores the Buffer class and its children.

Channels

Forcing a CPU to perform I/O tasks and wait for I/O completions (such a CPU is said to be *I/O bound*) is wasteful of this resource. Performance can be improved by offloading these tasks to DMA controllers so that the processor can get on with other work.

A *channel* serves as a conduit for communicating (via the operating system) with a DMA controller to efficiently drain byte buffers to or fill byte buffers from a disk. JDK 1.4's java.nio.channels.Channel interface, its subinterfaces, and various classes implement the channel architecture.

One of these classes is called java.nio.channels.FileChannel, and it abstracts a channel for reading, writing, mapping, and manipulating a file. One interesting feature of FileChannel is its support for file locking, upon which sophisticated applications such as database management systems rely.

File locking lets a process prevent or limit access to a file while the process is accessing the file. Although file locking can be applied to an entire file, it is often narrowed to a smaller region. A lock ranges from a starting byte offset in the file and continues for a specific number of bytes.

Another interesting FileChannel feature is *memory-mapped file I/O* via the map() method. map() returns a java.nio.MappedByteBuffer whose content is a memory-mapped region of a file. File content is accessed via memory accesses; buffer copies and read-write system calls are eliminated.

You can obtain a channel by calling the java.nio.channels.Channels class's methods or the methods in classic I/O classes such as RandomAccessFile.

Chapter 7 explores Channel, Channels, and more.

Selectors

I/O is classified as block-oriented or stream-oriented. Reading from or writing to a file is an example of block-oriented I/O. In contrast, reading from the keyboard or writing to a network connection is an example of stream-oriented I/O.

Stream I/O is often slower than block I/O. Furthermore, input tends to be intermittent. For example, the user might pause while entering a stream of characters or momentary slowness in a network connection causes a playing video to proceed in a jerky fashion.

Many operating systems allow streams to be configured to operate in *nonblocking mode* in which a thread continually checks for available input without blocking when no input is available. The thread can handle incoming data or perform other tasks until data arrives.

This "polling for available input" activity can be wasteful, especially when the thread needs to monitor many input streams (such as in a web server context). Modern operating systems can perform this checking efficiently, which is known as *readiness selection*, and which is often built on top of nonblocking mode. The operating system monitors a collection of streams and returns an indication to the thread of which streams are ready to perform I/O. As a result, a single thread can multiplex many active streams via common code and makes it possible, in a web server context, to manage a huge number of network connections.

JDK 1.4 supports readiness selection by providing *selectors*, which are instances of the java.nio.channels.Selector class that can examine one or more channels and determine which channels are ready for reading or writing. This way a single thread can manage multiple channels (and, therefore, multiple network connections) efficiently. Being able to use fewer threads is advantageous where thread creation and thread context switching is expensive in terms of performance and/or memory use. See Figure 1-3.

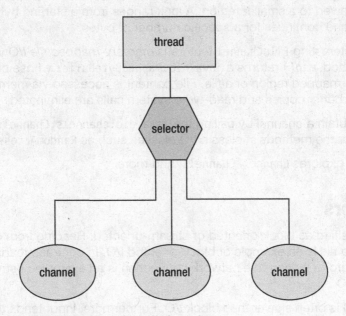

Figure 1-3. A thread manages three channels via a selector

Chapter 8 explores Selector and its related types.

Regular Expressions

Regular expressions were introduced as part of NIO. Although you might wonder about the rationale for doing this (what have regular expressions got to do with I/O?), regular expressions are commonly used to scan textual data that is read from a file or other source. The need to perform these scans as quickly as possible mandated their inclusion. JDK 1.4 supports regular expressions via the java.util.regex package and its Pattern and Matcher classes.

Chapter 9 explores the Pattern and Matcher classes.

Charsets

I previously mentioned that JDK 1.1 introduced writer/reader classes that take character encodings into account. Originally, classes such as `java.io.InputStreamReader` worked with the `java.io.ByteToCharConverter` class to perform conversions based on encodings. `ByteToCharConverter` was eventually deprecated and removed from JDK 6 and successors. In its place, the more capable `java.nio.charset` package along with its `Charset`, `CharsetEncoder`, `CharsetDecoder`, and related types was introduced.

Chapter 10 explores the `Charset` class.

Formatter

JSR 51 mentions a simple `printf`-style formatting facility. Such a facility offers significant value in preparing data for presentation, to which many C programmers can attest. However, JDK 1.4 did not include this capability because it relies on variable argument lists, a language feature that did not debut until JDK 5. Fortunately, JDK 5 also included a `java.util.Formatter` class with a wealth of formatting capabilities along with related types that support custom formatting, and added `printf()` (and related `format()`) methods to the `PrintStream` class.

Chapter 11 explores `Formatter` and demonstrates `printf()`.

NIO.2

JSR 51 specifies that NIO would introduce an improved file system interface that overcomes various problems with the legacy `File` class. However, lack of time prevented this feature from being included. Also, it wasn't possible to support asynchronous I/O and complete socket channel functionality. JSR 203 (`www.jcp.org/en/jsr/detail?id=203`) was subsequently created to address these omissions, which debuted in JDK 7.

Note Before the official JDK 7 release, *big buffers* (buffers with 64-bit addressability) were considered for NIO.2. Classes such as `BigByteBuffer` and `MappedBigByteBuffer` were planned for inclusion in package `java.nio` or a different package. However, as explained in the "BigByteBuffer/Mapped BigByteBuffer" OpenJDK discussion topic (`http://mail.openjdk.java .net/pipermail/nio-discuss/2009-June/000207.html`), this capability was abandoned in favor of pursuing "64-bit arrays or collections."

Improved File System Interface

The legacy File class suffers from various problems. For example, the renameTo() method doesn't work consistently across operating systems. Also, many of File's methods don't scale; requesting a large directory listing from a server could result in a hang. The new file system interface mentioned in JSR 203 fixes these and other problems. For example, it supports bulk access to file attributes, provides a change notification facility, offers the ability to escape to file system-specific APIs, and has a service provider interface for pluggable file system implementations.

Chapter 12 explores the improved file system interface.

Asynchronous I/O

Nonblocking mode improves performance by preventing a thread that performs a read or write operation on a channel from blocking until input is available or the output has been fully written. However, it doesn't let an application determine if it can perform an operation without actually performing the operation. For example, when a nonblocking read operation succeeds, the application learns that the read operation is possible but also has read some data that must be managed. This duality prevents you from separating code that checks for stream readiness from the data-processing code without making your code significantly complicated.

Asynchronous I/O overcomes this problem by letting the thread initiate the operation and immediately proceed to other work. The thread specifies some kind of *callback function* that is invoked when the operation finishes.

Chapter 13 explores asynchronous I/O.

Completion of Socket Channel Functionality

JDK 1.4 added the DatagramChannel, ServerSocketChannel, and SocketChannel classes to the java.nio.channels package. However, lack of time prevented these classes from supporting binding and option configuration. Also, channel-based multicast datagrams were not supported. JDK 7 added binding support and option configuration to the aforementioned classes. Also, it introduced a new java.nio.channels .MulticastChannel interface.

Chapter 14 explores the completion of socket channel functionality.

EXERCISES

The following exercises are designed to test your understanding of Chapter 1's content:

1. Identify the API categories that comprise classic I/O.

2. What benefit is offered by the `try`-with-resources statement?

3. Identify the API categories that comprise NIO.

4. Which API class lets Java programs leverage readiness selection?

5. Identify the API categories that comprise NIO.2.

6. How does NIO.2 complete socket channel functionality?

Summary

I/O is fundamental to operating systems, computer languages, and language libraries. Java supports I/O through its classic I/O, NIO, and NIO.2 API categories.

Classic I/O provides APIs to access the file system, access file content randomly (as opposed to sequentially), stream byte-oriented data between sources and destinations, and support character streams.

NIO provides APIs to manage buffers, communicate buffered data over channels, leverage readiness selection via selectors, scan textual data quickly via regular expressions, specify character encodings via charsets, and support `printf`-style formatting.

NIO.2 provides APIs to improve the file system interface; support asynchronous I/O; and complete socket channel functionality by upgrading `DatagramChannel`, `ServerSocketChannel`, and `SocketChannel`, and by introducing a new `MulticastChannel` interface.

Chapter 2 presents classic I/O's `File` class.

Part **II**

Classic I/O APIs

File

Applications often interact with a *file system*, which is usually implemented as a hierarchy of files and directories starting from a *root directory*. Operating systems on which a Java virtual machine (JVM) runs typically support at least one file system. For example, Unix/Linux combines all *mounted* (attached and prepared) disks into one virtual file system. In contrast, Windows associates a separate file system with each active disk drive. Java offers access to the underlying operating system's available file system(s) via its concrete java.io.File class, which this chapter explores.

Constructing File Instances

An instance of the File class contains an abstract representation of a file or directory *path* (a compact map that locates and identifies a file system object). To create a File instance, call a constructor such as File(String path), which creates a File instance that stores the path string:

```
File file1 = new File("/x/y");
File file2 = new File("C:\\temp\\x.dat");
```

The first line assumes a Unix/Linux operating system, starts the path with root directory symbol /, and continues with directory name x, separator character /, and file or directory name y. (It also works on Windows, which assumes this path begins at the root directory on the current drive.)

> **Note** An operating system-dependent *separator character* (such as the Windows backslash [\] character) appears between a path's consecutive names.

The second line assumes a Windows operating system, starts the path with drive specifier C:, and continues with root directory symbol \, directory name temp, separator character \, and file name x.dat (although x.dat might refer to a directory). (You could also use forward slashes [/] on Windows.)

> **Caution**   Always double backslash characters that appear in a string literal, especially when specifying a path; otherwise, you run the risk of introducing bugs or receiving compiler error messages. For example, I doubled the backslash characters in the second statement to denote a backslash and not a tab (\t) and to avoid a compiler error message (\x is illegal).

Each statement's path is *absolute*, which is a path that starts with the root directory symbol; no other information is required to locate the file/directory that it denotes. In contrast, a *relative path* doesn't start with the root directory symbol; it's interpreted via information taken from another path.

> **Note**   The java.io package's classes default to resolving relative paths against the current user (also known as working) directory, which is identified by the system property user.dir and which is typically the directory in which the JVM was launched. (You obtain a system property value by calling the java.lang.System class's getProperty() method.)

File instances contain abstract representations of file and directory paths (these files or directories may or may not exist in their file systems) by storing *abstract paths*, which offer operating system-independent views of hierarchical paths. In contrast, user interfaces and operating systems use operating system-dependent *path strings* to name files and directories.

An abstract path consists of an optional operating system-dependent prefix string, such as a disk drive specifier, "/" for the Unix/Linux root directory, or "\\" for a Windows Universal Naming Convention (UNC) path, and a sequence of zero or more string names. The first name in an abstract path may be a directory name or, in the case of Windows UNC paths, a hostname. Each subsequent name denotes a directory; the last name may denote a directory or a file. The *empty abstract path* has no prefix and an empty name sequence.

The conversion of a path string to or from an abstract path is inherently operating system-dependent. When a path string is converted into an abstract path, the names within this string may be separated by the default name-separator character or by any other name-separator character that is supported by the underlying operating system. When an abstract path is converted into a path string, each name is separated from the next by a single copy of the default name-separator character.

> **Note** The *default name-separator character* is defined by the system property `file.separator` and is made available in `File`'s `public static separator` and `separatorChar` fields—the first field stores the character in a `java.lang.String` instance and the second field stores it as a `char` value.

`File` offers additional constructors for instantiating this class. For example, the following constructors merge parent and child paths into combined paths that are stored in `File` objects:

- `File(String parent, String child)` creates a new `File` instance from a parent path string and a child path string.

- `File(File parent, String child)` creates a new `File` instance from a parent path `File` instance and a child path string.

Each constructor's parent parameter is passed a *parent path*, a path that consists of all path components except for the last name, which is specified by `child`. The following statement demonstrates this concept via the first constructor:

```
File file3 = new File("prj/books/", "io");
```

The constructor merges the parent path `prj/books/` with the child path `io` into the `prj/books/io` path. (If I had specified `prj/books` as the parent path, the constructor would have added the separator character after `books`.)

> **Tip** Because `File(String path)`, `File(String parent, String child)`, and `File(File parent, String child)` don't detect invalid path arguments (apart from throwing a `java.lang.NullPointerException` when `path` or `child` is null), you must be careful when specifying paths. You should strive to only specify paths that are valid for all operating systems on which the application will run. For example, instead of hard-coding a drive specifier (such as `C:`) in a path, use a root returned from `listRoots()`, which I discuss later. Even better, keep your paths relative to the current user/working directory (returned from the `user.dir` system property).

Learning About Stored Abstract Paths

After obtaining a File object, you can interrogate it to learn about its stored abstract path by calling the methods described in Table 2-1.

Table 2-1. File *Methods for Learning About a Stored Abstract Path*

Method	Description
File getAbsoluteFile()	Return the absolute form of this File object's abstract path. This method is equivalent to new File(this.getAbsolutePath()).
String getAbsolutePath()	Return the absolute path string of this File object's abstract path. When it's already absolute, the path string is returned as if by calling getPath(). When it's the empty abstract path, the path string of the current user directory (identified via user.dir) is returned. Otherwise, the abstract path is resolved in an operating system-dependent manner. On Unix/Linux operating systems, a relative path is made absolute by resolving it against the current user directory. On Windows operating systems, the path is made absolute by resolving it against the current directory of the drive named by the path, or the current user directory when there is no drive.
File getCanonicalFile()	Return the *canonical* (simplest possible, absolute and unique) form of this File object's abstract path. This method throws java.io.IOException when an I/O error occurs (creating the canonical path may require file system queries); it equates to new File(this.getCanonicalPath()).
String getCanonicalPath()	Return the canonical path string of this File object's abstract path. This method first converts this path to the absolute form when necessary, as if by invoking getAbsolutePath(), and then maps it to its unique form in an operating system-dependent way. Doing so typically involves removing redundant names such as "." and ".." from the path, resolving symbolic links (on Unix/Linux operating systems), and converting drive letters to a standard case (on Windows operating systems). This method throws IOException when an I/O error occurs (creating the canonical path may require file system queries).

(continued)

Table 2-1. (*continued*)

Method	Description
String getName()	Return the file name or directory name denoted by this File object's abstract path. This name is the last in a path's name sequence. The empty string is returned when the path's name sequence is empty.
String getParent()	Return the parent path string of this File object's path, or return null when this path doesn't name a parent directory.
File getParentFile()	Return a File object storing this File object's abstract path's parent abstract path; return null when the parent path isn't a directory.
String getPath()	Convert this File object's abstract path into a path string where the names in the sequence are separated by the character stored in File's separator field. Return the resulting path string.
boolean isAbsolute()	Return true when this File object's abstract path is absolute; otherwise, return false when it's relative. The definition of absolute path is system dependent. For Unix/Linux operating systems, a path is absolute when its prefix is "/". For Windows operating systems, a path is absolute when its prefix is a drive specifier followed by "\" or when its prefix is "\\".
String toString()	A synonym for getPath().

Table 2-1 refers to IOException, which is the common exception superclass for those exception classes that describe various kinds of I/O errors such as java.io.FileNotFoundException.

Listing 2-1 instantiates File with its path command-line argument and calls some of the File methods described in Table 2-1 to learn about this path.

Listing 2-1. Obtaining Abstract Path Information

```
import java.io.File;
import java.io.IOException;

public class PathInfo
{
   public static void main(final String[] args) throws IOException
   {
      if (args.length != 1)
```

```
    {
        System.err.println("usage: java PathInfo path");
        return;
    }
    File file = new File(args[0]);
    System.out.println("Absolute path = " + file.getAbsolutePath());
    System.out.println("Canonical path = " + file.getCanonicalPath());
    System.out.println("Name = " + file.getName());
    System.out.println("Parent = " + file.getParent());
    System.out.println("Path = " + file.getPath());
    System.out.println("Is absolute = " + file.isAbsolute());
    }
}
```

Compile Listing 2-1 as follows:

```
javac PathInfo.java
```

Run the resulting application as follows:

```
java PathInfo .
```

The period represents the current directory on my Windows 7 operating system; use your own equivalent. I observed the following output:

```
Absolute path = C:\prj\books\io\ch02\code\PathInfo\.
Canonical path = C:\prj\books\io\ch02\code\PathInfo
Name = .
Parent = null
Path = .
Is absolute = false
```

This output reveals that the canonical path doesn't include the period. It also shows that there is no parent path and that the path is relative.

Continuing, specify java PathInfo C:\reports\2015\..\2014\February. You should observe the following output:

```
Absolute path = C:\reports\2015\..\2014\February
Canonical path = C:\reports\2014\February
Name = February
Parent = C:\reports\2015\..\2014
Path = C:\reports\2015\..\2014\February
Is absolute = true
```

This output reveals that the canonical path doesn't include 2015. It also shows that the path is absolute.

Finally, specify java `PathInfo` `""` to obtain information for the empty path. I observed the following output:

```
Absolute path = C:\prj\books\io\ch02\code\PathInfo
Canonical path = C:\prj\books\io\ch02\code\PathInfo
Name =
Parent = null
Path =
Is absolute = false
```

The output reveals that `getName()` and `getPath()` return the empty string (`""`) because the empty path is empty. Also, `C:` is the default drive.

Learning About a Path's File or Directory

You can interrogate the file system to learn about the file or directory represented by a `File` object's stored path by calling the methods that are described in Table 2-2.

Table 2-2. *File Methods for Learning About a File or Directory*

Method	Description
`boolean exists()`	Return true if and only if the file or directory that's denoted by this `File` object's abstract path exists.
`boolean isDirectory()`	Return true when this `File` object's abstract path refers to an existing directory.
`boolean isFile()`	Return true when this `File` object's abstract path refers to an existing normal file. A file is *normal* when it's not a directory and satisfies other operating system-dependent criteria. It's not a symbolic link or a named pipe, for example. Any nondirectory file created by a Java application is guaranteed to be a normal file.
`boolean isHidden()`	Return true when the file denoted by this `File` object's abstract path is hidden. The exact definition of *hidden* is operating system dependent. On Unix/Linux operating systems, a file is hidden when its name begins with a period character. On Windows operating systems, a file is hidden when it has been marked as such in the file system.

(continued)

Table 2-2. (*continued*)

Method	Description
`long lastModified()`	Return the time that the file denoted by this `File` object's abstract path was last modified, or 0 when the file doesn't exist or an I/O error occurred during this method call. The returned value is measured in milliseconds since the Unix epoch (00:00:00 GMT, January 1, 1970).
`long length()`	Return the length of the file denoted by this `File` object's abstract path. The return value is unspecified when the path denotes a directory and will be 0 when the file doesn't exist.

Listing 2-2 instantiates `File` with its path command-line argument and calls all of the `File` methods described in Table 2-2 to learn about the path's file/directory.

Listing 2-2. Obtaining File/Directory Information

```java
import java.io.File;
import java.io.IOException;

import java.util.Date;

public class FileDirectoryInfo
{
   public static void main(final String[] args) throws IOException
   {
      if (args.length != 1)
      {
         System.err.println("usage: java FileDirectoryInfo pathname");
         return;
      }
      File file = new File(args[0]);
      System.out.println("About " + file + ":");
      System.out.println("Exists = " + file.exists());
      System.out.println("Is directory = " + file.isDirectory());
      System.out.println("Is file = " + file.isFile());
      System.out.println("Is hidden = " + file.isHidden());
      System.out.println("Last modified = " +
                         new Date(file.lastModified()));
      System.out.println("Length = " + file.length());
   }
}
```

Compile Listing 2-2 as follows:

```
javac FileDirectoryInfo.java
```

Run the resulting application as follows:

```
java FileDirectoryInfo x.dat
```

Assuming the existence of a three-byte file named x.dat, you should observe output similar to that shown here:

```
About x.dat:
Exists = true
Is directory = false
Is file = true
Is hidden = false
Last modified = Sat Jul 25 15:49:41 CDT 2015
Length = 3
```

Listing File System Root Directories

File declares the File[] listRoots() class method to return the root directories (roots) of available file systems as an array of File objects.

> **Note**   The set of available file system roots is affected by operating system-level operations, such as inserting or ejecting removable media, and disconnecting or unmounting physical or virtual disk drives.

Listing 2-3 presents a DumpRoots application that uses listRoots() to obtain an array of available file system roots and then outputs the array's contents.

Listing 2-3. Dumping Available File System Roots to Standard Output

```java
import java.io.File;

public class DumpRoots
{
    public static void main(String[] args)
    {
        File[] roots = File.listRoots();
        for (File root: roots)
            System.out.println(root);
    }
}
```

Compile Listing 2-3 as follows:

```
javac DumpRoots.java
```

Run the resulting application as follows:

```
java DumpRoots
```

When I run this application on my Windows 7 operating system, I receive the following output, which reveals four available roots:

```
C:\
D:\
E:\
F:\
```

If I ran DumpRoots on a Unix or Linux operating system, I would receive one line of output that consists of the virtual file system root (/).

Obtaining Disk Space Information

A *partition* is an operating system-specific portion of storage for a file system. Obtaining the amount of partition free space is important to installers and other applications. Until Java 6 arrived, the only portable way to accomplish this task was to guess by creating files of different sizes.

Java 6 added to the File class long getFreeSpace(), long getTotalSpace(), and long getUsableSpace() methods that return space information about the partition described by the File instance's abstract path:

- long getFreeSpace() returns the number of unallocated bytes in the partition identified by this File object's abstract path; it returns zero when the abstract path doesn't name a partition.

- long getTotalSpace() returns the size (in bytes) of the partition identified by this File object's abstract path; it returns zero when the abstract path doesn't name a partition.

- long getUsableSpace() returns the number of bytes available to the current JVM on the partition identified by this File object's abstract path; it returns zero when the abstract path doesn't name a partition.

Although getFreeSpace() and getUsableSpace() appear to be equivalent, they differ in the following respect: unlike getFreeSpace(), getUsableSpace() checks for write permissions and other operating system restrictions, resulting in a more accurate estimate.

> **Note** The getFreeSpace() and getUsableSpace() methods return a hint
> (not a guarantee) that a Java application can use all (or most) of the unallocated
> or available bytes. These values are hints because a program running outside
> the JVM can allocate partition space, resulting in actual unallocated and
> available values being lower than the values returned by these methods.

Listing 2-4 presents an application that demonstrates these methods. After
obtaining an array of all available file system roots, this application obtains
and outputs the free, total, and usable space for each partition identified by
the array.

Listing 2-4. Outputting the Free, Usable, and Total Space on All Partitions

```java
import java.io.File;

public class PartitionSpace
{
   public static void main(String[] args)
   {
      File[] roots = File.listRoots();
      for (File root: roots)
      {
         System.out.println("Partition: " + root);
         System.out.println("Free space on this partition = " +
                             root.getFreeSpace());
         System.out.println("Usable space on this partition = " +
                             root.getUsableSpace());
         System.out.println("Total space on this partition = " +
                             root.getTotalSpace());
         System.out.println("***");
      }
   }
}
```

Compile Listing 2-4 as follows:

```
javac PartitionSpace.java
```

Run the resulting application as follows:

```
java PartitionSpace
```

When run on my Windows 7 machine with a hard drive designated as C:, a
DVD drive designated as D:, an external hard drive designated as E:, and a
flash drive designated as F:, I observed the following output (usually with
different free/usable space amounts on C:, E:, and F:):

```
Partition: C:\
Free space on this partition = 143271129088
Usable space on this partition = 143271129088
Total space on this partition = 499808989184
***
Partition: D:\
Free space on this partition = 0
Usable space on this partition = 0
Total space on this partition = 0
***
Partition: E:\
Free space on this partition = 733418569728
Usable space on this partition = 733418569728
Total space on this partition = 1000169533440
***
Partition: F:\
Free space on this partition = 33728192512
Usable space on this partition = 33728192512
Total space on this partition = 64021835776
***
```

Listing Directories

File declares five methods that return the names of files and directories
located in the directory identified by a File object's abstract path. Table 2-3
describes these methods.

Table 2-3. File Methods for Obtaining Directory Content

Method	Description
String[] list()	Return a potentially empty array of strings naming the files and directories in the directory denoted by this File object's abstract path. If the path doesn't denote a directory, or if an I/O error occurs, this method returns null. Otherwise, it returns an array of strings, one string for each file or directory in the directory.
	Names denoting the directory itself and the directory's parent directory are not included in the result. Each string is a file name rather than a complete path. Also, there is no guarantee that the name strings in the resulting array will appear in alphabetical or any other order.
String[] list(FilenameFilter filter)	A convenience method for calling list() and returning only those Strings that satisfy filter.
File[] listFiles()	A convenience method for calling list(), converting its array of Strings to an array of Files, and returning the Files array.
File[] listFiles(FileFilter filter)	A convenience method for calling list(), converting its array of Strings to an array of Files, but only for those Strings that satisfy filter, and returning the Files array.
File[] listFiles(FilenameFilter filter)	A convenience method for calling list(), converting its array of Strings to an array of Files, but only for those Strings that satisfy filter, and returning the Files array.

The overloaded list() methods return arrays of Strings denoting file and directory names. The second method lets you return only those names of interest (such as only those names that end with the.txt extension) via a java.io.FilenameFilter-based filter object.

The FilenameFilter interface declares a single boolean accept(File dir, String name) method that is called for each file/directory located in the directory identified by the File object's path:

- dir identifies the parent portion of the path (the directory path).

- name identifies the final directory name or the file name portion of the path.

The accept() method uses the arguments passed to these parameters to determine whether or not the file or directory satisfies its criteria for what is acceptable. It returns true when the file/directory name should be included in the returned array; otherwise, this method returns false.

Listing 2-5 presents a Dir(ectory) application that uses list(FilenameFilter) to obtain only those names that end with a specific extension.

Listing 2-5. Listing Specific Names

```
import java.io.File;
import java.io.FilenameFilter;

public class Dir
{
   public static void main(final String[] args)
   {
      if (args.length != 2)
      {
         System.err.println("usage: java Dir dirpath ext");
         return;
      }
      File file = new File(args[0]);
      FilenameFilter fnf = new FilenameFilter()
                           {
                              @Override
                              public boolean accept(File dir, String name)
                              {
                                 return name.endsWith(args[1]);
                              }
                           };
      String[] names = file.list(fnf);
      for (String name: names)
         System.out.println(name);
   }
}
```

Compile Listing 2-5 as follows:

```
javac Dir.java
```

Assuming Windows, run the resulting application as follows:

```
java Dir C:\windows exe
```

I observe the following output, which consists of those file system objects that have an .exe extension:

```
bfsvc.exe
explorer.exe
fveupdate.exe
HelpPane.exe
hh.exe
IsUninst.exe
kindlegen.exe
notepad.exe
regedit.exe
splwow64.exe
twunk_16.exe
twunk_32.exe
winhlp32.exe
write.exe
```

The overloaded listFiles() methods return arrays of Files. For the most part, they're symmetrical with their list() counterparts. However, listFiles(FileFilter) introduces an asymmetry.

The java.io.FileFilter interface declares a single boolean accept(String path) method that Is called for each file/directory located in the directory identified by the File object's path. The argument passed to path identifies the complete path of the file or directory.

The accept() method uses this argument to determine whether or not the file or directory satisfies its criteria for what is acceptable. It returns true when the file/directory name should be included in the returned array; otherwise, this method returns false.

Note   Because each interface's accept() method accomplishes the same task, you might be wondering which interface to use. If you prefer a path broken into its directory and name components, use FilenameFilter. However, if you prefer a complete path, use FileFilter; you can always call getParent() and getName() to get these components.

Creating/Modifying Files and Directories

File also declares several methods for creating new files and directories and modifying existing files and directories. Table 2-4 describes these methods.

Table 2-4. File Methods for Creating New and Manipulating Existing Files and Directories

Method	Description
`boolean createNewFile()`	Atomically create a new, empty file named by this File object's abstract path if and only if a file with this name doesn't yet exist. The check for file existence and the creation of the file when it doesn't exist are a single operation that's atomic with respect to all other file system activities that might affect the file. This method returns true when the named file doesn't exist and was successfully created, and returns false when the named file already exists. It throws IOException when an I/O error occurs.
`static File createTempFile(String prefix, String suffix)`	Create an empty file in the default temporary file directory using the given prefix and suffix to generate its name. This overloaded class method calls its three-parameter variant, passing prefix, suffix, and null to this other method, and returning the other method's return value.
`static File createTempFile(String prefix, String suffix, File directory)`	Create an empty file in the specified directory using the given prefix and suffix to generate its name. The name begins with the character sequence specified by prefix and ends with the character sequence specified by suffix; ".tmp" is used as the suffix when suffix is null. This method returns the created file's path when successful. It throws java.lang.IllegalArgumentException when prefix contains fewer than three characters and IOException when the file can't be created.
`boolean delete()`	Delete the file or directory denoted by this File object's path. Return true when successful; otherwise, return false. If the path denotes a directory, the directory must be empty in order to be deleted.
`void deleteOnExit()`	Request that the file or directory denoted by this File object's abstract path be deleted when the JVM terminates. Reinvoking this method on the same File object has no effect. Once deletion has been requested, it's not possible to cancel the request. Therefore, this method should be used with care.

(continued)

Table 2-4. (continued)

Method	Description
`boolean mkdir()`	Create the directory named by this `File` object's abstract path. Return true when successful; otherwise, return false.
`boolean mkdirs()`	Create the directory and any necessary intermediate directories named by this `File` object's abstract path. Return true when successful; otherwise, return false.
`boolean renameTo(File dest)`	Rename the file denoted by this `File` object's abstract path to dest. Return true when successful; otherwise, return false. This method throws `NullPointerException` when dest is null.
	Many aspects of this method's behavior are operating system-dependent. For example, the rename operation might not be able to move a file from one file system to another, the operation might not be atomic, or it might not succeed when a file with the destination path already exists. The return value should always be checked to make sure that the rename operation was successful.
`boolean setLastModified(long time)`	Set the last-modified time of the file or directory named by this `File` object's abstract path. Return true when successful; otherwise, return false. This method throws `IllegalArgumentException` when time is negative.
	All operating systems support file-modification times to the nearest second, but some provide more precision. The time value will be truncated to fit the supported precision. If the operation succeeds and no intervening operations on the file take place, the next call to `lastModified()` will return the (possibly truncated) time value passed to this method.

Suppose you're designing a text editor application that a user will use to open a text file and make changes to its content. Until the user explicitly saves these changes to the file, you want the text file to remain unchanged.

Because the user doesn't want to lose these changes when the application crashes or the computer loses power, you design the application to save these changes to a temporary file every few minutes. This way, the user has a backup of the changes.

You can use the overloaded createTempFile() methods to create the temporary file. If you don't specify a directory in which to store this file, it's created in the directory identified by the java.io.tmpdir system property.

You probably want to remove the temporary file after the user tells the application to save or discard the changes. The deleteOnExit() method lets you register a temporary file for deletion; it's deleted when the JVM ends without a crash/power loss.

Listing 2-6 presents a TempFileDemo application for experimenting with the createTempFile() and deleteOnExit() methods.

Listing 2-6. Experimenting with Temporary Files

```
import java.io.File;
import java.io.IOException;

public class TempFileDemo
{
   public static void main(String[] args) throws IOException
   {
      System.out.println(System.getProperty("java.io.tmpdir"));
      File temp = File.createTempFile("text", ".txt");
      System.out.println(temp);
      temp.deleteOnExit();
   }
}
```

After outputting the location where temporary files are stored, TempFileDemo creates a temporary file whose name begins with text and which ends with the .txt extension. TempFileDemo next outputs the temporary file's name and registers the temporary file for deletion upon the successful termination of the application.

Compile Listing 2-6 as follows:

```
javac TempFileDemo.java
```

Run the resulting application as follows:

```
java TempFileDemo
```

I observed the following output during one run of TempFileDemo (and the file disappeared on exit):

```
C:\Users\Owner\AppData\Local\Temp\
C:\Users\Owner\AppData\Local\Temp\text8621896953150462138.txt
```

Setting and Getting Permissions

Java 1.2 added a boolean setReadOnly() method to the File class to mark a file or directory as read-only. However, a method to revert the file or directory to the writable state wasn't added. More importantly, until Java 6's arrival, File offered no way to manage an abstract path's read, write, and execute permissions.

Java 6 added to the File class boolean setExecutable(boolean executable), boolean setExecutable(boolean executable, boolean ownerOnly), boolean setReadable(boolean readable), boolean setReadable(boolean readable, boolean ownerOnly), boolean setWritable(boolean writable), and boolean setWritable(boolean writable, boolean ownerOnly) methods that let you set the owner's or everybody's execute, read, and write permissions for the file identified by the File object's abstract path:

- boolean setExecutable(boolean executable, boolean ownerOnly) enables (pass true to executable) or disables (pass false to executable) this abstract path's execute permission for its owner (pass true to ownerOnly) or everyone (pass false to ownerOnly). When the file system doesn't differentiate between the owner and everyone, this permission always applies to everyone. It returns true when the operation succeeds. It returns false when the user doesn't have permission to change this abstract path's access permissions or when executable is false and the file system doesn't implement an execute permission.

- boolean setExecutable(boolean executable) is a convenience method that invokes the previous method to set the execute permission for the owner.

- boolean setReadable(boolean readable, boolean ownerOnly) enables (pass true to readable) or disables (pass false to readable) this abstract path's read permission for its owner (pass true to ownerOnly) or everyone (pass false to ownerOnly). When the file system doesn't differentiate between the owner and everyone, this permission always applies to everyone. It returns true when the operation succeeds. It returns false when the user doesn't have permission to change this abstract path's access permissions or when readable is false and the file system doesn't implement a read permission.

■ boolean setReadable(boolean readable) is a convenience method that invokes the previous method to set the read permission for the owner.

■ boolean setWritable(boolean writable, boolean ownerOnly) enables (pass true to writable) or disables (pass false to writable) this abstract path's write permission for its owner (pass true to ownerOnly) or everyone (pass false to ownerOnly). When the file system doesn't differentiate between the owner and everyone, this permission always applies to everyone. It returns true when the operation succeeds. It returns false when the user doesn't have permission to change this abstract path's access permissions.

■ boolean setWritable(boolean writable) is a convenience method that invokes the previous method to set the write permission for the owner.

Along with these methods, Java 6 retrofitted File's boolean canRead() and boolean canWrite() methods, and introduced a boolean canExecute() method to return an abstract path's access permissions. These methods return true when the file or directory object identified by the abstract path exists and when the appropriate permission is in effect. For example, canWrite() returns true when the abstract path exists and when the application has permission to write to the file.

The canRead(), canWrite(), and canExecute() methods can be used to implement a simple utility that identifies which permissions have been assigned to an arbitrary file or directory. This utility's source code is presented in Listing 2-7.

Listing 2-7. Checking a File's or Directory's Permissions

```java
import java.io.File;

public class Permissions
{
    public static void main(String[] args)
    {
        if (args.length != 1)
        {
            System.err.println("usage: java Permissions filespec");
            return;
        }
        File file = new File(args[0]);
        System.out.println("Checking permissions for " + args[0]);
        System.out.println("  Execute = " + file.canExecute());
```

```
        System.out.println("  Read = " + file.canRead());
        System.out.println("  Write = " + file.canWrite());
    }
}
```

Compile Listing 2-7 as follows:

```
javac Permissions.java
```

Assuming a readable and executable (only) file named x in the current directory, run the resulting application as follows:

```
java Permissions x
```

You should observe the following output:

```
Checking permissions for x
  Execute = true
  Read = true
  Write = false
```

Exploring Miscellaneous Capabilities

Finally, File implements the java.lang.Comparable interface's compareTo() method and overrides equals() and hashCode(). Table 2-5 describes these miscellaneous methods.

Table 2-5. File's Miscellaneous Methods

Method	Description
int compareTo(File path)	Compare two paths lexicographically. The ordering defined by this method depends on the underlying operating system. For Unix/Linux operating systems, alphabetic case is significant when comparing paths; for Windows operating systems, alphabetic case is insignificant. Return zero when path's abstract path equals this File object's abstract path, a negative value when this File object's abstract path is less than path, and a positive value otherwise. To accurately compare two File objects, call getCanonicalFile() on each File object and then compare the returned File objects.

(continued)

Table 2-5. (continued)

Method	Description
boolean equals(Object obj))	Compare this File object with obj for equality. Abstract path equality depends on the underlying operating system. For Unix/Linux operating systems, alphabetic case is significant when comparing paths; for Windows operating systems, alphabetic case is insignificant. Return true if and only if obj is not null and is a File object whose abstract path denotes the same file/directory as this File object's abstract path.
int hashCode()	Calculate and return a hash code for this path. This calculation depends on the underlying operating system. On Unix/Linux operating systems, a path's hash code equals the exclusive OR of its path string's hash code and decimal value 1234321. On Windows operating systems, the hash code is the exclusive OR of the lowercased path string's hash code and decimal value 1234321. The current *locale* (geographical, political, or cultural region) is not taken into account when lowercasing the path string.

Listing 2-8 presents an application that demonstrates compareTo() along with getCanonicalFile().

Listing 2-8. Comparing Files

```java
import java.io.File;
import java.io.IOException;

public class Compare
{
   public static void main(String[] args) throws IOException
   {
      if (args.length != 2)
      {
         System.err.println("usage: java Compare filespec1 filespec2");
         return;
      }

      File file1 = new File(args[0]);
      File file2 = new File(args[1]);
      System.out.println(file1.compareTo(file2));
      System.out.println(file1.getCanonicalFile()
                              .compareTo(file2.getCanonicalFile()));
   }
}
```

Compile Listing 2-8 as follows:

```
javac Compare.java
```

Assuming Windows, run the resulting application as follows:

```
java Compare Compare.class .\Compare.class
```

You should observe the following output:

```
53
0
```

The 53 indicates that file1's abstract path is lexicographically greater than file2's abstract path. However, when comparing their canonical representations, these abstract paths are considered to be identical (as indicated by the 0).

<hr>

EXERCISE

The following exercises are designed to test your understanding of Chapter 2's content:

1.   What is the purpose of the File class?

2.   What do instances of the File class contain?

3.   What is a path?

4.   What is the difference between an absolute path and a relative path?

5.   How do you obtain the current user (also known as working) directory?

6.   Define parent path.

7.   File's constructors normalize their path arguments. What does normalize mean?

8.   How do you obtain the default name-separator character?

9.   What is a canonical path?

10. What is the difference between File's getParent() and getName() methods?

11. True or false: File's exists() method only determines whether or not a file exists.

12. What is a normal file?

13. What does File's lastModified() method return?

14.   What does File's listRoots() method accomplish?

15.   True or false: File's list() method returns an array of Strings where each entry is a file name rather than a complete path.

16.   What is the difference between the FilenameFilter and FileFilter interfaces?

17.   True or false: File's createNewFile() method doesn't check for file existence and create the file when it doesn't exist in a single operation that's atomic with respect to all other file system activities that might affect the file.

18.   File's createTempFile(String, String) method creates a temporary file in the default temporary directory. How can you locate this directory?

19.   Temporary files should be removed when no longer needed after an application exits (to avoid cluttering the file system). How do you ensure that a temporary file is removed when the JVM ends normally (it doesn't crash and the power isn't lost)?

20.   Which one of the boolean canRead(), boolean canWrite(), and boolean canExecute() methods was introduced by Java 6?

21.   How would you accurately compare two File objects?

22.   Create a Java application named Touch for setting a file's or directory's timestamp to the current time. This application has the following usage syntax: java Touch pathname.

Summary

The File class provides access to the underlying operating system's available file system(s). Each File instance stores the abstract path for some file system object. Various File methods (such as void delete()) affect the file system object represented by the abstract path.

You first learned how to construct File instances. You then explored methods for obtaining information about stored abstract paths and their files or directories, obtaining a list of roots and disk space, listing directories, creating/modifying files/directories, setting/getting permissions, and more.

Chapter 3 presents classic I/O's java.io.RandomAccessFile class.

RandomAccessFile

Files can be created and/or opened for *random access* in which a mixture of write and read operations at various locations can occur until the file is closed. Java supports this random access by providing a `java.io.RandomAccessFile` class. I explore `RandomAccessFile` in this chapter.

Exploring RandomAccessFile

`RandomAccessFile` declares the following constructors:

- ▪ `RandomAccessFile(File file, String mode)`: Create and open a new file when it doesn't exist or open an existing file. The file is identified by `file`'s abstract path and is created and/or opened according to `mode`.

- ▪ `RandomAccessFile(String path, String mode)`: Create and open a new file when it doesn't exist or open an existing file. The file is identified by `path` and is created and/or opened according to `mode`.

Either constructor's mode argument must be one of `"r"`, `"rw"`, `"rws"`, or `"rwd"`; otherwise, the constructor throws `java.lang.IllegalArgumentException`. These string literals have the following meanings:

- ▪ `"r"` informs the constructor to open an existing file for reading only. Any attempt to write to the file results in a thrown instance of the `java.io.IOException` class.

- ▪ `"rw"` informs the constructor to create and open a new file when it doesn't exist for reading and writing or open an existing file for reading and writing.

43

- ■ "rwd" informs the constructor to create and open a new file when it doesn't exist for reading and writing or open an existing file for reading and writing. Furthermore, each update to the file's content must be written synchronously to the underlying storage device.

- ■ "rws" informs the constructor to create and open a new file when it doesn't exist for reading and writing or open an existing file for reading and writing. Furthermore, each update to the file's content or metadata must be written synchronously to the underlying storage device.

> **Note**   A file's *metadata* is data about the file and not the actual file contents. Examples of metadata include the file's length and the time the file was last modified.

The "rwd" and "rws" modes ensure than any writes to a file located on a local storage device are written to the device, which guarantees that critical data isn't lost when the operating system crashes. No guarantee is made when the file doesn't reside on a local device.

> **Note**   Operations on a random access file opened in "rwd" or "rws" mode are slower than these same operations on a random access file opened in "rw" mode.

These constructors throw java.io.FileNotFoundException when mode is "r" and the file identified by path cannot be opened (it might not exist or it might be a directory) or when mode is "rw" and path is read-only or a directory. The following example demonstrates the second constructor by attempting to open an existing file for read access via the "r" mode string:

```
RandomAccessFile raf = new RandomAccessFile("employee.dat", "r");
```

A random access file is associated with a *file pointer*, a cursor that identifies the location of the next byte to write or read. When an existing file is opened, the file pointer is set to its first byte at offset 0. The file pointer is also set to 0 when the file is created.

Write or read operations start at the file pointer and advance it past the number of bytes written or read. Operations that write past the current end of the file cause the file to be extended. These operations continue until the file is closed.

RandomAccessFile declares many methods. I present a representative sample of these methods in Table 3-1.

Table 3-1. RandomAccessFile Methods

Method	Description
void close()	Close the file and release any associated operating system resources. Subsequent writes or reads result in IOException. Also, the file cannot be reopened with this RandomAccessFile object. This method throws IOException when an I/O error occurs.
FileDescriptor getFD()	Return the file's associated file descriptor object. This method throws IOException when an I/O error occurs.
long getFilePointer()	Return the file pointer's current zero-based byte offset into the file. This method throws IOException when an I/O error occurs.
long length()	Return the length (measured in bytes) of the file. This method throws IOException when an I/O error occurs.
int read()	Read and return (as an int in the range 0 to 255) the next byte from the file or return -1 when the end of the file is reached. This method blocks when no input is available and throws IOException when an I/O error occurs.
int read(byte[] b)	Read up to b.length bytes of data from the file into byte array b. This method blocks until at least one byte of input is available. It returns the number of bytes read into the array, or returns -1 when the end of the file is reached. It throws java.lang.NullPointerException when b is null and IOException when an I/O error occurs.
char readChar()	Read and return a character from the file. This method reads two bytes from the file starting at the current file pointer. If the bytes read, in order, are b1 and b2, where $0 <= b1, b2 <= 255$, the result is equal to (char) ((b1 << 8)	b2). This method blocks until the two bytes are read, the end of the file is detected, or an exception is thrown. It throws java.io.EOFException (a subclass of IOException) when the end of the file is reached before reading both bytes and IOException when an I/O error occurs.

(continued)

Table 3-1. (*continued*)

Method	Description
int readInt()	Read and return a 32-bit integer from the file. This method reads four bytes from the file starting at the current file pointer. If the bytes read, in order, are b1, b2, b3, and b4, where 0 <= b1, b2, b3, b4 <= 255, the result is equal to (b1 << 24)	(b2 << 16)	(b3 << 8)	b4. This method blocks until the four bytes are read, the end of the file is detected, or an exception is thrown. It throws EOFException when the end of the file is reached before reading the four bytes and IOException when an I/O error occurs.
void seek(long pos)	Set the file pointer's current offset to pos (which is measured in bytes from the beginning of the file). If the offset is set beyond the end of the file, the file's length doesn't change. The file length will only change by writing after the offset has been set beyond the end of the file. This method throws IOException when the value in pos is negative or when an I/O error occurs.
void setLength(long newLength)	Set the file's length. If the present length as returned by length() is greater than newLength, the file is truncated. In this case, if the file offset as returned by getFilePointer() is greater than newLength, the offset will be equal to newLength after setLength() returns. If the present length is smaller than newLength, the file is extended. In this case, the contents of the extended portion of the file are not defined. This method throws IOException when an I/O error occurs.
int skipBytes(int n)	Attempt to skip over n bytes. This method skips over a smaller number of bytes (possibly zero) when the end of file is reached before n bytes have been skipped. It doesn't throw EOFException in this situation. If n is negative, no bytes are skipped. The actual number of bytes skipped is returned. This method throws IOException when an I/O error occurs.
void write(byte[] b)	Write b.length bytes from byte array b to the file starting at the current file pointer position. This method throws IOException when an I/O error occurs.

(*continued*)

Table 3-1. (*continued*)

Method	Description
void write(int b)	Write the lower eight bits of b as a 32-bit integer to the file at the current file pointer position. This method throws IOException when an I/O error occurs.
void writeChars(String s)	Write string s to the file as a sequence of characters starting at the current file pointer position. This method throws IOException when an I/O error occurs.
void writeInt(int i)	Write 32-bit integer i to the file starting at the current file pointer position. The four bytes are written with the high byte first. This method throws IOException when an I/O error occurs.

Most of Table 3-1's methods are fairly self-explanatory. However, the getFD() method requires further enlightenment.

Note   RandomAccessFile's read-prefixed methods and skipBytes() originate in the java.io.DataInput interface, which this class implements. Furthermore, RandomAccessFile's write-prefixed methods originate in the java.io.DataOutput interface, which this class also implements.

When a file is opened, the underlying operating system creates an operating system-dependent structure to represent the file. A handle to this structure is stored in an instance of the java.io.FileDescriptor class, which getFD() returns.

Note   A *handle* is an identifier that Java passes to the underlying operating system to identify, in this case, a specific open file when it requires that the underlying operating system perform a file operation.

FileDescriptor is a small class that declares three FileDescriptor constants named in, out, and err. These constants let System.in, System. out, and System.err provide access to the standard input, standard output, and standard error streams.

FileDescriptor also declares the following pair of methods:

- ■ void sync() tells the underlying operating system to *flush* (empty) the contents of the open file's output buffers to their associated local disk device. sync() returns after all modified data and attributes have been written to the relevant device. It throws java. io.SyncFailedException when the buffers cannot be flushed or because the operating system cannot guarantee that all the buffers have been synchronized with physical media.

- ■ boolean valid() determines whether this file descriptor object is valid. It returns true when the file descriptor object represents an open file or other active I/O connection; otherwise, it returns false.

Data that is written to an open file is stored in the underlying operating system's output buffers. When the buffers fill to capacity, the operating system empties them to the disk. Buffers improve performance because disk access is much slower than access to the computer's internal memory.

However, when you write data to a random access file that's been opened via mode "rwd" or "rws", each write operation's data is written straight to the disk. As a result, write operations are slower than when the random access file is opened in "rw" mode.

Suppose you have a situation that combines writing data through the output buffers and writing data directly to the disk. The following example addresses this hybrid scenario by opening the file in mode "rw" and selectively calling FileDescriptor's sync() method.

```
RandomAccessFile raf = new RandomAccessFile("employee.dat", "rw");
FileDescriptor fd = raf.getFD();
// Perform a critical write operation.
raf.write(...);
// Synchronize with the underlying disk by flushing the operating system
// output buffers to the disk.
fd.sync();
// Perform a non-critical write operation where synchronization isn't
// necessary.
raf.write(...);
// Do other work.
// Close the file, emptying output buffers to the disk.
raf.close();
```

Using RandomAccessFile

RandomAccessFile is useful for creating a *flat file database*, a single file organized into records and fields. A *record* stores a single entry (such as a part in a parts database) and a *field* stores a single attribute of the entry (such as a part number).

> **Note**   The term *field* is also used to refer to a variable declared within a class. To avoid confusion with this overloaded terminology, think of a field variable as being analogous to a record's field attribute.

A flat file database typically organizes its content into a sequence of fixed-length records. Each record is further organized into one or more fixed-length fields. Figure 3-1 illustrates this concept in the context of a parts database.

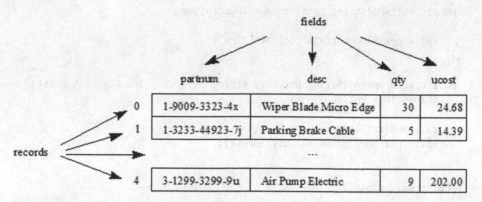

Figure 3-1. A flat file database of automotive parts is divided into records and fields

According to Figure 3-1, each field has a name (partnum, desc, qty, and ucost). Also, each record is assigned a number starting at 0. This example consists of five records, of which only three are shown for brevity.

To show you how to implement a flat file database in terms of
RandomAccessFile, I've created a simple PartsDB class to model Figure 3-1.
Check out Listing 3-1.

Listing 3-1. Implementing the Parts Flat File Database

```java
import java.io.IOException;
import java.io.RandomAccessFile;

public class PartsDB
{
   public final static int PNUMLEN = 20;
   public final static int DESCLEN = 30;
   public final static int QUANLEN = 4;
   public final static int COSTLEN = 4;

   private final static int RECLEN = 2 * PNUMLEN + 2 * DESCLEN + QUANLEN +
                                     COSTLEN;
   private RandomAccessFile raf;

   public PartsDB(String path) throws IOException
   {
      raf = new RandomAccessFile(path, "rw");
   }

   public void append(String partnum, String partdesc, int qty, int ucost)
      throws IOException
   {
      raf.seek(raf.length());
      write(partnum, partdesc, qty, ucost);
   }

   public void close()
   {
      try
      {
         raf.close();
      }
      catch (IOException ioe)
      {
         System.err.println(ioe);
      }
   }

   public int numRecs() throws IOException
   {
      return (int) raf.length() / RECLEN;
   }
```

```java
public Part select(int recno) throws IOException
{
   if (recno < 0 || recno >= numRecs())
      throw new IllegalArgumentException(recno + " out of range");
   raf.seek(recno * RECLEN);
   return read();
}

public void update(int recno, String partnum, String partdesc, int qty,
                   int ucost) throws IOException
{
   if (recno < 0 || recno >= numRecs())
      throw new IllegalArgumentException(recno + " out of range");
   raf.seek(recno * RECLEN);
   write(partnum, partdesc, qty, ucost);
}

private Part read() throws IOException
{
   StringBuffer sb = new StringBuffer();
   for (int i = 0; i < PNUMLEN; i++)
      sb.append(raf.readChar());
   String partnum = sb.toString().trim();
   sb.setLength(0);
   for (int i = 0; i < DESCLEN; i++)
      sb.append(raf.readChar());
   String partdesc = sb.toString().trim();
   int qty = raf.readInt();
   int ucost = raf.readInt();
   return new Part(partnum, partdesc, qty, ucost);
}

private void write(String partnum, String partdesc, int qty, int ucost)
   throws IOException
{
   StringBuffer sb = new StringBuffer(partnum);
   if (sb.length() > PNUMLEN)
      sb.setLength(PNUMLEN);
   else
   if (sb.length() < PNUMLEN)
   {
      int len = PNUMLEN - sb.length();
      for (int i = 0; i < len; i++)
         sb.append(" ");
   }
   raf.writeChars(sb.toString());
   sb = new StringBuffer(partdesc);
   if (sb.length() > DESCLEN)
      sb.setLength(DESCLEN);
```

```java
      else
      if (sb.length() < DESCLEN)
      {
         int len = DESCLEN - sb.length();
         for (int i = 0; i < len; i++)
            sb.append(" ");
      }
      raf.writeChars(sb.toString());
      raf.writeInt(qty);
      raf.writeInt(ucost);
   }

   public static class Part
   {
      private String partnum;
      private String desc;
      private int qty;
      private int ucost;

      public Part(String partnum, String desc, int qty, int ucost)
      {
         this.partnum = partnum;
         this.desc = desc;
         this.qty = qty;
         this.ucost = ucost;
      }

      String getDesc()
      {
         return desc;
      }

      String getPartnum()
      {
         return partnum;
      }

      int getQty()
      {
         return qty;
      }

      int getUnitCost()
      {
         return ucost;
      }
   }
}
```

PartsDB first declares constants that identify the lengths of the string and 32-bit integer fields. It then declares a constant that calculates the record length in terms of bytes. The calculation takes into account the fact that a character occupies two bytes in the file.

These constants are followed by a field named raf that is of type RandomAccessFile. This field is assigned an instance of the RandomAccessFile class in the subsequent constructor, which creates/opens a new file or opens an existing file because of "rw".

PartsDB next declares append(), close(), numRecs(), select(), and update(). These methods append a record to the file, close the file, return the number of records in the file, select and return a specific record, and update a specific record:

- The append() method first calls length() and seek(). Doing so ensures that the file pointer is positioned at the end of the file before calling the private write() method to write a record containing this method's arguments.

- RandomAccessFile's close() method can throw IOException. Because this is a rare occurrence, I chose to handle this exception in PartDB's close() method, which keeps that method's signature simple. However, I print a message when IOException occurs.

- The numRecs() method returns the number of records in the file. These records are numbered starting with 0 and ending with numRecs() - 1. Each of the select() and update() methods verifies that its recno argument lies within this range.

- The select() method calls the private read() method to return the record identified by recno as an instance of the nested Part class. Part's constructor initializes a Part object to a record's field values, and its getter methods return these values.

- The update() method is equally simple. As with select(), it first positions the file pointer to the start of the record identified by recno. As with append(), it calls write() to write out its arguments but replaces a record instead of adding one.

Records are written with the private write() method. Because fields must have exact sizes, write() pads String-based values that are shorter than a field size with spaces on the right and truncates these values to the field size when needed.

Records are read via the private read() method. read() removes the padding before saving a String-based field value in the Part object.

By itself, PartsDB is useless. You need an application that lets you experiment with this class, and Listing 3-2 fulfills this requirement.

Listing 3-2. Experimenting with the Parts Flat File Database

```
import java.io.IOException;

public class UsePartsDB
{
   public static void main(String[] args)
   {
      PartsDB pdb = null;
      try
      {
         pdb = new PartsDB("parts.db");
         if (pdb.numRecs() == 0)
         {
            // Populate the database with records.
            pdb.append("1-9009-3323-4x", "Wiper Blade Micro Edge", 30,
                       2468);
            pdb.append("1-3233-44923-7j", "Parking Brake Cable", 5, 1439);
            pdb.append("2-3399-6693-2m", "Halogen Bulb H4 55/60W", 22, 813);
            pdb.append("2-599-2029-6k", "Turbo Oil Line O-Ring ", 26, 155);
            pdb.append("3-1299-3299-9u", "Air Pump Electric", 9, 20200);
         }
         dumpRecords(pdb);
         pdb.update(1, "1-3233-44923-7j", "Parking Brake Cable", 5, 1995);
         dumpRecords(pdb);
      }
      catch (IOException ioe)
      {
         System.err.println(ioe);
      }
      finally
      {
         if (pdb != null)
            pdb.close();
      }
   }

   static void dumpRecords(PartsDB pdb) throws IOException
   {
      for (int i = 0; i < pdb.numRecs(); i++)
      {
         PartsDB.Part part = pdb.select(i);
         System.out.print(format(part.getPartnum(), PartsDB.PNUMLEN, true));
```

```
        System.out.print(" | ");
        System.out.print(format(part.getDesc(), PartsDB.DESCLEN, true));
        System.out.print(" | ");
        System.out.print(format("" + part.getQty(), 10, false));
        System.out.print(" | ");
        String s = part.getUnitCost() / 100 + "." + part.getUnitCost() %
                   100;
        if (s.charAt(s.length() - 2) == '.') s += "0";
        System.out.println(format(s, 10, false));
    }
    System.out.println("Number of records = " + pdb.numRecs());
    System.out.println();
}

static String format(String value, int maxWidth, boolean leftAlign)
{
    StringBuffer sb = new StringBuffer();
    int len = value.length();
    if (len > maxWidth)
    {
        len = maxWidth;
        value = value.substring(0, len);
    }
    if (leftAlign)
    {
        sb.append(value);
        for (int i = 0; i < maxWidth - len; i++)
            sb.append(" ");
    }
    else
    {
        for (int i = 0; i < maxWidth - len; i++)
            sb.append(" ");
        sb.append(value);
    }
    return sb.toString();
}
}
```

Listing 3-2's main() method begins by instantiating PartsDB, with parts.db as the name of the database file. When this file has no records, numRecs() returns 0 and several records are appended to the file via the append() method.

main() next dumps the five records stored in parts.db to the standard output stream, updates the unit cost in the record whose number is 1, once again dumps these records to the standard output stream to show this change, and closes the database.

> **Note** I store unit cost values as integer-based penny amounts. For example, I specify literal 1995 to represent 1995 pennies, or $19.95. If I were to use java.math.BigDecimal objects to store currency values, I would have to refactor PartsDB to take advantage of object serialization, and I'm not prepared to do that right now. (I discuss object serialization in Chapter 4.)

main() relies on a dumpRecords() helper method to dump these records, and dumpRecords() relies on a format() helper method to format field values so that they can be presented in properly aligned columns—I could have used java.util.Formatter (see Chapter 11) instead.

Compile Listings 3–1 and 3–2 as follows:

```
javac *.java
```

Run the resulting application as follows:

```
java UsePartsDB
```

The following output reveals the alignment achieved by format():

```
1-9009-3323-4x      | Wiper Blade Micro Edge      |       30 |      24.68
1-3233-44923-7j     | Parking Brake Cable         |        5 |      19.95
2-3399-6693-2m      | Halogen Bulb H4 55/60W      |       22 |       8.13
2-599-2029-6k       | Turbo Oil Line O-Ring       |       26 |       1.55
3-1299-3299-9u      | Air Pump Electric           |        9 |     202.00
Number of records = 5

1-9009-3323-4x      | Wiper Blade Micro Edge      |       30 |      24.68
1-3233-44923-7j     | Parking Brake Cable         |        5 |      19.95
2-3399-6693-2m      | Halogen Bulb H4 55/60W      |       22 |       8.13
2-599-2029-6k       | Turbo Oil Line O-Ring       |       26 |       1.55
3-1299-3299-9u      | Air Pump Electric           |        9 |     202.00
Number of records = 5
```

And there you have it: a simple flat file database. Despite its lack of support for advanced database features such as indexes and transaction management, a flat file database might be all that your Java application requires.

> **Note**   Check out Wikipedia's "Flat file database" entry
> (https://en.wikipedia.org/wiki/Flat_file_database) to learn
> more about flat file databases.

EXERCISES

The following exercises are designed to test your understanding of Chapter 3's content:

1. What is the purpose of the RandomAccessFile class?

2. What is a file's metadata?

3. What is the purpose of the "rwd" and "rws" mode arguments?

4. What is a file pointer?

5. What happens when you write past the end of the file?

6. True or false: When you call RandomAccessFile's seek(long) method to set the file pointer's value, and when this value is greater than the length of the file, the file's length changes.

7. What does method void write(int b) accomplish?

8. What does FileDescriptor's sync() method accomplish?

9. Define flat file database.

10. Write a small Java application named RAFDemo that opens file data in read/write mode, uses void write(int b) to write byte value 127 followed by void writeChars(String s) to write string "Test" (minus the quotes) to this file, resets the file pointer to the start of the file, and read/outputs these values.

Summary

Files can be opened for random access in which a mixture of write and read operations at various locations can occur until the file is closed. Java supports this random access by providing the RandomAccessFile class (in the java.io package).

You first learned about RandomAccessFile's constructors, operation modes, and the file pointer. You then explored a sample of this class's methods. Next, you learned about the FileDescriptor class and its methods. Lastly, you learned how to use RandomAccessFile to create a flat file database.

Chapter 4 presents classic I/O's stream classes.

Streams

Along with `java.io.File` and `java.io.RandomAccessFile`, Java's classic I/O infrastructure provides streams for performing I/O operations. A *stream* is an ordered sequence of bytes of an arbitrary length. Bytes flow over an *output stream* from an application to a destination and flow over an *input stream* from a source to an application.

Java provides classes in the `java.io` package that identify various stream destinations for writing; for example, byte arrays, files, and thread pipes. Java also provides classes in this package that identify various stream sources for reading. Examples include byte arrays, files, and thread pipes. This chapter explores many of these classes.

Stream Classes Overview

The `java.io` package provides several output stream and input stream classes that are descendants of its abstract `OutputStream` and `InputStream` classes. Figure 4-1 reveals the hierarchy of output stream classes.

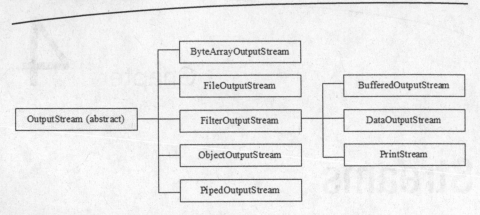

Figure 4-1. All output stream classes except for `PrintStream` are denoted by their `OutputStream` suffixes

Figure 4-2 reveals the hierarchy of input stream classes.

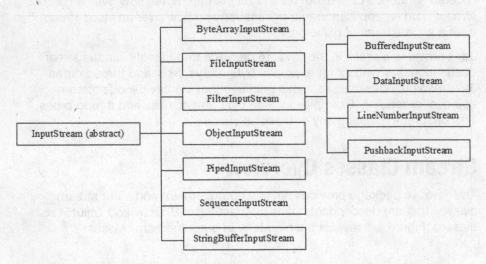

Figure 4-2. `LineNumberInputStream` and `StringBufferInputStream` are deprecated

LineNumberInputStream and StringBufferInputStream have been deprecated because they don't support different character encodings, a topic I discuss in Chapter 5. java.io.LineNumberReader and java.io.StringReader are their replacements. (I discuss readers along with writers in Chapter 5.)

> **Note** PrintStream is another class that should be deprecated because it
> doesn't support different character encodings; java.io.PrintWriter is its
> replacement. However, it's doubtful that Oracle will deprecate this class because
> PrintStream is the type of the java.lang.System class's out and err
> class fields, and too much legacy code depends on this fact.

Other Java packages provide additional output stream and input stream
classes. For example, java.util.zip provides four output stream classes
that compress uncompressed data into various formats and four matching
input stream classes that uncompress compressed data from the same
formats:

- CheckedOutputStream
- CheckedInputStream
- DeflaterOutputStream
- GZIPOutputStream
- GZIPInputStream
- InflaterInputStream
- ZipOutputStream
- ZipInputStream

Also, the java.util.jar package provides a pair of stream classes for
writing content to a JAR file and for reading content from a JAR file:

- JarOutputStream
- JarInputStream

Touring the Stream Classes

In the next several sections, I take you on a tour of most of java.io's
output stream and input stream classes, beginning with OutputStream and
InputStream.

OutputStream and InputStream

Java provides the abstract OutputStream and InputStream classes to describe
classes that perform stream I/O. OutputStream is the superclass of all output
stream subclasses. Table 4-1 describes OutputStream's methods.

Table 4-1. OutputStream Methods

Method	Description
void close()	Close this output stream and release any operating system resources associated with the stream. This method throws java.io.IOException when an I/O error occurs.
void flush()	Flush this output stream by writing any buffered output bytes to the destination. If the intended destination of this output stream is an abstraction provided by the underlying operating system (for example, a file), flushing the stream only guarantees that bytes previously written to the stream are passed to the underlying operating system for writing; it doesn't guarantee that they're actually written to a physical device such as a disk drive. This method throws IOException when an I/O error occurs.
void write(byte[] b)	Write b.length bytes from byte array b to this output stream. In general, write(b) behaves as if you specified write(b, 0, b.length). This method throws java.lang .NullPointerException when b is null and IOException when an I/O error occurs.
void write(byte[] b, int off, int len)	Write len bytes from byte array b starting at offset off to this output stream. This method throws NullPointerException when b is null; java.lang .IndexOutOfBoundsException when off is negative, len is negative, or off + len is greater than b.length; and IOException when an I/O error occurs.
void write(int b)	Write byte b to this output stream. Only the eight low-order bits are written; the 24 high-order bits are ignored. This method throws IOException when an I/O error occurs.

The flush() method is useful in a long-running application that needs to save changes every so often, for example, a text editor application that saves changes to a temporary file every few minutes. Remember that flush() only flushes bytes to the operating system; doing so doesn't necessarily result in the operating system flushing these bytes to the disk.

> **Note** The close() method automatically flushes the output stream. If an application ends before close() is called, the output stream is automatically closed and its data is flushed.

InputStream is the superclass of all input stream subclasses. Table 4-2 describes InputStream's methods.

Table 4-2. InputStream Methods

Method	Description
int available()	Return an estimate of the number of bytes that can be read from this input stream via the next read() method call (or skipped over via skip()) without blocking the calling thread. This method throws IOException when an I/O error occurs. It's never correct to use this method's return value to allocate a buffer for holding all of the stream's data because a subclass might not return the total size of the stream.
void close()	Close this input stream and release any operating system resources associated with the stream. This method throws IOException when an I/O error occurs.
void mark(int readlimit)	Mark the current position in this input stream. A subsequent call to reset() repositions this stream to the last marked position so that subsequent read operations re-read the same bytes. The readlimit argument tells this input stream to allow that many bytes to be read before invalidating this mark (so that the stream cannot be reset to the marked position).
boolean markSupported()	Return true when this input stream supports mark() and reset(); otherwise, return false.
int read()	Read and return (as an int in the range 0 to 255) the next byte from this input stream, or return -1 when the end of the stream is reached. This method blocks until input is available, the end of the stream is detected, or an exception is thrown. It throws IOException when an I/O error occurs.
int read(byte[] b)	Read some number of bytes from this input stream and store them in byte array b. Return the number of bytes actually read (which might be less than b's length but is never more than its length), or return -1 when the end of the stream is reached (no byte is available to read). This method blocks until input is available, the end of the stream is detected, or an exception is thrown. It throws NullPointerException when b is null and IOException when an I/O error occurs.

(continued)

Table 4-2. (*continued*)

Method	Description
int read(byte[] b, int off, int len)	Read no more than len bytes from this input stream and store them in byte array b, starting at the offset specified by off. Return the number of bytes actually read (which might be less than len but is never more than len), or return -1 when the end of the stream is reached (no byte is available to read). This method blocks until input is available, the end of the stream is detected, or an exception is thrown. It throws NullPointerException when b is null; IndexOutOfBoundsException when off is negative, len is negative, or len is greater than b.length - off; and IOException when an I/O error occurs.
void reset()	Reposition this input stream to the position at the time mark() was last called. This method throws IOException when this input stream has not been marked or the mark has been invalidated.
long skip(long n)	Skip over and discard n bytes of data from this input stream. This method might skip over some smaller number of bytes (possibly zero), for example, when the end of the file is reached before n bytes have been skipped. The actual number of bytes skipped is returned. When n is negative, no bytes are skipped. This method throws IOException when this input stream doesn't support skipping or when some other I/O error occurs.

InputStream subclasses such as ByteArrayInputStream support marking the current read position in the input stream via the mark() method and later return to that position via the reset() method.

> **Caution**   Don't forget to call markSupported() to find out if the subclass supports mark() and reset().

ByteArrayOutputStream and ByteArrayInputStream

Byte arrays are often useful as stream destinations and sources. The ByteArrayOutputStream class lets you write a stream of bytes to a byte array; the ByteArrayInputStream class lets you read a stream of bytes from a byte array.

ByteArrayOutputStream declares two constructors. Each constructor creates a byte array output stream with an internal byte array; a copy of this array can be returned by calling ByteArrayOutputStream's byte[] toByteArray() method:

- ByteArrayOutputStream() creates a byte array output stream with an internal byte array whose initial size is 32 bytes. This array grows as necessary.

- ByteArrayOutputStream(int size) creates a byte array output stream with an internal byte array whose initial size is specified by size and grows as necessary. This constructor throws java.lang.IllegalArgumentException when size is less than zero.

The following example uses ByteArrayOutputStream() to create a byte array output stream with an internal byte array set to the default size:

```
ByteArrayOutputStream baos = new ByteArrayOutputStream();
```

ByteArrayInputStream also declares a pair of constructors. Each constructor creates a byte array input stream based on the specified byte array and keeps track of the next byte to read from the array and the number of bytes to read:

- ByteArrayInputStream(byte[] ba) creates a byte array input stream that uses ba as its byte array (ba is used directly; a copy isn't created). The position is set to 0 and the number of bytes to read is set to ba.length.

- ByteArrayInputStream(byte[] ba, int offset, int count) creates a byte array input stream that uses ba as its byte array (no copy is made). The position is set to offset and the number of bytes to read is set to count.

The following example uses ByteArrayInputStream(byte[]) to create a byte array input stream whose source is a copy of the previous byte array output stream's byte array:

```
ByteArrayInputStream bais = new ByteArrayInputStream(baos.toByteArray());
```

ByteArrayOutputStream and ByteArrayInputStream are useful when you need to convert an image to an array of bytes, process these bytes in some manner, and convert the bytes back to the image.

For example, suppose you're writing an Android-based image-processing application. You decode a file containing the image into an Android-specific android.graphics.BitMap instance, compress this instance into a ByteArrayOutputStream instance, obtain a copy of the byte array output stream's array, process this array in some manner, convert this array to a

ByteArrayInputStream instance, and use the byte array input stream to decode these bytes into another BitMap instance, as follows:

```
String path = ... ; // Assume a legitimate path to an image.
Bitmap bm = BitmapFactory.decodeFile(path);
ByteArrayOutputStream baos = new ByteArrayOutputStream();
if (bm.compress(Bitmap.CompressFormat.PNG, 100, baos))
{
   byte[] imageBytes = baos.toByteArray();
   // Do something with imageBytes.
   bm = BitMapFactory.decodeStream(new ByteArrayInputStream(imageBytes));
}
```

This example obtains an image file's path and then calls the concrete android.graphics.BitmapFactory class's Bitmap decodeFile(String path) class method. This method decodes the image file identified by path into a bitmap and returns a Bitmap instance that represents this bitmap.

After creating a ByteArrayOutputStream object, the example uses the returned BitMap instance to call BitMap's boolean compress(Bitmap.CompressFormat format, int quality, OutputStream stream) method to write a compressed version of the bitmap to the byte array output stream:

- format identifies the format of the compressed image. I've chosen to use the popular Portable Network Graphics (PNG) format.

- quality hints to the compressor as to how much compression is required. This value ranges from 0 to 100, where 0 means maximum compression at the expense of quality and 100 means maximum quality at the expense of compression. Formats such as PNG ignore quality because they employ lossless compression.

- stream identifies the stream on which to write the compressed image data.

When compress() returns true, which means that it successfully compressed the image onto the byte array output stream in the PNG format, the ByteArrayOutputStream object's toByteArray() method is called to create and return a byte array with the image's bytes.

Next, the array is processed, a ByteArrayInputStream object is created with the processed bytes as the source of this stream, and BitmapFactory's BitMap decodeStream(InputStream is) class method is called to convert the byte array input stream's source of bytes to a BitMap instance.

FileOutputStream and FileInputStream

Files are common stream destinations and sources. The concrete FileOutputStream class lets you write a stream of bytes to a file; the concrete FileInputStream class lets you read a stream of bytes from a file.

FileOutputStream subclasses OutputStream and declares five constructors for creating file output streams. For example, FileOutputStream(String name) creates a file output stream to the existing file identified by name. This constructor throws java.io.FileNotFoundException when the file doesn't exist and cannot be created, it is a directory rather than a normal file, or there is some other reason why the file cannot be opened for output.

The following example uses FileOutputStream(String path) to create a file output stream with employee.dat as its destination:

```
FileOutputStream fos = new FileOutputStream("employee.dat");
```

> **Tip** FileOutputStream(String name) overwrites an existing file. To append data instead of overwriting existing content, call a FileOutputStream constructor that includes a boolean append parameter and pass true to this parameter.

FileInputStream subclasses InputStream and declares three constructors for creating file input streams. For example, FileInputStream(String name) creates a file input stream from the existing file identified by name. This constructor throws FileNotFoundException when the file doesn't exist, it is a directory rather than a normal file, or there is some other reason that the file cannot be opened for input.

The following example uses FileInputStream(String name) to create a file input stream with employee.dat as its source:

```
FileInputStream fis = new FileInputStream("employee.dat");
```

FileOutputStream and FileInputStream are useful in a file-copying context. Listing 4-1 presents the source code to a Copy application that provides a demonstration.

Listing 4-1. Copying a Source File to a Destination File

```java
import java.io.FileInputStream;
import java.io.FileNotFoundException;
import java.io.FileOutputStream;
import java.io.IOException;

public class Copy
{
   public static void main(String[] args)
   {
      if (args.length != 2)
      {
         System.err.println("usage: java Copy srcfile dstfile");
         return;
      }
      FileInputStream fis = null;
      FileOutputStream fos = null;
      try
      {
         fis = new FileInputStream(args[0]);
         fos = new FileOutputStream(args[1]);
         int b; // I chose b instead of byte because byte is a reserved
                // word.
         while ((b = fis.read()) != -1)
            fos.write(b);
      }
      catch (FileNotFoundException fnfe)
      {
         System.err.println(args[0] + " could not be opened for input, or "
                             + args[1] + " could not be created for output");
      }
      catch (IOException ioe)
      {
         System.err.println("I/O error: " + ioe.getMessage());
      }
      finally
      {
         if (fis != null)
            try
            {
               fis.close();
            }
            catch (IOException ioe)
            {
               assert false; // shouldn't happen in this context
            }
```

```
        if (fos != null)
           try
           {
               fos.close();
           }
           catch (IOException ioe)
           {
               assert false; // shouldn't happen in this context
           }
       }
    }
}
```

Listing 4-1's main() method first verifies that two command-line arguments, identifying the names of source and destination files, are specified. It then proceeds to instantiate FileInputStream and FileOutputStream and enter a while loop that repeatedly reads bytes from the file input stream and writes them to the file output stream.

Of course, something might go wrong. Perhaps the source file doesn't exist, or perhaps the destination file cannot be created (a same-named read-only file might exist, for example). In either scenario, FileNotFoundException is thrown and must be handled. Another possibility is that an I/O error occurred during the copy operation. Such an error results in IOException.

Regardless of an exception being thrown or not, the input and output streams are closed via the finally block. In a simple application like this, you could ignore the close() method calls and let the application terminate. Although Java automatically closes open files at this point, it's good form to explicitly close files upon exit.

Because close() is capable of throwing an instance of the checked IOException class, a call to this method is wrapped in a try statement with an appropriate catch block that catches this exception. Notice the if statement that precedes each try statement. The if statement is necessary to avoid a thrown NullPointerException instance when either fis or fos contain the null reference.

Java 7's try-with-resources statement can save you a lot of coding by automatically closing open streams. To see the savings for yourself, check out Listing 4-2, which presents the source code to another Copy application that uses try-with-resources.

Listing 4-2. Copying a Source File to a Destination File, Version 2

```java
import java.io.FileInputStream;
import java.io.FileNotFoundException;
import java.io.FileOutputStream;
import java.io.IOException;

public class Copy
{
   public static void main(String[] args)
   {
      if (args.length != 2)
      {
         System.err.println("usage: java Copy srcfile dstfile");
         return;
      }
      try (FileInputStream fis = new FileInputStream(args[0]);
           FileOutputStream fos = new FileOutputStream(args[1]))
      {
         int b; // I chose b instead of byte because byte is a reserved
                // word.
         while ((b = fis.read()) != -1)
            fos.write(b);
      }
      catch (FileNotFoundException fnfe)
      {
         System.err.println(args[0] + " could not be opened for input, or "
                            + args[1] + " could not be created for output");
      }
      catch (IOException ioe)
      {
         System.err.println("I/O error: " + ioe.getMessage());
      }
   }
}
```

Compile Listing 4-1 or 4-2 as follows:

```
javac Copy.java
```

Run the resulting application as follows:

```
java Copy Copy.java Copy.bak
```

If all goes well, you should observe a Copy.bak file whose length and contents are identical to that of Copy.java.

PipedOutputStream and PipedInputStream

Threads must often communicate. One approach involves using shared variables. Another approach involves using piped streams via the PipedOutputStream and PipedInputStream classes. The PipedOutputStream class lets a sending thread write a stream of bytes to an instance of the PipedInputStream class, which a receiving thread uses to subsequently read those bytes.

> **Caution** Attempting to use a PipedOutputStream object and a PipedInputStream object from a single thread is not recommended because it might deadlock the thread.

PipedOutputStream declares a pair of constructors for creating piped output streams:

- PipedOutputStream() creates a piped output stream that's not yet connected to a piped input stream. It must be connected to a piped input stream, either by the receiver or the sender, before being used.

- PipedOutputStream(PipedInputStream dest) creates a piped output stream that's connected to the piped input stream dest. Bytes written to the piped output stream can be read from dest. This constructor throws IOException when an I/O error occurs.

PipedOutputStream declares a void connect(PipedInputStream dest) method that connects this piped output stream to dest. This method throws IOException when this piped output stream is already connected to another piped input stream.

PipedInputStream declares four constructors for creating piped input streams:

- PipedInputStream() creates a piped input stream that's not yet connected to a piped output stream. It must be connected to a piped output stream before being used.

- PipedInputStream(int pipeSize) creates a piped input stream that's not yet connected to a piped output stream and uses pipeSize to size the piped input stream's buffer. It must be connected to a piped output stream before being used. This constructor throws IllegalArgumentException when pipeSize is less than or equal to 0.

■ PipedInputStream(PipedOutputStream src) creates a piped input stream that's connected to the piped output stream src. Bytes written to src can be read from this piped input stream. This constructor throws IOException when an I/O error occurs.

■ PipedInputStream(PipedOutputStream src, int pipeSize) creates a piped input stream that's connected to the piped output stream src and uses pipeSize to size the piped input stream's buffer. Bytes written to src can be read from this piped input stream. This constructor throws IOException when an I/O error occurs and IllegalArgumentException when pipeSize is less than or equal to 0.

PipedInputStream declares a void connect(PipedOutputStream src) method that connects this piped input stream to src. This method throws IOException when this piped input stream is already connected to another piped output stream.

The easiest way to create a pair of piped streams is in the same thread and in either order. For example, you can first create the piped output stream:

```
PipedOutputStream pos = new PipedOutputStream();
PipedInputStream pis = new PipedInputStream(pos);
```

Alternatively, you can first create the piped input stream:

```
PipedInputStream pis = new PipedInputStream();
PipedOutputStream pos = new PipedOutputStream(pis);
```

You can leave both streams unconnected and later connect them to each other using the appropriate piped stream's connect() method, as follows:

```
PipedOutputStream pos = new PipedOutputStream();
PipedInputStream pis = new PipedInputStream();
// ...
pos.connect(pis);
```

Listing 4-3 presents a PipedStreamsDemo application whose sender thread streams a sequence of randomly generated byte integers to a receiver thread, which outputs this sequence.

Listing 4-3. Piping Randomly Generated Bytes from a Sender Thread to a Receiver Thread

```java
import java.io.IOException;
import java.io.PipedInputStream;
import java.io.PipedOutputStream;

public class PipedStreamsDemo
{
   final static int LIMIT = 10;

   public static void main(String[] args) throws IOException
   {
      final PipedOutputStream pos = new PipedOutputStream();
      final PipedInputStream pis = new PipedInputStream(pos);
      Runnable senderTask = () -> {
                                try
                                {
                                   for (int i = 0 ; i < LIMIT; i++)
                                      pos.write((byte)
                                               (Math.random() * 256));
                                }
                                catch (IOException ioe)
                                {
                                   ioe.printStackTrace();
                                }
                                finally
                                {
                                   try
                                   {
                                      pos.close();
                                   }
                                   catch (IOException ioe)
                                   {
                                      ioe.printStackTrace();
                                   }
                                }
                             };
         Runnable receiverTask = () -> {
                                try
                                {
                                   int b;
                                   while ((b = pis.read()) != -1)
                                      System.out.println(b);
                                }
                                catch (IOException ioe)
                                {
                                   ioe.printStackTrace();
                                }
```

```
                                      finally
                                      {
                                          try
                                          {
                                              pis.close();
                                          }
                                          catch (IOException ioe)
                                          {
                                              ioe.printStackTrace();
                                          }
                                      }
                                  };
        Thread sender = new Thread(senderTask);
        Thread receiver = new Thread(receiverTask);
        sender.start();
        receiver.start();
    }
}
```

Listing 4-3's main() method creates piped output and piped input streams that will be used by the senderTask thread to communicate a sequence of randomly generated byte integers and by the receiverTask thread to receive this sequence.

The sender task's run() method explicitly closes its pipe stream when it finishes sending the data. If it didn't do this, an IOException instance with a "write end dead" message would be thrown when the receiver thread invoked read() for the final time (which would otherwise return -1 to indicate end of stream). For more information on this message, check out Daniel Ferber's "What's this? IOException: Write End Dead" blog post (http://techtavern.wordpress.com/2008/07/16/whats-this-ioexception-write-end-dead/).

Compile Listing 4-3 as follows:

```
javac PipedStreamsDemo.java
```

Run the resulting application as follows:

```
java PipedStreamsDemo
```

You'll discover output similar to the following:

```
243
147
34
68
174
```

251
99
44
7
19

FilterOutputStream and FilterInputStream

Byte array, file, and piped streams pass bytes unchanged to their destinations. Java also supports *filter streams* that buffer, compress/uncompress, encrypt/decrypt, or otherwise manipulate a stream's byte sequence (that is input to the filter) before it reaches its destination.

A *filter output stream* takes the data passed to its write() methods (the input stream), filters it, and writes the filtered data to an underlying output stream, which might be another filter output stream or a destination output stream such as a file output stream.

Filter output streams are created from subclasses of the concrete FilterOutputStream class, an OutputStream subclass. FilterOutputStream declares a single FilterOutputStream(OutputStream out) constructor that creates a filter output stream built on top of out, the underlying output stream.

Listing 4-4 reveals that it's easy to subclass FilterOutputStream. At a minimum, you declare a constructor that passes its OutputStream argument to FilterOutputStream's constructor and override FilterOutputStream's write(int) method.

Listing 4-4. Scrambling a Stream of Bytes

```java
import java.io.FilterOutputStream;
import java.io.IOException;
import java.io.OutputStream;

public class ScrambledOutputStream extends FilterOutputStream
{
    private int[] map;

    public ScrambledOutputStream(OutputStream out, int[] map)
    {
        super(out);
        if (map == null)
            throw new NullPointerException("map is null");
        if (map.length != 256)
            throw new IllegalArgumentException("map.length != 256");
        this.map = map;
    }
```

```
    @Override
    public void write(int b) throws IOException
    {
        out.write(map[b]);
    }
}
```

Listing 4-4 presents a ScrambledOutputStream class that performs trivial encryption on its input stream by scrambling the input stream's bytes via a remapping operation. This constructor declares two parameters:

- out identifies the output stream on which to write the scrambled bytes.

- map identifies an array of 256 byte-integer values to which input stream bytes map.

The constructor first passes its out argument to the FilterOutputStream parent via a super(out); call. It then verifies its map argument's integrity (map must be non-null and have a length of 256; a byte stream offers exactly 256 bytes to map) before saving map.

The write(int) method is trivial: it calls the underlying output stream's write(int) method with the byte to which argument b maps. FilterOutputStream declares out to be protected (for performance), which is why you can directly access this field.

> **Note**   It's only essential to override write(int) because FilterOutputStream's other two write() methods are implemented via this method.

Listing 4-5 presents the source code to a Scramble application for experimenting with scrambling a source file's bytes via ScrambledOutputStream and writing these scrambled bytes to a destination file.

Listing 4-5. Scrambling a File's Bytes

```
import java.io.FileInputStream;
import java.io.FileOutputStream;
import java.io.IOException;

import java.util.Random;
```

```
public class Scramble
{
   public static void main(String[] args)
   {
      if (args.length != 2)
      {
         System.err.println("usage: java Scramble srcpath destpath");
         return;
      }
      FileInputStream fis = null;
      ScrambledOutputStream sos = null;
      try
      {
         fis = new FileInputStream(args[0]);
         FileOutputStream fos = new FileOutputStream(args[1]);
         sos = new ScrambledOutputStream(fos, makeMap());
         int b;
         while ((b = fis.read()) != -1)
            sos.write(b);
      }
      catch (IOException ioe)
      {
         ioe.printStackTrace();
      }
      finally
      {
         if (fis != null)
            try
            {
               fis.close();
            }
            catch (IOException ioe)
            {
               ioe.printStackTrace();
            }
         if (sos != null)
            try
            {
               sos.close();
            }
            catch (IOException ioe)
            {
               ioe.printStackTrace();
            }
      }
   }
}
```

```
static int[] makeMap()
{
    int[] map = new int[256];
    for (int i = 0; i < map.length; i++)
        map[i] = i;
    // Shuffle map.
    Random r = new Random(0);
    for (int i = 0; i < map.length; i++)
    {
        int n = r.nextInt(map.length);
        int temp = map[i];
        map[i] = map[n];
        map[n] = temp;
    }
    return map;
}
}
```

Scramble's main() method first verifies the number of command-line arguments. The first argument identifies the source path of the file with unscrambled content; the second argument identifies the destination path of the file that stores scrambled content.

Assuming that two command-line arguments have been specified, main() instantiates FileInputStream, creating a file input stream that's connected to the file identified by args[0].

Continuing, main() instantiates FileOutputStream, creating a file output stream that's connected to the file identified by args[1]. It then instantiates ScrambledOutputStream and passes the FileOutputStream instance to ScrambledOutputStream's constructor.

> **Note**   When a stream instance is passed to another stream class's constructor, the two streams are *chained together*. For example, the scrambled output stream is chained to the file output stream.

main() now enters a loop, reading bytes from the file input stream and writing them to the scrambled output stream by calling ScrambledOutputStream's write(int) method. This loop continues until FileInputStream's read() method returns -1 (end of file).

The finally block closes the file input stream and scrambled output stream by calling their close() methods. It doesn't call the file output stream's close() method because FilterOutputStream automatically calls the underlying output stream's close() method.

The makeMap() method is responsible for creating the map array that's passed to ScrambledOutputStream's constructor. The idea is to populate the array with all 256 byte-integer values, storing them in random order.

> **Note** I pass 0 as the seed argument when creating the java.util.Random object in order to return a predictable sequence of random numbers. I need to use the same sequence of random numbers when creating the complementary map array in the Unscramble application, which I will present shortly. Unscrambling will not work without the same sequence.

Compile Listings 4-4 and 4-5 as follows:

```
javac *.java
```

Assuming that you have a simple 15-byte file named hello.txt that contains "Hello, World!" (followed by a carriage return and a line feed), run the resulting application with this file as follows:

```
java Scramble hello.txt hello.out
```

On a Windows 7 operating system, I observe Figure 4-3's scrambled output.

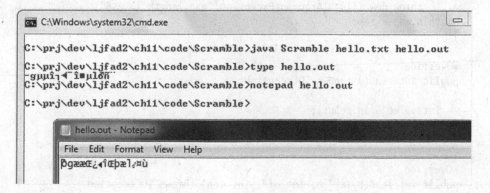

Figure 4-3. Different fonts yield different-looking scrambled output

A *filter input stream* takes the data obtained from its underlying input stream—which might be another filter input stream or a source input stream such as a file input stream—filters it, and makes this data available via its read() methods (the output stream).

Filter input streams are created from subclasses of the concrete
FilterInputStream class, an InputStream subclass. FilterInputStream
declares a single FilterInputStream(InputStream in) constructor that
creates a filter input stream built on top of in, the underlying input stream.

Listing 4-6 shows that it's easy to subclass FilterInputStream. At a
minimum, declare a constructor that passes its InputStream argument to
FilterInputStream's constructor and override FilterInputStream's read()
and read(byte[], int, int) methods.

Listing 4-6. Unscrambling a Stream of Bytes

```java
import java.io.FilterInputStream;
import java.io.InputStream;
import java.io.IOException;

public class ScrambledInputStream extends FilterInputStream
{
   private int[] map;

   public ScrambledInputStream(InputStream in, int[] map)
   {
      super(in);
      if (map == null)
         throw new NullPointerException("map is null");
      if (map.length != 256)
         throw new IllegalArgumentException("map.length != 256");
      this.map = map;
   }

   @Override
   public int read() throws IOException
   {
      int value = in.read();
      return (value == -1) ? -1 : map[value];
   }

   @Override
   public int read(byte[] b, int off, int len) throws IOException
   {
      int nBytes = in.read(b, off, len);
      if (nBytes <= 0)
         return nBytes;
      for (int i = 0; i < nBytes; i++)
         b[off + i] = (byte) map[off + i];
      return nBytes;
   }
}
```

Listing 4-6 presents a `ScrambledInputStream` class that performs trivial decryption on its underlying input stream by unscrambling the underlying input stream's scrambled bytes via a remapping operation.

The `read()` method first reads the scrambled byte from its underlying input stream. If the returned value is -1 (end of file), this value is returned to its caller. Otherwise, the byte is mapped to its unscrambled value, which is returned.

The `read(byte[], int, int)` method is similar to `read()`, but stores bytes read from the underlying input stream in a byte array, taking an offset into this array and a length (number of bytes to read) into account.

Once again, -1 might be returned from the underlying `read()` method call. If so, this value must be returned. Otherwise, each byte in the array is mapped to its unscrambled value, and the number of bytes read is returned.

> **Note**   It's only essential to override `read()` and `read(byte[], int, int)` because `FilterInputStream`'s `read(byte[])` method is implemented via the latter method.

Listing 4-7 presents the source code to an `Unscramble` application for experimenting with `ScrambledInputStream` by unscrambling a source file's bytes and writing these unscrambled bytes to a destination file.

Listing 4-7. Unscrambling a File's Bytes

```java
import java.io.FileInputStream;
import java.io.FileOutputStream;
import java.io.IOException;

import java.util.Random;

public class Unscramble
{
    public static void main(String[] args)
    {
        if (args.length != 2)
        {
            System.err.println("usage: java Unscramble srcpath destpath");
            return;
        }
        ScrambledInputStream sis = null;
        FileOutputStream fos = null;
```

```java
      try
      {
         FileInputStream fis = new FileInputStream(args[0]);
         sis = new ScrambledInputStream(fis, makeMap());
         fos = new FileOutputStream(args[1]);
         int b;
         while ((b = sis.read()) != -1)
            fos.write(b);
      }
      catch (IOException ioe)
      {
         ioe.printStackTrace();
      }
      finally
      {
         if (sis != null)
            try
            {
               sis.close();
            }
            catch (IOException ioe)
            {
               ioe.printStackTrace();
            }
         if (fos != null)
            try
            {
               fos.close();
            }
            catch (IOException ioe)
            {
               ioe.printStackTrace();
            }
      }
   }

   static int[] makeMap()
   {
      int[] map = new int[256];
      for (int i = 0; i < map.length; i++)
         map[i] = i;
      // Shuffle map.
      Random r = new Random(0);
      for (int i = 0; i < map.length; i++)
      {
         int n = r.nextInt(map.length);
         int temp = map[i];
         map[i] = map[n];
         map[n] = temp;
      }
```

```
    int[] temp = new int[256];
    for (int i = 0; i < temp.length; i++)
        temp[map[i]] = i;
    return temp;
    }
}
```

Unscramble's `main()` method first verifies the number of command-line arguments: the first argument identifies the source path of the file with scrambled content; the second argument identifies the destination path of the file that stores unscrambled content.

Assuming that two command-line arguments have been specified, `main()` instantiates `FileInputStream`, creating a file input stream that's connected to the file identified by `args[1]`.

Continuing, `main()` instantiates `FileInputStream`, creating a file input stream that's connected to the file identified by `args[0]`. It then instantiates `ScrambledInputStream` and passes the `FileInputStream` instance to `ScrambledInputStream`'s constructor.

> **Note**   When a stream instance is passed to another stream class's constructor, the two streams are *chained together*. For example, the scrambled input stream is chained to the file input stream.

`main()` now enters a loop, reading bytes from the scrambled input stream and writing them to the file output stream. This loop continues until `ScrambledInputStream`'s `read()` method returns -1 (end of file).

The `finally` block closes the scrambled input stream and file output stream by calling their `close()` methods. It doesn't call the file input stream's `close()` method because `FilterOutputStream` automatically calls the underlying input stream's `close()` method.

The `makeMap()` method is responsible for creating the map array that's passed to `ScrambledInputStream`'s constructor. The idea is to duplicate Listing 4-5's map array and then invert it so that unscrambling can be performed.

Compile Listings 4-6 and 4-7 as follows:

```
javac *.java
```

Assuming that you have copied the previously generated hello.out file to the current directory, run the resulting application with this file as follows:

```
java Unscramble hello.out hello.bak
```

You should see the same unscrambled content in hello.bak that's present in hello.txt.

> **Note**   For an additional example of a filter output stream and its complementary filter input stream, check out the "Extending Java Streams to Support Bit Streams" article (www.drdobbs.com/184410423) on the Dr. Dobb's web site. This article introduces BitStreamOutputStream and BitStreamInputStream classes that are useful for outputting and inputting bit streams. The article then demonstrates these classes in a Java implementation of the Lempel-Zif-Welch (LZW) data compression and decompression algorithm.

BufferedOutputStream and BufferedInputStream

FileOutputStream and FileInputStream have a performance problem. Each file output stream write() method call and file input stream read() method call results in a native method call to one of the underlying operating system's functions, and these native method calls slow down I/O.

The concrete BufferedOutputStream and BufferedInputStream filter stream classes improve performance by minimizing underlying output stream write() and underlying input stream read() method calls. Instead, calls to BufferedOutputStream's write() and BufferedInputStream's read() methods take Java buffers into account:

- When a write buffer is full, write() calls the underlying output stream write() method to empty the buffer. Subsequent calls to BufferedOutputStream's write() methods store bytes in this buffer until it's once again full.

- When the read buffer is empty, read() calls the underlying input stream read() method to fill the buffer. Subsequent calls to BufferedInputStream's read() methods return bytes from this buffer until it's once again empty.

BufferedOutputStream declares the following constructors:

- ■ BufferedOutputStream(OutputStream out) creates a buffered output stream that streams its output to out. An internal buffer is created to store bytes written to out.

- ■ BufferedOutputStream(OutputStream out, int size) creates a buffered output stream that streams its output to out. An internal buffer of length size is created to store bytes written to out.

The following example chains a BufferedOutputStream instance to a FileOutputStream instance. Subsequent write() method calls on the BufferedOutputStream instance buffer bytes and occasionally result in internal write() method calls on the encapsulated FileOutputStream instance:

```
FileOutputStream fos = new FileOutputStream("employee.dat");
BufferedOutputStream bos = new BufferedOutputStream(fos); // Chain bos
                                                           // to fos.
bos.write(0); // Write to employee.dat through the buffer.
// Additional write() method calls.
bos.close(); // This method call internally calls fos's close() method.
```

BufferedInputStream declares the following constructors:

- ■ BufferedInputStream(InputStream in) creates a buffered input stream that streams its input from in. An internal buffer is created to store bytes read from in.

- ■ BufferedInputStream(InputStream in, int size) creates a buffered input stream that streams its input from in. An internal buffer of length size is created to store bytes read from in.

The following example chains a BufferedInputStream instance to a FileInputStream instance. Subsequent read() method calls on the BufferedInputStream instance unbuffer bytes and occasionally result in internal read() method calls on the encapsulated FileInputStream instance:

```
FileInputStream fis = new FileInputStream("employee.dat");
BufferedInputStream bis = new BufferedInputStream(fis); // Chain bis to fis.
int ch = bis.read(); // Read employee.dat through the buffer.
// Additional read() method calls.
bis.close(); // This method call internally calls fis's close() method.
```

DataOutputStream and DataInputStream

FileOutputStream and FileInputStream are useful for writing and reading bytes and arrays of bytes. However, they provide no support for writing and reading primitive-type values (such as integers) and strings.

For this reason, Java provides the concrete DataOutputStream and DataInputStream filter stream classes. Each class overcomes this limitation by providing methods to write or read primitive-type values and strings in an operating system-independent way:

- Integer values are written and read in *big-endian format* (the most significant byte comes first). Check out Wikipedia's "Endianness" entry (http://en.wikipedia .org/wiki/Endianness) to learn about the concept of *endianness*.

- Floating-point and double precision floating-point values are written and read according to the IEEE 754 standard, which specifies four bytes per floating-point value and eight bytes per double precision floating-point value.

- Strings are written and read according to a modified version of *UTF-8*, a variable-length encoding standard for efficiently storing two-byte Unicode characters. Check out Wikipedia's "UTF-8" entry (http://en.wikipedia.org/wiki/Utf-8) to learn more about UTF-8.

DataOutputStream declares a single DataOutputStream(OutputStream out) constructor. Because this class implements the java.io.DataOutput interface, DataOutputStream also provides access to the same-named write methods as provided by java.io.RandomAccessFile.

DataInputStream declares a single DataInputStream(InputStream in) constructor. Because this class implements the java.io.DataInput interface, DataInputStream also provides access to the same-named read methods as provided by RandomAccessFile.

Listing 4-8 presents the source code to a DataStreamsDemo application that uses a DataOutputStream instance to write multibyte values to a FileOutputStream instance and uses a DataInputStream instance to read multibyte values from a FileInputStream instance.

Listing 4-8. Outputting and then Inputting a Stream of Multibyte Values

```java
import java.io.DataInputStream;
import java.io.DataOutputStream;
import java.io.FileInputStream;
import java.io.FileOutputStream;
import java.io.IOException;

public class DataStreamsDemo
{
   final static String FILENAME = "values.dat";

   public static void main(String[] args)
   {
      try (FileOutputStream fos = new FileOutputStream(FILENAME);
           DataOutputStream dos = new DataOutputStream(fos))
      {
         dos.writeInt(1995);
         dos.writeUTF("Saving this String in modified UTF-8 format!");
         dos.writeFloat(1.0F);
      }
      catch (IOException ioe)
      {
         System.err.println("I/O error: " + ioe.getMessage());
      }

      try (FileInputStream fis = new FileInputStream(FILENAME);
           DataInputStream dis = new DataInputStream(fis))
      {
         System.out.println(dis.readInt());
         System.out.println(dis.readUTF());
         System.out.println(dis.readFloat());
      }
      catch (IOException ioe)
      {
         System.err.println("I/O error: " + ioe.getMessage());
      }
   }
}
```

`DataStreamsDemo` creates a file named `values.dat`; calls `DataOutputStream` methods to write an integer, a string, and a floating-point value to this file; and calls `DataInputStream` methods to read back these values.

Compile Listing 4-8 as follows:

```
javac DataStreamsDemo.java
```

Run the resulting application as follows:

```
java DataStreamsDemo
```

You should observe the following output:

```
1995
Saving this String in modified UTF-8 format!
1.0
```

> **Caution**   When reading a file of values written by a sequence of
> DataOutputStream method calls, make sure to use the same method-
> call sequence. Otherwise, you're bound to end up with erroneous data and,
> in the case of the readUTF() methods, thrown instances of the java.
> io.UTFDataFormatException class (a subclass of IOException).

Object Serialization and Deserialization

Java provides the DataOutputStream and DataInputStream classes to
stream primitive-type values and String objects. However, you cannot use
these classes to stream non-String objects. Instead, you must use object
serialization and deserialization to stream objects of arbitrary types.

Object serialization is a Java virtual machine (JVM) mechanism for *serializing*
object state into a stream of bytes. Its *deserialization* counterpart is a JVM
mechanism for *deserializing* this state from a byte stream.

> **Note**   An object's state consists of instance fields that store primitive-type
> values and/or references to other objects. When an object is serialized, the
> objects that are part of this state are also serialized (unless you prevent them
> from being serialized). Furthermore, the objects that are part of those objects'
> states are serialized (unless you prevent this), and so on.

Java supports default serialization and deserialization, custom serialization
and deserialization, and externalization.

Default Serialization and Deserialization

Default serialization and deserialization is the easiest form to use but offers little control over how objects are serialized and deserialized. Although Java handles most of the work on your behalf, there are a couple of tasks that you must perform.

Your first task is to have the class of the object that's to be serialized implement the java.io.Serializable interface, either directly or indirectly via the class's superclass. The rationale for implementing Serializable is to avoid unlimited serialization.

Note Serializable is an empty marker interface (there are no methods to implement) that a class implements to tell the JVM that it's okay to serialize the class's objects. When the serialization mechanism encounters an object whose class doesn't implement Serializable, it throws an instance of the java.io.NotSerializableException class (an indirect subclass of IOException).

Unlimited serialization is the process of serializing an entire object graph. Java doesn't support unlimited serialization for the following reasons:

- *Security*: If Java automatically serialized an object containing sensitive information (such as a password or a credit card number), it would be easy for a hacker to discover this information and wreak havoc. It's better to give the developer a choice to prevent this from happening.

- *Performance*: Serialization leverages the Reflection API, which tends to slow down application performance. Unlimited serialization could really hurt an application's performance.

- *Objects not amenable to serialization*: Some objects exist only in the context of a running application and it's meaningless to serialize them. For example, a file stream object that's deserialized no longer represents a connection to a file.

Listing 4-9 declares an Employee class that implements the Serializable interface to tell the JVM that it's okay to serialize Employee objects.

Listing 4-9. Implementing Serializable

```java
import java.io.Serializable;

public class Employee implements Serializable
{
   private String name;
   private int age;

   public Employee(String name, int age)
   {
      this.name = name;
      this.age = age;
   }

   public String getName() { return name; }

   public int getAge() { return age; }
}
```

Because Employee implements Serializable, the serialization mechanism will not throw a NotSerializableException instance when serializing an Employee object. Not only does Employee implement Serializable, the java.lang.String class also implements this interface.

Your second task is to work with the ObjectOutputStream class and its writeObject() method to serialize an object and the OutputInputStream class and its readObject() method to deserialize the object.

> **Note**   Although ObjectOutputStream extends OutputStream instead of FilterOutputStream, and although ObjectInputStream extends InputStream instead of FilterInputStream, these classes behave as filter streams.

Java provides the concrete ObjectOutputStream class to initiate the serialization of an object's state to an object output stream. This class declares an ObjectOutputStream(OutputStream out) constructor that chains the object output stream to the output stream specified by out.

When you pass an output stream reference to out, this constructor attempts to write a serialization header to that output stream. It throws NullPointerException when out contains the null reference and IOException when an I/O error prevents it from writing this header.

ObjectOutputStream serializes an object via its void writeObject(Object obj) method. This method attempts to write information about obj's class followed by the values of obj's instance fields to the underlying output stream.

writeObject() doesn't serialize the contents of static fields. In contrast, it serializes the contents of all instance fields that are not explicitly prefixed with the transient reserved word. For example, consider the following field declaration:

```
public transient char[] password;
```

This declaration specifies transient to avoid serializing a password for some hacker to encounter. The JVM's serialization mechanism ignores any instance field that's marked transient.

> **Note**   Check out my "Transience" blog post (www.javaworld.com/community/node/13451) to learn more about transient.

writeObject() throws an instance of IOException or an IOException subclass when something goes wrong. For example, this method throws NotSerializableException when it encounters an object whose class doesn't implement Serializable.

> **Note**   Because ObjectOutputStream implements DataOutput, it also declares methods for writing primitive-type values and strings to an object output stream.

Java provides the concrete ObjectInputStream class to initiate the deserialization of an object's state from an object input stream. This class declares an ObjectInputStream(InputStream in) constructor that chains the object input stream to the input stream specified by in.

When you pass an input stream reference to in, this constructor attempts to read a serialization header from that input stream. It throws NullPointerException when in is null, IOException when an I/O error prevents it from reading this header, and java.io.StreamCorruptedException (an indirect subclass of IOException) when the stream header is incorrect.

ObjectInputStream deserializes an object via its Object readObject() method. This method attempts to read information about obj's class followed by the values of obj's instance fields from the underlying input stream.

readObject() throws an instance of java.lang.ClassNotFoundException, IOException, or an IOException subclass when something goes wrong. For example, this method throws java.io.OptionalDataException when it encounters primitive-type values instead of objects.

> **Note**   Because ObjectInputStream implements DataInput, it also declares methods for reading primitive-type values and strings from an object input stream.

Listing 4-10 presents an application that uses these classes to serialize and deserialize an instance of Listing 4-9's Employee class to and from an employee.dat file.

Listing 4-10.   Serializing and Deserializing an Employee Object

```java
import java.io.FileInputStream;
import java.io.FileOutputStream;
import java.io.IOException;
import java.io.ObjectInputStream;
import java.io.ObjectOutputStream;

public class SerializationDemo
{
    final static String FILENAME = "employee.dat";

    public static void main(String[] args)
    {
        ObjectOutputStream oos = null;
        ObjectInputStream ois = null;
        try
        {
            FileOutputStream fos = new FileOutputStream(FILENAME);
            oos = new ObjectOutputStream(fos);
            Employee emp = new Employee("John Doe", 36);
            oos.writeObject(emp);
            oos.close();
            oos = null;
            FileInputStream fis = new FileInputStream(FILENAME);
            ois = new ObjectInputStream(fis);
            emp = (Employee) ois.readObject(); // (Employee) cast is necessary.
            ois.close();
            System.out.println(emp.getName());
            System.out.println(emp.getAge());
        }
```

```
catch (ClassNotFoundException cnfe)
{
    System.err.println(cnfe.getMessage());
}
catch (IOException ioe)
{
    System.err.println(ioe.getMessage());
}
finally
{
    if (oos != null)
        try
        {
            oos.close();
        }
        catch (IOException ioe)
        {
            assert false; // shouldn't happen in this context
        }
    if (ois != null)
        try
        {
            ois.close();
        }
        catch (IOException ioe)
        {
            assert false; // shouldn't happen in this context
        }
    }
}
}
```

Listing 4-10's main() method first instantiates Employee and serializes this instance via writeObject() to employee.dat. It then deserializes this instance from this file via readObject() and invokes the instance's getName() and getAge() methods.

Compile Listings 4-9 and 4-10 as follows:

javac *.java

Run the resulting application as follows:

java SerializationDemo

Along with employee.dat, you should discover the following output:

John Doe
36

There's no guarantee that the same class will exist when a serialized object is deserialized (perhaps an instance field has been deleted). During deserialization, this mechanism causes readObject() to throw java.io.InvalidClassException—an indirect subclass of the IOException class—when it detects a difference between the deserialized object and its class.

Every serialized object has an identifier. The deserialization mechanism compares the identifier of the object being deserialized with the serialized identifier of its class (all serializable classes are automatically given unique identifiers unless they explicitly specify their own identifiers) and causes InvalidClassException to be thrown when it detects a mismatch.

Perhaps you've added an instance field to a class, and you want the deserialization mechanism to set the instance field to a default value rather than have readObject() throw an InvalidClassException instance. (The next time you serialize the object, the new field's value will be written out.)

You can avoid the thrown InvalidClassException instance by adding a static final long serialVersionUID = long integer value; declaration to the class. The long integer value must be unique and is known as a *stream unique identifier (SUID)*.

During deserialization, the JVM will compare the deserialized object's SUID to its class's SUID. If they match, readObject() will not throw InvalidClassException when it encounters a *compatible class change* (such as adding an instance field). However, it will still throw this exception when it encounters an *incompatible class change* (such as changing an instance field's name or type).

> **Note** Whenever you change a class in some fashion, you must calculate a new SUID and assign it to serialVersionUID.

The JDK provides a serialver tool for calculating the SUID. For example, to generate an SUID for Listing 4-9's Employee class, change to the directory containing Employee.class and execute the following command:

```
serialver Employee
```

In response, serialver generates the following output, which you paste (except for Employee:) into Employee.java:

```
Employee:    static final long serialVersionUID = 1517331364702470316L;
```

The Windows version of `serialver` also provides a graphical user interface that you might find more convenient to use. To access this interface, specify the following command line:

```
serialver -show
```

When the `serialver` window appears, enter **Employee** into the Full Class Name text field and click the Show button, as demonstrated in Figure 4-4.

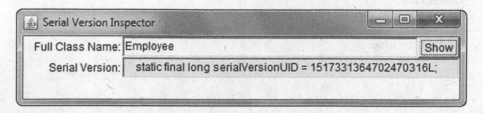

Figure 4-4. The `serialver` user interface reveals Employee's SUID

Custom Serialization and Deserialization

The previous discussion focused on default serialization and deserialization (with the exception of marking an instance field `transient` to prevent it from being included during serialization). However, situations arise where you need to customize these tasks.

For example, suppose you want to serialize instances of a class that doesn't implement `Serializable`. As a workaround, you subclass this other class, have the subclass implement `Serializable`, and forward the subclass constructor calls to the superclass.

Although this workaround lets you serialize subclass objects, you cannot deserialize these serialized objects when the superclass doesn't declare a noargument constructor, which is required by the deserialization mechanism. Listing 4-11 demonstrates this problem.

Listing 4-11. Problematic Deserialization

```
import java.io.FileInputStream;
import java.io.FileOutputStream;
import java.io.IOException;
import java.io.ObjectInputStream;
import java.io.ObjectOutputStream;
import java.io.Serializable;
```

```
class Employee
{
   private String name;

   Employee(String name)
   {
      this.name = name;
   }

   @Override
   public String toString()
   {
      return name;
   }
}

class SerEmployee extends Employee implements Serializable
{
   SerEmployee(String name)
   {
      super(name);
   }
}

public class SerializationDemo
{
   public static void main(String[] args)
   {
      ObjectOutputStream oos = null;
      ObjectInputStream ois = null;
      try
      {
         oos = new ObjectOutputStream(new FileOutputStream("employee.dat"));
         SerEmployee se = new SerEmployee("John Doe");
         System.out.println(se);
         oos.writeObject(se);
         oos.close();
         oos = null;
         System.out.println("se object written to file");
         ois = new ObjectInputStream(new FileInputStream("employee.dat"));
         se = (SerEmployee) ois.readObject();
         System.out.println("se object read from file");
         System.out.println(se);
      }
      catch (ClassNotFoundException cnfe)
      {
         cnfe.printStackTrace();
      }
```

```
        catch (IOException ioe)
        {
            ioe.printStackTrace();
        }
        finally
        {
            if (oos != null)
                try
                {
                    oos.close();
                }
                catch (IOException ioe)
                {
                    assert false; // shouldn't happen in this context
                }
            if (ois != null)
                try
                {
                    ois.close();
                }
                catch (IOException ioe)
                {
                    assert false; // shouldn't happen in this context
                }
        }
    }
}
```

Listing 4-11's main() method instantiates SerEmployee with an employee name. This class's SerEmployee(String) constructor passes this argument to its Employee counterpart.

main() next calls Employee's toString() method indirectly via System.out.println(), to obtain this name, which is then output.

Continuing, main() serializes the SerEmployee instance to an employee.dat file via writeObject(). It then attempts to deserialize this object via readObject(), and this is where the trouble occurs, as revealed by the following output:

```
John Doe
se object written to file
java.io.InvalidClassException: SerEmployee; no valid constructor
        at java.io.ObjectStreamClass$ExceptionInfo.newInvalidClassException
        (ObjectStreamClass.java:150)
        at java.io.ObjectStreamClass.checkDeserialize(ObjectStreamClass.java:768)
        at java.io.ObjectInputStream.readOrdinaryObject(ObjectInputStream.java:1775)
        at java.io.ObjectInputStream.readObject0(ObjectInputStream.java:1351)
        at java.io.ObjectInputStream.readObject(ObjectInputStream.java:371)
        at SerializationDemo.main(SerializationDemo.java:48)
```

This output reveals a thrown instance of the `InvalidClassException` class. This exception object was thrown during deserialization because `Employee` doesn't possess a noargument constructor.

You can overcome this problem by taking advantage of the adapter pattern (`https://en.wikipedia.org/wiki/Adapter_pattern`). Furthermore, you declare a pair of private methods in the subclass that the serialization and deserialization mechanisms look for and call.

Normally, the serialization mechanism writes out a class's instance fields to the underlying output stream. However, you can prevent this from happening by declaring a private void `writeObject(ObjectOutputStream oos)` method in that class.

When the serialization mechanism discovers this method, it calls the method instead of automatically outputting instance field values. The only values that are output are those explicitly output via the method.

Conversely, the deserialization mechanism assigns values to a class's instance fields that it reads from the underlying input stream. However, you can prevent this from happening by declaring a private void `readObject(ObjectInputStream ois)` method.

When the deserialization mechanism discovers this method, it calls the method instead of automatically assigning values to instance fields. The only values that are assigned to instance fields are those explicitly assigned via the method.

Because `SerEmployee` doesn't introduce any fields, and because `Employee` doesn't offer access to its internal fields (assume you don't have the source code for this class), what would a serialized `SerEmployee` object include?

Although you cannot serialize `Employee`'s internal state, you can serialize the argument(s) passed to its constructors, such as the employee name.

Listing 4-12 reveals the refactored `SerEmployee` and `SerializationDemo` classes.

Listing 4-12. Solving Problematic Deserialization

```
import java.io.FileInputStream;
import java.io.FileOutputStream;
import java.io.IOException;
import java.io.ObjectInputStream;
import java.io.ObjectOutputStream;
import java.io.Serializable;
```

```
class Employee
{
    private String name;

    Employee(String name)
    {
        this.name = name;
    }

    @Override
    public String toString()
    {
        return name;
    }
}

class SerEmployee implements Serializable
{
    private Employee emp;
    private String name;

    SerEmployee(String name)
    {
        this.name = name;
        emp = new Employee(name);
    }

    private void writeObject(ObjectOutputStream oos) throws IOException
    {
        oos.writeUTF(name);
    }

    private void readObject(ObjectInputStream ois)
        throws ClassNotFoundException, IOException
    {
        name = ois.readUTF();
        emp = new Employee(name);
    }

    @Override
    public String toString()
    {
        return name;
    }
}
```

```
public class SerializationDemo
{
   public static void main(String[] args)
   {
      ObjectOutputStream oos = null;
      ObjectInputStream ois = null;
      try
      {
         oos = new ObjectOutputStream(new FileOutputStream("employee.dat"));
         SerEmployee se = new SerEmployee("John Doe");
         System.out.println(se);
         oos.writeObject(se);
         oos.close();
         oos = null;
         System.out.println("se object written to file");
         ois = new ObjectInputStream(new FileInputStream("employee.dat"));
         se = (SerEmployee) ois.readObject();
         System.out.println("se object read from file");
         System.out.println(se);
      }
      catch (ClassNotFoundException cnfe)
      {
         cnfe.printStackTrace();
      }
      catch (IOException ioe)
      {
         ioe.printStackTrace();
      }
      finally
      {
         if (oos != null)
            try
            {
               oos.close();
            }
            catch (IOException ioe)
            {
               assert false; // shouldn't happen in this context
            }
         if (ois != null)
            try
            {
               ois.close();
            }
```

```
            catch (IOException ioe)
            {
                assert false; // shouldn't happen in this context
            }
        }
    }
}
```

SerEmployee's writeObject() and readObject() methods rely on DataOutput and DataInput methods: they don't need to call ObjectOutputStream's writeObject() method and ObjectInputStream's readObject() method to perform their tasks.

When you run this application, it generates the following output:

```
John Doe
se object written to file
se object read from file
John Doe
```

The writeObject() and readObject() methods can be used to serialize/ deserialize data items beyond the normal state (non-transient instance fields), for example, serializing/deserializing the contents of a static field.

However, before serializing or deserializing the additional data items, you must tell the serialization and deserialization mechanisms to serialize or deserialize the object's normal state. The following methods help you accomplish this task:

- ObjectOutputStream's defaultWriteObject() method outputs the object's normal state. Your writeObject() method first calls this method to output that state and then outputs additional data items via ObjectOutputStream methods such as writeUTF().

- ObjectInputStream's defaultReadObject() method inputs the object's normal state. Your readObject() method first calls this method to input that state and then inputs additional data items via ObjectInputStream methods such as readUTF().

Externalization

Along with default serialization/deserialization and custom serialization/ deserialization, Java supports externalization. Unlike default/custom serialization/deserialization, *externalization* offers complete control over the serialization and deserialization tasks.

> **Note**   Externalization helps you improve the performance of the reflection-based serialization and deserialization mechanisms by giving you complete control over what fields are serialized and deserialized.

Java supports externalization via java.io.Externalizable. This interface declares the following pair of public methods:

- void writeExternal(ObjectOutput out) saves the calling object's contents by calling various methods on the out object. This method throws IOException when an I/O error occurs. (java.io.ObjectOutput is a subinterface of DataOutput and is implemented by ObjectOutputStream.)

- void readExternal(ObjectInput in) restores the calling object's contents by calling various methods on the in object. This method throws IOException when an I/O error occurs and ClassNotFoundException when the class of the object being restored cannot be found. (java.io.ObjectInput is a subinterface of DataInput and is implemented by ObjectInputStream.)

If a class implements Externalizable, its writeExternal() method is responsible for saving all field values that are to be saved. Also, its readExternal() method is responsible for restoring all saved field values and in the order they were saved.

Listing 4-13 presents a refactored version of Listing 4-9's Employee class to show you how to take advantage of externalization.

Listing 4-13. Refactoring Listing 4-9's Employee Class to Support Externalization

```
import java.io.Externalizable;
import java.io.IOException;
import java.io.ObjectInput;
import java.io.ObjectOutput;

public class Employee implements Externalizable
{
   private String name;
   private int age;

   public Employee()
   {
      System.out.println("Employee() called");
   }
```

```
    public Employee(String name, int age)
    {
        this.name = name;
        this.age = age;
    }

    public String getName() { return name; }

    public int getAge() { return age; }

    @Override
    public void writeExternal(ObjectOutput out) throws IOException
    {
        System.out.println("writeExternal() called");
        out.writeUTF(name);
        out.writeInt(age);
    }

    @Override
    public void readExternal(ObjectInput in)
        throws IOException, ClassNotFoundException
    {
        System.out.println("readExternal() called");
        name = in.readUTF();
        age = in.readInt();
    }
}
```

Employee declares a `public Employee()` constructor because each class that participates in externalization must declare a public noargument constructor. The deserialization mechanism calls this constructor to instantiate the object.

> **Caution** The deserialization mechanism throws `InvalidClassException` with a "no valid constructor" message when it doesn't detect a `public` noargument constructor.

Initiate externalization by instantiating `ObjectOutputStream` and calling its `writeObject(Object)` method, or by instantiating `ObjectInputStream` and calling its `readObject()` method.

> **Note**   When passing an object whose class (directly/indirectly) implements
> `Externalizable` to `writeObject()`, the `writeObject()`-initiated
> serialization mechanism writes only the identity of the object's class to the
> object output stream.

Suppose you compiled Listing 4-10's `SerializationDemo.java` source code
and Listing 4-13's `Employee.java` source code in the same directory. Now
suppose you executed `java SerializationDemo`. In response, you would
observe the following output:

```
writeExternal() called
Employee() called
readExternal() called
John Doe
36
```

Before serializing an object, the serialization mechanism checks the object's
class to see if it implements `Externalizable`. If so, the mechanism calls
`writeExternal()`. Otherwise, it looks for a private `writeObject(ObjectOutput
Stream)` method and calls this method when present. When this method isn't
present, this mechanism performs default serialization, which includes only
non-transient instance fields.

Before deserializing an object, the deserialization mechanism checks the
object's class to see if it implements `Externalizable`. If so, the mechanism
attempts to instantiate the class via the `public` noargument constructor.
Assuming success, it calls `readExternal()`.

When the object's class doesn't implement `Externalizable`, the
deserialization mechanism looks for a private `readObject(ObjectInputStream)`
method. When this method isn't present, this mechanism performs default
deserialization, which includes only non-transient instance fields.

PrintStream

Of all the stream classes, `PrintStream` is an oddball: it should have been
named `PrintOutputStream` for consistency with the naming convention. This
filter output stream class writes string representations of input data items to
the underlying output stream.

> **Note** `PrintStream` uses the default character encoding to convert a string's characters to bytes. (I'll discuss character encodings when I introduce you to writers and readers in Chapter 5.) Because `PrintStream` doesn't support different character encodings, you should use the equivalent `PrintWriter` class instead of `PrintStream`. However, you need to know about `PrintStream` because of standard I/O.

`PrintStream` instances are print streams whose various `print()` and `println()` methods print string representations of integers, floating-point values, and other data items to the underlying output stream. Unlike the `print()` methods, `println()` methods append a line terminator to their output.

> **Note** The line terminator (also known as line separator) isn't necessarily the newline (also commonly referred to as line feed). Instead, to promote portability, the line separator is the sequence of characters defined by system property `line.separator`. On Windows operating systems, `System.getProperty("line.separator")` returns the actual carriage return code (13), which is symbolically represented by `\r`, followed by the actual newline/line feed code (10), which is symbolically represented by `\n`. In contrast, `System.getProperty("line.separator")` returns only the actual newline/line feed code on Unix and Linux operating systems.

The `println()` methods call their corresponding `print()` methods followed by the equivalent of the `void println()` method, which eventually results in `line.separator`'s value being output. For example, `void println(int x)` outputs x's string representation and calls this method to output the line separator.

> **Caution** Never hard-code the \n escape sequence in a string literal that you are going to output via a print() or println() method. Doing so isn't portable. For example, when Java executes System.out.print("first line\n"); followed by System.out.println("second line");, you will see first line on one line followed by second line on a subsequent line when this output is viewed at the Windows command line. In contrast, you'll see first linesecond line when this output is viewed in the Windows Notepad application (which requires a carriage return/line feed sequence to terminate lines). When you need to output a blank line, the easiest way to do this is to execute System.out.println();, which is why you find this method call used elsewhere in my book. I confess that I don't always follow my own advice, so you might find instances of \n in literal strings being passed to System.out.print() or System.out.println() elsewhere in this book.

PrintStream offers three other features that you'll find useful:

- Unlike other output streams, a print stream never rethrows an IOException instance thrown from the underlying output stream. Instead, exceptional situations set an internal flag that can be tested by calling PrintStream's boolean checkError() method, which returns true to indicate a problem.

- PrintStream objects can be created to automatically flush their output to the underlying output stream. In other words, the flush() method is automatically called after a byte array is written, one of the println() methods is called, or a newline is written.

- PrintStream declares a PrintStream format(String format, Object... args) method for achieving formatted output. Behind the scene, this method works with the Formatter class that I introduce in Chapter 11. PrintStream also declares a printf(String format, Object... args) convenience method that delegates to the format() method. For example, invoking printf() via out.printf(format, args) is identical to invoking out.format(format, args).

Revisiting Standard I/O

Java supports standard I/O. You input data items from the standard input stream by making `System.in.read()` method calls, you output data items to the standard output stream by making `System.out.print()` and `System.out.println()` method calls, and you output data items to the standard error stream by making `System.err.print()` and `System.err.println()` method calls.

`System.in`, `System.out`, and `System.err` are formally described by the following class fields in the `System` class:

- `public static final InputStream in`
- `public static final PrintStream out`
- `public static final PrintStream err`

These fields contain references to `InputStream` and `PrintStream` objects that represent the standard input, standard output, and standard error streams.

When you invoke `System.in.read()`, the input is originating from the source identified by the `InputStream` instance assigned to `in`. Similarly, when you invoke `System.out.print()` or `System.err.println()`, the output is being sent to the destination identified by the `PrintStream` instance assigned to `out` or `err`, respectively.

Java initializes `in` to refer to the keyboard or a file when the standard input stream is redirected to the file. Similarly, Java initializes `out`/`err` to refer to the screen or a file when the standard output/error stream is redirected to the file. You can programmatically specify the input source, output destination, and error destination by calling the following `System` class methods:

- `void setIn(InputStream in)`
- `void setOut(PrintStream out)`
- `void setErr(PrintStream err)`

Listing 4-14 presents a `RedirectIO` application that shows you how to use these methods to programmatically redirect the standard input, standard output, and standard error destinations.

Listing 4-14. Programmatically Specifying the Standard Input Source and Standard Output/Error Destinations

```
import java.io.FileInputStream;
import java.io.IOException;
import java.io.PrintStream;
```

```java
public class RedirectIO
{
   public static void main(String[] args) throws IOException
   {
      if (args.length != 3)
      {
         System.err.println("usage: java RedirectIO stdinfile " +
                            "stdoutfile stderrfile");
         return;
      }

      System.setIn(new FileInputStream(args[0]));
      System.setOut(new PrintStream(args[1]));
      System.setErr(new PrintStream(args[2]));

      int ch;
      while ((ch = System.in.read()) != -1)
         System.out.print((char) ch);

      System.err.println("Redirected error output");
   }
}
```

Listing 4-14 lets you specify (via command-line arguments) the name of a file from which `System.in.read()` obtains its content as well as the names of the files to which `System.out.print()` and `System.err.println()` send their content. It then proceeds to copy standard input to standard output and then demonstrates outputting content to standard error.

`new FileInputStream(args[0])` provides access to the input sequence of bytes that is stored in the file identified by `args[0]`. Similarly, `new PrintStream(args[1])` provides access to the file identified by `args[1]`, which will store the output sequence of bytes, and `new PrintStream(args[2])` provides access to the file identified by `args[2]`, which will store the error sequence of bytes.

Compile Listing 4-14 as follows:

`javac RedirectIO.java`

Run the resulting application as follows:

`java RedirectIO RedirectIO.java out.txt err.txt`

This command line produces no visual output on the screen. Instead, it copies the contents of `RedirectIO.java` to `out.txt`. It also stores `Redirected error output` in `err.txt`.

EXERCISES

The following exercises are designed to test your understanding of Chapter 4's content:

1. What is a stream?

2. What is the purpose of OutputStream's flush() method?

3. True or false: OutputStream's close() method automatically flushes the output stream.

4. What is the purpose of InputStream's mark(int) and reset() methods?

5. How would you access a copy of a ByteArrayOutputStream instance's internal byte array?

6. True or false: FileOutputStream and FileInputStream provide internal buffers to improve the performance of write and read operations.

7. Why would you use PipedOutputStream and PipedInputStream?

8. Define filter stream.

9. What does it mean for two streams to be chained together?

10. How do you improve the performance of a file output stream or a file input stream?

11. How do DataOutputStream and DataInputStream support FileOutputStream and FileInputStream?

12. What is object serialization and deserialization?

13. What three forms of serialization and deserialization does Java support?

14. What is the purpose of the Serializable interface?

15. What does the serialization mechanism do when it encounters an object whose class doesn't implement Serializable?

16. Identify the three stated reasons for Java not supporting unlimited serialization.

17. How do you initiate serialization? How do you initiate deserialization?

18. True or false: Class fields are automatically serialized.

19. What is the purpose of the transient reserved word?

20. What does the deserialization mechanism do when it attempts to deserialize an object whose class has changed?

21. How does the deserialization mechanism detect that a serialized object's class has changed?

22. How can you add an instance field to a class and avoid trouble when deserializing an object that was serialized before the instance field was added? What JDK tool can you use to help with this task?

23. How do you customize the default serialization and deserialization mechanisms without using externalization?

24. How do you tell the serialization and deserialization mechanisms to serialize or deserialize the object's normal state before serializing or deserializing additional data items?

25. How does externalization differ from default and custom serialization and deserialization?

26. How does a class indicate that it supports externalization?

27. True or false: During externalization, the deserialization mechanism throws `InvalidClassException` with a "no valid constructor" message when it doesn't detect a `public` noargument constructor.

28. What is the difference between `PrintStream`'s `print()` and `println()` methods?

29. What does `PrintStream`'s noargument `void println()` method accomplish?

30. How do you redirect the standard input, standard output, and standard error streams?

31. Improve Listing 4-1's Copy application (performance wise) by using `BufferedInputStream` and `BufferedOutputStream`. Copy should read the bytes to be copied from the buffered input stream and write these bytes to the buffered output stream.

32. Create a Java application named `Split` for splitting a large file into a number of smaller `partx` files (where x starts at 0 and increments; for example, `part0`, `part1`, `part2`, and so on). Each `partx` file (except possibly the last `partx` file, which holds the remaining bytes) will have the same size. This application has the following usage syntax: `java Split path`. Furthermore, your implementation must use the `BufferedInputStream`, `BufferedOutputStream`, `File`, `FileInputStream`, and `FileOutputStream` classes.

Summary

Java uses streams to perform I/O operations. A stream is an ordered sequence of bytes of an arbitrary length. Bytes flow over an output stream from an application to a destination and flow over an input stream from a source to an application.

The `java.io` package provides several classes that identify various stream destinations and sources. These classes are descendants of the abstract `OutputStream` and `InputStream` classes. `FileOutputStream` and `BufferedInputStream` are examples.

This chapter explored `OutputStream` and `InputStream`, followed by the byte array, file, piped, filter, buffered, data, object, and print streams. While covering object streams, it introduced the topics of serialization and externalization. The chapter concluded by revisiting standard I/O.

Chapter 5 presents classic I/O's writer and reader classes.

Chapter **5**

Writers and Readers

Java's stream classes are good for streaming sequences of bytes, but they're not good for streaming sequences of characters because bytes and characters are two different things: a byte represents an 8-bit data item and a character represents a 16-bit data item. Also, Java's char and java.lang. String types naturally handle characters instead of bytes.

More importantly, byte streams have no knowledge of *character sets* (sets of mappings between integer values, known as *code points*, and symbols, such as Unicode) and their *character encodings* (mappings between the members of a character set and sequences of bytes that encode these characters for efficiency, such as UTF-8).

A BRIEF HISTORY OF CHARACTER SETS AND CHARACTER ENCODINGS

Early computers and programming languages were created mainly by English-speaking programmers in countries where English was the native language. They developed a standard mapping between code points 0 through 127 and the 128 commonly used characters in the English language (such as A–Z). The resulting character set/encoding was named *American Standard Code for Information Interchange (ASCII)*.

The problem with ASCII is that it's inadequate for most non-English languages. For example, ASCII doesn't support diacritical marks such as the cedilla used in French. Because a byte can represent a maximum of 256 different characters, developers around the world started creating different character sets/encodings that encoded the 128 ASCII characters, but also encoded extra characters to meet the needs of languages such as French, Greek, and Russian. Over the years, many legacy (and still important) data files have been created whose bytes represent characters defined by specific character sets/encodings.

The International Organization for Standardization (ISO) and the International Electrotechnical Commission (IEC) worked to standardize these 8-bit character sets/encodings under a joint umbrella standard called ISO/IEC 8859. The result is a series of substandards named ISO/IEC 8859-1, ISO/IEC 8859-2, and so on. For example, ISO/IEC 8859-1 (also known as Latin-1) defines a character set/encoding that consists of ASCII plus the characters covering most Western European countries. Also, ISO/IEC 8859-2 (also known as Latin-2) defines a similar character set/encoding covering Central and Eastern European countries.

Despite the ISO's/IEC's best efforts, a plethora of character sets/encodings is still inadequate. For example, most character sets/encodings only allow you to create documents in a combination of English and one other language (or a small number of other languages). You cannot, for example, use an ISO/IEC character set/encoding to create a document using a combination of English, French, Turkish, Russian, and Greek characters.

This and other problems are being addressed by an international effort that has created and is continuing to develop *Unicode*, a single universal character set. Because Unicode characters are bigger than ISO/IEC characters, Unicode uses one of several variable-length encoding schemes known as *Unicode Transformation Format (UTF)* to encode Unicode characters for efficiency. For example, UTF-8 encodes every character in the Unicode character set in one to four bytes (and is backward-compatible with ASCII).

Finally, the terms *character set* and *character encoding* are often used interchangeably. They mean the same thing in the context of ISO/IEC character sets in which a code point is the encoding. However, these terms are different in the context of Unicode in which Unicode is the character set and UTF-8 is one of several possible character encodings for Unicode characters.

If you need to stream characters, you should take advantage of Java's writer and reader classes, which were designed to support character I/O (they work with char instead of byte). Furthermore, the writer and reader classes take character encodings into account. Chapter 5 introduces you to Java's writer and reader classes.

Writer and Reader Classes Overview

The java.io package provides several writer and reader classes that are descendants of this package's abstract Writer and Reader classes. Figure 5-1 reveals the hierarchy of writer classes.

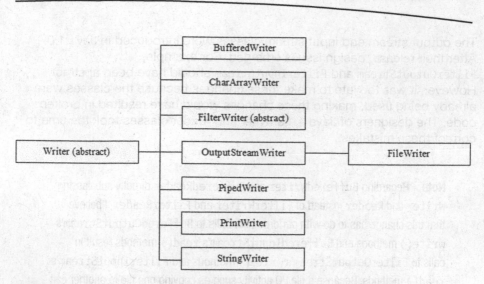

Figure 5-1. *Unlike* `java.io.FilterOutputStream,` `FilterWriter` *is abstract*

Figure 5-2 reveals the hierarchy of reader classes.

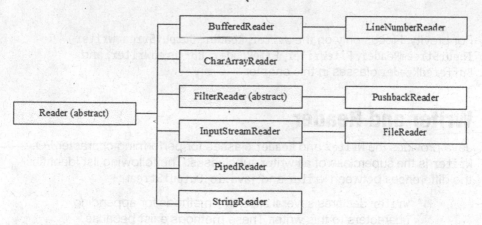

Figure 5-2. *Unlike* `java.io.FilterInputStream,` `FilterReader` *is abstract*

Although the writer and reader class hierarchies are similar to their output stream and input stream counterparts, there are differences. For example, `FilterWriter` and `FilterReader` are abstract, whereas their `FilterOutputStream` and `FilterInputStream` equivalents are not abstract. Also, `BufferedWriter` and `BufferedReader` don't extend `FilterWriter` and `FilterReader`, whereas `java.io.BufferedOutputStream` and `java.io.BufferedInputStream` extend `FilterOutputStream` and `FilterInputStream`.

The output stream and input stream classes were introduced in Java 1.0. After their release, design issues emerged. For example, FilterOutputStream and FilterInputStream should have been abstract. However, it was too late to make these changes because the classes were already being used; making these changes would have resulted in broken code. The designers of Java 1.1's writer and reader classes took the time to correct these mistakes.

> **Note**   Regarding BufferedWriter and BufferedReader directly subclassing Writer and Reader instead of FilterWriter and FilterReader, I believe that this change has to do with performance. Calls to BufferedOutputStream's write() methods and BufferedInputStream's read() methods result in calls to FilterOutputStream's write() methods and FilterInputStream's read() methods. Because a file I/O activity such as copying one file to another can involve many write()/read() method calls, you want the best performance possible. By not subclassing FilterWriter and FilterReader, BufferedWriter and BufferedReader achieve better performance.

For brevity, I focus only on the Writer, Reader, OutputStreamWriter, InputStreamReader, FileWriter, FileReader, BufferedWriter, and BufferedReader classes in this chapter.

Writer and Reader

Java provides the Writer and Reader classes for performing character I/O. Writer is the superclass of all writer subclasses. The following list identifies the differences between Writer and java.io.OutputStream:

- Writer declares several append() methods for appending characters to this writer. These methods exist because Writer implements the java.lang.Appendable interface, which is used in partnership with the java.util.Formatter class (discussed in Chapter 11) to output formatted strings.

- Writer declares additional write() methods, including a convenient void write(String str) method for writing a String object's characters to this writer.

Reader is the superclass of all reader subclasses. The following list identifies differences between Reader and java.io.InputStream:

- Reader declares read(char[]) and read(char[], int, int) methods instead of read(byte[]) and read(byte[], int, int) methods.

- Reader doesn't declare an available() method.

- Reader declares a boolean ready() method that returns true when the next read() call is guaranteed not to block for input.

- Reader declares an int read(CharBuffer target) method for reading characters from a character buffer. (I discuss CharBuffer in Chapter 6.)

OutputStreamWriter and InputStreamReader

The concrete OutputStreamWriter class (a Writer subclass) is a bridge between an incoming sequence of characters and an outgoing stream of bytes. Characters written to this writer are encoded into bytes according to the default or specified character encoding.

> **Note**   The default character encoding is accessible via the file.encoding system property.

Each call to one of OutputStreamWriter's write() methods causes an encoder to be called on the given character(s). The resulting bytes are accumulated in a buffer before being written to the underlying output stream. The characters passed to the write() methods are not buffered.

OutputStreamWriter declares four constructors, including the following pair:

- OutputStreamWriter(OutputStream out) creates a bridge between an incoming sequence of characters (passed to OutputStreamWriter via its append() and write() methods) and the underlying output stream out. The default character encoding is used to encode characters into bytes.

- OutputStreamWriter(OutputStream out, String charsetName) creates a bridge between an incoming sequence of characters (passed to OutputStreamWriter via its append() and write() methods) and the underlying output stream out. charsetName identifies the character encoding used to encode characters into bytes. This constructor throws java.io.UnsupportedEncodingException when the named character encoding isn't supported.

> **Note** OutputStreamWriter depends on the abstract java.nio.charset. Charset and java.nio.charset.CharsetEncoder classes (see Chapter 10) to perform character encoding.

The following example uses the second constructor to create a bridge to an underlying file output stream so that Polish text can be written to an ISO/IEC 8859-2-encoded file.

```
FileOutputStream fos = new FileOutputStream("polish.txt");
OutputStreamWriter osw = new OutputStreamWriter(fos, "8859_2");
char ch = '\u0323'; // Accented N.
osw.write(ch);
```

The concrete InputStreamReader class (a Reader subclass) is a bridge between an incoming stream of bytes and an outgoing sequence of characters. Characters read from this reader are decoded from bytes according to the default or specified character encoding.

Each call to one of InputStreamReader's read() methods may cause one or more bytes to be read from the underlying input stream. To enable the efficient conversion of bytes to characters, more bytes may be read ahead from the underlying stream than are necessary to satisfy the current read operation.

InputStreamReader declares four constructors, including the following pair:

- InputStreamReader(InputStream in) creates a bridge between the underlying input stream in and an outgoing sequence of characters (returned from InputStreamReader via its read() methods). The default character encoding is used to decode bytes into characters.

- InputStreamReader(InputStream in, String charsetName) creates a bridge between the underlying input stream in and an outgoing sequence of characters (returned from InputStreamReader via its read() methods). charsetName identifies the character encoding used to decode bytes into characters. This constructor throws UnsupportedEncodingException when the named character encoding is not supported.

> **Note** InputStreamReader depends on the abstract Charset and java.nio.charset.CharsetDecoder classes (see Chapter 10) to perform character decoding.

The following example uses the second constructor to create a bridge to an underlying file input stream so that Polish text can be read from an ISO/IEC 8859-2-encoded file.

```
FileInputStream fis = new FileInputStream("polish.txt");
InputStreamReader isr = new InputStreamReader(fis, "8859_2");
char ch = isr.read(ch);
```

> **Note** OutputStreamWriter and InputStreamReader declare a String getEncoding() method that returns the name of the character encoding in use. If the encoding has a historical name, that name is returned; otherwise, the encoding's canonical name is returned.

FileWriter and FileReader

FileWriter is a convenience class for writing characters to files. It subclasses OutputStreamWriter, and its constructors, such as FileWriter(String path), call OutputStreamWriter(OutputStream). An instance of this class is equivalent to the following code fragment:

```
FileOutputStream fos = new FileOutputStream(path);
OutputStreamWriter osw;
osw = new OutputStreamWriter(fos, System.getProperty("file.encoding"));
```

FileReader is a convenience class for reading characters from files. It subclasses InputStreamReader, and its constructors, such as FileReader(String path), call InputStreamReader(InputStream). An instance of this class is equivalent to the following code fragment:

```
FileInputStream fis = new FileInputStream(path);
InputStreamReader isr;
isr = new InputStreamReader(fis, System.getProperty("file.encoding"));
```

Neither FileWriter nor FileReader supply their own methods. Instead, you call their inherited methods, such as the following:

- void write(String str, int off, int len): Write len characters of string str starting at zero-based offset off. Throw java.io.IOException when an I/O error occurs.

- int read(char[] cbuf, int off, int len): Read len characters into cbuf starting at zero-based offset off. Throw IOException when an I/O error occurs.

Listing 5-1 presents a short application that demonstrates FileWriter, FileReader, and these methods.

Listing 5-1. Demonstrating the FileWriter and FileReader Classes

```
import java.io.FileReader;
import java.io.FileWriter;
import java.io.IOException;

public class FWFRDemo
{
    final static String MSG = "Test message";

    public static void main(String[] args) throws IOException
    {
        try (FileWriter fw = new FileWriter("temp"))
        {
            fw.write(MSG, 0, MSG.length());
        }
        char[] buf = new char[MSG.length()];
        try (FileReader fr = new FileReader("temp"))
        {
            fr.read(buf, 0, MSG.length());
            System.out.println(buf);
        }
    }
}
```

FWFRDemo first creates a FileWriter instance connected to a file named temp. It then invokes void write(String str, int off, int len) to write a message to this file. The try-with-resources statement automatically closes the file following this operation.

Next, FWFRDemo creates a buffer for storing a line of text, and then creates a FileReader instance connected to temp. It then invokes int read(char[] cbuf, int off, int len) to read the previously written message and output it to the standard output stream. The file is then closed.

Compile Listing 5-1 as follows:

```
javac FWFRDemo.java
```

Run this application as follows:

```
java FWFRDemo
```

You should observe the following output (and a file named temp):

```
Test message
```

BufferedWriter and BufferedReader

BufferedWriter writes text to a character-output stream (a Writer instance), buffering characters so as to provide for the efficient writing of single characters, arrays, and strings. Invoke either of the following constructors to construct a buffered writer:

- BufferedWriter(Writer out)
- BufferedWriter(Writer out, int size)

The buffer size may be specified, or the default size (8,192 bytes) may be accepted. The default is large enough for most purposes.

BufferedWriter includes a handy void newLine() method for writing a line-separator string, which effectively terminates the current line.

BufferedReader reads text from a character-input stream (a Reader instance), buffering characters so as to provide for the efficient reading of characters, arrays, and lines. Invoke either of the following constructors to construct a buffered reader:

- BufferedReader(Reader in)
- BufferedReader(Reader in, int size)

The buffer size may be specified, or the default size (8,192 bytes) may be used. The default is large enough for most purposes.

BufferedReader includes a handy String readLine() method for reading a line of text, not including any line-termination characters.

Listing 5-2 presents a short application that demonstrates BufferedWriter, BufferedReader, and these methods.

Listing 5-2. Demonstrating the BufferedWriter and BufferedReader Classes

```java
import java.io.BufferedReader;
import java.io.BufferedWriter;
import java.io.FileReader;
import java.io.FileWriter;
import java.io.IOException;

public class BWBRDemo
{
   static String[] lines =
   {
      "It was the best of times, it was the worst of times,",
      "it was the age of wisdom, it was the age of foolishness,",
      "it was the epoch of belief, it was the epoch of incredulity,",
      "it was the season of Light, it was the season of Darkness,",
      "it was the spring of hope, it was the winter of despair."
   };

   public static void main(String[] args) throws IOException
   {
      try (BufferedWriter bw = new BufferedWriter(new FileWriter("temp")))
      {
         for (String line: lines)
         {
            bw.write(line, 0, line.length());
            bw.newLine();
         }
      }
      try (BufferedReader br = new BufferedReader(new FileReader("temp")))
      {
         String line;
         while ((line = br.readLine()) != null)
            System.out.println(line);
      }
   }
}
```

BWBRDemo first creates a BufferedWriter instance that wraps a created FileWriter instance that is connected to a file named temp. It then iterates over the line of strings, writing each line followed by a newline sequence.

Next, BWBRDemo creates a BufferedReader instance that wraps a created FileReader instance that is connected to temp. It then reads and outputs each line from the file until readLine() returns null.

Compile Listing 5-2 as follows:

```
javac BWBRDemo.java
```

Run this application as follows:

```
java BWBRDemo
```

You should observe the following output (and a file named temp):

```
It was the best of times, it was the worst of times,
it was the age of wisdom, it was the age of foolishness,
it was the epoch of belief, it was the epoch of incredulity,
it was the season of Light, it was the season of Darkness,
it was the spring of hope, it was the winter of despair.
```

EXERCISES

The following exercises are designed to test your understanding of Chapter 5's content:

1. Why are Java's stream classes not good at streaming characters?

2. What does Java provide as the preferred alternative to stream classes when it comes to character I/O?

3. True or false: Reader declares an available() method.

4. What is the purpose of the OutputStreamWriter class? What is the purpose of the InputStreamReader class?

5. How do you identify the default character encoding?

6. What is the purpose of the FileWriter class? What is the purpose of the FileReader class?

7.   What method does `BufferedWriter` provide for writing a line separator?

8.   It's often convenient to read lines of text from standard input, and the `InputStreamReader` and `BufferedReader` classes make this task possible. Create a Java application named `CircleInfo` that, after obtaining a `BufferedReader` instance that is chained to standard input, presents a loop that prompts the user to enter a radius, parses the entered radius into a `double` value, and outputs a pair of messages that report the circle's circumference and area based on this radius.

Summary

Java's stream classes are good for streaming sequences of bytes, but they're not good for streaming sequences of characters because bytes and characters are two different things. A byte represents an 8-bit data item and a character represents a 16-bit data item. Also, Java's char and String types naturally handle characters instead of bytes. More importantly, byte streams have no knowledge of character sets and their encodings.

Java provides writer and reader classes to stream characters. They support character I/O (they work with char instead of byte) and take character encodings into account. The abstract Writer and Reader classes describe what it means to be a writer and a reader.

Writer and Reader are subclassed by OutputStreamWriter and InputStreamReader, which bridge the gap between character and byte streams. These classes are subclassed by the FileWriter and FileReader convenience classes, which facilitate writing/reading characters to/from files. Writer and Reader are also subclassed by BufferedWriter and BufferedReader, which buffer characters for efficiency.

Chapter 6 presents NIO's buffer classes.

Part III

New I/O APIs

Buffers

NIO is based on buffers, whose contents are sent to or received from I/O services via channels. This chapter introduces you to NIO's buffer classes.

Introducing Buffers

A *buffer* is an object that stores a fixed amount of data to be sent to or received from an *I/O service* (an operating system component for performing input/output). It sits between an application and a *channel* that writes the buffered data to the service or reads the data from the service and deposits it into the buffer.

Buffers possess four properties:

- *Capacity*: The total number of data items that can be stored in the buffer. The capacity is specified when the buffer is created and cannot be changed later.

- *Limit*: The zero-based index of the first element that should not be read or written. In other words, it identifies the number of "live" data items in the buffer.

- *Position*: The zero-based index of the next data item that can be read or the location where the data item can be written.

- *Mark*: A zero-based index to which the buffer's position will be reset when the buffer's reset() method (presented shortly) is called. The mark is initially undefined.

These four properties are related as follows: 0 <= mark <= position <= limit <= capacity

Figure 6-1 reveals a newly created and byte-oriented buffer with a capacity of 7.

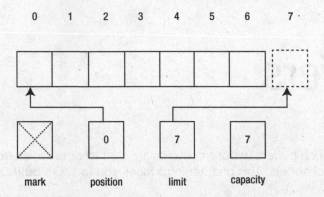

Figure 6-1. *The logical layout of a byte-oriented buffer includes an undefined mark, a current position, a limit, and a capacity*

Figure 6-1's buffer can store a maximum of seven elements. The mark is initially undefined, the position is initially set to 0, and the limit is initially set to the capacity (7), which specifies the maximum number of bytes that can be stored in the buffer. You can only access positions 0 through 6. Position 7 lies beyond the buffer.

Buffer and its Children

Buffers are implemented by classes that derive from the abstract java.nio.Buffer class. Table 6-1 describes Buffer's methods.

Table 6-1. Buffer Methods

Method	Description
Object array()	Return the array that backs this buffer. This method is intended to allow array-backed buffers to be passed to *native code* more efficiently. Concrete subclasses override this method and provide more strongly typed return values via covariant return types. This method throws java.nio.ReadOnlyBufferException when this buffer is backed by an array but is read-only and throws java.lang.UnsupportedOperationException when this buffer isn't backed by an accessible array.
int arrayOffset()	Return the offset of the first buffer element within this buffer's backing array. When this buffer is backed by an array, buffer position p corresponds to array index p + arrayOffset(). Invoke hasArray() before invoking this method to ensure that this buffer has an accessible backing array. This method throws ReadOnlyBufferException when this buffer is backed by an array but is read-only and throws UnsupportedOperationException when this buffer isn't backed by an accessible array.
int capacity()	Return this buffer's capacity.
Buffer clear()	Clear this buffer. The position is set to 0, the limit is set to the capacity, and the mark is discarded. This method doesn't erase the data in the buffer but is named as if it did because it will most often be used in situations in which that might as well be the case.
Buffer flip()	Flip this buffer. The limit is set to the current position and then the position is set to 0. When the mark is defined, it's discarded.
boolean hasArray()	Return true when this buffer is backed by an array and isn't read-only; otherwise, return false. When this method returns true, array() and arrayOffset() may be invoked safely.
boolean hasRemaining()	Return true when at least one element remains in this buffer (that is, between the current position and the limit); otherwise, return false.
boolean isDirect()	Return true when this buffer is a direct byte buffer (discussed later in this chapter); otherwise, return false.
boolean isReadOnly()	Return true when this buffer is read-only, otherwise, return false.

(continued)

Table 6-1. (*continued*)

Method	Description
int limit()	Return this buffer's limit.
Buffer limit(int newLimit)	Set this buffer's limit to newLimit. When the position is larger than newLimit, the position is set to newLimit. When the mark is defined and is larger than newLimit, the mark is discarded. This method throws java.lang.IllegalArgumentException when newLimit is negative or larger than this buffer's capacity; otherwise, it returns this buffer.
Buffer mark()	Set this buffer's mark to its position and return this buffer.
int position()	Return this buffer's position.
Buffer position (int newPosition)	Set this buffer's position to newPosition. When the mark is defined and is larger than newPosition, the mark is discarded. This method throws IllegalArgumentException when newPosition is negative or larger than this buffer's current limit; otherwise, it returns this buffer.
int remaining()	Return the number of elements between the current position and the limit.
Buffer reset()	Reset this buffer's position to the previously marked position. Invoking this method neither changes nor discards the mark's value. This method throws java.nio.InvalidMarkException when the mark hasn't been set; otherwise, it returns this buffer.
Buffer rewind()	Rewind and then return this buffer. The position is set to 0 and the mark is discarded.

Table 6-1 shows that many of Buffer's methods return Buffer references so that you can chain instance method calls together. For example, instead of specifying the following three lines:

```
buf.mark();
buf.position(2);
buf.reset();
```

you can more conveniently specify the following line:

```
buf.mark().position(2).reset();
```

Table 6-1 also shows that all buffers can be read but not all buffers can be written—for example, a buffer backed by a memory-mapped file that's read-only. You must not write to a read-only buffer; otherwise, ReadOnlyBufferException is thrown. Call isReadOnly() when you're unsure that a buffer is writable before attempting to write to that buffer.

> **Caution**   Buffers are not thread-safe. You must employ synchronization when you want to access a buffer from multiple threads.

The java.nio package includes several abstract classes that extend Buffer, one for each primitive type except for Boolean: ByteBuffer, CharBuffer, DoubleBuffer, FloatBuffer, IntBuffer, LongBuffer, and ShortBuffer. Furthermore, this package includes MappedByteBuffer as an abstract ByteBuffer subclass.

> **Note**   Operating systems perform byte-oriented I/O and you use ByteBuffer to create byte-oriented buffers that store the bytes to write to a destination or that are read from a source. The other primitive-type buffer classes let you create multibyte view buffers (discussed later) so that you can conceptually perform I/O in terms of characters, double precision floating-point values, 32-bit integers, and so on. However, the I/O operation is really being carried out as a flow of bytes.

Listing 6-1 demonstrates the Buffer class in terms of ByteBuffer, capacity, limit, position, and remaining elements.

Listing 6-1. Demonstrating a Byte-Oriented Buffer

```java
import java.nio.Buffer;
import java.nio.ByteBuffer;

public class BufferDemo
{
   public static void main(String[] args)
   {
      Buffer buffer = ByteBuffer.allocate(7);
      System.out.println("Capacity: " + buffer.capacity());
      System.out.println("Limit: " + buffer.limit());
      System.out.println("Position: " + buffer.position());
      System.out.println("Remaining: " + buffer.remaining());
```

```
        System.out.println("Changing buffer limit to 5");
        buffer.limit(5);
        System.out.println("Limit: " + buffer.limit());
        System.out.println("Position: " + buffer.position());
        System.out.println("Remaining: " + buffer.remaining());
        System.out.println("Changing buffer position to 3");
        buffer.position(3);
        System.out.println("Position: " + buffer.position());
        System.out.println("Remaining: " + buffer.remaining());
        System.out.println(buffer);
    }
}
```

Listing 6-1's `main()` method first needs to obtain a buffer. It cannot instantiate the `Buffer` class because that class is abstract. Instead, it uses the `ByteBuffer` class and its `allocate()` class method to allocate the seven-byte buffer shown in Figure 6-1. `main()` then calls assorted `Buffer` methods to demonstrate capacity, limit, position, and remaining elements.

Compile Listing 6-1 as follows:

```
javac BufferDemo.java
```

Run the resulting application as follows:

```
java BufferDemo
```

You should observe the following output:

```
Capacity: 7
Limit: 7
Position: 0
Remaining: 7
Changing buffer limit to 5
Limit: 5
Position: 0
Remaining: 5
Changing buffer position to 3
Position: 3
Remaining: 2
java.nio.HeapByteBuffer[pos=3 lim=5 cap=7]
```

The final output line reveals that the `ByteBuffer` instance assigned to buffer is actually an instance of the package-private `java.nio.HeapByteBuffer` class.

Buffers in Depth

The previous discussion of the Buffer class has given you some insight into NIO buffers. However, there's much more to explore. This section takes you deeper into buffers by exploring buffer creation, buffer writing and reading, buffer flipping, buffer marking, Buffer subclass operations, byte ordering, and direct buffers.

> **Note** Although the primitive-type buffer classes have similar capabilities, ByteBuffer is the largest and most versatile. After all, bytes are the basic unit used by operating systems to transfer data items. I'll therefore use ByteBuffer to demonstrate most buffer operations. I'll also use CharBuffer to add variety.

Buffer Creation

ByteBuffer and the other primitive-type buffer classes declare various class methods for creating a buffer of that type. For example, ByteBuffer declares the following class methods for creating ByteBuffer instances:

- ByteBuffer allocate(int capacity): Allocate a new byte buffer with the specified capacity value. Its position is 0, its limit is its capacity, its mark is undefined, and each element is initialized to 0. It has a backing array, and its array offset is 0. This method throws IllegalArgumentException when capacity is negative.

- ByteBuffer allocateDirect(int capacity): Allocate a new direct byte buffer (discussed later) with the specified capacity value. Its position is 0, its limit is its capacity, its mark is undefined, and each element is initialized to 0. Whether or not it has a backing array is unspecified. This method throws IllegalArgumentException when capacity is negative.

  Before JDK 7, direct buffers allocated via this method were aligned on a page boundary. In JDK 7, the implementation changed so that direct buffers are no longer page-aligned. This should reduce the memory requirements of applications that create lots of small buffers. (To learn about an operating system's paging memory-management mechanism, which is based on pages, check out Wikipedia's "Paging" topic at https://en.wikipedia.org/wiki/Paging.)

- ■ ByteBuffer wrap(byte[] array): Wrap a byte array
  into a buffer. The new buffer is backed by array; that
  is, modifications to the buffer will cause the array to be
  modified and vice versa. The new buffer's capacity and
  limit are set to array.length, its position is set to 0, and
  its mark is undefined. Its array offset is 0.

- ■ ByteBuffer wrap(byte[] array, int offset, int
  length): Wrap a byte array into a buffer. The new buffer
  is backed by array. The new buffer's capacity is set to
  array.length, its position is set to offset, its limit is
  set to offset + length, and its mark is undefined. Its
  array offset is 0. This method throws java.lang.
  IndexOutOfBoundsException when offset is negative or
  greater than array.length or when length is negative or
  greater than array.length - offset.

These methods show two ways to create a byte buffer: create the
ByteBuffer object and allocate an internal array that stores capacity bytes
or create the ByteBuffer object and use the specified array to store these
bytes. Consider these examples:

```
ByteBuffer buffer = ByteBuffer.allocate(10);
byte[] bytes = new byte[200];
ByteBuffer buffer2 = ByteBuffer.wrap(bytes);
```

The first line creates a byte buffer with an internal byte array that stores a
maximum of 10 bytes, and the second and third lines create a byte array
and a byte buffer that uses this array to store a maximum of 200 bytes.

Now consider the following example, which extends the previous example:

```
buffer = ByteBuffer.wrap(bytes, 10, 50);
```

This example creates a byte buffer with a position of 10, a limit of 50, and a
capacity of bytes.length (which happens to be 200). Although it appears
that the buffer can only access a subrange of this array, it actually has
access to the entire array: values 10 and 50 are only the starting values for
the position and limit.

ByteBuffers (and other primitive-type buffers) created via allocate() or
wrap() are nondirect byte buffers—you'll learn about direct byte buffers
later. Nondirect byte buffers have backing arrays, and you can access these
backing arrays via the array() method (which happens to be declared as
byte[] array() in the ByteArray class) as long as hasArray() returns true.
(When hasArray() returns true, you'll need to call arrayOffset() to obtain
the location of the first data item in the array.)

Listing 6-2 demonstrates buffer allocation and wrapping.

Listing 6-2. Creating Byte-Oriented Buffers via Allocation and Wrapping

```java
import java.nio.ByteBuffer;

public class BufferDemo
{
    public static void main(String[] args)
    {
        ByteBuffer buffer1 = ByteBuffer.allocate(10);
        if (buffer1.hasArray())
        {
            System.out.println("buffer1 array: " + buffer1.array());
            System.out.println("Buffer1 array offset: " +
                                buffer1.arrayOffset());
            System.out.println("Capacity: " + buffer1.capacity());
            System.out.println("Limit: " + buffer1.limit());
            System.out.println("Position: " + buffer1.position());
            System.out.println("Remaining: " + buffer1.remaining());
            System.out.println();
        }

        byte[] bytes = new byte[200];
        ByteBuffer buffer2 = ByteBuffer.wrap(bytes);
        buffer2 = ByteBuffer.wrap(bytes, 10, 50);
        if (buffer2.hasArray())
        {
            System.out.println("buffer2 array: " + buffer2.array());
            System.out.println("Buffer2 array offset: " +
                                buffer2.arrayOffset());
            System.out.println("Capacity: " + buffer2.capacity());
            System.out.println("Limit: " + buffer2.limit());
            System.out.println("Position: " + buffer2.position());
            System.out.println("Remaining: " + buffer2.remaining());
        }
    }
}
```

Compile Listing 6-2 (javac BufferDemo.java) and run this application (java BufferDemo). You should observe output that is similar to the following:

```
buffer1 array: [B@659e0bfd
Buffer1 array offset: 0
Capacity: 10
Limit: 10
Position: 0
Remaining: 10
```

```
buffer2 array: [B@2a139a55
Buffer2 array offset: 0
Capacity: 200
Limit: 60
Position: 10
Remaining: 50
```

As well as managing data elements stored in external arrays (via the wrap() methods), buffers can manage data stored in other buffers. When you create a buffer that manages another buffer's data, the created buffer is known as a *view buffer*. Changes made in either buffer are reflected in the other.

View buffers are created by calling a Buffer subclass's duplicate() method. The resulting view buffer is equivalent to the original buffer; both buffers share the same data items and have equivalent capacities. However, each buffer has its own position, limit, and mark. When the buffer being duplicated is read-only or direct, the view buffer is also read-only or direct.

Consider the following example:

```
ByteBuffer buffer = ByteBuffer.allocate(10);
ByteBuffer bufferView = buffer.duplicate();
```

The ByteBuffer instance identified by bufferView shares the same internal array of 10 elements as buffer. At the moment, these buffers have the same position, limit, and (undefined) mark. However, these properties in one buffer can be changed independently of the properties in the other buffer.

View buffers are also created by calling one of ByteBuffer's asxBuffer() methods. For example, LongBuffer asLongBuffer() returns a view buffer that conceptualizes the byte buffer as a buffer of long integers.

> **Note**   Read-only view buffers can be created by calling a method such as ByteBuffer asReadOnlyBuffer(). Any attempt to change a read-only view buffer's content results in ReadOnlyBufferException. However, the original buffer content (provided that it isn't read-only) can be changed, and the read-only view buffer will reflect these changes.

Buffer Writing and Reading

ByteBuffer and the other primitive-type buffer classes declare several overloaded put() and get() methods for writing data items to and reading data items from a buffer. These methods are absolute when they require an index argument or relative when they don't require an index.

For example, ByteBuffer declares the absolute ByteBuffer put(int index, byte b) method to store byte b in the buffer at the index value and the absolute byte get(int index) method to fetch the byte located at position index. This class also declares the relative ByteBuffer put(byte b) method to store byte b in the buffer at the current position and then increment the current position, and the relative byte get() method to fetch the byte located at the buffer's current position and increment the current position.

The absolute put() and get() methods throw IndexOutOfBoundsException when index is negative or greater than or equal to the buffer's limit. The relative put() method throws java.nio.BufferOverflowException when the current position is greater than or equal to the limit, and the relative get() method throws java.nio.BufferUnderflowException when the current position is greater than or equal to the limit. Furthermore, the absolute and relative put() methods throw ReadOnlyBufferException when the buffer is read-only.

Listing 6-3 demonstrates the relative put() method and the absolute get() method.

Listing 6-3. Writing Bytes to and Reading Them from a Buffer

```java
import java.nio.ByteBuffer;

public class BufferDemo
{
   public static void main(String[] args)
   {
      ByteBuffer buffer = ByteBuffer.allocate(7);
      System.out.println("Capacity = " + buffer.capacity());
      System.out.println("Limit = " + buffer.limit());
      System.out.println("Position = " + buffer.position());
      System.out.println("Remaining = " + buffer.remaining());

      buffer.put((byte) 10).put((byte) 20).put((byte) 30);

      System.out.println("Capacity = " + buffer.capacity());
      System.out.println("Limit = " + buffer.limit());
      System.out.println("Position = " + buffer.position());
      System.out.println("Remaining = " + buffer.remaining());

      for (int i = 0; i < buffer.position(); i++)
         System.out.println(buffer.get(i));
   }
}
```

Compile Listing 6-3 (javac BufferDemo.java) and run this application
(java BufferDemo). You should observe the following output:

```
Capacity = 7
Limit = 7
Position = 0
Remaining = 7
Capacity = 7
Limit = 7
Position = 3
Remaining = 4
10
20
30
```

Figure 6-2 illustrates the state of the buffer following the three put() method
calls and presented in the previous output.

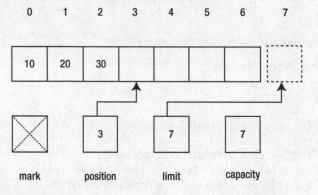

Figure 6-2. The buffer can store four more data items before reaching its capacity

The subsequent calls to the absolute get() method don't change the
position, which remains set to 3.

> **Tip** For maximum efficiency, you can perform bulk data transfers by using
> the ByteBuffer put(byte[] src), ByteBuffer put(byte[] src,
> int offset, int length), ByteBuffer get(byte[] dst), and
> ByteBuffer get(byte[] dst, int offset, int length) methods to
> write and read an array of bytes.

Flipping Buffers

After filling a buffer, you must prepare it for draining by a channel. When you pass the buffer as is, the channel accesses undefined data beyond the current position.

To solve this problem, you could reset the position to 0, but how would the channel know when the end of the inserted data had been reached? The solution is to work with the limit property, which indicates the end of the active portion of the buffer. Basically, you set the limit to the current position and then reset the current position to 0.

You could accomplish this task by executing the following code, which also clears any defined mark:

```
buffer.limit(buffer.position()).position(0);
```

However, there's an easier way to accomplish the same task, as shown here:

```
buffer.flip();
```

In either case, the buffer is ready to be drained.

Assuming that `buffer.flip();` is executed at the end of Listing 6-3's `main()` method, Figure 6-3 reveals what the buffer state would look like after calling `flip()`.

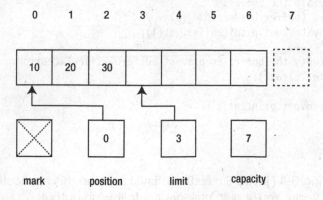

Figure 6-3. The buffer is ready to be drained

A call to `buffer.remaining()` would return 3. This value indicates the number of bytes available for draining (10, 20, and 30).

Listing 6-4 provides another buffer-flipping demonstration, which uses a character buffer.

Listing 6-4. Writing Characters to and Reading Them from a Character Buffer

```java
import java.nio.CharBuffer;

public class BufferDemo
{
   public static void main(String[] args)
   {
      String[] poem =
      {
         "Roses are red",
         "Violets are blue",
         "Sugar is sweet",
         "And so are you."
      };

      CharBuffer buffer = CharBuffer.allocate(50);

      for (int i = 0; i < poem.length; i++)
      {
         // Fill the buffer.
         for (int j = 0; j < poem[i].length(); j++)
            buffer.put(poem[i].charAt(j));

         // Flip the buffer so that its contents can be read.
         buffer.flip();

         // Drain the buffer.
         while (buffer.hasRemaining())
            System.out.print(buffer.get());

         // Empty the buffer to prevent BufferOverflowException.
         buffer.clear();

         System.out.println();
      }
   }
}
```

Compile Listing 6-4 (javac BufferDemo.java) and run this application (java BufferDemo). You should observe the following output:

```
Roses are red
Violets are blue
Sugar is sweet
And so are you.
```

> **Note** rewind() is similar to flip() but ignores the limit. Also, calling flip() twice doesn't return you to the original state. Instead, the buffer has a zero size. Calling a put() method results in BufferOverflowException, and calling a get() method results in BufferUnderflowException or (in the case of get(int)), IndexOutOfBoundsException.

Marking Buffers

You can mark a buffer by invoking the mark() method and later return to the marked position by invoking reset(). For example, suppose you've executed ByteBuffer buffer = ByteBuffer.allocate(7);, followed by buffer.put((byte) 10).put((byte) 20).put((byte) 30).put((byte) 40);, followed by buffer.limit(4);. The current position and limit are set to 4.

Continuing, suppose you execute buffer.position(1).mark(). position(3);. Figure 6-4 reveals the buffer state at this point.

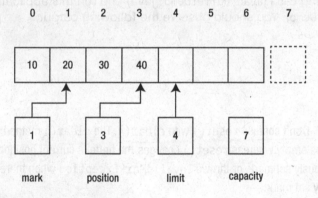

Figure 6-4. The mark has been set to position 1

If you sent this buffer to a channel, byte 40 would be sent (the current position is 3 because of position(3)) and the position would advance to 4. If you subsequently executed buffer.reset(); and sent this buffer to the channel, the position would be set to the mark (1) and bytes 20, 30, and 40 (all bytes from the current position to one position below the limit) would be sent to the channel (and in that order).

Listing 6-5 demonstrates this mark/reset scenario.

Listing 6-5. Marking the Current Buffer Position and Resetting the Current Position to the Marked Position

```java
import java.nio.ByteBuffer;

public class BufferDemo
{
   public static void main(String[] args)
   {
      ByteBuffer buffer = ByteBuffer.allocate(7);
      buffer.put((byte) 10).put((byte) 20).put((byte) 30).put((byte) 40);
      buffer.limit(4);
      buffer.position(1).mark().position(3);
      System.out.println(buffer.get());
      System.out.println();
      buffer.reset();
      while (buffer.hasRemaining())
         System.out.println(buffer.get());
   }
}
```

Compile Listing 6-5 (javac BufferDemo.java) and run this application
(java BufferDemo). You should observe the following output:

```
40
20
30
40
```

> **Caution**   Don't confuse reset() with clear(). The clear() method marks
> a buffer as empty whereas reset() changes the buffer's current position to
> the previously set mark, or throws InvalidMarkException when there's no
> previously set mark.

Buffer Subclass Operations

ByteBuffer and the other primitive-type buffer classes declare a compact()
method that's useful for compacting a buffer by copying all bytes between
the current position and the limit to the beginning of the buffer. The byte at
index p = position() is copied to index 0, the byte at index p + 1 is copied
to index 1, and so on until the byte at index limit() - 1 is copied to index
n = limit() - 1 - p. The buffer's current position is then set to n + 1 and
its limit is set to its capacity. The mark, when defined, is discarded.

You invoke compact() after writing data from a buffer to handle situations where not all of the buffer's content is written. Consider the following example, which copies content from an in channel to an out channel via buffer buf:

```
buf.clear(); // Prepare buffer for use
while (in.read(buf) != -1)
{
   buf.flip(); // Prepare buffer for draining.
   out.write(buf); // Write the buffer.
   buf.compact(); // Do this in case of a partial write.
}
```

The compact() method call moves unwritten buffer data to the beginning of the buffer so that the next read() method call appends read data to the buffer's data instead of overwriting that data when compact() isn't specified.

You may occasionally need to compare buffers for equality or order. All Buffer subclasses except for ByteBuffer's MappedByteBuffer subclass override the equals() and compareTo() methods to perform these comparisons—MappedByteBuffer inherits these methods from its ByteBuffer superclass. The following example shows you how to compare the byte buffers bytBuf1 and bytBuf2 for equality and ordering:

```
System.out.println(bytBuf1.equals(bytBuf2));
System.out.println(bytBuf1.compareTo(bytBuf2));
```

The equals() contract for ByteBuffer states that two byte buffers are equal if and only if they have the same element type; they have the same number of remaining elements; and the two sequences of remaining elements, considered independently of their starting positions, are individually equal. This contract is the same for the other Buffer subclasses.

The compareTo() method for ByteBuffer states that two byte buffers are compared for order by comparing their sequences of remaining elements lexicographically, without regard to the starting position of each sequence within its corresponding buffer. Pairs of byte elements are compared as if by invoking Byte.compare(byte, byte). Similar descriptions apply to the other Buffer subclasses.

Byte Ordering

Nonbyte primitive types except for Boolean (which might be represented by a bit or by a byte) are composed of several bytes: a character or a short integer occupies two bytes, a 32-bit integer or a floating-point value occupies four bytes, and a long integer or a double precision floating-point value occupies eight bytes. Each value of one of these multibyte types is stored in a sequence of contiguous memory locations. However, the order of these bytes can differ from operating system to operating system.

For example, consider 32-bit long integer 0x10203040. This value's four bytes could be stored in memory (from low address to high address) as 10, 20, 30, 40; this arrangement is known as *big endian order* (the most-significant byte, the "big" end, is stored at the lowest address). Alternatively, these bytes could be stored as 40, 30, 20, 10; this arrangement is known as *little endian order* (the least-significant byte, the "little" end, is stored at the lowest address).

Java provides the java.nio.ByteOrder class to help you deal with byte-order issues when writing/reading multibyte values to/from a multibyte buffer. ByteOrder declares a ByteOrder nativeOrder() method that returns the operating system's byte order as a ByteOrder instance. Because this instance is one of ByteOrder's BIG_ENDIAN and LITTLE_ENDIAN constants, and because no other ByteOrder instances can be created, you can compare nativeOrder()'s return value to one of these constants via the == or != operator.

Also, each multibyte class (such as FloatBuffer) declares a ByteOrder order() method that returns the buffer's byte order. This method returns ByteOrder.BIG_ENDIAN or ByteOrder.LITTLE_ENDIAN.

The ByteOrder value returned from order() can take on a different value based on how the buffer was created. If a multibyte buffer (such as a floating-point buffer) was created by allocation or by wrapping an existing array, the buffer's byte order is the native order of the underlying operating system. However, if a multibyte buffer was created as a view of a byte buffer, the view buffer's byte order is that of the byte buffer when the view was created. The view buffer's byte order cannot be subsequently changed.

ByteBuffer differs from the multibyte classes when it comes to byte order. Its default byte order is always big endian, even when the underlying operating system's byte order is little endian. ByteBuffer defaults to big endian because Java's default byte order is also big endian, which lets classfiles and serialized objects store data consistently across Java virtual machines (JVMs).

Because this big endian default can impact performance on little endian operating systems, ByteBuffer also declares a ByteBuffer order(ByteOrder bo) method to change the byte buffer's byte order.

Although it may seem unusual to change the byte order of a byte buffer (where only single-byte data items are accessed), this method is useful because ByteBuffer also declares several convenience methods for writing and reading multibyte values (ByteBuffer putInt(int value) and int getInt(), for example). These convenience methods write these values according to the byte buffer's current byte order. Furthermore, you can subsequently call ByteBuffer's LongBuffer asLongBuffer() or another asxBuffer() method to return a view buffer whose order will reflect the byte buffer's changed byte order.

Direct Byte Buffers

Unlike multibyte buffers, byte buffers can serve as the sources and/or targets of channel-based I/O. This shouldn't come as a surprise because operating systems perform I/O on memory areas that are contiguous sequences of 8-bit bytes (not floating-point values, not 32-bit integers, and so on).

Operating systems can directly access the address space of a process. For example, an operating system could directly access a JVM process's address space to perform a data transfer operation based on a byte array. However, a JVM might not store the array of bytes contiguously or its garbage collector might move the byte array to another location. Because of these limitations, direct byte buffers were created.

A *direct byte buffer* is a byte buffer that interacts with channels and native code to perform I/O. The direct byte buffer attempts to store byte elements in a memory area that a channel uses to perform *direct* (raw) access via native code that tells the operating system to drain or fill the memory area directly.

Direct byte buffers are the most efficient means for performing I/O on the JVM. Although you can also pass nondirect byte buffers to channels, a performance problem might arise because nondirect byte buffers are not always able to serve as the target of native I/O operations.

When passed a nondirect byte buffer, a channel might have to create a temporary direct byte buffer, copy the nondirect byte buffer's content to the direct byte buffer, perform the I/O operation on the temporary direct byte buffer, and copy the temporary direct byte buffer's content to the nondirect byte buffer. The temporary direct byte buffer will then be subject to garbage collection.

Although optimal for I/O, a direct byte buffer can be expensive to create because memory extraneous to the JVM's heap will need to be allocated by the operating system, and setting up/tearing down this memory might take longer than when the buffer was located within the heap.

After your code is working and should you want to experiment with performance optimization, you can easily obtain a direct byte buffer by invoking ByteBuffer's allocateDirect() method, which I discussed earlier.

```
                              EXERCISES
```

The following exercises are designed to test your understanding of Chapter 6's content:

1. What is a buffer?

2. Identify a buffer's four properties.

3. What happens when you invoke Buffer's array() method on a buffer backed by a read-only array?

4. What happens when you invoke Buffer's flip() method on a buffer?

5. What happens when you invoke Buffer's reset() method on a buffer where a mark has not been set?

6. True or false: Buffers are thread-safe.

7. Identify the classes that extend the abstract Buffer class.

8. How do you create a byte buffer?

9. Define view buffer.

10. How is a view buffer created?

11. How do you create a read-only view buffer?

12. Identify ByteBuffer's methods for storing a single byte in a byte buffer and fetching a single byte from a byte buffer.

13. What causes BufferOverflowException or BufferUnderflowException to occur?

14. What is the equivalent of executing buffer.flip();?

15. True or false: Calling flip() twice returns you to the original state.

16. What is the difference between Buffer's clear() and reset() methods?

17. What does ByteBuffer's compact() method accomplish?

18. What is the purpose of the ByteOrder class?

19. Define direct byte buffer.

20. How do you obtain a direct byte buffer?

21. Why could it be expensive to create a direct byte buffer?

22. Create a ViewBufferDemo application that populates a byte buffer with the values 0, 0x6e, 0, 0x69, 0, 0x6f; creates a character view buffer; and iterates over the view buffer, outputting each character.

Summary

A buffer is an NIO object that stores a fixed amount of data to be sent to or received from an I/O service. It sits between an application and a channel that writes the buffered data to the service or reads the data from the service and deposits it into the buffer.

Buffers possess capacity, limit, position, and mark properties. These four properties are related as follows: 0 <= mark <= position <= limit <= capacity.

Buffers are implemented by abstract classes that derive from the abstract Buffer class. These classes include ByteBuffer, CharBuffer, DoubleBuffer, FloatBuffer, IntBuffer, LongBuffer, and ShortBuffer. Furthermore, ByteBuffer is subclassed by the abstract MappedByteBuffer class.

In this chapter, you learned how to create buffers (including view buffers), write and read buffer contents, flip buffers, mark buffers, and perform additional operations on buffers such as compaction. You also learned about byte ordering and direct byte buffers.

Chapter 7 presents NIO's channel types.

Channels

Channels partner with buffers to achieve high-performance I/O. This chapter introduces you to NIO's channel types.

Introducing Channels

A *channel* is an object that represents an open connection to a hardware device, a file, a network socket, an application component, or another entity that's capable of performing writes, reads, and other I/O operations. Channels efficiently transfer data between byte buffers and operating system-based I/O service sources or destinations.

> **Note**   Channels are gateways through which I/O services are accessed.
> Channels use byte buffers as the endpoints for sending and receiving data.

There often exists a one-to-one correspondence between an operating system file handle or file descriptor and a channel. When you work with channels in a file context, the channel will often be connected to an open file descriptor. Despite channels being more abstract than file descriptors, they are still capable of modeling an operating system's I/O facilities.

Channel and Its Children

Java supports channels via its java.nio.channels and java.nio.channels.spi packages. Applications interact with the types located in the former package; developers who are defining new selector providers work with the latter package. (I will discuss selectors in the next chapter.)

All channels are instances of classes that ultimately implement the java.nio.channels.Channel interface. Channel declares the following methods:

- void close(): Close this channel. When this channel is already closed, invoking close() has no effect. When another thread has already invoked close(), a new close() invocation blocks until the first invocation finishes, after which close() returns without effect. This method throws java.io.IOException when an I/O error occurs. After the channel is closed, any further attempts to invoke I/O operations on it result in java.nio.channels.ClosedChannelException being thrown.

- boolean isOpen(): Return this channel's open status. This method returns true when the channel is open; otherwise, it returns false.

These methods indicate that only two operations are common to all channels: close the channel and determine whether the channel is open or closed. To support I/O, Channel is extended by the java.nio.channels.WritableByteChannel and java.nio.channels.ReadableByteChannel interfaces:

- WritableByteChannel declares an abstract int write(ByteBuffer buffer) method that writes a sequence of bytes from buffer to the current channel. This method returns the number of bytes actually written. It throws java.nio.channels.NonWritableChannelException when the channel was not opened for writing, java.nio.channels.ClosedChannelException when the channel is closed, java.nio.channels.AsynchronousCloseException when another thread closes the channel during the write, java.nio.channels.ClosedByInterruptException when another thread interrupts the current thread while the write operation is in progress (thereby closing the channel and setting the current thread's interrupt status), and IOException when some other I/O error occurs.

- ReadableByteChannel declares an abstract int read(ByteBuffer buffer) method that reads bytes from the current channel into buffer. This method returns the number of bytes actually read (or -1 when there are no more bytes to read). It throws java.nio.channels.NonReadableChannelException when the channel was not opened for reading; ClosedChannelException when the channel is closed; AsynchronousCloseException when another thread closes the channel during the read; ClosedByInterruptException when another thread interrupts the current thread while the write operation is in progress, thereby closing the channel and setting the current thread's interrupt status; and IOException when some other I/O error occurs.

Note   A channel whose class implements only WritableByteChannel or ReadableByteChannel is *unidirectional.* Attempting to read from a writable byte channel or write to a readable byte channel results in a thrown exception.

You can use the instanceof operator to determine if a channel instance implements either interface. Because it's somewhat awkward to test for both interfaces, Java supplies the java.nio.channels.ByteChannel interface, which is an empty marker interface that subtypes WritableByteChannel and ReadableByteChannel. When you need to learn whether or not a channel is *bidirectional*, it's more convenient to specify an expression such as channel instanceof ByteChannel.

Channel is also extended by the java.nio.channels.InterruptibleChannel interface. InterruptibleChannel describes a channel that can be asynchronously closed and interrupted. This interface overrides its Channel superinterface's close() method header, presenting the following additional stipulation to Channel's contract for this method: Any thread currently blocked in an I/O operation on this channel will receive AsynchronousCloseException (an IOException descendent).

A channel that implements this interface is asynchronously *closeable*: When a thread is blocked in an I/O operation on an interruptible channel, another thread may invoke the channel's close() method. This causes the blocked thread to receive a thrown AsynchronousCloseException instance.

A channel that implements this interface is also *interruptible*: When a thread is blocked in an I/O operation on an interruptible channel, another thread may invoke the blocked thread's interrupt() method. Doing this causes the channel to be closed, the blocked thread to receive a thrown ClosedByInterruptException instance, and the blocked thread to have its interrupt status set. (When a thread's interrupt status is already set and it invokes a blocking I/O operation on a channel, the channel is closed and the thread will immediately receive a thrown ClosedByInterruptException instance; its interrupt status will remain set.)

NIO's designers chose to shut down a channel when a blocked thread is interrupted because they couldn't find a way to reliably handle interrupted I/O operations in the same manner across operating systems. The only way to guarantee deterministic behavior was to shut down the channel.

> **Tip**   You can determine whether or not a channel supports asynchronous closing and interruption by using the `instanceof` operator in an expression such as `channel instanceof InterruptibleChannel`.

In Chapter 6, you learned that you must call a class method on a `java.nio.Buffer` subclass to obtain a buffer. Regarding channels, there are two ways to obtain a channel:

- The `java.nio.channels` package provides a `Channels` utility class that offers two methods for obtaining channels from streams. For each of the following methods, the underlying stream is closed when the channel is closed, and the channel isn't buffered:

  - `WritableByteChannel newChannel(OutputStream outputStream)` returns a writable byte channel for the given `outputStream`.

  - `ReadableByteChannel newChannel(InputStream inputStream)` returns a readable byte channel for the given `inputStream`.

- Various classic I/O classes have been retrofitted to support channel creation. For example, `java.io.RandomAccessFile` declares a `FileChannel getChannel()` method for returning a file channel, and `java.net.Socket` declares a `SocketChannel getChannel()` method for returning a socket channel.

Listing 7-1 uses the `Channels` class to obtain channels for the standard input and output streams and then uses these channels to copy bytes from the input channel to the output channel.

Listing 7-1. Copying Bytes from an Input Channel to an Output Channel

```
import java.io.IOException;

import java.nio.ByteBuffer;

import java.nio.channels.Channels;
import java.nio.channels.ReadableByteChannel;
import java.nio.channels.WritableByteChannel;
```

```java
public class ChannelDemo
{
   public static void main(String[] args)
   {
      ReadableByteChannel src = Channels.newChannel(System.in);
      WritableByteChannel dest = Channels.newChannel(System.out);

      try
      {
         copy(src, dest); // or copyAlt(src, dest);
      }
      catch (IOException ioe)
      {
         System.err.println("I/O error: " + ioe.getMessage());
      }
      finally
      {
         try
         {
            src.close();
            dest.close();
         }
         catch (IOException ioe)
         {
            ioe.printStackTrace();
         }
      }
   }

   static void copy(ReadableByteChannel src, WritableByteChannel dest)
      throws IOException
   {
      ByteBuffer buffer = ByteBuffer.allocateDirect(2048);
      while (src.read(buffer) != -1)
      {
         buffer.flip();
         dest.write(buffer);
         buffer.compact();
      }
      buffer.flip();
      while (buffer.hasRemaining())
         dest.write(buffer);
   }

   static void copyAlt(ReadableByteChannel src, WritableByteChannel dest)
      throws IOException
   {
      ByteBuffer buffer = ByteBuffer.allocateDirect(2048);
      while (src.read(buffer) != -1)
```

```
   {
      buffer.flip();
      while (buffer.hasRemaining())
         dest.write(buffer);
      buffer.clear();
   }
  }
}
```

Listing 7-1 presents two approaches to copying bytes from the standard input stream to the standard output stream. In the first approach, which is exemplified by the copy() method, the goal is to minimize operating system I/O calls (via the write() method calls), although more data may end up being copied as a result of the compact() method calls. In the second approach, as demonstrated by copyAlt(), the goal is to eliminate data copying, although more operating system I/O calls might occur.

The copy() and copyAlt() methods first allocate a direct byte buffer (recall that a direct byte buffer is the most efficient means for performing I/O on the Java virtual machine [JVM]) and enter a while loop that continually reads bytes from the source channel until end-of-input (read() returns -1). Following the read, the buffer is flipped so that it can be drained. Here is where the methods diverge.

- The copy() method while loop makes a single call to write(). Because write() might not completely drain the buffer, compact() is called to compact the buffer before the next read. Compaction ensures that unwritten buffer content isn't overwritten during the next read operation. Following the while loop, copy() flips the buffer in preparation for draining any remaining content, and then works with hasRemaining() and write() to completely drain the buffer.

- The copyAlt() method while loop contains a nested while loop that works with hasRemaining() and write() to continue draining the buffer until the buffer is empty. This is followed by a clear() method call, which empties the buffer so that it can be filled on the next read() call.

Note   It's important to realize that a single write() method call may not output the entire content of a buffer. Similarly, a single read() call may not completely fill a buffer.

Compile Listing 7-1 as follows:

```
javac ChannelDemo.java
```

Run the resulting application as follows:

```
java ChannelDemo
java ChannelDemo <ChannelDemo.java >ChannelDemo.bak
```

The first command line copies the standard input to the standard output. The second command line copies the contents of `ChannelDemo.java` to `ChannelDemo.bak`. After testing the `copy()` method, replace `copy(src, dest);` with `copyAlt(src, dest);` and repeat.

Channels in Depth

The previous discussion of the `Channel` interface and its direct descendants has given you some insight into channels. However, there's much more to explore. This section takes you deeper into channels by exploring scatter/gather I/O, file channels, socket channels, and pipes.

Scatter/Gather I/O

Channels provide the ability to perform a single I/O operation across multiple buffers. This capability is known as *scatter/gather I/O* (and is also known as *vectored I/O*).

In the context of a write operation, the contents of several buffers are *gathered* (drained) in sequence and then sent through the channel to a destination. These buffers are not required to have identical capacities. In the context of a read operation, the contents of a channel are *scattered* (filled) to multiple buffers in sequence; each buffer is filled to its limit until the channel is empty or until the total buffer space is used.

Note   Modern operating systems provide APIs that support vectored I/O to eliminate (or at least reduce) system calls or buffer copies, and hence improve performance. For example, the Win32/Win64 APIs provide `ReadFileScatter()` and `WriteFileGather()` functions for this purpose.

Java provides the java.nio.channels.ScatteringByteChannel interface to support scattering and the java.nio.channels.GatheringByteChannel interface to support gathering.

ScatteringByteChannel offers the following methods:

- long read(ByteBuffer[] buffers, int offset, int length)

- long read(ByteBuffer[] buffers)

GatheringByteChannel offers the following methods:

- long write(ByteBuffer[] buffers, int offset, int length)

- long write(ByteBuffer[] buffers)

The first read() method and the first write() method let you identify the first buffer to read/write by passing a zero-based offset to offset, and the number of buffers to read/write by passing a value to length. The second read() method and the second write() method read and write all buffers in sequence.

Listing 7-2 demonstrates read(ByteBuffer[] buffers) and write(ByteBuffer[] buffers).

Listing 7-2. Demonstrating Scatter/Gather

```
import java.io.FileInputStream;
import java.io.FileOutputStream;
import java.io.IOException;

import java.nio.ByteBuffer;

import java.nio.channels.Channels;
import java.nio.channels.GatheringByteChannel;
import java.nio.channels.ReadableByteChannel;
import java.nio.channels.ScatteringByteChannel;

public class ChannelDemo
{
    public static void main(String[] args) throws IOException
    {
        ScatteringByteChannel src;
        FileInputStream fis = new FileInputStream("x.dat");
        src = (ScatteringByteChannel) Channels.newChannel(fis);
        ByteBuffer buffer1 = ByteBuffer.allocateDirect(5);
        ByteBuffer buffer2 = ByteBuffer.allocateDirect(3);
        ByteBuffer[] buffers = { buffer1, buffer2 };
        src.read(buffers);
```

```
    buffer1.flip();
    while (buffer1.hasRemaining())
        System.out.println(buffer1.get());
    System.out.println();
    buffer2.flip();
    while (buffer2.hasRemaining())
        System.out.println(buffer2.get());
    buffer1.rewind();
    buffer2.rewind();
    GatheringByteChannel dest;
    FileOutputStream fos = new FileOutputStream("y.dat");
    dest = (GatheringByteChannel) Channels.newChannel(fos);
    buffers[0] = buffer2;
    buffers[1] = buffer1;
    dest.write(buffers);
    }
}
```

Listing 7-2's main() method first obtains a scattering byte channel by instantiating java.io.FileInputStream and passing this instance to the Channels class's ReadableByteChannel newChannel(InputStream inputStream) method. The returned ReadableByteChannel instance is cast to ScatteringByteChannel because this instance is actually a file channel (discussed later) that implements ScatteringByteChannel.

Next, main() creates a couple of direct byte buffers; the first buffer has a capacity of five bytes and the second buffer has a capacity of three bytes. These buffers are subsequently stored in an array and this array is passed to read(ByteBuffer[]) to fill them.

After filling the buffers, main() flips them so that it can output their contents to standard output. After these contents have been output, the buffers are rewound in preparation for being drained via a gather operation.

main() now obtains a gathering byte channel by instantiating java.io.FileOutputStream and passing this instance to the Channels class's WritableByteChannel newChannel(OutputStream outputStream) method. The returned WritableByteChannel instance is cast to GatheringByteChannel because this instance is actually a file channel (discussed later) that implements GatheringByteChannel.

Finally, main() assigns these buffers to the buffers array in reverse order to how they were originally assigned, and then passes this array to write(ByteBuffer[]) to drain them.

Create a file named x.dat and store the following text in this file:

12345abcdefg

Now compile Listing 7-2 (javac ChannelDemo.java) and run this application (java ChannelDemo). You should observe the following Unicode values for the first eight characters:

49
50
51
52
53

97
98
99

Additionally, you should observe a newly created y.dat file with the following content:

abc12345

File Channels

I previously mentioned that RandomAccessFile declares a FileChannel getChannel() method for returning a file channel instance, which describes an open connection to a file. It turns out that FileInputStream and FileOutputStream also provide the same method. In contrast, java.io.FileReader and java.io.FileWriter don't offer a way to obtain a file channel.

Caution   The file channel returned from FileInputStream's getChannel() method is read-only, and the file channel returned from FileOutputStream's getChannel() method is write-only. Attempting to write to a read-only file channel or read from a write-only file channel results in an exception.

The abstract java.nio.channels.FileChannel class describes a file channel. Because this class implements the InterruptibleChannel interface, file channels are interruptible. Because this class implements the ByteChannel, GatheringByteChannel, and ScatteringByteChannel interfaces, you can write to, read from, and perform scatter/gather I/O on underlying files. However, there's more.

Note   Unlike buffers, which are not thread-safe, file channels are thread-safe.

A file channel maintains a current position into the file, which `FileChannel` lets you obtain and change. It also lets you request that cached data be forced to the disk, read/write file content, obtain the size of the file underlying the channel, truncate a file, attempt to lock the entire file or just a region of the file, perform memory-mapped file I/O, and transfer data directly to another channel in a manner that has the potential to be optimized by the operating system.

Table 7-1 describes a few of `FileChannel`'s methods.

Table 7-1. `FileChannel Methods`

Method	Description
`void force(boolean metadata)`	Request that all updates to this file channel be committed to the storage device. When this method returns, all modifications made to the file underlying this channel have been committed when the file resides on a local storage device. However, when the file isn't hosted locally (it's on a networked file system, for example), applications cannot be certain that the modifications have been committed. (No assurances are given that changes made to the file using methods defined elsewhere will be committed. For example, changes made via a mapped byte buffer may not be committed.)
	The `metadata` value indicates whether the update should include the file's metadata (such as last modification time and last access time), when `true` is passed, or not include the file's metadata, when `false` is passed. Passing `true` may invoke an underlying write to the operating system (if the operating system is maintaining metadata, such as last access time), even when the channel is opened as a read-only channel.
	This method throws `ClosedChannelException` when the channel is already closed and throws `IOException` when any other I/O error occurs.
`long position()`	Return the current zero-based file position maintained by this file channel. This method throws `ClosedChannelException` when the file channel is closed and `IOException` when another I/O error occurs.

(continued)

Table 7-1. (*continued*)

Method	Description
FileChannel position(long newPosition)	Set this file channel's current file position to newPosition. The argument is the number of bytes counted from the start of the file. The position cannot be set to a negative value. However, it can be set beyond the current file size. If it's set beyond the current file size, attempts to read will return end of file. Write operations will succeed, but they will fill the bytes between the current end of file and the new position with the required number of (unspecified) byte values. This method throws java.lang.IllegalArgumentException when offset is negative, ClosedChannelException when the file channel is closed, and IOException when another I/O error occurs.
int read(ByteBuffer buffer)	Read bytes from this file channel into the given buffer. The maximum number of bytes that will be read is the remaining number of bytes in the buffer when the method is invoked. The bytes will be copied into the buffer starting at the buffer's current position. The call may block when other threads are also attempting to read from this channel. Upon completion, the buffer's position is set to the end of the bytes that have been read. The buffer's limit isn't changed. This method returns the number of bytes actually read and throws the same exceptions as previously discussed regarding ReadableByteChannel.
int read(ByteBuffer dst, long position)	Equivalent to the previous method except that bytes are read starting at the specified file position. IllegalArgumentException is thrown when position is negative.
long size()	Return the size (in bytes) of the file underlying this file channel. This method throws ClosedChannelException when the file channel is closed and IOException when another I/O error occurs.

(*continued*)

Table 7-1. *(continued)*

Method	Description
FileChannel truncate(long size)	Truncate the file underlying this file channel to size. Any bytes beyond the given size are removed from the file. When there are no bytes beyond the given size, the file contents are unmodified. When the current file position is greater than the given size, it's set to size.
int write(ByteBuffer buffer)	Write a sequence of bytes to this file channel from the given buffer. Bytes are written starting at the channel's current file position unless the channel is in append mode, in which case the position is first advanced to the end of the file. The file is grown (when necessary) to accommodate the written bytes, and then the file position is updated with the number of bytes actually written. Otherwise this method behaves exactly as specified by the WritableByteChannel interface. This method returns the number of bytes actually written and throws the same exceptions as previously discussed regarding WritableByteChannel.
int write(ByteBuffer src, long position)	Equivalent to the previous method except that bytes are written starting at the specified file position. IllegalArgumentException is thrown when position is negative.

The force(boolean) method ensures that all changes made to a file residing in the local file system and since this method was previously invoked are written to the disk. This capability is vital for critical tasks such as transaction processing, where you must maintain data integrity and ensure reliable recovery. However, this guarantee doesn't apply to remote file systems.

Passing true to force(boolean) results in metadata (last modification time, access permissions, and so on) also being synchronized to the disk. Because metadata isn't usually critical to file recovery, you can often pass false and gain a small performance increase because an extra I/O operation isn't required to output the metadata.

FileChannel objects support the concept of a current file position, which determines the location where the next data item will be read from or written to. The position() method returns the current position and the position(long newPosition) method sets the current position to newPosition. The value passed to newPosition must be non-negative or IllegalArgumentException will be thrown.

There are two forms of the read() and write() methods. The relative forms don't take position arguments and ensure that the current file position is updated after a call to either method. The absolute forms of these methods take a position argument and don't update the position. Absolute reads and writes can be more efficient because the channel's state doesn't need to be updated.

If you attempt to perform an absolute read past the end of a file, which size() returns, -1 is returned to signify end of file. Attempting to perform an absolute write past the end of a file causes the file to grow to accommodate the bytes being written. The values of the bytes located between the previous end of file and the first newly written byte are file system-specific and may constitute a hole.

A *hole* occurs in a file when the amount of disk space allocated for the file is smaller than the file's size. Modern file systems typically allocate space only for data that's written to the file. When data is written to noncontiguous areas, holes can appear. When the file is read, holes typically appear to be zero-filled but don't take up disk space.

The truncate(long size) method is useful for reducing a file's size. This method truncates all data beyond the specified size. When the file's size is greater than the specified size, all bytes past the specified size are discarded. When the specified size is greater than or equal to the current size, the file isn't changed.

Listing 7-3 demonstrates various methods from Table 7-1.

Listing 7-3. Demonstrating a File Channel

```
import java.io.IOException;
import java.io.RandomAccessFile;

import java.nio.ByteBuffer;

import java.nio.channels.FileChannel;

public class ChannelDemo
{
   public static void main(String[] args) throws IOException
   {
      RandomAccessFile raf = new RandomAccessFile("temp", "rw");
      FileChannel fc = raf.getChannel();
      long pos;
      System.out.println("Position = " + (pos = fc.position()));
      System.out.println("size: " + fc.size());
      String msg = "This is a test message.";
      ByteBuffer buffer = ByteBuffer.allocateDirect(msg.length() * 2);
      buffer.asCharBuffer().put(msg);
```

```
        fc.write(buffer);
        fc.force(true);
        System.out.println("position: " + fc.position());
        System.out.println("size: " + fc.size());
        buffer.clear();
        fc.position(pos);
        fc.read(buffer);
        buffer.flip();
        while (buffer.hasRemaining())
            System.out.print(buffer.getChar());
    }
}
```

Listing 7-3's main() method first creates a randomly-accessible file named temp for writing and reading. It then obtains a file channel for communicating with this file and reports the file channel's current position and the file's size, which are both 0 for a newly created file.

main() next allocates a direct byte buffer for storing a message to be written to the file, treats this buffer as a character buffer, and calls the character buffer's put() method to store the message in the buffer, which is then output to the file.

main() now calls force(true) to recommend to the underlying operating system that the data be committed to the underlying storage device.

After reporting the new current position and file size, main() clears the buffer, resets the file position to where it was before the message was written, and reads the previously written content back into the buffer. It then flips the buffer and outputs its contents.

Compile Listing 7-3 (javac ChannelDemo.java) and run this application (java ChannelDemo). You should observe the following output:

```
Position = 0
size: 0
position: 46
size: 46
This is a test message.
```

On subsequent runs, the presence of a file named temp will change the output to the following:

```
Position = 0
size: 46
position: 46
size: 46
This is a test message.
```

Locking Files

The ability to lock all or part of a file was an important but missing feature from Java until Java 1.4 arrived. This capability lets a JVM process prevent other processes from accessing all or part of a file until it's finished with the entire file or part of the file.

Although an entire file can be locked, it's often desirable to lock a smaller region. For example, a database management system might lock individual table rows that are being updated instead of locking the entire table so that read requests can be honored, which improves throughput.

Locks that are associated with files are known as *file locks*. Each file lock starts at a certain byte position in the file and has a specific length (in bytes) from this position. Together, they define the region governed by the lock. File locks let processes coordinate access to various regions in a file.

There are two kinds of file locks: exclusive and shared. An *exclusive lock* gives a single writer process access to a file region; it prohibits additional file locks from being applied simultaneously to the region. A *shared lock* gives one of multiple reader processes access to the same file region; it does not prohibit other shared locks but does prohibit an exclusive lock from being applied simultaneously to the region.

Exclusive and shared locks are commonly used in scenarios where a shared file is primarily read and occasionally updated. A process that needs to read from the file acquires a shared lock to the entire file or to the desired subregion. A second process that also needs to read from the file acquires a shared lock to the desired region. Both processes can read the file without interfering with each other.

Suppose a third process wants to perform updates. To do so, it would request an exclusive lock. The process would block until all exclusive or shared locks that overlap with its region were released. Once the exclusive lock was granted to the updater process, any reader process requesting a shared lock would block until the exclusive lock was released. The updater process could then update the file without the reader processes observing inconsistent data.

There are a couple more items to keep in mind regarding file locking:

- When an operating system doesn't support shared locks, a shared lock request is quietly promoted to a request for an exclusive lock. Although correctness is assured, performance may be impacted.

- Locks are applied on a per-file basis. They are not applied on a per-thread or per-channel basis. Two threads running on the same JVM that request, via different channels, an exclusive lock to the same file region are granted access. However, if these threads were running on different JVMs, the second thread would block. Locks are ultimately arbitrated by the operating system's file system, and almost always at the process level. They are not arbitrated at the thread level. Locks associate with files and not with file handles or channels.

FileChannel declares four methods for obtaining exclusive and shared locks:

- FileLock lock(): Obtain an exclusive lock on this file channel's underlying file. This convenience method is equivalent to executing fileChannel.lock(0L, Long. MAX_VALUE, false);, where fileChannel references a file channel.

  This method returns a java.nio.channels.FileLock object representing the locked area. It throws ClosedChannelException when the file channel is closed; NonWritableChannelException when the channel isn't open for writing; java.nio.channels.OverlappingFileLockException when either a lock that overlaps the requested region is already held by this JVM, or another thread is already blocked in this method and is attempting to lock an overlapping region of the same file; java.nio.channels. FileLockInterruptionException when the calling thread was interrupted while waiting to acquire the lock; AsynchronousCloseException when the channel was closed while the calling thread was waiting to acquire the lock; and IOException when some other I/O error occurs while obtaining the requested lock.

- FileLock lock(long position, long size, boolean shared): This method is similar to the previous method except that it attempts to acquire a lock on the given region of this channel's file. Pass non-negative values to position and size to delimit the region. Pass true to shared to request a shared lock and false to shared to request an exclusive lock.

- `FileLock tryLock()`: Attempt to obtain an exclusive lock on this file channel's underlying file without blocking. This convenience method is equivalent to executing `fileChannel.tryLock(0L, Long.MAX_VALUE, false)`; where `fileChannel` references a file channel.

  This method returns a `FileLock` object representing the locked area or `null` when the lock would overlap with an existing exclusive lock in another operating system process. It throws `ClosedChannelException` when the file channel is closed; `OverlappingFileLockException` when a lock that overlaps the requested region is already held by this JVM, or when another thread is already blocked in this method and is attempting to lock an overlapping region; and `IOException` when some other I/O error occurs while obtaining the requested lock.

- `FileLock tryLock(long position, long size, boolean shared)`: This method is similar to the previous method except that it attempts to acquire a lock on the given region of this channel's file. Pass non-negative values to `position` and `size` to delimit the region. Pass `true` to `shared` to request a shared lock and `false` to `shared` to request an exclusive lock.

The `lock()` methods block when the desired region to be locked is already locked (unless both locks are shared locks). In contrast, the `tryLock()` methods return immediately with a `null` value (when the lock would overlap with an existing exclusive lock in another operating system process).

Each method returns a `FileLock` instance, which encapsulates a locked region in the file. `FileLock`'s methods are described next:

- `FileChannel channel()`: Return the file channel on whose file this lock was acquired or `null` when the lock wasn't acquired by a file channel.

- `void close()`: Invoke the `release()` method to release the lock.

- `boolean isShared()`: Return `true` to identify the lock as a shared lock or `false` to identify it as an exclusive lock.

- `boolean isValid()`: Return `true` to identify a valid lock; otherwise, return `false`. A lock is valid until it's released or the associated file channel is closed, whichever comes first.

- boolean overlaps(long position, long size): Indicate whether (return true) or not (return false) this lock's region overlaps the region described in the parameter list.

- long position(): Return the position within the file of the first byte of the locked region. A locked region doesn't need to be contained within or even overlap the underlying file, so the value returned by this method may exceed the file's current size.

- void release(): Release this lock. If this lock object is valid, invoking this method releases the lock and renders the object invalid. If this lock object is invalid, invoking this method has no effect.

- long size(): Return the length of the file lock (in bytes).

- String toString(): Return a string describing the range, type, and validity of this lock.

A FileLock instance is associated with a FileChannel instance but the file lock represented by the FileLock instance associates with the underlying file and not with the file channel. Without care, you can run into conflicts (and possibly even a deadlock) when you don't release a file lock after you're finished using it. To avoid these problems, you should adopt a pattern such as the following one to ensure that the file lock is always released:

```
FileLock lock = fileChannel.lock();
try
{
   // interact with the file channel
}
catch (IOException ioe)
{
   // handle the exception
}
finally
{
   lock.release();
}
```

I've created an application that demonstrates file locking. It follows this pattern to ensure that the lock is released. Listing 7-4 presents its source code.

Listing 7-4. Demonstrating File Locking

```java
import java.io.IOException;
import java.io.RandomAccessFile;

import java.nio.ByteBuffer;
import java.nio.IntBuffer;

import java.nio.channels.FileChannel;
import java.nio.channels.FileLock;

public class ChannelDemo
{
    final static int MAXQUERIES = 150000;
    final static int MAXUPDATES = 150000;

    final static int RECLEN = 16;

    static ByteBuffer buffer = ByteBuffer.allocate(RECLEN);
    static IntBuffer intBuffer = buffer.asIntBuffer();

    static int counter = 1;

    public static void main(String[] args) throws IOException
    {
        boolean writer = false;
        if (args.length != 0)
            writer = true;
        RandomAccessFile raf = new RandomAccessFile("temp",
                                                    (writer) ? "rw" : "r");
        FileChannel fc = raf.getChannel();
        if (writer)
            update(fc);
        else
            query(fc);
    }

    static void query(FileChannel fc) throws IOException
    {
        for (int i = 0; i < MAXQUERIES; i++)
        {
            System.out.println("acquiring shared lock");
            FileLock lock = fc.lock(0, RECLEN, true);
            try
            {
                buffer.clear();
                fc.read(buffer, 0);
                int a = intBuffer.get(0);
                int b = intBuffer.get(1);
```

```
            int c = intBuffer.get(2);
            int d = intBuffer.get(3);
            System.out.println("Reading: " + a + " " +
                                b + " " +
                                c + " " +
                                d);
            if (a * 2 != b || a * 3 != c || a * 4 != d)
            {
                System.out.println("error");
                return;
            }
        }
        finally
        {
            lock.release();
        }
    }
}

static void update(FileChannel fc) throws IOException
{
    for (int i = 0; i < MAXUPDATES; i++)
    {
        System.out.println("acquiring exclusive lock");
        FileLock lock = fc.lock(0, RECLEN, false);
        try
        {
            intBuffer.clear();
            int a = counter;
            int b = counter * 2;
            int c = counter * 3;
            int d = counter * 4;
            System.out.println("Writing: " + a + " " +
                                b + " " +
                                c + " " +
                                d);
            intBuffer.put(a);
            intBuffer.put(b);
            intBuffer.put(c);
            intBuffer.put(d);
            counter++;
            buffer.clear();
            fc.write(buffer, 0);
        }
```

```
        finally
        {
           lock.release();
        }
     }
   }
}
```

Listing 7-4 describes an application that either updates a file named `temp` or queries this file. Because file locking applies at the process level and not at the thread level, you need to run two copies of this application to demonstrate file locking for yourself. One copy will behave as a writer, updating the file. The other copy will behave as a reader, querying the file.

The `ChannelDemo` class first declares a pair of constants for controlling the duration of the update and query loops, along with a constant that denotes the length of a record. It then allocates a byte buffer that can accommodate the entire 16-byte record and an `int`-based view buffer for treating the byte buffer as a sequence of four `int` values. Finally, a `counter` variable initialized to 1 is declared.

The `main()` method first determines whether the application runs as a writer or reader. If you specify any command-line arguments, writer is assumed. This method then either opens (for a reader) or creates (for a writer) `temp` as a random access file. If this file doesn't exist when you run the application as a reader, an exception is thrown.

After opening or creating `temp`, a file channel to this file is obtained. This channel is then passed to either the `update()` or `query()` method.

Consider `update()`. This method receives the file channel argument and enters a fixed-length `for` loop whose duration is governed by the `MAXUPDATES` constant. After outputting a lock-acquisition message, it attempts to obtain an exclusive lock to the entire 16-byte record. If the reader process has locked that record via a shared lock, `lock()` blocks until the shared lock is released.

Once the lock is obtained, the view buffer is cleared, which sets the position to 0 and the limit to the capacity. The buffer is ready to be completely filled.

The `counter` variable's current value is now accessed and saved in a variable. This value is multiplied by 2, 3, and 4, and the results are also saved in their own variables. After outputting a writing message that identifies these values, `update()` makes four `put()` calls on the view buffer to store the values in the byte buffer. The `counter` variable is incremented and the byte buffer is cleared to ensure that it can be completely drained. Finally, the file channel's `write()` method is called to drain the buffer to the underlying `temp` file.

The query() method has a similar structure to the update() method. However, it uses the file channel to read the temp file's record and stores the results in the byte buffer. After outputting a message to display the read results, it verifies that the values are correct. Any deviation from what is expected causes the method to terminate after outputting an error message.

Compile Listing 7-4 (javac ChannelDemo.java) and execute the following command line in one command window:

```
java ChannelDemo w
```

You should observe messages similar to the following:

```
acquiring exclusive lock
Writing: 1 2 3 4
acquiring exclusive lock
Writing: 2 4 6 8
acquiring exclusive lock
Writing: 3 6 9 12
acquiring exclusive lock
Writing: 4 8 12 16
acquiring exclusive lock
Writing: 5 10 15 20
```

In a second command window, execute the following command line:

```
java ChannelDemo
```

You should observe messages similar to the following:

```
acquiring shared lock
Reading: 2500 5000 7500 10000
acquiring shared lock
Reading: 2501 5002 7503 10004
acquiring shared lock
Reading: 2502 5004 7506 10008
acquiring shared lock
Reading: 2503 5006 7509 10012
acquiring shared lock
Reading: 2504 5008 7512 10016
```

If you run these applications until they finish, you should observe no error messages. The file locking ensures that only the writer process or the reader process can access temp's 16-byte record. The other process is denied while these bytes are locked. As a result, there can be no corruption to this record's values.

To prove to yourself that the file locking is actually working, comment out the following four lines from the previous listing, recompile ChannelDemo.java, and re-run this application as a writer and as a reader:

```
FileLock lock = fc.lock(0, RECLEN, true);
FileLock lock = fc.lock(0, RECLEN, false);
lock.release();
lock.release();
```

At some point during the execution, you should observe output similar to that shown here:

```
acquiring shared lock
Reading: 803 1606 2412 3216
error
```

The output is invalid—it should be 803 1606 2409 3212 but isn't because the reader and writer were able to access the record at the same time.

> **Note**   The more ChannelDemo reader processes that run, the slower a ChannelDemo writer process will run. Eventually, the ChannelDemo writer process will block during a lock acquisition attempt and not unblock because there will always be a shared lock in use.

Mapping Files into Memory

FileChannel declares a map() method that lets you create a virtual memory mapping between a region of an open file and a java.nio.MappedByteBuffer instance that wraps itself around this region. This mapping mechanism offers an efficient way to access a file because no time-consuming system calls are needed to perform I/O.

> **Note**   *Virtual memory* is a kind of memory in which virtual addresses (also known as artificial addresses) replace physical (RAM memory) addresses. Check out Wikipedia's "Virtual Memory" topic (http://en.wikipedia.org/wiki/Virtual_memory) to learn more about virtual memory.

The map()method has the following signature:

```
MappedByteBuffer map(FileChannel.MapMode mode, long position, long size)
```

The mode parameter defines the mapping mode and receives one of the following constants defined by the FileChannel.MapMode enumerated type:

- READ_ONLY: Any attempt to modify the buffer will cause java.nio.ReadOnlyBufferException to be thrown.

- READ_WRITE: Changes made to the resulting buffer will eventually be propagated to the file; they might not be made visible to other programs that have mapped the same file.

- PRIVATE: Changes made to the resulting buffer will not be propagated to the file and will not be visible to other programs that have mapped the same file. Instead, changes will cause private copies of the modified portions of the buffer to be created. These changes are lost when the buffer is garbage collected.

The specified mapping mode is constrained by the invoking FileChannel object's access permissions. For example, if the file channel was opened as a read-only channel, and if you request READ_WRITE mode, map()will throw NonWritableChannelException because it cannot write to the file channel. Similarly, NonReadableChannelException is thrown when the channel was opened as write-only and you request READ_ONLY mode. (You can request READ_ONLY for a file channel opened as a read-write channel.)

Tip Invoke MappedByteBuffer's isReadOnly() method to determine whether or not you can modify the mapped file.

The position and size parameters define the start and extent of the mapped region. Arguments passed to these parameters must be non-negative. Furthermore, the argument passed to size must not exceed Integer.MAX_VALUE.

The specified range shouldn't exceed the file's size because the file will be made larger to accommodate the range. For example, if you pass Integer.MAX_VALUE to size, the file will grow to more than two gigabytes. Also, for a read-only mapping, map()will probably throw IOException.

The returned MappedByteBuffer object behaves like a memory-mapped buffer but its contents are stored in a file. When you invoke get() on this object, the current contents of the file are obtained, even when these contents have been modified by an external program. Similarly, when you have write permission, invoking put() updates the file and changes are available to external programs.

> **Note**   Because mapped byte buffers are direct byte buffers, the memory space assigned to them exists outside of the JVM's heap.

Consider the following example:

```
MappedByteBuffer buffer = fileChannel.map(FileChannel.MapMode.READ_ONLY, 50, 100);
```

This example maps a subrange, from location 50 through location 149, of the file described by `fileChannel`. In contrast, the following example maps the entire file:

```
MappedByteBuffer buffer =
fileChannel.map(FileChannel.MapMode.READ_ONLY, 0, fileChannel.size());
```

There is no `unmap()` method. Once a mapping is established, it remains until the `MappedByteBuffer` object is garbage collected (or the application exits, whichever happens first). Because a mapped byte buffer isn't connected to the file channel by which it was created, the mapping isn't destroyed when the file channel is closed.

`MappedByteBuffer` inherits methods from its `java.nio.ByteBuffer` superclass. It also declares the following methods:

- `MappedByteBuffer load()`: Attempt to load all of the mapped file content into memory. This results in much faster access for large files because the virtual memory manager doesn't have to load portions of the file into memory as those portions are requested (by reading from/writing to their locations) while traversing the mapped buffer. Although `load()` makes a best effort, it may not succeed because external programs may cause the virtual memory manager to remove portions of the loaded file content to make room for their requests to load content into physical memory. Also, `load()` can be expensive time-wise because it can cause the virtual memory manager to perform many I/O operations; it may take time for this method to complete.

- `boolean isLoaded()`: Return `true` when all of the mapped file content has been loaded into memory; otherwise, return `false`. If this method returns `true`, you can probably access all of the content with few or no I/O operations. If this method returns `false`, it's still possible that buffer access will be fast and that the mapped content will be entirely resident in memory. Think of `isLoaded()` as hinting at the mapped byte buffer's status.

■ MappedByteBuffer force(): Cause changes made to the mapped byte buffer to be written out to permanent storage. When working with mapped byte buffers, you should invoke this method instead of the file channel's force() method because the channel might be unaware of various changes made through the mapped byte buffer. Calling this method has no effect on READ_ONLY and PRIVATE mappings.

Listing 7-5 presents an application that demonstrates file mapping.

Listing 7-5. Demonstrating File Mapping

```java
import java.io.IOException;
import java.io.RandomAccessFile;

import java.nio.ByteBuffer;
import java.nio.MappedByteBuffer;

import java.nio.channels.FileChannel;

public class ChannelDemo
{
    public static void main(String[] args) throws IOException
    {
        if (args.length != 1)
        {
            System.out.println("usage: java ChannelDemo filespec");
            return;
        }
        RandomAccessFile raf = new RandomAccessFile(args[0], "rw");
        FileChannel fc = raf.getChannel();
        long size = fc.size();
        System.out.println("Size: " + size);
        MappedByteBuffer mbb = fc.map(FileChannel.MapMode.READ_WRITE, 0,
                                      size);
        while (mbb.remaining() > 0)
            System.out.print((char) mbb.get());
        System.out.println();
        System.out.println();
        for (int i = 0; i < mbb.limit() / 2; i++)
        {
            byte b1 = mbb.get(i);
            byte b2 = mbb.get(mbb.limit() - i - 1);
            mbb.put(i, b2);
            mbb.put(mbb.limit() - i - 1, b1);
        }
```

```
        mbb.flip();
        while (mbb.remaining() > 0)
            System.out.print((char) mbb.get());
        fc.close();
    }
}
```

After verifying that you've specified a single command-line argument, which should identify an existing file, main() creates a RandomAccessFile object for accessing this file in read/write mode. It then obtains a file channel for communicating with this file.

After using the file channel to obtain the file size, which is subsequently output, main() uses the file channel to invoke map()to obtain a read/write mapping of the entire file. It subsequently outputs the contents of the returned mapped byte buffer.

Later on, main() enters a for loop whose purpose is to reverse the file's contents. In each of the iterations, two bytes that mirror each other are obtained and then swapped. After leaving this loop, main() flips the buffer for draining and outputs its reversed contents.

Compile Listing 7-5 (javac ChannelDemo.java) and, assuming the existence of a poem.txt file, execute the following command line to reverse this file's contents:

```
java ChannelDemo poem.txt
```

You should observe output similar to the following:

```
Size: 67
Roses are red,
Violets are blue,
Sugar is sweet,
And so are you!

!uoy era os dnA
,teews si raguS
,eulb era steloiV
,der era sesoR
```

Note that the blank lines in the reversed text result from reversing the carriage return (13)/line feed (10) sequences on Windows operating systems.

Furthermore, the contents of poem.txt should be reversed.

Transferring Bytes Among Channels

To optimize the common practice of performing bulk transfers, two methods have been added to `FileChannel` that avoid the need for intermediate buffers:

- `long transferFrom(ReadableByteChannel src, long position, long count)`

- `long transferTo(long position, long count, WritableByteChannel target)`

`transferFrom(ReadableByteChannel, long, long)` transfers bytes into this channel's file from the given readable byte channel. Parameter `src` identifies the source channel, `position` identifies the non-negative start position in the file where the transfer is to start, and `count` identifies the non-negative maximum number of bytes that are to be transferred.

This method returns the number of bytes (possibly 0) that were actually transferred. It throws `IllegalArgumentException` when a precondition on a parameter (such as `position` being non-negative) doesn't hold; `NonReadableChannelException` when the source channel wasn't opened for reading; `NonWritableChannelException` when this channel wasn't opened for writing; `ClosedChannelException` when this channel or the source channel is closed; `ClosedByInterruptException` when another thread interrupts the current thread while the transfer is in progress, thereby closing both channels and setting the current thread's interrupt status; and `IOException` when some other I/O error occurs.

`transferTo(long, long, WritableByteChannel)` transfers bytes from this channel's file to the given writable byte channel. Parameter `position` identifies the non-negative start position in the file where the transfer is to start, `count` identifies the non-negative maximum number of bytes that are to be transferred, and `target` identifies the target channel.

This method returns the number of bytes (possibly 0) that were actually transferred. It throws `IllegalArgumentException` when a precondition on a parameter doesn't hold; `NonReadableChannelException` when this channel wasn't opened for reading; `NonWritableChannelException` when the target channel wasn't opened for writing; `ClosedChannelException` when this channel or the target channel is closed; `ClosedByInterruptException` when another thread interrupts the current thread while the transfer is in progress, thereby closing both channels and setting the current thread's interrupt status; and `IOException` when some other I/O error occurs.

If you're using `transferTo()` with a file channel as the transfer source, the transfer stops at the end of the file when `position` plus `count` exceeds the file's size. Similarly, `transferFrom()` stops when `src` is a file channel and its end of file is reached.

Listing 7-6 presents an application that demonstrates channel transfer.

Listing 7-6. Demonstrating Channel Transfer

```java
import java.io.FileInputStream;
import java.io.IOException;

import java.nio.channels.Channels;
import java.nio.channels.FileChannel;
import java.nio.channels.WritableByteChannel;

public class ChannelDemo
{
   public static void main(String[] args)
   {
      if (args.length != 1)
      {
         System.err.println("usage: java ChannelDemo filespec");
         return;
      }

      try (FileInputStream fis = new FileInputStream(args[0]))
      {
         FileChannel inChannel = fis.getChannel();
         WritableByteChannel outChannel = Channels.newChannel(System.out);
         inChannel.transferTo(0, inChannel.size(), outChannel);
      }
      catch (IOException ioe)
      {
         System.out.println("I/O error: " + ioe.getMessage());
      }
   }
}
```

Listing 7-6's main() method verifies that a single command-line argument has been specified. This argument identifies a file whose contents are to be copied to the standard output stream.

Next, main() creates a file input stream to the file identified by the command-line argument and a file channel for reading from this file.

Finally, an output channel for sending bytes to the standard output stream is obtained and the input file channel's transferTo()method is called to transfer the file content to standard output.

Compile Listing 7-6 (javac ChannelDemo.java) and execute the following command line to make a copy of ChannelDemo.java:

```
java ChannelDemo ChannelDemo.java >ChannelDemo.bak
```

You should observe a `ChannelDemo.bak` file with size and contents identical to `ChannelDemo.java`.

Socket Channels

I previously mentioned that `Socket` declares a `SocketChannel getChannel()` method for returning a socket channel instance, which describes an open connection to a socket. Unlike sockets, socket channels are selectable and can function in nonblocking mode. These capabilities (discussed later in this chapter) enhance the scalability and flexibility of large applications (such as web servers).

Socket channels are described by the `java.nio.channels` package's abstract `ServerSocketChannel`, `SocketChannel`, and `DatagramChannel` classes. Each class ultimately extends `java.nio.channels.SelectableChannel` and implements `InterruptibleChannel`, making `ServerSocketChannel`, `SocketChannel`, and `DatagramChannel` instances selectable and interruptible. Because `SocketChannel` and `DatagramChannel` implement the `ByteChannel`, `GatheringByteChannel`, and `ScatteringByteChannel` interfaces, you can write to, read from, and perform scatter/gather I/O on their underlying sockets.

> **Note** Unlike buffers, which are not thread-safe, server socket channels, socket channels, and datagram channels are thread-safe.

Each `ServerSocketChannel`, `SocketChannel`, and `DatagramChannel` instance creates a peer socket object from the `java.net.ServerSocket`, `Socket`, or `java.net.DatagramSocket` class. Each class has been retrofitted to work with channels. You can obtain the peer socket object by invoking `ServerSocketChannel`'s, `SocketChannel`'s, or `DatagramChannel`'s `socket()` method.

> **Note** When invoked on the socket instance returned from `socket()`, `getChannel()` returns the associated socket channel. However, when invoked on a socket obtained by instantiating `ServerSocket`, `Socket`, or `DatagramSocket`, `getChannel()` returns null.

Understanding Nonblocking Mode

The blocking nature of sockets created from Java's socket classes is a serious limitation to a network-oriented Java application's scalability. For example, the ServerSocket class's Socket accept() method blocks until an incoming connection arrives, at which point it creates and returns a Socket instance that lets the server communicate with the client. If this method didn't block, scalability would improve because the server could be accomplishing other useful work instead of having to wait.

The abstract SelectableChannel class is a common ancestor of the ServerSocketChannel, SocketChannel, and DatagramChannel classes. As well as letting the socket channel work in a selector context (I discuss selectors in Chapter 8), SelectableChannel lets socket channels choose to block or operate in *nonblocking mode*, in which a thread can check for input or send output without blocking when no input is available or when the output buffer is full.

> **Note** SelectableChannel merges functionality related to selectors with nonblocking mode because nonblocking mode is most useful in conjunction with selector-based multiplexing.

SelectableChannel offers the following methods to enable blocking or nonblocking, determine whether the channel is blocking or nonblocking, and obtain the blocking lock:

- SelectableChannel configureBlocking(boolean block): Specify the calling selectable channel's blocking status. Pass true to make the channel blocking and false to make the channel nonblocking. The method returns the selectable channel or throws an exception: ClosedChannelException when the channel is closed, java.net.channels.IllegalBlockingModeException when block is true and the channel has been registered with one or more selectors, and IOException when an I/O error occurs.

- boolean isBlocking(): This method returns true when the calling selectable channel is blocking; otherwise, it returns false. Newly created channels default to blocking.

- Object blockingLock(): Return the object on which configureBlocking() synchronizes. The returned object is useful in the implementation of adaptors that require the current blocking mode value to not change for a short period of time.

It's trivial to set or reset a selectable channel's blocking/nonblocking status. To enable nonblocking, pass `false` to an invocation of `configureBlocking()`, which the following example demonstrates:

```
ServerSocketChannel ssc = ServerSocketChannel.open();
ssc.configureBlocking(false); // enable nonblocking mode
```

Although nonblocking sockets are commonly used in server-oriented applications, they are also beneficial on the client side. For example, a GUI-based application can leverage nonblocking sockets to keep the user interface responsive while communicating simultaneously with several server applications.

The `blockingLock()` method lets you prevent other threads from changing a socket channel's blocking/nonblocking status. This method returns the object that a channel implementation uses for synchronizing when changing this status. Only the thread that holds the lock on this object can change the status and the lock is often obtained by using Java's synchronized keyword. Consider the following example:

```
ServerSocketChannel ssc = ServerSocketChannel.open();
SocketChannel sc = null;
Object lock = ssc.blockingLock();

// Thread might block when obtaining the lock associated with
// the lock object.
synchronized(lock)
{
    // Current thread owns the lock. No other thread can
    // change blocking mode.

    // Obtaining server socket channel's current blocking mode.
    boolean blocking = ssc.isBlocking();

    // Set server socket channel to nonblocking.
    ssc.configureBlocking(false);

    // Obtain next connection, which is null when there is no
    // connection.
    sc = ssc.accept();

    // Restore previous blocking mode.
    ssc.configureBlocking(blocking);
}

// The lock is released and some other thread may modify the
// server socket channel's blocking mode.
if (sc != null)
    communicateWithSocket(sc);
```

Exploring Server Socket Channels

ServerSocketChannel is the simplest of the three socket channel classes. This class includes the following methods:

- static ServerSocketChannel open(): Attempt to open a server-socket channel, which is initially unbound; it must be bound to a specific address via one of its peer socket's bind() methods before connections can be accepted. If the channel cannot be opened, IOException is thrown.

- ServerSocket socket(): Return the peer ServerSocket instance associated with this server socket channel.

- SocketChannel accept(): Accept the connection made to this channel's socket. If this channel is nonblocking, accept() immediately returns null when there are no pending connections or returns a socket channel that represents the connection. Otherwise, when the channel is blocking, accept() blocks indefinitely until a new connection is available or an I/O error occurs. The socket channel returned by accept() is blocking regardless of whether the server socket channel is blocking or nonblocking. This method throws ClosedChannelException when the server socket channel is closed, AsynchronousCloseException when another thread closes this server socket channel while the accept operation is in progress, java.nio.channels. NotYetBoundException when the server socket channel hasn't been bound, or IOException when an I/O error occurs.

A server socket channel behaves as a server in the TCP/IP stream protocol. You use server socket channels to listen for incoming connections with clients.

You create a new server socket channel by invoking the static open() factory method. If all goes well, open() returns a ServerSocketChannel instance associated with an unbound peer ServerSocket object. You can obtain this object by invoking socket(), and then invoke ServerSocket's bind() method to bind the server socket (and ultimately the server socket channel) to a specific address.

You can then invoke ServerSocketChannel's accept() method to accept an incoming connection. Depending on whether or not you have configured the server socket channel to be nonblocking, this method either returns immediately with null or a socket channel to an incoming connection, or blocks until there is an incoming connection.

> **Note**   Alternatively, you can invoke accept()on the peer ServerSocket object
> that socket() returns. However, this accept() method will always block.

Listing 7-7 presents a ChannelServer application that demonstrates
ServerSocketChannel.

Listing 7-7. Demonstrating ServerSocketChannel

```java
import java.io.IOException;

import java.net.InetSocketAddress;

import java.nio.ByteBuffer;

import java.nio.channels.ServerSocketChannel;
import java.nio.channels.SocketChannel;

public class ChannelServer
{
    public static void main(String[] args) throws IOException
    {
        System.out.println("Starting server...");
        ServerSocketChannel ssc = ServerSocketChannel.open();
        ssc.socket().bind(new InetSocketAddress(9999));
        ssc.configureBlocking(false);
        String msg = "Local address: " + ssc.socket().getLocalSocketAddress();
        ByteBuffer buffer = ByteBuffer.wrap(msg.getBytes());
        while (true)
        {
            System.out.print(".");
            SocketChannel sc = ssc.accept();
            if (sc != null)
            {
                System.out.println();
                System.out.println("Received connection from " +
                                    sc.socket().getRemoteSocketAddress());
                buffer.rewind();
                sc.write(buffer);
                sc.close();
            }
            else
                try
                {
                    Thread.sleep(100);
                }
```

```
        catch (InterruptedException ie)
        {
            assert false; // shouldn't happen
        }
    }
}
}
```

Listing 7-7's `main()` method first outputs a startup message and then obtains a server socket channel. Continuing, it accesses the `ServerSocket` peer object and uses this object to bind the socket/channel to port 9999.

Next, `main()` configures the server socket channel to be nonblocking and creates a byte buffer based on a message that identifies the server socket channel's local socket address.

`main()` now enters a `while` loop that repeatedly prints a single period character to demonstrate the channel's nonblocking status and checks for an incoming connection. If a connection is detected, its `SocketChannel` instance is used to obtain the remote socket address, which is output to the standard output stream. The buffer is then rewound and its content is written to the socket channel, which is then closed. However, if a connection isn't detected, `main()` sleeps for a fraction of a second.

Compile Listing 7-7 as follows:

```
javac ChannelServer.java
```

Execute the following command line to start the server:

```
java ChannelServer
```

You should observe a `starting server...` message followed by a growing sequence of periods across the screen from left to right. At this point, there's nothing further to observe.

Exploring Socket Channels

`SocketChannel` is the most commonly used of the three socket channel classes and models a connection-oriented stream protocol (such as TCP/IP). This class includes the following methods:

- `static SocketChannel open()`: Attempt to open a socket channel. If the channel cannot be opened, `IOException` is thrown.

- `static SocketChannel open(InetSocketAddress remoteAddr)`: Attempt to open a socket channel and connect it to `remoteAddr`. This convenience method works as if by invoking the `open()` method, invoking the `connect()` method on the resulting socket channel, passing it `remoteAddr`, and then returning that channel. This method throws five different exceptions. It throws `AsynchronousCloseException` when another thread closes this channel while the connect operation is in progress; `ClosedByInterruptException` when another thread interrupts the current thread while the connect operation is in progress, thereby closing the channel and setting the current thread's interrupt status; `java.nio.channels.UnresolvedAddressException` when the given remote address isn't fully resolved; `java.nio.channels.UnsupportedAddressTypeException` when the type of the given remote address isn't supported; and `IOException` when some other I/O error occurs.

- `Socket socket()`: Return the peer Socket instance associated with this socket channel.

- `boolean connect(SocketAddress remoteAddr)`: Attempt to connect this socket channel's socket object to the remote address. If this channel is nonblocking, an invocation of this method initiates a nonblocking connection operation. If the connection is established immediately, as can happen with a local connection, this method returns `true`. Otherwise, this method returns `false` and the connection operation must be subsequently completed by repeatedly invoking the `finishConnect()` method until this method returns `true`. This method throws `java.nio.channels.AlreadyConnectedException` when this channel is already connected; `java.nio.channels.ConnectionPendingException` when a nonblocking connection operation is already in progress on this channel; `ClosedChannelException` when this channel is closed; `AsynchronousCloseException` when another thread closes this channel while the connect operation is in progress; `ClosedByInterruptException` when another thread interrupts the current thread while the connect operation is in progress, thereby closing the channel and setting the current thread's interrupt status; `UnresolvedAddressException` when the given remote address isn't fully resolved; `UnsupportedAddressTypeException` when the type of the given remote address isn't supported; and IOException when some other I/O error occurs.

- boolean isConnectionPending(): Return true when a connection operation is pending completion; otherwise, return false.

- boolean finishConnect(): Finish the process of connecting a socket channel. This method returns true when the socket channel is fully connected; otherwise, it returns false. This method throws java.nio.channels. NoConnectionPendingException when this channel isn't connected and a connection operation hasn't been initiated; ClosedChannelException when this channel is closed; AsynchronousCloseException when another thread closes this channel while the connect operation is in progress; ClosedByInterruptException when another thread interrupts the current thread while the connect operation is in progress, thereby closing the channel and setting the current thread's interrupt status; and IOException when some other I/O error occurs.

- boolean isConnected(): Return true when this channel's socket is open and connected; otherwise, return false.

A socket channel behaves as a client in the TCP/IP stream protocol. You use socket channels to initiate connections to listening servers.

Create a new socket channel by calling either of the open() methods. Behind the scenes, a peer Socket object is created. Invoke SocketChannel's socket() method to return this peer object. Also, you can return the original socket channel by invoking getChannel() on the peer Socket object.

A socket channel obtained from the noargument open() method isn't connected. Attempting to read from or write to this socket channel results in java.nio.channels.NotYetConnectedException. To connect the socket, call the connect() method on the socket channel or on its peer socket.

After a socket channel has been connected, it remains connected until closed. To determine if a socket channel is connected, invoke SocketChannel's boolean isConnected() method.

The open() method that takes a java.net.InetSocketAddress argument also lets you connect to another host at the specified remote address, as follows:

```
SocketChannel sc = SocketChannel.open(new InetSocketAddress("localhost", 9999));
```

This convenience method is equivalent to invoking the following code sequence:

```
SocketChannel sc = SocketChannel.open();
sc.connect(new InetSocketAddress("localhost", 9999));
```

When connecting to a server via the peer Socket object or via SocketChannel's connect()/second open() method on a blocking socket channel, the thread that invokes connect() blocks until the socket channel is connected. However, when the socket channel isn't blocking, connect() returns immediately, typically with false to indicate that the connection hasn't been made (although it might return true for a local loopback connection). Because a connection must be established before you can perform I/O on the socket channel, you need to repeatedly invoke finishConnect() until this method returns true.

Listing 7-8 presents a ChannelClient application that demonstrates SocketChannel.

Listing 7-8. Demonstrating SocketChannel

```
import java.io.IOException;

import java.net.InetSocketAddress;

import java.nio.ByteBuffer;

import java.nio.channels.SocketChannel;

public class ChannelClient
{
   public static void main(String[] args)
   {
      try
      {
         SocketChannel sc = SocketChannel.open();
         sc.configureBlocking(false);
         InetSocketAddress addr = new InetSocketAddress("localhost", 9999);
         sc.connect(addr);

         while (!sc.finishConnect())
            System.out.println("waiting to finish connection");

         ByteBuffer buffer = ByteBuffer.allocate(200);
         while (sc.read(buffer) >= 0)
         {
            buffer.flip();
            while (buffer.hasRemaining())
```

```
            System.out.print((char) buffer.get());
         buffer.clear();
      }
      sc.close();
   }
   catch (IOException ioe)
   {
      System.err.println("I/O error: " + ioe.getMessage());
   }
}
}
```

Listing 7-8's main() method first obtains a socket channel and configures it to be nonblocking. It then creates an address to the previous channel server application and initiates a connection to this address. Because of the nonblocking status, it's necessary to repeatedly invoke finishConnect() until this method returns true, which indicates a connection to the remote server application.

main() subsequently creates a byte buffer and enters a loop that repeatedly reads content into this buffer and outputs this content to the standard output stream. The channel is then closed.

Compile Listing 7-8 as follows:

```
javac ChannelClient.java
```

Assuming that the channel server is running, execute the following command line to start the client:

```
java ChannelClient
```

You should observe a message similar to the following on the channel server output stream:

```
Received connection from /127.0.0.1:51177
```

You should also observe the following message on the channel client output stream:

```
Local address: /0:0:0:0:0:0:0:0:9999
```

Exploring Datagram Channels

DatagramChannel models a connectionless packet-oriented protocol (such as UDP/IP). This class includes the following methods:

- static DatagramChannel open(): Attempt to open a datagram channel. If the channel cannot be opened, IOException is thrown.

- DatagramSocket socket(): Return the peer DatagramSocket instance associated with this datagram channel.

- DatagramChannel connect(SocketAddress remoteAddr): Attempt to connect this datagram channel's socket object to the remote address. The channel's socket is configured so that it only receives datagrams from and sends datagrams to the given address. Once connected, datagrams cannot be received from or sent to any other address. A datagram socket remains connected until explicitly disconnected or closed. This method returns the datagram channel upon success. It throws ClosedChannelException when the datagram channel is closed; AsynchronousCloseException when another thread closes this channel while the connect operation is in progress; ClosedByInterruptException when another thread interrupts the current thread while the connect operation is in progress, thereby closing the channel and setting the current thread's interrupt status; and IOException when some other I/O error occurs.

- boolean isConnected(): Return true when this channel's socket is open and connected; otherwise, return false.

- DatagramChannel disconnect(): Disconnect this channel's socket. This method may be invoked at any time and has no effect on read or write operations that are already in progress. When the socket isn't connected or when the channel is closed, invoking this method has no effect.

- SocketAddress receive(ByteBuffer buffer): Receive a datagram via this channel. If a datagram is immediately available or if this channel is blocking and a datagram becomes available, the datagram is copied into the given byte buffer and its source address is returned. If this channel is nonblocking and a datagram isn't immediately available, this method immediately returns null. The datagram is transferred into the given byte buffer starting at its current position, as if by a regular read operation. If there are fewer bytes remaining in the buffer than are required to hold the datagram, the remainder of the datagram is silently discarded. This method returns the datagram's source address or `null` when the channel isn't blocking and no datagram is available. It throws `ClosedChannelException` when the datagram channel is closed; `AsynchronousCloseException` when another thread closes this channel while the read operation is in progress; `ClosedByInterruptException` when another thread interrupts the current thread while the read operation is in progress, thereby closing the channel and setting the current thread's interrupt status; and `IOException` when some other I/O error occurs.

- `int send(ByteBuffer buffer, SocketAddress destAddr)`: Send a datagram via this channel. If this channel is nonblocking and there is sufficient room in the underlying output buffer, or if this channel is blocking and sufficient room becomes available, the remaining bytes in the given buffer are transmitted as a single datagram to the given destination address. The datagram is transferred from the byte buffer as if by a regular write operation. This method returns the number of bytes sent, which will be the number of bytes that were remaining in the source buffer when this method was invoked or, when this channel is nonblocking, may be zero if there was insufficient room for the datagram in the underlying output buffer. It throws `ClosedChannelException` when the datagram channel is closed; `AsynchronousCloseException` when another thread closes this channel while the write operation is in progress; `ClosedByInterruptException` when another thread interrupts the current thread while the write operation is in progress, thereby closing the channel and setting the current thread's interrupt status; and `IOException` when some other I/O error occurs.

Additionally, there are several `read()` and `write()` methods that you might like to use. Unlike `send()` and `receive()`, which don't require the datagram channel to be connected, the `read()` and `write()` methods require a connection.

As with ServerSocketChannel and SocketChannel, you obtain a DatagramChannel instance by invoking the static open() method. The new datagram channel is associated with a peer DatagramSocket object, which you can obtain by invoking DatagramChannel's socket() method.

A datagram channel can behave as both a client (the sender) and a server (the listener). To act as a listener, the datagram channel must be bound to a port and an optional address. Accomplish this task by obtaining the DatagramSocket object and invoking bind() on this object, as follows:

```
DatagramChannel dc = DatagramChannel.open();
DatagramSocket ds = dc.socket();
ds.bind(new InetSocketAddress(9999)); // bind to port 9999
```

The receive() method copies the incoming datagram's data payload into the byte buffer argument and returns a socket address identifying the datagram's source address. If the channel is blocking, receive() sleeps until the packet arrives or some event results in a thrown exception. If the channel is nonblocking, receive() returns null when a datagram isn't available. If the data payload is larger than will fit in the buffer, excess bytes are quietly removed.

The send() method sends the given byte buffer's content, starting from the current position and ranging to the buffer's limit, to the destination address/port number specified by the socket address argument. If the datagram channel is blocking, send()sleeps until the datagram is queued for sending or some event results in a thrown exception. If the channel isn't blocking, this method returns with one of two values: the entire length of the buffer content that was sent or 0 indicating that the buffer content wasn't sent (nothing is sent when there isn't room to store the entire datagram before transmission).

> **Note**   Datagram protocols aren't reliable. For one thing, they don't guarantee delivery. As a result, a nonzero return value from send() doesn't mean that the datagram reached its destination. Also, the underlying network might fragment the datagram into multiple smaller packets. When a datagram is fragmented, it's more probable for one or more of these packets to not arrive at the destination. Because the receiver cannot reassemble all of the packets, the entire datagram is discarded. For this reason, data payloads should be restricted to several hundred bytes maximum.

An example of where you might require a datagram channel is a stock ticker that offers the latest stock prices for a given company. A client would submit a company's stock symbol (such as MSFT for Microsoft) as a datagram payload and receive a datagram in response whose payload provides the requested stock prices. Because the latest information is desired, the client would re-request the stock prices when a response datagram doesn't arrive.

Listing 7-9 presents a ChannelServer application that leverages DatagramChannel to implement the server portion of the stock ticker.

Listing 7-9. Using DatagramChannel to Implement a Stock Ticker Server

```java
import java.io.IOException;

import java.net.InetSocketAddress;
import java.net.SocketAddress;

import java.nio.ByteBuffer;

import java.nio.channels.DatagramChannel;

public class ChannelServer
{
   final static int PORT = 9999;

   public static void main(String[] args) throws IOException
   {
      System.out.println("server starting and listening on port " +
                         PORT + " for incoming requests...");
      DatagramChannel dcServer = DatagramChannel.open();
      dcServer.socket().bind(new InetSocketAddress(PORT));
      ByteBuffer symbol = ByteBuffer.allocate(4);
      ByteBuffer payload = ByteBuffer.allocate(16);
      while (true)
      {
         payload.clear();
         symbol.clear();
         SocketAddress sa = dcServer.receive(symbol);
         if (sa == null)
            return;
         System.out.println("Received request from " + sa);
         String stockSymbol = new String(symbol.array(), 0, 4);
         System.out.println("Symbol: " + stockSymbol);
         if (stockSymbol.toUpperCase().equals("MSFT"))
         {
            payload.putFloat(0, 37.40f); // open share price
            payload.putFloat(4, 37.22f); // low share price
```

```
        payload.putFloat(8, 37.48f); // high share price
        payload.putFloat(12, 37.41f); // close share price
    }
    else
    {
        payload.putFloat(0, 0.0f);
        payload.putFloat(4, 0.0f);
        payload.putFloat(8, 0.0f);
        payload.putFloat(12, 0.0f);
    }
    dcServer.send(payload, sa);
   }
  }
}
```

Listing 7-9's `main()` method first creates a datagram channel and binds it to port 9999. It then creates two byte buffers to hold a four-byte stock symbol and a 16-byte response, which is organized into four four-byte floating-point values representing open share price, low share price, high share price, and close share price.

> **Note** For convenience, I'm representing currency amounts as floating-point values. This is not a good idea in practice and `java.math.BigDecimal` should be used instead. Also, you wouldn't embed stock prices in the source code but would dynamically obtain them from some kind of external server or database.

`main()` now enters an infinite loop that clears both byte buffers in preparation for receiving new information from a client and receives the next stock symbol. The subsequent `if` statement that tests `sa` for `null` isn't necessary for this application but is present in case you want to configure the channel for nonblocking mode.

After outputting a message identifying the request, `main()` checks the stock symbol to see if it equals `MSFT`. If so, the `payload` byte buffer is configured to store four stock prices for Microsoft stock; otherwise, the `payload` byte buffer is configured to store four 0 prices (to indicate unknown stock symbol).

Finally, `main()` sends the `payload` datagram payload to the receiver and continues to loop.

Compile Listing 7-9 as follows:

```
javac ChannelServer.java
```

Run the resulting application as follows:

```
java ChannelServer
```

You should observe the following message:

```
server starting and listening on port 9999 for incoming requests...
```

Listing 7-10 presents a ChannelClient application that leverages DatagramChannel to implement the client portion of the stock ticker.

Listing 7-10. Using DatagramChannel to Implement a Stock Ticker Client

```java
import java.io.IOException;

import java.net.InetSocketAddress;

import java.nio.ByteBuffer;

import java.nio.channels.DatagramChannel;

public class ChannelClient
{
   final static int PORT = 9999;

   public static void main(String[] args) throws IOException
   {
      if (args.length != 1)
      {
         System.err.println("usage: java ChannelClient stocksymbol");
         return;
      }

      DatagramChannel dcClient = DatagramChannel.open();

      ByteBuffer symbol = ByteBuffer.wrap(args[0].getBytes());
      ByteBuffer response = ByteBuffer.allocate(16);

      InetSocketAddress sa = new InetSocketAddress("localhost", PORT);
      dcClient.send(symbol, sa);
      System.out.println("Receiving datagram from " +
                      dcClient.receive(response));
      System.out.println("Open price: " + response.getFloat(0));
      System.out.println("Low price: " + response.getFloat(4));
      System.out.println("High price: " + response.getFloat(8));
      System.out.println("Close price: " + response.getFloat(12));
   }
}
```

Listing 7-10's main() method first verifies that a single command-line argument has been specified. This argument identifies a stock symbol. It then creates a datagram channel and a pair of byte buffers: symbol stores the specified symbol and response stores the response from the server.

Next, main() creates a socket address for communicating with and sends the symbol buffer to the server. It then receives a response datagram from the server, storing its payload in the response buffer.

Finally, main() accesses the response buffer, using getFloat() to convert each set of four bytes to a floating-point value, which is subsequently output.

Compile Listing 7-10 as follows:

```
javac ChannelClient.java
```

Run the resulting application as follows:

```
java ChannelClient msft
```

Assuming that the server is still running, you should observe the following messages (with, possibly, a different port number) in the server window:

```
Received request from /127.0.0.1:64837
Symbol: msft
```

Also, you should observe the following output in the client window:

```
Receiving datagram from /127.0.0.1:9999
Open price: 37.4
Low price: 37.22
High price: 37.48
Close price: 37.41
```

Pipes

The java.nio.channels package includes a Pipe class. Pipe describes a pair of channels that implement a unidirectional *pipe*, which is a conduit for passing data in one direction between two entities, such as two file channels or two socket channels. Pipe is analogous to the java.io.PipedInputStream and java.io.PipedOutputStream classes—see Chapter 4.

Pipe declares nested SourceChannel and SinkChannel classes that serve as readable and writable byte channels, respectively. Pipe also declares the following methods:

- ■ static Pipe open(): This class method opens a new pipe, throwing IOException when an I/O error occurs.

- ■ SourceChannel source(): This method returns the pipe's source channel (from which data originates).

- ■ SinkChannel sink(): This method returns the pipe's sink channel (to which data is sent).

Pipes can be used to pass data within the same JVM; you cannot use them to pass data between the JVM and an external program. Pipes are ideal in producer/consumer scenarios because of encapsulation: you can use the same code to write data to files, sockets, or pipes depending on the kind of channel presented to the pipe.

Listing 7-11 presents a producer/consumer application that uses a pipe to achieve communication between two threads.

Listing 7-11. Producing and Consuming Bytes via a Pipe

```java
import java.io.IOException;

import java.nio.ByteBuffer;

import java.nio.channels.Pipe;
import java.nio.channels.ReadableByteChannel;
import java.nio.channels.WritableByteChannel;

public class ChannelDemo
{
   final static int BUFSIZE = 10;
   final static int LIMIT = 3;

   public static void main(String[] args) throws IOException
   {
      final Pipe pipe = Pipe.open();

      Runnable senderTask =
         new Runnable()
         {
            @Override
            public void run()
            {
               WritableByteChannel src = pipe.sink();
               ByteBuffer buffer = ByteBuffer.allocate(BUFSIZE);
               for (int i = 0; i < LIMIT; i++)
```

```
        {
            buffer.clear();
            for (int j = 0; j < BUFSIZE; j++)
                buffer.put((byte) (Math.random() * 256));
            buffer.flip();
            try
            {
                while (src.write(buffer) > 0);
            }
            catch (IOException ioe)
            {
                System.err.println(ioe.getMessage());
            }
        }
        try
        {
            src.close();
        }
        catch (IOException ioe)
        {
            ioe.printStackTrace();
        }
    }
};

Runnable receiverTask =
    new Runnable()
    {
        @Override
        public void run()
        {
            ReadableByteChannel dst = pipe.source();
            ByteBuffer buffer = ByteBuffer.allocate(BUFSIZE);
            try
            {
                while (dst.read(buffer) >= 0)
                {
                    buffer.flip();
                    while (buffer.remaining() > 0)
                        System.out.println(buffer.get() & 255);
                    buffer.clear();
                }
            }
            catch (IOException ioe)
            {
                System.err.println(ioe.getMessage());
            }
        }
    };
```

```
        Thread sender = new Thread(senderTask);
        Thread receiver = new Thread(receiverTask);
        sender.start();
        receiver.start();
    }
}
```

Listing 7-11's main() method first obtains a pipe and then creates sender and receiver tasks that serve as producer and consumer. main() then creates sender and receiver threads and starts them.

The sender task's run() method first obtains a writable byte channel from the pipe by invoking Pipe's sink() method. It then allocates a byte buffer for storing content to be written.

run()continues by entering a pair of for loops for sending byte-oriented data to the writable byte channel. Each of the outer for loop iterations clears the buffer in preparation for filling by the inner for loop. The buffer is then flipped in preparation for draining, which is accomplished by passing the buffer to the writable byte channel's write() method. Because a single method call might not drain the entire buffer, write()is invoked in a loop until it returns 0, which means that there is no more content to write. The channel is then closed so that the receiver task doesn't block when reading from the channel because it expects to receive more data.

The receiver task's run() method first obtains a readable byte channel from the pipe by invoking Pipe's source() method. It then allocates a buffer for storing read content.

Continuing, run()enters a while loop that continually reads from the channel until the read() method returns -1, which indicates that the channel has reached the end of the stream. This method wouldn't reach the end of the stream if the sender's run()method hadn't closed the channel.

At this point, the buffer is flipped to prepare it for draining. It's then drained by printing its byte values to the standard output stream. Each byte is bitwise ANDed with 255 to prevent a negative value from being output. Basically, get() returns an 8-bit integer value that's converted to a 32-bit integer during the System.out.println() method call. This conversion applies sign extension, which means that some byte values become negative 32-bit integers. By bitwise ANDing the byte value with 255, the conversion ensures that no byte value is turned into a negative 32-bit integer.

Finally, the buffer is cleared in preparation for filling and the loop continues.

Compile Listing 7-11 (javac ChannelDemo.java) and run the application (java ChannelDemo). You should observe a sequence of 30 random integers similar to that shown here:

```
245
56
137
166
52
183
252
166
246
124
163
11
159
68
203
118
157
70
54
148
186
17
12
203
75
223
224
175
205
47
```

EXERCISES

The following exercises are designed to test your understanding of Chapter 7's content:

1. What is a channel?

2. What capabilities does the Channel interface provide?

3. Identify the three interfaces that directly extend Channel.

4. True or false: A channel that implements InterruptibleChannel is asynchronously closeable.

5. Identify the two ways to obtain a channel.

6. Define scatter/gather I/O.

7. What interfaces are provided for achieving scatter/gather I/O?

8. Define file channel.

9. True or false: File channels don't support scatter/gather I/O.

10. Define exclusive lock and shared lock.

11. What is the fundamental difference between FileChannel's lock() and tryLock() methods?

12. What does the FileLock lock() method do when either a lock is already held that overlaps this lock request or another thread is waiting to acquire a lock that will overlap with this request?

13. Specify the pattern that you should adopt to ensure that an acquired file lock is always released.

14. What method does FileChannel provide for mapping a region of a file into memory?

15. Identify the three file-mapping modes.

16. Which file-mapping mode corresponds to copy-on-write?

17. Identify the FileChannel methods that optimize the common practice of performing bulk transfers.

18. True or false: Socket channels are selectable and can function in nonblocking mode.

19. Identify the three classes that describe socket channels.

20. True or false: Datagram channels are not thread-safe.

21. Why do socket channels support nonblocking mode?

22. How would you obtain a socket channel's associated socket?

23. How do you obtain a server socket channel?

24. Create a Copy application that uses the ByteBuffer and FileChannel classes in partnership with FileInputStream and FileOutputStream to copy a source file to a destination file.

Summary

Channels partner with buffers to achieve high-performance I/O. A channel is an object that represents an open connection to a hardware device, a file, a network socket, an application component, or another entity that's capable of performing write, read, and other I/O operations. Channels efficiently transfer data between byte buffers and operating system-based I/O service sources or destinations.

Java supports channels by providing the Channel interface, its WritableByteChannel and ReadableByteChannel subinterfaces, the Channels class, and other types in the java.nio.channels package. While exploring this package, you learned about scatter/gather I/O, file channels (in terms of the FileChannel class with emphasis on its file locking, memory-mapped file I/O, and byte-transfer capabilities), socket channels, and pipes.

Chapter 8 presents NIO's support for selectors.

Selectors

I/O is either block-oriented (such as file I/O) or stream-oriented (such as network I/O). Streams are often slower than block devices (such as fixed disks) and read/write operations often cause the calling thread to block until input is available or output has been fully written. To compensate, modern operating systems let streams operate in *nonblocking mode*, which makes it possible for a thread to read or write data without blocking. The operation fully succeeds or indicates partial success. Either way, the thread is able to perform other useful work instead of waiting.

Nonblocking mode doesn't let an application determine if it can perform an operation without actually performing the operation. For example, when a nonblocking read operation succeeds, the application learns that the read operation is possible but also has read some data that must be managed. This duality prevents you from separating code that checks for stream readiness from the data-processing code without making your code significantly complicated.

Nonblocking mode serves as a foundation for performing *readiness selection*, which offloads to the operating system the work involved in checking for I/O stream readiness to perform write, read, and other operations without actually performing the operations. The operating system is instructed to observe a group of streams and return some indication of which streams are ready to perform a specific operation (such as read) or operations (such as accept and read). This capability lets a thread *multiplex* a potentially huge number of active streams by using the readiness information provided by the operating system. In this way, network servers can handle large numbers of network connections; they are vastly scalable.

> **Note**   Modern operating systems make readiness selection available to applications by providing system calls such as the POSIX `select()` call.

Selectors let you achieve readiness selection in a Java context. This chapter introduces you to selector fundamentals and then provides a demonstration.

Selector Fundamentals

A *selector* is an object created from a subclass of the abstract `java.nio.channels.Selector` class. The selector maintains a set of channels that it examines to determine which channels are ready for reading, writing, completing a connection sequence, accepting another connection, or some combination of these tasks. The actual work is delegated to the operating system via a POSIX `select()` or similar system call.

> **Note**   The ability to check a channel without having to wait when something isn't ready (such as bytes are not available for reading) and without also having to perform the operation while checking is the key to scalability. A single thread can manage a huge number of channels, which reduces code complexity and potential threading issues.

Selectors are used with *selectable channels*, which are objects whose classes ultimately inherit from the abstract `java.nio.channels.SelectableChannel` class, which describes a channel that can be multiplexed by a selector. Socket channels, server socket channels, datagram channels, and pipe source/sink channels are selectable channels because `java.nio.channels.SocketChannel`, `java.nio.channels.ServerSocketChannel`, `java.nio.channels.DatagramChannel`, `java.nio.channels.Pipe.SinkChannel`, and `java.nio.channels.Pipe.SourceChannel` are derived from `SelectableChannel`. In contrast, file channels are not selectable channels because `java.nio.channels.FileChannel` doesn't include `SelectableChannel` in its ancestry.

One or more previously created selectable channels are registered with a selector. Each registration returns an instance of a subclass of the abstract `SelectionKey` class, which is a token signifying the relationship between one channel and the selector. This *key* keeps track of two sets of operations: interest set and ready set. The *interest set* identifies the operation categories that will be tested for readiness the next time one of the selector's selection methods is invoked. The *ready set* identifies the operation categories for which the key's channel has been found to be ready by the key's selector.

When a selection method is invoked, the selector's associated keys are updated by checking all channels registered with that selector. The application can then obtain a set of keys whose channels were found ready and iterate over these keys to service each channel that has become ready since the previous select method call.

> **Note**   A selectable channel can be registered with more than one selector. It has no knowledge of the selectors to which it's currently registered.

To work with selectors, you first need to create one. You can accomplish this task by invoking Selector's Selector open() class method, which returns a Selector instance on success or throws java.io.IOException on failure. The following code fragment demonstrates this task:

```
Selector selector = Selector.open();
```

You can create your selectable channels before or after creating your selector. However, you must ensure that each channel is in nonblocking mode before registering the channel with the selector. You register a selectable channel with a selector by invoking either of the following SelectableChannel registration methods:

- SelectionKey register(Selector sel, int ops)
- SelectionKey register(Selector sel, int ops, Object att)

Each method requires that you pass a previously created selector to sel and a bitwise ORed combination of the following SelectionKey int-based constants to ops, which signifies the interest set:

- OP_ACCEPT: Operation-set bit for socket-accept operations.
- OP_CONNECT: Operation-set bit for socket-connect operations.
- OP_READ: Operation-set bit for read operations.
- OP_WRITE: Operation-set bit for write operations.

The second method also lets you pass an arbitrary java.lang.Object or a subclass instance (or null) to att. The non-null object is known as an *attachment* and is a convenient way of recognizing a given channel or attaching additional information to the channel. It's stored in the SelectionKey instance returned from this method.

Upon success, each method returns a SelectionKey instance that relates the selectable channel with the selector. Upon failure, an exception is thrown. For example, java.nio.channels.ClosedChannelException is thrown when the channel is closed and java.nio.channels. IllegalBlockingModeException is thrown when the channel hasn't been set to nonblocking mode.

The following code fragment extends the previous code fragment by configuring a previously created channel to nonblocking mode and registering the channel with the selector. The selection methods test the channel for accept, read, and write readiness:

```
channel.configureBlocking(false);
SelectionKey key = channel.register(selector, SelectionKey.OP_ACCEPT |
                                              SelectionKey.OP_READ |
                                              SelectionKey.OP_WRITE);
```

At this point, the application typically enters an infinite loop where it accomplishes the following tasks:

1. Performs a selection operation.

2. Obtains the selected keys followed by an iterator over the selected keys.

3. Iterates over these keys and performs channel operations.

A selection operation is performed by invoking one of Selector's selection methods. For example, int select() performs a blocking selection operation. It doesn't return until at least one channel is selected, until this selector's wakeup() method is invoked, or until the current thread is interrupted, whichever comes first.

> **Note**   Selector also declares an int select(long timeout) method that doesn't return until at least one channel is selected, until this selector's wakeup()method is invoked, until the current thread is interrupted, or until the timeout value expires, whichever comes first. Additionally, Selector declares int selectNow(), which is a nonblocking version of select().

The select() method returns the number of channels that have become ready since the last time it was called. For example, if you call select() and it returns 1 because one channel has become ready, and if you call select()

again and a second channel has become ready, select() will once again return 1. If you've not yet serviced the first ready channel, you now have two ready channels to service. However, only one channel became ready between the two select() calls.

A set of the selected keys (the ready set) is now obtained by invoking Selector's Set<SelectionKey> selectedKeys() method. Invoke the set's iterator() method to obtain an iterator over these keys.

Finally, the application iterates over the keys. For each of the iterations, a SelectionKey instance is returned. Some combination of SelectionKey's boolean isAcceptable(), boolean isConnectable(), boolean isReadable(), and boolean isWritable() methods is called to determine if the key indicates that a channel is ready to accept a connection, is finished connecting, is readable, or is writable.

> **Note** The aforementioned methods offer a convenient alternative to specifying expressions such as key.readyOps() & OP_READ != 0. SelectionKey's int readyOps() method returns the key's ready set. The returned set will only contain operation bits that are valid for this key's channel. For example, it never returns an operation bit that indicates that a read-only channel is ready for writing. Note that every selectable channel also declares an int validOps() method, which returns a bitwise ORed set of operations that are valid for the channel.

Once the application determines that a channel is ready to perform a specific operation, it can call SelectionKey's SelectableChannel channel() method to obtain the channel and then perform work on that channel.

> **Note** SelectionKey also declares a Selector selector() method that returns the selector for which the key was created.

When you're finished processing a channel, you must remove the key from the set of keys; the selector doesn't perform this task. The next time the channel becomes ready, the Selector will add the key to the selected key set.

The following code fragment continues from the previous code fragment and demonstrates the aforementioned tasks:

```
while (true)
{
   int numReadyChannels = selector.select();
   if (numReadyChannels == 0)
      continue; // there are no ready channels to process

   Set<SelectionKey> selectedKeys = selector.selectedKeys();
   Iterator<SelectionKey> keyIterator = selectedKeys.iterator();

   while (keyIterator.hasNext())
   {
      SelectionKey key = keyIterator.next();

      if (key.isAcceptable())
      {
         // A connection was accepted by a ServerSocketChannel.
         ServerSocketChannel server = (ServerSocketChannel) key.channel();
         SocketChannel client = server.accept();
         if (client == null) // in case accept() returns null
            continue;
         client.configureBlocking(false); // must be nonblocking
         // Register socket channel with selector for read operations.
         client.register(selector, SelectionKey.OP_READ);
      }
      else
      if (key.isReadable())
      {
         // A socket channel is ready for reading.
         SocketChannel client = (SocketChannel) key.channel();
         // Perform work on the socket channel.
      }
      else
      if (key.isWritable())
      {
         // A socket channel is ready for writing.
         SocketChannel client = (SocketChannel) key.channel();
         // Perform work on the socket channel.
      }

      keyIterator.remove();
   }
}
```

As well as registering the server socket channel with the selector, each incoming client socket channel is also registered with the server socket channel. When a client socket channel becomes ready for read or write operations, either key.isReadable() or key.isWritable() for the associated socket channel return true and the socket channel can be read or written.

A key represents a relationship between a selectable channel and a selector. This relationship can be terminated by invoking SelectionKey's void cancel() method. Upon return, the key will be invalid and will have been added to its selector's cancelled-key set. The key will be removed from all of the selector's key sets during the next selection operation.

When you're finished with a selector, call Selector's void close() method. If a thread is currently blocked in one of this selector's selection methods, it's interrupted as if by invoking the selector's wakeup() method. Any uncancelled keys still associated with this selector are invalidated, their channels are deregistered, and any other resources associated with this selector are released. If this selector is already closed, invoking close() has no effect.

Selector Demonstration

Selectors are commonly used in server applications. Listing 8-1 shows the source code of a server application that sends its local time to clients.

Listing 8-1. Serving Time to Clients

```
import java.io.IOException;

import java.net.InetSocketAddress;
import java.net.ServerSocket;

import java.nio.ByteBuffer;

import java.nio.channels.SelectionKey;
import java.nio.channels.Selector;
import java.nio.channels.ServerSocketChannel;
import java.nio.channels.SocketChannel;

import java.util.Iterator;

public class SelectorServer
{
    final static int DEFAULT_PORT = 9999;

    static ByteBuffer bb = ByteBuffer.allocateDirect(8);
```

```java
    public static void main(String[] args) throws IOException
    {
        int port = DEFAULT_PORT;
        if (args.length > 0)
            port = Integer.parseInt(args[0]);
        System.out.println("Server starting ... listening on port " + port);

        ServerSocketChannel ssc = ServerSocketChannel.open();
        ServerSocket ss = ssc.socket();
        ss.bind(new InetSocketAddress(port));
        ssc.configureBlocking(false);

        Selector s = Selector.open();
        ssc.register(s, SelectionKey.OP_ACCEPT);

        while (true)
        {
            int n = s.select();
            if (n == 0)
                continue;
            Iterator it = s.selectedKeys().iterator();
            while (it.hasNext())
            {
                SelectionKey key = (SelectionKey) it.next();
                if (key.isAcceptable())
                {
                    SocketChannel sc;
                    sc = ((ServerSocketChannel) key.channel()).accept();
                    if (sc == null)
                        continue;
                    System.out.println("Receiving connection");
                    bb.clear();
                    bb.putLong(System.currentTimeMillis());
                    bb.flip();
                    System.out.println("Writing current time");
                    while (bb.hasRemaining())
                        sc.write(bb);
                    sc.close();
                }
                it.remove();
            }
        }
    }
}
```

Listing 8-1's server application consists of a SelectorServer class. This class allocates a direct byte buffer after this class is loaded.

When the `main()` method is executed, it first checks for a command-line argument, which is assumed to represent a port number. If no argument is specified, a default port number is used; otherwise, `main()` tries to convert it to an integer representing the port by passing the argument to `Integer.parseInt()`. (This method throws `java.lang.NumberFormatException` when a noninteger argument is passed.)

After outputting a startup message that identifies the listening port, `main()` obtains a server socket channel followed by the underlying socket, which is bound to the specified port. The server socket channel is then configured for nonblocking mode in preparation for registering this channel with a selector.

A selector is now obtained and the server socket channel registers itself with the selector so that it can learn when the channel is ready to perform an accept operation. The returned key isn't saved because it's never cancelled (and the selector is never closed).

`main()` now enters an infinite loop, first invoking the selector's `select()` method. If the server socket channel isn't ready (`select()` returns 0), the rest of the loop is skipped.

The selected keys (just one key in the example) along with an iterator for iterating over them are now obtained and `main()` enters an inner loop to loop over these keys. Each key's `isAcceptable()` method is invoked to find out if the server socket channel is ready to perform an accept operation. If this is the case, the channel is obtained and cast to `ServerSocketChannel`, and `ServerSocketChannel`'s `accept()` method is called to accept the new connection.

To guard against the unlikely possibility of the returned `SocketChannel` instance being null (`accept()` returns `null` when the server socket channel is in nonblocking mode and no connection is available to be accepted), `main()` tests for this scenario and continues the loop when `null` is detected.

A message about receiving a connection is output and the byte buffer is cleared in preparation for storing the local time. After this long integer has been stored in the buffer, the buffer is flipped in preparation for draining. A message about writing the current time is output and the buffer is drained. The socket channel is then closed and the key is removed from the set of keys.

Compile Listing 8-1 as follows:

```
javac SelectorServer.java
```

Run the resulting application as follows:

```
java SelectorServer
```

You should observe the following output and the server should continue to run:

```
Server starting ... listening on port 9999
```

We need a client to exercise this server. Listing 8-2 shows the source code of a sample client application.

Listing 8-2. Receiving Time from the Server

```java
import java.io.IOException;

import java.net.InetSocketAddress;

import java.nio.ByteBuffer;

import java.nio.channels.SocketChannel;

import java.util.Date;

public class SelectorClient
{
    final static int DEFAULT_PORT = 9999;

    static ByteBuffer bb = ByteBuffer.allocateDirect(8);

    public static void main(String[] args)
    {
        int port = DEFAULT_PORT;
        if (args.length > 0)
            port = Integer.parseInt(args[0]);

        try
        {
            SocketChannel sc = SocketChannel.open();
            InetSocketAddress addr = new InetSocketAddress("localhost", port);
            sc.connect(addr);

            long time = 0;
            while (sc.read(bb) != -1)
            {
                bb.flip();
                while (bb.hasRemaining())
                {
                    time <<= 8;
                    time |= bb.get() & 255;
                }
                bb.clear();
            }
            System.out.println(new Date(time));
```

```
        sc.close();
      }
   catch (IOException ioe)
   {
      System.err.println("I/O error: " + ioe.getMessage());
   }
  }
}
```

Listing 8-2 is much simpler than Listing 8-1 because selectors aren't used. There's no need for a selector in this simple application. You would typically use selectors in a client context when the client interacts with several servers.

There are a couple of interesting items in the source code:

- `bb.get()` returns a 32-bit integer representation of an 8-bit byte. Sign extension is used for byte values greater than 127, which are regarded as negative numbers. Because leading one bits affect the result after bitwise ORing them with `time`, they are removed by bitwise ANDing the integer with 255.

- This value in `time` is passed to the `java.util.Date(long time)` constructor when a new Date object is constructed. In turn, the Date object is passed to `System.out.println()`, which invokes Date's `toString()` method to obtain a human-readable date/time string.

Compile Listing 8-2 as follows:

```
javac SelectorClient.java
```

In a second command window, run the resulting application as follows:

```
java SelectorClient
```

You should observe output similar to the following:

```
Tue Jul 28 13:38:20 CDT 2015
```

In the server command window, you should observe the following messages:

```
Receiving connection
Writing current time
```

```
                        EXERCISES
```

The following exercises are designed to test your understanding of Chapter 8's content:

1. Define selector.

2. Identify the three main types that support selectors.

3. True or false: File channels can be used with selectors.

4. What does `SelectionKey` provide as a convenient alternative to the expression `key.readyOps() & OP_READ != 0`?

Summary

A selector is an object created from a subclass of the abstract `Selector` class. The selector maintains a set of channels that it examines to determine which channels are ready for reading, writing, completing a connection sequence, accepting another connection, or some combination of these tasks.

Selectors are used with selectable channels, which are objects whose classes ultimately inherit from the abstract `SelectableChannel` class, which describes a channel that can be multiplexed by a selector.

One or more previously created selectable channels are registered with a selector. Each registration returns an instance of a subclass of the abstract `SelectionKey` class, which is a token signifying the relationship between one channel and the selector. When a selection method is invoked, the selector's associated keys are updated by checking all channels registered with that selector. The application can then obtain a set of keys whose channels were found ready and iterate over these keys to service each channel that has become ready since the previous select method call.

Chapter 9 presents NIO's support for regular expressions.

Chapter **9**

Regular Expressions

Text-processing applications often need to match text against *patterns* (character strings that concisely describe sets of strings that are considered to be matches). For example, an application might need to locate all occurrences of a specific word pattern in a text file so that it can replace those occurrences with another word. NIO includes regular expressions to help text-processing applications perform pattern matching with high performance. This chapter introduces regular expressions.

Pattern, PatternSyntaxException, and Matcher

A *regular expression* (also known as a *regex* or *regexp*) is a string-based pattern that represents the set of strings that match this pattern. The pattern consists of literal characters and *metacharacters*, which are characters with special meanings instead of literal meanings.

The Regular Expressions API provides the java.util.regex.Pattern class to represent patterns via compiled regexes. Regexes are compiled for performance reasons; pattern matching via compiled regexes is much faster than if the regexes were not compiled. Table 9-1 describes Pattern's methods.

Table 9-1. `Pattern Methods`

Method	Description
`static Pattern compile(String regex)`	Compile regex and return its `Pattern` object. This method throws `java.util.regex.PatternSyntaxException` when regex's syntax is invalid.
`static Pattern compile(String regex,int flags)`	Compile regex according to the given flags (a bitset consisting of some combination of Pattern's `CANON_EQ`, `CASE_INSENSITIVE`, `COMMENTS`, `DOTALL`, `LITERAL`, `MULTILINE`, `UNICODE_CASE`, and `UNIX_LINES` constants) and return its `Pattern` object. This method throws `PatternSyntaxException` when regex's syntax is invalid, and throws `java.lang.IllegalArgumentException` when bit values other than those corresponding to the defined match flags are set in `flags`.
`int flags()`	Return this `Pattern` object's match flags. This method returns 0 for `Pattern` instances created via `compile(String)` and the bitset of flags for `Pattern` instances created via `compile(String, int)`.
`Matcher matcher(CharSequence input)`	Return a `java.util.regex.Matcher` that will match input against this `Pattern`'s compiled regex.
`static boolean matches(String regex, CharSequence input)`	Compile regex and attempt to match input against the compiled regex. Return `true` when there is a match; otherwise, return `false`. This convenience method is equivalent to `Pattern.compile(regex).matcher(input).matches()` and throws `PatternSyntaxException` when regex's syntax is invalid.
`String pattern()`	Return this `Pattern`'s uncompiled regex.
`static String quote(String s)`	Quote s using `"\Q"` and `"\E"` so that all other metacharacters lose their special meaning. When the returned `java.lang.String` object is later compiled into a `Pattern` instance, it only can be matched literally.

(continued)

Table 9-1. (*continued*)

Method	Description
String[] split(CharSequence input)	Split input around matches of this Pattern's compiled regex and return an array containing the matches.
String[] split(CharSequence input, int limit)	Split input around matches of this Pattern's compiled regex; limit controls the number of times the compiled regex is applied and thus affects the length of the resulting array.
String toString()	Return this Pattern's uncompiled regex.

Table 9-1 reveals the java.lang.CharSequence interface, which describes a readable and immutable sequence of char values—the underlying implementation may be mutable. Instances of any class that implements this interface (such as String, java.lang.StringBuffer, and java.lang.StringBuilder) can be passed to Pattern methods that take CharSequence arguments (such as split(CharSequence)).

Table 9-1 also reveals that each of Pattern's compile() methods and its matches() method (which calls the compile(String) method) throws PatternSyntaxException when a syntax error is encountered while compiling the pattern argument. Table 9-2 describes PatternSyntaxException's methods.

Table 9-2. PatternSyntaxException *Methods*

Method	Description
String getDescription()	Return a description of the syntax error.
int getIndex()	Return the approximate index of where the syntax error occurred in the pattern or -1 when the index isn't known.
String getMessage()	Return a multiline string containing the description of the syntax error and its index, the erroneous pattern, and a visual indication of the error index within the pattern.
String getPattern()	Return the erroneous pattern.

Finally, Table 9-1's `Matcher matcher(CharSequence input)` method reveals that the Regular Expressions API also provides the `Matcher` class, whose *matchers* attempt to match compiled regexes against input text. `Matcher` declares the following methods to perform matching operations:

- `boolean matches()`: Attempt to match the entire region against the pattern. When the match succeeds, more information can be obtained by calling `Matcher`'s `start()`, `end()`, and `group()` methods. For example, `int start()` returns the start index of the previous match, `int end()` returns the offset of the first character following the previous match, and `String group()` returns the input subsequence matched by the previous match. Each method throws `java.lang.IllegalStateException` when a match has not yet been attempted or the previous match attempt failed.

- `boolean lookingAt()`: Attempt to match the input sequence, starting at the beginning of the region, against the pattern. As with `matches()`, this method always starts at the beginning of the region. Unlike `matches()`, `lookingAt()` doesn't require that the entire region be matched. When the match succeeds, more information can be obtained by calling `Matcher`'s `start()`, `end()`, and `group()` methods.

- `boolean find()`: Attempt to find the next instance of the input sequence that matches the pattern. It can start at the beginning of this matcher's region. Or, if a previous call to this method was successful and the matcher hasn't since been reset (by calling `Matcher`'s `Matcher reset()` or `Matcher reset(CharSequence input)` method), it will start at the first character not matched by the previous match. When the match succeeds, more information can be obtained by calling `Matcher`'s `start()`, `end()`, and `group()` methods.

> **Note**   A matcher finds matches in a subset of its input called the *region*. By default, the region contains all of the matcher's input. The region can be modified by calling `Matcher`'s `Matcher region(int start, int end)` method (set the limits of this matcher's region) and queried by calling `Matcher`'s `int regionStart()` and `int regionEnd()` methods.

I've created a simple application that demonstrates `Pattern`, `PatternSyntaxException`, and `Matcher`. Listing 9-1 presents this application's source code.

Listing 9-1. Playing with Regular Expressions

```java
import java.util.regex.Matcher;
import java.util.regex.Pattern;
import java.util.regex.PatternSyntaxException;

public class RegExDemo
{
   public static void main(String[] args)
   {
      if (args.length != 2)
      {
         System.err.println("usage: java RegExDemo regex input");
         return;
      }
      try
      {
         System.out.println("regex = " + args[0]);
         System.out.println("input = " + args[1]);
         Pattern p = Pattern.compile(args[0]);
         Matcher m = p.matcher(args[1]);
         while (m.find())
            System.out.println("Located [" + m.group() + "] starting at "
                               + m.start() + " and ending at " +
                               (m.end() - 1));
      }
      catch (PatternSyntaxException pse)
      {
         System.err.println("Bad regex: " + pse.getMessage());
         System.err.println("Description: " + pse.getDescription());
         System.err.println("Index: " + pse.getIndex());
         System.err.println("Incorrect pattern: " + pse.getPattern());
      }
   }
}
```

Compile Listing 9-1 as follows:

```
javac RegExDemo.java
```

Run the resulting application as follows:

```
java RegExDemo ox ox
```

You'll discover the following output:

```
regex = ox
input = ox
Located [ox] starting at 0 and ending at 1
```

`find()` searches for a match by comparing regex characters with the input characters in left-to-right order and returns `true` because o equals o and x equals x.

Continue by executing the following command line:

```
java RegExDemo box ox
```

This time, you'll discover the following output:

```
regex = box
input = ox
```

`find()` first compares regex character b with input character o. Because these characters are not equal and because there are not enough characters in the input to continue the search, `find()` doesn't output a "Located" message to indicate a match. However, if you execute `java RegExDemo ox box`, you'll discover a match:

```
regex = ox
input = box
Located [ox] starting at 1 and ending at 2
```

The ox regex consists of literal characters. More sophisticated regexes combine literal characters with *metacharacters* (such as the period [.]) and other regex constructs.

Tip   To specify a metacharacter as a literal character, precede the metacharacter with a backslash character (as in \.) or place the metacharacter between \Q and \E (as in \Q.\E). In either case, make sure to double the backslash character when the escaped metacharacter appears in a string literal; for example, "\\." or "\\Q.\\E".

The period metacharacter matches all characters except for the line terminator. For example, java RegExDemo .ox box and java RegExDemo .ox fox both report a match because the period matches the b in box and the f in fox.

> **Note**   Pattern recognizes the following line terminators: carriage return (\r), newline (line feed) (\n), carriage return immediately followed by newline (\r\n), next line (\u0085), line separator (\u2028), and paragraph separator (\u2029). The period metacharacter can be made to also match these line terminators by specifying the Pattern.DOTALL flag when calling Pattern. compile(String, int).

Character Classes

A *character class* is a set of characters appearing between [and]. There are six kinds of character classes:

- A *simple character class* consists of literal characters placed side by side and matches only these characters. For example, [abc] consists of characters a, b, and c. Also, java RegExDemo t[aiou]ck tack reports a match because a is a member of [aiou]. It also reports a match when the input is tick, tock, or tuck because i, o, and u are members.

- A *negation character class* consists of a circumflex metacharacter (^), followed by literal characters placed side by side, and matches all characters except for the characters in the class. For example, [^abc] consists of all characters except for a, b, and c. Also, java RegExDemo "[^b]ox" box doesn't report a match because b isn't a member of [^b], whereas java RegExDemo "[^b]ox" fox reports a match because f is a member. (The double quotes surrounding [^b]ox are necessary on my Windows 7 operating system because ^ is treated specially at the command line.)

- A *range character class* consists of successive literal characters expressed as a starting literal character, followed by the hyphen metacharacter (-), followed by an ending literal character, and matches all characters in this range. For example, [a-z] consists of all

characters from a through z. Also, java RegExDemo
[h-l]ouse house reports a match because h is a
member of the class, whereas java RegExDemo [h-l]
ouse mouse doesn't report a match because m lies
outside of the range and is therefore not part of the
class. You can combine multiple ranges within the same
range character class by placing them side by side;
for example, [A-Za-z] consists of all uppercase and
lowercase Latin letters.

- A *union character class* consists of multiple nested
character classes and matches all characters that
belong to the resulting union. For example, [abc[u-z]]
consists of characters a, b, c, u, v, w, x, y, and z.
Also, java RegExDemo [[0-9][A-F][a-f]] e reports a
match because e is a hexadecimal character. (I could
have alternatively expressed this character class as
[0-9A-Fa-f] by combining multiple ranges.)

- An *intersection character class* consists of multiple
&&–separated nested character classes and matches all
characters that are common to these nested character
classes. For example, [a-c&&[c-f]] consists of
character c, which is the only character common to
[a-c] and [c-f]. Also, java RegExDemo "[aeiouy&&[y]]"
y reports a match because y is common to classes
[aeiouy] and [y].

- A *subtraction character class* consists of multiple
&&-separated nested character classes, where at least
one nested character class is a negation character
class, and matches all characters except for those
indicated by the negation character class/classes.
For example, [a-z&&[^x-z]] consists of characters a
through w. (The square brackets surrounding ^x-z are
necessary; otherwise, ^ is ignored and the resulting
class consists of only x, y, and z.) Also, java RegExDemo
"[a-z&&[^aeiou]]" g reports a match because g is a
consonant and only consonants belong to this class.
(I'm ignoring y, which is sometimes regarded as a
consonant and sometimes regarded as a vowel.)

A *predefined character class* is a regex construct for a commonly specified
character class. Table 9-3 identifies Pattern's predefined character classes.

Table 9-3. Predefined Character Classes

Predefined Character Class	Description
\d	Match any digit character. \d is equivalent to [0-9].
\D	Match any nondigit character. \D is equivalent to [^\d].
\s	Match any whitespace character. \s is equivalent to [\t\n\x0B\f\r].
\S	Match any nonwhitespace character. \S is equivalent to [^\s].
\w	Match any word character. \w is equivalent to [a-zA-Z0-9].
\W	Match any nonword character. \W is equivalent to [^\w].

For example, the following command line reports a match because \w matches the word character a in abc:

```
java RegExDemo \wbc abc
```

Capturing Groups

A *capturing group* saves a match's characters for later recall during pattern matching and is expressed as a character sequence surrounded by parentheses metacharacters (and). All characters within a capturing group are treated as a unit. For example, the (Java) capturing group combines J, a, v, and a into a unit. It matches the Java pattern against all occurrences of Java in the input. Each match replaces the previous match's saved Java characters with the next match's Java characters.

Capturing groups can appear inside other capturing groups. For example, capturing groups (A) and (B(C)) appear inside capturing group ((A)(B(C))), and capturing group (C) appears inside capturing group (B(C)). Each nested or non-nested capturing group receives its own number, numbering starts at 1, and capturing groups are numbered from left to right. For example, ((A)(B(C))) is assigned 1, (A) is assigned 2, (B(C)) is assigned 3, and (C) is assigned 4.

A capturing group saves its match for later recall via a *back reference*, which is a backslash character followed by a digit character denoting a capturing group number. The back reference causes the matcher to use the back reference's capturing group number to recall the capturing group's saved match and then use that match's characters to attempt a further match. The following example uses a back reference to determine if the input consists of two consecutive Java patterns:

```
java RegExDemo "(Java) \1" "Java Java"
```

RegExDemo reports a match because the matcher detects Java, followed by a space, followed by Java in the input.

Boundary Matchers and Zero-Length Matches

A *boundary matcher* is a regex construct for identifying the beginning of a line, a word boundary, the end of text, and other commonly occurring boundaries. See Table 9-4.

Table 9-4. Boundary Matchers

Boundary Matcher	Description
^	Match beginning of line.
$	Match end of line.
\b	Match word boundary.
\B	Match nonword boundary.
\A	Match beginning of text.
\G	Match end of previous match.
\Z	Match end of text except for line terminator (when present).
\z	Match end of text.

Consider the following example:

```
java RegExDemo \b\b "I think"
```

This example reports several matches, as revealed in the following output:

```
regex = \b\b
input = I think
Located [] starting at 0 and ending at -1
Located [] starting at 1 and ending at 0
Located [] starting at 2 and ending at 1
Located [] starting at 7 and ending at 6
```

This output reveals several *zero-length matches*. When a zero-length match occurs, the starting and ending indexes are equal, although the output shows the ending index to be one less than the starting index because I specified end() - 1 in Listing 9-1 (so that a match's end index identifies a non-zero-length match's last character, not the character following the non-zero-length match's last character).

> **Note** A zero-length match occurs in empty input text, at the beginning of input text, after the last character of input text, or between any two characters of that text. Zero-length matches are easy to identify because they always start and end at the same index position.

Quantifiers

The final regex construct I present is the *quantifier*, a numeric value implicitly or explicitly bound to a pattern. Quantifiers are categorized as greedy, reluctant, or possessive:

- A *greedy quantifier* (?, *, or +) attempts to find the longest match. Specify X? to find one or no occurrences of X, X* to find zero or more occurrences of X, X+ to find one or more occurrences of X, X{n} to find n occurrences of X, X{n,} to find at least n (and possibly more) occurrences of X, and X{n,m} to find at least n but no more than m occurrences of X.

- A *reluctant quantifier* (??, *?, or +?) attempts to find the shortest match. Specify X?? to find one or no occurrences of X, X*? to find zero or more occurrences of X, X+? to find one or more occurrences of X, X{n}? to find n occurrences of X, X{n,}? to find at least n (and possibly more) occurrences of X, and X{n,m}? to find at least n but no more than m occurrences of X.

- A *possessive quantifier* (?+, *+, or ++) is similar to a greedy quantifier except that a possessive quantifier makes only one attempt to find the longest match, whereas a greedy quantifier can make multiple attempts. Specify X?+ to find one or no occurrences of X, X*+ to find zero or more occurrences of X, X++ to find one or more occurrences of X, X{n}+ to find n occurrences of X, X{n,}+ to find at least n (and possibly more) occurrences of X, and X{n,m}+ to find at least n but no more than m occurrences of X.

For an example of a greedy quantifier, execute the following command line:

```
java RegExDemo .*end "wend rend end"
```

You'll discover the following output:

```
regex = .*end
input = wend rend end
Located [wend rend end] starting at 0 and ending at 12
```

The greedy quantifier (.*) matches the longest sequence of characters that terminates in end. It starts by consuming all of the input text and then is forced to back off until it discovers that the input text terminates with these characters.

For an example of a reluctant quantifier, execute the following command line:

```
java RegExDemo .*?end "wend rend end"
```

You'll discover the following output:

```
regex = .*?end
input = wend rend end
Located [wend] starting at 0 and ending at 3
Located [ rend] starting at 4 and ending at 8
Located [ end] starting at 9 and ending at 12
```

The reluctant quantifier (.*?) matches the shortest sequence of characters that terminates in end. It begins by consuming nothing and then slowly consumes characters until it finds a match. It then continues until it exhausts the input text.

For an example of a possessive quantifier, execute the following command line:

```
java RegExDemo .*+end "wend rend end"
```

You'll discover the following output:

```
regex = .*+end
input = wend rend end
```

The possessive quantifier (.*+) doesn't detect a match because it consumes the entire input text, leaving nothing left over to match end at the end of the regex. Unlike a greedy quantifier, a possessive quantifier doesn't back off.

While working with quantifiers, you'll probably encounter zero-length matches. For example, execute the following command line:

```
java RegExDemo 1? 101101
```

You should observe the following output:

```
regex = 1?
input = 101101
Located [1] starting at 0 and ending at 0
Located [] starting at 1 and ending at 0
Located [1] starting at 2 and ending at 2
Located [1] starting at 3 and ending at 3
Located [] starting at 4 and ending at 3
Located [1] starting at 5 and ending at 5
Located [] starting at 6 and ending at 5
```

The result of this greedy quantifier is that 1 is detected at locations 0, 2, 3, and 5 in the input text, and nothing is detected (a zero-length match) at locations 1, 4, and 6.

This time, execute the following command line:

```
java RegExDemo 1?? 101101
```

You should observe the following output:

```
regex = 1??
input = 101101
Located [] starting at 0 and ending at -1
Located [] starting at 1 and ending at 0
Located [] starting at 2 and ending at 1
Located [] starting at 3 and ending at 2
Located [] starting at 4 and ending at 3
Located [] starting at 5 and ending at 4
Located [] starting at 6 and ending at 5
```

This output might look surprising, but remember that a reluctant quantifier looks for the shortest match, which (in this case) is no match at all.

Finally, execute the following command line:

```
java RegExDemo 1+? 101101
```

You should observe the following output:

```
regex = 1+?
input = 101101
Located [1] starting at 0 and ending at 0
Located [1] starting at 2 and ending at 2
Located [1] starting at 3 and ending at 3
Located [1] starting at 5 and ending at 5
```

This possessive quantifier only matches the locations where 1 is detected in the input text. It doesn't perform zero-length matches.

> **Note**   Check out the Java documentation on the `Pattern` class to learn about additional regex constructs.

Practical Regular Expressions

Most of the previous regex examples haven't been practical, except to help you grasp how to use the various regex constructs. In contrast, the following examples reveal a regex that matches phone numbers of the form (ddd) ddd-dddd or ddd-dddd. A single space appears between (ddd) and ddd; there's no space on either side of the hyphen.

```
java RegExDemo "(\(\d{3}\))?\s*\d{3}-\d{4}" "(800) 555-1212"
regex = (\(\d{3}\))?\s*\d{3}-\d{4}
input = (800) 555-1212
Located [(800) 555-1212] starting at 0 and ending at 13

java RegExDemo "(\(\d{3}\))?\s*\d{3}-\d{4}" 555-1212
regex = (\(\d{3}\))?\s*\d{3}-\d{4}
input = 555-1212
Located [555-1212] starting at 0 and ending at 7
```

> **Note**   To learn more about regular expressions, check out "Lesson: Regular Expressions" at `http://download.oracle.com/javase/tutorial/essential/regex/index.html` in *The Java Tutorials*.

EXERCISES

The following exercises are designed to test your understanding of Chapter 9's content:

1. Define regular expression.

2. What does the `Pattern` class accomplish?

3. What do `Pattern`'s `compile()` methods do when they discover illegal syntax in their regular expression arguments?

4. What does the `Matcher` class accomplish?

5. What is the difference between `Matcher`'s `matches()` and `lookingAt()` methods?

6. Define character class.

7. Identify the various kinds of character classes.

8. True or false: An intersection character class consists of multiple &&-separated nested character classes, where at least one nested character class is a negation character class, and matches all characters except for those indicated by the negation character class/classes.

9. Define capturing group.

10. What is a zero-length match?

11. Define quantifier.

12. What is the difference between greedy and reluctant quantifiers?

13. How do possessive and greedy quantifiers differ?

14. Create a `ReplaceText` application that takes input text, a pattern that specifies text to replace, and replacement text command-line arguments, and uses `Matcher`'s `String replaceAll(String replacement)` method to replace all matches of the pattern with the replacement text (passed to `replacement`). For example, `java ReplaceText "too many embedded spaces" "\s+" " "` should output too many embedded spaces with only a single space character between successive words.

Summary

Text-processing applications often need to match text against patterns. NIO includes regular expressions to help these applications perform pattern matching with high performance. Java supports regular expressions by providing the `Pattern`, `PatternSyntaxException`, and `Matcher` classes.

In this chapter, you explored `Pattern`, `PatternSyntaxException`, and `Matcher`. You then learned about character classes, capturing groups, boundary matchers and zero-length matches, and quantifiers. Finally, you observed a practical use case for regexes: phone number matching.

Chapter 10 presents NIO's support for charsets.

Chapter 10

Charsets

In Chapter 5, I briefly introduced the concepts of character set and character encoding. I also referred to some of the types located in the java.nio.charset package. In this chapter, I expand on these topics and explore this package. I also discuss the part of the java.lang.String class that's relevant to these topics.

A Brief Review of the Fundamentals

Java uses Unicode to represent characters. (*Unicode* is a 16-bit character set standard [actually, more of an encoding standard because some characters are represented by multiple numeric values; each value is known as a *code point*] whose goal is to map all of the world's significant character sets into an all-encompassing map.) Although Unicode makes it much easier to work with characters from different languages, it doesn't automate everything and you often need to work with charsets. Before I dig into this topic, you should understand the following terms:

- *Character*: A meaningful symbol. For example, "$" and "E" are characters. These symbols predate the computer era.

- *Character set*: A set of characters. For example, uppercase letters A through Z could be considered to form a character set. No numeric values are assigned to the characters in the set. There is no relationship to Unicode, ASCII, EBCDIC, or any other kind of character set standard.

- *Coded character set*: A character set where each character is assigned a unique numeric value. Standards bodies such as US-ASCII or ISO-8859-1 define mappings from characters to numeric values.

- *Character-encoding scheme*: An encoding of a coded character set's numeric values to sequences of bytes that represent these values. Some encodings are one-to-one. For example, in ASCII, character A is mapped to integer 65 and encoded as integer 65. For some other mappings, encodings are one-to-one or one-to-many. For example, UTF-8 encodes Unicode characters. Each character whose numeric value is less than 128 is encoded as a single byte to be compatible with ASCII. Other Unicode characters are encoded as two-to-six-byte sequences. See `www.ietf.org/rfc/rfc2279.txt` for more information.

- *Charset*: A coded character set combined with a character-encoding scheme. Charsets are described by the abstract `java.nio.charset.Charset` class.

Although Unicode is widely used and increasing in popularity, other character set standards are also used. Because operating systems perform I/O at the byte level, and because files store data as byte sequences, it's necessary to translate between byte sequences and the characters that are encoded into these sequences. `Charset` and the other classes located in the `java.nio.charset` package address this translation task.

Working with Charsets

Beginning with JDK 1.4, Java virtual machines (JVMs) were required to support a standard collection of charsets and could support additional charsets. They also support the default charset, which doesn't have to be one of the standard charsets and is obtained when the JVM starts running. Table 10-1 identifies and describes the standard charsets.

Table 10-1. *Standard Charsets*

Charset Name	Description
US-ASCII	Seven-bit ASCII, which forms the American-English character set. Also known as the basic Latin block in Unicode.
ISO-8859-1	The 8-bit character set used by most European languages. It's a superset of ASCII and includes most non-English European characters.
UTF-8	An 8-bit byte-oriented character encoding for Unicode. Characters are encoded in one to six bytes.
UTF-16BE	A 16-bit encoding using big-endian order for Unicode. Characters are encoded in two bytes with the high-order eight bits written first.
UTF-16LE	A 16-bit encoding using little-endian order for Unicode. Characters are encoded in two bytes with the low-order eight bits written first.
UTF-16	A 16-bit encoding whose endian order is determined by an optional byte-order mark.

Charset names are case-insensitive and are maintained by the Internet Assigned Names Authority (IANA). The names in Table 10-1 are included in IANA's official registry.

UTF-16BE and UTF-16LE encode each character as a two-byte sequence in big-endian or little-endian order, respectively. A decoder for a UTF-16BE- or UTF-16LE-encoded byte sequence needs to know how the byte sequence was encoded or have a way to detect the byte order from the encoded data. In contrast, UTF-16 relies on a *byte order mark* that appears at the beginning of the sequence. If this mark is absent, decoding proceeds according to UTF-16BE (Java's native byte order). If this mark equals \uFEFF, the sequence is decoded according to UTF-16BE. If this mark equals \uFFFE, the sequence is decoded according to UTF-16LE.

Each charset name is associated with a Charset object, which you obtain by invoking one of this class's factory methods. Listing 10-1 presents an application that shows you how to use this class to obtain the default and standard charsets, which are then used to encode characters into byte sequences.

Listing 10-1. *Using Charsets to Encode Characters into Byte Sequences*

```
import java.nio.ByteBuffer;

import java.nio.charset.Charset;

public class CharsetDemo
```

```java
{
    public static void main(String[] args)
    {
        String msg = "façade touché";
        String[] csNames =
        {
            "US-ASCII",
            "ISO-8859-1",
            "UTF-8",
            "UTF-16BE",
            "UTF-16LE",
            "UTF-16"
        };

        encode(msg, Charset.defaultCharset());
        for (String csName: csNames)
            encode(msg, Charset.forName(csName));
    }

    static void encode(String msg, Charset cs)
    {
        System.out.println("Charset: " + cs.toString());
        System.out.println("Message: " + msg);

        ByteBuffer buffer = cs.encode(msg);
        System.out.println("Encoded: ");

        for (int i = 0; buffer.hasRemaining(); i++)
        {
            int _byte = buffer.get() & 255;
            char ch = (char) _byte;
            if (Character.isWhitespace(ch) || Character.isISOControl(ch))
                ch = '\u0000';
            System.out.printf("%2d: %02x (%c)%n", i, _byte, ch);
        }
        System.out.println();
    }
}
```

Listing 10-1's `main()` method first creates a message consisting of two French words and an array of names for the standard collection of charsets. Next, it invokes the `encode()` method to encode the message according to the default charset, which it obtains by calling `Charset`'s `Charset defaultCharset()` factory method.

Continuing, `main()` invokes `encode()` for each of the standard charsets. `Charset`'s `Charset forName(String charsetName)` factory method is used to obtain the `Charset` instance that corresponds to `charsetName`.

> **Caution** forName() throws java.nio.charset.
> IllegalCharsetNameException when the specified charset name is illegal
> and throws java.nio.charset.UnsupportedCharsetException when
> the desired charset isn't supported by the JVM.

The encode() method first identifies the charset and the message. It then invokes Charset's ByteBuffer encode(String s) method to return a new java.nio.ByteBuffer object containing the bytes that encode the characters from s.

main() next iterates over the bytes in the byte buffer, converting each byte to a character. It uses java.lang.Character's isWhitespace() and isISOControl() methods to determine if the character is whitespace or a control character (neither is regarded as printable) and converts such a character to Unicode 0 (an empty string). (A carriage return or newline would screw up the output, for example.)

Finally, the index of the character, its hexadecimal value, and the character itself are printed to the standard output stream. I chose to use System.out.printf() for this task. You'll learn about this method in the next chapter.

Compile Listing 10-1 as follows:

```
javac CharsetDemo.java
```

Run the resulting application as follows:

```
java CharsetDemo
```

You should observe the following output:

```
Charset: windows-1252
Message: façade touché
Encoded:
 0: 66 (f)
 1: 61 (a)
 2: e7 (ç)
 3: 61 (a)
 4: 64 (d)
 5: 65 (e)
 6: 20 ( )
 7: 74 (t)
 8: 6f (o)
 9: 75 (u)
```

```
10: 63 (c)
11: 68 (h)
12: e9 (é)
```

```
Charset: US-ASCII
Message: façade touché
Encoded:
 0: 66 (f)
 1: 61 (a)
 2: 3f (?)
 3: 61 (a)
 4: 64 (d)
 5: 65 (e)
 6: 20 ( )
 7: 74 (t)
 8: 6f (o)
 9: 75 (u)
10: 63 (c)
11: 68 (h)
12: 3f (?)
```

```
Charset: ISO-8859-1
Message: façade touché
Encoded:
 0: 66 (f)
 1: 61 (a)
 2: e7 (ç)
 3: 61 (a)
 4: 64 (d)
 5: 65 (e)
 6: 20 ( )
 7: 74 (t)
 8: 6f (o)
 9: 75 (u)
10: 63 (c)
11: 68 (h)
12: e9 (é)
```

```
Charset: UTF-8
Message: façade touché
Encoded:
 0: 66 (f)
 1: 61 (a)
 2: c3 (Ã)
 3: a7 (§)
 4: 61 (a)
 5: 64 (d)
 6: 65 (e)
 7: 20 ( )
```

```
 8: 74 (t)
 9: 6f (o)
10: 75 (u)
11: 63 (c)
12: 68 (h)
13: c3 (Ã)
14: a9 (©)
```

Charset: UTF-16BE
Message: façade touché
Encoded:
```
 0: 00 ( )
 1: 66 (f)
 2: 00 ( )
 3: 61 (a)
 4: 00 ( )
 5: e7 (ç)
 6: 00 ( )
 7: 61 (a)
 8: 00 ( )
 9: 64 (d)
10: 00 ( )
11: 65 (e)
12: 00 ( )
13: 20 ( )
14: 00 ( )
15: 74 (t)
16: 00 ( )
17: 6f (o)
18: 00 ( )
19: 75 (u)
20: 00 ( )
21: 63 (c)
22: 00 ( )
23: 68 (h)
24: 00 ( )
25: e9 (é)
```

Charset: UTF-16LE
Message: façade touché
Encoded:
```
 0: 66 (f)
 1: 00 ( )
 2: 61 (a)
 3: 00 ( )
 4: e7 (ç)
 5: 00 ( )
 6: 61 (a)
 7: 00 ( )
```

```
 8: 64 (d)
 9: 00 ( )
10: 65 (e)
11: 00 ( )
12: 20 ( )
13: 00 ( )
14: 74 (t)
15: 00 ( )
16: 6f (o)
17: 00 ( )
18: 75 (u)
19: 00 ( )
20: 63 (c)
21: 00 ( )
22: 68 (h)
23: 00 ( )
24: e9 (é)
25: 00 ( )
```

```
Charset: UTF-16
Message: façade touché
Encoded:
 0: fe (þ)
 1: ff (ÿ)
 2: 00 ( )
 3: 66 (f)
 4: 00 ( )
 5: 61 (a)
 6: 00 ( )
 7: e7 (ç)
 8: 00 ( )
 9: 61 (a)
10: 00 ( )
11: 64 (d)
12: 00 ( )
13: 65 (e)
14: 00 ( )
15: 20 ( )
16: 00 ( )
17: 74 (t)
18: 00 ( )
19: 6f (o)
20: 00 ( )
21: 75 (u)
22: 00 ( )
23: 63 (c)
24: 00 ( )
25: 68 (h)
26: 00 ( )
27: e9 (é)
```

As well as providing encoding methods such as the aforementioned `ByteBuffer encode(String s)` method, `Charset` provides a complementary `CharBuffer decode(ByteBuffer buffer)` decoding method. The return type is `java.nio.CharBuffer` because byte sequences are decoded into characters.

> **Note** `ByteBuffer encode(String s)` is a convenience method for specifying `CharBuffer.wrap(s)` and passing the result to the `ByteBuffer encode(CharBuffer buffer)` method.

If you dig deeper into `Charset`, you'll encounter the following pair of methods:

- `CharsetEncoder newEncoder()`
- `CharsetDecoder newDecoder()`

These methods perform the actual work of encoding and decoding. `Charset`'s `encode()` and `decode()` methods delegate to the `java.nio.charset.CharsetEncoder` and `java.nio.charset.CharsetDecoder` objects returned from `newEncoder()` and `newDecoder()`, and invoke their `encode()` and `decode()` (along with additional) methods. (For brevity, I don't discuss `CharsetEncoder` and `CharsetDecoder`.)

Charsets and the String Class

The `String` class describes a string as a sequence of characters. It declares constructors that can be passed byte arrays. Because a byte array contains an encoded character sequence, a charset is required to decode them. Here is a partial list of `String` constructors that work with charsets:

- `String(byte[] data)`: Constructs a new `String` instance by decoding the specified array of bytes using the platform's default charset.

- `String(byte[] data, int offset, int byteCount)`: Constructs a new `String` instance by decoding the specified subsequence of the byte array using the platform's default charset.

- `String(byte[] data, String charsetName)`: Constructs a new `String` instance by decoding the specified array of bytes using the named charset.

Furthermore, String declares methods that encode its sequence of characters into a byte array with help from the default charset or a named charset. Two of these methods are described here:

- byte[] getBytes(): Returns a new byte array containing the characters of this string encoded using the platform's default charset.

- byte[] getBytes(String charsetName): Returns a new byte array containing the characters of this string encoded using the named charset.

Note that String(byte[] data, String charsetName) and byte[] getBytes(String charsetName) throw java.io.UnsupportedEncodingException when the charset isn't supported.

I've created a small application that demonstrates String and charsets. Listing 10-2 presents the source code.

Listing 10-2. Using Charsets with String

```
import java.io.UnsupportedEncodingException;

public class CharsetDemo
{
   public static void main(String[] args)
      throws UnsupportedEncodingException
   {
      byte[] encodedMsg =
      {
         0x66, 0x61, (byte) 0xc3, (byte) 0xa7, 0x61, 0x64, 0x65, 0x20, 0x74,
         0x6f, 0x75, 0x63, 0x68, (byte) 0xc3, (byte) 0xa9
      };
      String s = new String(encodedMsg, "UTF-8");
      System.out.println(s);
      System.out.println();
      byte[] bytes = s.getBytes();
      for (byte _byte: bytes)
         System.out.print(Integer.toHexString(_byte & 255) + " ");
      System.out.println();
   }
}
```

Listing 10-2's main() method first creates a byte array containing a UTF-8 encoded message. It then converts this array to a String object via the UTF-8 charset. After outputting the resulting String object, it extracts this object's bytes into a new byte array and proceeds to output these bytes in hexadecimal format. As demonstrated earlier in this chapter, I bitwise AND each byte value with 255 to remove the 0xFF sign extension bytes for negative integers when the 8-bit byte integer value is converted to a 32-bit integer value. These sign extension bytes would otherwise be output.

Compile Listing 10-2 (javac CharsetDemo.java) and run this application (java CharsetDemo). You should observe the following output:

façade touché

66 61 e7 61 64 65 20 74 6f 75 63 68 e9

You might be wondering why you observe e7 instead of c3 a7 (Latin small letter c with a *cedilla* [a hook or tail]) and e9 instead of c3 a9 (Latin small letter e with an acute accent). The answer is that I invoked the noargument getBytes() method to encode the string. This method uses the default charset, which is windows-1252 on my platform. According to this charset, e7 is equivalent to c3 a7 and e9 is equivalent to c3 a9. The result is a shorter encoded sequence.

EXERCISES

The following exercises are designed to test your understanding of Chapter 10's content:

1. Define charset.

2. What is the purpose of the Charset class?

3. Identify the standard charsets supported by the JVM.

4. What is the purpose of the byte order mark?

5. How do you obtain the default charset?

6. What does Charset's Charset forName(String charsetName) factory method do when the desired charset isn't supported by the JVM?

7. How would you typically encode a string via a Charset instance?

8. Identify the Charset methods that perform the actual encoding and decoding tasks.

9. What does String's byte[] getBytes() method accomplish?

10. Write an AvailCharsets application that obtains and outputs a map of all charsets that the current JVM supports. (Hint: You'll find the method that returns this map in the Charset class.)

Summary

Charsets combine coded character sets with character-encoding schemes. They're used to translate between byte sequences and the characters that are encoded into these sequences. Java supports charsets by providing Charset and related classes. It also uses charsets with the String class.

Chapter 11 presents NIO's java.util.Formatter class and related types.

Formatter

The description of JSR 51 (http://jcp.org/en/jsr/detail?id=51) indicates that a simple printf-style formatting facility was proposed for inclusion in NIO. If you're familiar with the C language, you've probably worked with the printf() family of functions that support formatted output.

One feature that makes the printf() functions useful is *varargs*, which lets you pass a variable number of arguments to these functions. Because support for varargs wasn't added to Java until JDK 5, and because this support is very useful for achieving formatted output, the printf-style formatting facility was deferred to JDK 5.

This chapter explores JDK 5's printf-style formatting facility.

Exploring Formatter

JDK 5 introduced the java.util.Formatter class as an interpreter for printf()-style format strings. This class provides support for layout justification and alignment; common formats for numeric, string, and date/time data; and more. Commonly used Java types (such as byte and java.math.BigDecimal) are supported.

Formatter declares several constructors for creating Formatter objects. These constructors let you specify where you want formatted output to be sent. For example, Formatter() writes formatted output to an internal java.lang.StringBuilder instance and Formatter(OutputStream os) writes formatted output to the specified output stream. You can access the destination by calling Formatter's Appendable out() method.

> **Note**   The `java.lang.Appendable` interface describes an object to
> which `char` values and character sequences can be appended. Classes
> (such as `StringBuilder`) whose instances are to receive formatted output
> (via the `Formatter` class) implement `Appendable`. This interface declares
> methods such as `Appendable append(char c)`—append c's character
> to this appendable. When an I/O error occurs, this method throws
> `java.io.IOException`.

After creating a `Formatter` object, you would call a `format()` method to
format a varying number of values. For example, `Formatter format(String
format, Object... args)` formats the `args` array according to the string of
format specifiers passed to the `format` parameter, and returns a reference
to the invoking `Formatter` so that you can chain `format()` calls together
(for convenience).

Each format specifier has one of the following syntaxes:

- %[*argument_index*$][*flags*][*width*][.*precision*]*conversion*
- %[*argument_index*$][*flags*][*width*]*conversion*
- %[*flags*][*width*]*conversion*

The first syntax describes a format specifier for general (such as string),
character, and numeric types. The second syntax describes a format
specifier for types that are used to represent dates and times. The third
syntax describes a format specifier that doesn't correspond to arguments.

The optional *argument_index* is a decimal integer indicating the position of
the argument in the argument list. The first argument is referenced by 1$, the
second argument is referenced by 2$, and so on.

The optional *flags* represents a set of characters that modify the output
format. The set of valid flags depends on the conversion.

The optional *width* is a positive decimal integer indicating the minimum
number of characters to be written to the output.

The optional *precision* is a nonnegative decimal integer typically used to
restrict the number of characters. The specific behavior depends on the
conversion.

The required conversion depends on the syntax. For the first syntax, it's a
character indicating how the argument should be formatted. The set of valid
conversions for a given argument depends on the argument's data type.

For the second syntax, it's a two-character sequence. The first character is t or T. The second character indicates the format to be used. For the third syntax, it's a character indicating content to be inserted in the output.

Conversions are divided into six categories: general, character, numeric (integer or floating-point), date/time, percent, and line separator. The following list identifies a few example format specifiers and their conversions:

- %d: Formats the argument as a decimal integer.

- %x: Formats the argument as a hexadecimal integer.

- %c: Formats the argument as a character.

- %f: Formats the argument as a decimal number.

- %s: Formats the argument as a string.

- %n: Outputs an operating system-specific line separator.

- %10.2f: Formats the argument as a decimal number with 10 as the minimum number of characters to be written (leading spaces are written when the number is smaller than the width) and 2 as the number of characters to be written after the decimal point.

- %05d: Formats the argument as a decimal integer with 5 as the minimum number of characters to be written (leading 0s are written when the number is smaller than the width).

When you're finished with the formatter, you might want to invoke the void flush() method to ensure that any buffered output in the destination is written to the underlying stream. You would typically invoke flush() when the destination is a file.

Continuing, invoke the formatter's void close() method. As well as closing the formatter, this method also closes the underlying output destination when this destination's class implements the java.io.Closeable interface. If the formatter has been closed, this method has no effect. Attempting to format after calling close() results in java.util.FormatterClosedException.

Listing 11-1 provides a simple demonstration of Formatter using the aforementioned format specifiers.

Listing 11-1. Demonstrating the Formatter Class

```java
import java.util.Formatter;

public class FormatterDemo
{
   public static void main(String[] args)
   {
      Formatter formatter = new Formatter();
      formatter.format("%d", 123);
      System.out.println(formatter.toString());
      formatter.format("%x", 123);
      System.out.println(formatter.toString());
      formatter.format("%c", 'X');
      System.out.println(formatter.toString());
      formatter.format("%f", 0.1);
      System.out.println(formatter.toString());
      formatter.format("%s%n", "Hello, World");
      System.out.println(formatter.toString());
      formatter.format("%10.2f", 98.375);
      System.out.println(formatter.toString());
      formatter.format("%05d", 123);
      System.out.println(formatter.toString());
      formatter.format("%1$d %1$d", 123);
      System.out.println(formatter.toString());
      formatter.format("%d %d", 123);
      System.out.println(formatter.toString());
      formatter.close();
   }
}
```

Listing 11-1's main() method first creates a Formatter object via the Formatter() constructor, which sends formatted output to an internal StringBuilder instance. It then demonstrates the aforementioned format specifiers by invoking a format() method, followed by the toString() method to obtain the formatted content, which is subsequently output.

The formatter.format("%1$d %1$d", 123); method call accesses the single data item argument to be formatted (123) twice by referencing this argument via 1$. Without this reference, which is demonstrated via formatter.format("%d %d", 123);, an exception would be thrown because there must be a separate argument for each format specifier unless you use an argument index.

Lastly, the formatter is closed.

Compile Listing 11-1 as follows:

```
javac FormatterDemo.java
```

Run the resulting application as follows:

```
java FormatterDemo
```

You should observe the following output:

```
123
1237b
1237bX
1237bX0.100000
1237bX0.100000Hello, World

1237bX0.100000Hello, World
    98.38
1237bX0.100000Hello, World
    98.3800123
1237bX0.100000Hello, World
    98.3800123123 123
Exception in thread "main" java.util.MissingFormatArgumentException: Format
specifier '%d'
        at java.util.Formatter.format(Formatter.java:2519)
        at java.util.Formatter.format(Formatter.java:2455)
        at FormatterDemo.main(FormatterDemo.java:24)
```

The first thing to notice about the output is that each format() call appends formatted output to the previously formatted output. The second thing to notice is that java.util.MissingFormatArgumentException is thrown when you don't specify a needed argument.

> **Note** MissingFormatArgumentException is one of several formatter exception types, which subtype java.util.IllegalFormatException.

If you aren't happy with this concatenated output, there are two ways to solve the problem:

- Instantiate a new Formatter instance, as in formatter = new Formatter();, before calling format(). This ensures that a new default and empty string builder is created.

- Create your own StringBuilder instance and pass it to a constructor such as Formatter(Appendable a). After outputting the formatted content, invoke StringBuilder's void setLength(int newLength) method with 0 as the argument to erase the previous content.

It's cumbersome to have to create and manage a Formatter object when all you want to do is achieve something equivalent to the C language's printf() function. Java addresses this situation by adding format() and the equivalent printf() methods to the java.io.PrintStream class.

Of the various formatter-oriented methods added to PrintStream, you'll often invoke PrintStream printf(String format, Object... args). After sending its formatted content to the print stream, this method returns a reference to this stream so that you can chain method calls together.

Listing 11-2 provides a small printf() demonstration.

Listing 11-2. Formatting via printf()

```
public class FormatterDemo
{
   public static void main(String[] args)
   {
      System.out.printf("%04X%n", 478);
      System.out.printf("Current date: %1$tb %1$te, %1$tY%n",
                        System.currentTimeMillis());
   }
}
```

Listing 11-2's main() method invokes System.out.printf() twice. The first invocation formats 32-bit integer 478 into a four-digit hexadecimal string with a leading zero and uppercase hexadecimal digits. The second invocation formats the current millisecond value returned from System. currentTimeMillis() into a date. The tb conversion specifies an abbreviated month name (such as Jan), the te conversion specifies the day of the month (such as 1 through 31), and the tY conversion specifies the year (formatted with at least four digits, with leading 0s as necessary).

Compile Listing 11-2 (javac FormatterDemo.java) and run the application (java FormatterDemo). You should observe output similar to the output shown here:

```
01DE
Current date: Jul 28, 2015
```

> **Note** For more information on Formatter and its supported format specifiers, check out Formatter's Java documentation.

Exploring Formattable and FormattableFlags

Formatter is accompanied by a java.util.Formattable interface and a java.util.FormattableFlags class that collectively support limited formatting customization for arbitrary user-defined types.

Formattable is implemented by any class that needs to perform custom formatting using Formatter's "s" (format argument as string) conversion character. This interface allows basic control for formatting arbitrary objects.

Formattable declares the following method, which is called by Formatter's format() methods to perform custom formatting:

```
void formatTo(Formatter formatter, int flags, int width, int precision)
```

These parameters have the following meanings:

- formatter is the Formatter object that holds the locale and is where you send the output when it's done.

- flags is a bitmask of FormattableFlags constants: ALTERNATE (the user specified # for alternate formatting), LEFT_JUSTIFY (the user specified - for left justification), and UPPERCASE (the user specified S for locale-based conversion to uppercase).

- width is the minimum number of characters to be written to the output. If the length of the converted value is less than the width, the output will be padded by space characters until the total number of characters equals the width. By default, the padding is at the beginning of the output. If FormattableFlags.LEFT_JUSTIFY is specified, the padding will be at the end. If width is -1, there is no minimum.

- precision is the maximum number of characters to be written to the output. Because the precision is applied before the width, the output will be truncated to precision characters even when the width is greater than the precision. If precision is -1, there is no explicit limit on the number of characters in the output.

The width and precision parameters may seem confusing. To help you understand them, consider the following examples:

```
System.out.printf("[%10.2s]%n", "ABC");
System.out.printf("[%10.12s]%n", "ABC");
System.out.printf("[%10.2s]%n", "ABCDEFGHIJKLMNOP");
System.out.printf("[%10.12s]%n", "ABCDEFGHIJKLMNOP");
```

When you execute these statements, you should observe the following output:

```
[        AB]
[       ABC]
[        AB]
[ABCDEFGHIJKL]
```

The final example shows that 12 characters are output. Although this value exceeds the width of 10 characters, it does not exceed the precision of 12 characters. The value passed to width is most useful from an alignment perspective when fewer than width characters are output.

formatTo(Formatter, int, int, int) will build a string in a string builder and then, before returning, pass the string to the formatter's format() method. This method doesn't return a value. However, it should throw IllegalFormatException when any of the parameter values is invalid.

To put this discussion into a practical context, suppose you have created the Employee class that appears in Listing 11-3.

Listing 11-3. An Employee Consists of a Name and Number

```java
public class Employee
{
    private String name;

    private int empno;

    public Employee(String name, int empno)
    {
        this.name = name;
        this.empno = empno;
    }

    @Override
    public String toString()
    {
        return name + ": " + empno;
    }
}
```

Continuing, suppose you create the FormatterDemo application class that appears in Listing 11-4.

Listing 11-4. Exercising the Employee Class

```java
import java.util.Locale;

public class FormatterDemo
{
   public static void main(String[] args)
   {
      Employee emp = new Employee("John Doe", 1000);
      System.out.printf("[%s]%n", emp);
      System.out.printf(Locale.FRENCH, "[%s]%n", emp);
      System.out.printf("[%S]%n", emp);
      System.out.printf("[%10.3s]%n", emp);
      System.out.printf("[%-10.3s]%n", emp);
      System.out.printf("[%#s]%n", emp);
   }
}
```

The various System.out.printf() method calls attempt to format and then output the string returned from the Employee object's toString() method in different ways. For example, the first call outputs the value returned from toString() verbatim.

The second call attempts to output it in the French locale. You will see the English name because there is no customization. The third call outputs the name in uppercase; the fourth and fifth calls right-justify and left-justify the first three characters from toString() in a width of 10 characters.

The final call attempts to use a conversion-dependent alternate form, which is indicated by #s. However, because customization has not yet been added to Employee, java.util.FormatFlagsConversionMismatchException will be thrown when #s is detected.

Compile Listings 11-3 and 11-4 as follows:

```
javac *.java
```

Run the resulting application as follows:

```
java FormatterDemo
```

You should observe the following output:

```
[John Doe: 1000]
[John Doe: 1000]
[JOHN DOE: 1000]
[       Joh]
[Joh       ]
[
```

```
Exception in thread "main" java.util.FormatFlagsConversionMismatchException:
Conversion = s, Flags = #
      at java.util.Formatter$FormatSpecifier.failMismatch(Formatter.
      java:4298)
      at java.util.Formatter$FormatSpecifier.printString(Formatter.
      java:2882)
      at java.util.Formatter$FormatSpecifier.print(Formatter.java:2763)
      at java.util.Formatter.format(Formatter.java:2520)
      at java.io.PrintStream.format(PrintStream.java:970)
      at java.io.PrintStream.printf(PrintStream.java:871)
      at FormatterDemo.main(FormatterDemo.java:13)
```

We can improve on this output by having Employee implement Formattable.
For example, we can display an equivalent name for the French locale. Also,
we can display just the employee number when the precision is less than 8.
Listing 11-5 presents an improved Employee class.

Listing 11-5. Implementing Formattable

```java
import java.util.Formattable;
import java.util.FormattableFlags;
import java.util.Formatter;
import java.util.Locale;

public class Employee implements Formattable
{
   private String name;

   private int empno;

   public Employee(String name, int empno)
   {
      this.name = name;
      this.empno = empno;
   }

   @Override
   public void formatTo(Formatter formatter, int flags, int width,
                        int precision)
   {
      StringBuilder sb = new StringBuilder();

      String output = this.name;
      if (formatter.locale().equals(Locale.FRENCH) &&
          name.equals("John Doe"))
         output = "Jean Dupont";
      output += ": " + empno;
```

```
        if (((flags & FormattableFlags.UPPERCASE) ==
            FormattableFlags.UPPERCASE))
          output = output.toUpperCase();

        boolean alternate = (flags & FormattableFlags.ALTERNATE) ==
                            FormattableFlags.ALTERNATE;
        alternate |= (precision >= 0 && precision < 8);
        if (alternate)
          output = "" + empno;

        if (precision == -1 || output.length() <= precision)
          sb.append(output);
        else
          sb.append(output.substring(0, precision - 1)).append('*');

        int len = sb.length();
        if (len < width)
        {
          boolean leftJustified = (flags & FormattableFlags.LEFT_JUSTIFY)
                            == FormattableFlags.LEFT_JUSTIFY;
          for (int i = 0; i < width - len; i++)
            if (leftJustified)
                sb.append(' ');
            else
                sb.insert(0, ' ');
        }

        formatter.format(sb.toString());
    }

    @Override
    public String toString()
    {
        return name + ": " + empno;
    }
}
```

formatTo(Formatter, int, int, int) first creates a string builder to store the output string.

Next, the output string is defaulted to the employee's name. If the locale is French and the name equals John Doe, the output string is changed to Jean Dupont. A colon and the employee number are appended to this string. If the uppercase flag was specified, the output string is uppercased.

Continuing, if the alternate flag was specified or the precision is between 0 and 7 inclusive, the output string is shortened to the employee number.

If the precision equals -1 (unlimited) or the output string length doesn't exceed the precision, the output string is appended to the string buffer. Otherwise, no more than the left-most precision -1 characters followed by * (which signifies a truncated string) are appended.

At this point, if the number of characters in the string buffer is less than the specified width, the string buffer contents are either left- or right-justified.

The work is now finished so the final task is to convert the string builder to a string and then pass it to the formatter's format() method.

Compile Listings 11-4 and 11-5 as follows:

```
javac *.java
```

Run the resulting application as follows:

```
java FormatterDemo
```

You should observe the following output:

```
[John Doe: 1000]
[Jean Dupont: 1000]
[JOHN DOE: 1000]
[        10*]
[10*        ]
[1000]
```

EXERCISES

The following exercises are designed to test your understanding of Chapter 11's content:

1. Identify the three nonexception types that contribute to NIO's printf-style formatting facility.

2. How do you reference an argument from within a format specifier string?

3. What does the %n format specifier accomplish?

4. Modify Listing 11-1 so that FormatterDemo's output isn't concatenated into one long string.

Summary

JDK 5 introduced the Formatter class as an interpreter for printf()-style format strings. This class provides support for layout justification and alignment; common formats for numeric, string, and date/time data; and more. Commonly used Java types (such as byte and BigDecimal) are supported.

Formatter declares several constructors for creating Formatter objects. These constructors let you specify where you want formatted output to be sent. For example, Formatter() writes formatted output to an internal StringBuilder instance. You can access the destination by calling Formatter's Appendable out() method.

After creating a Formatter object, call a format() method to format a varying number of values. For example, Formatter format(String format, Object... args) formats the args array according to the string of format specifiers passed to the format parameter, and returns a reference to the invoking Formatter so that you can chain the format() calls together.

It's cumbersome to have to create and manage a Formatter object when all you want to do is achieve something equivalent to the C language's printf() function. Java addresses this situation by adding format() and equivalent printf() methods (such as PrintStream printf(String format, Object... args)) to the PrintStream class.

Formatter is accompanied by a Formattable interface and a FormattableFlags class that collectively support limited formatting customization for arbitrary user-defined types. Formattable is implemented by any class that needs to perform custom formatting using Formatter's "s" (format argument as string) conversion character.

Chapter 12 presents NIO.2's improved file system interface.

Part IV

More New I/O APIs

Improved File System Interface

NIO.2 improves the file system interface that was previously limited to the java.io.File class. This chapter introduces the improved file system interface's architecture and shows you how to use the new APIs to accomplish a wide range of file system tasks.

> **Note** A *file system* manages *files*, which are classified as regular files, directories, symbolic links (https://en.wikipedia.org/wiki/Symbolic_link), and hard links (https://en.wikipedia.org/wiki/Hard_link).

Architecting a Better File Class

The File-based file system interface is problematic. Several problems are listed here:

- Many methods return Boolean values rather than throw exceptions. As a result, you don't know why an operation fails. For example, when the delete() method returns false, you don't know why the file could not be deleted (such as the file not existing or the user not having the appropriate permission to perform the deletion).

- File doesn't support file system-specific symbolic links and hard links.

- File provides access to a limited set of file attributes. For example, it doesn't support access control lists (ACLs) (https://en.wikipedia.org/wiki/Access_control_list).

- File doesn't support efficient file-attribute access. Every query results in a call to the underlying operating system.

- File doesn't scale to large directories. Requesting a large directory listing over a server can result in a hung application. Large directories can also cause memory resource problems, resulting in a denial of service.

- File is limited to the *default file system* (the file system that is accessible to the Java Virtual Machine—JVM). It doesn't support alternatives, such as a memory-based file system.

- File doesn't offer a file-copy or a file-move capability. The renameTo() method, which is often used in a file-move context, doesn't work consistently across operating systems.

NIO.2 provides an improved file system interface that offers solutions to the previous problems. Some of its features are listed here:

- Methods throwing exceptions

- Support for symbolic links

- Broad and efficient support for file attributes

- Directory streams

- Support for alternative file systems via custom file system providers

- Support for file copying and file moving

- Support for walking the file tree/visiting files and watching directories

The improved file system interface is implemented mainly by the various types in the following packages:

- java.nio.file: Provides interfaces and classes for accessing file systems and their files.

- java.nio.file.attribute: Provides interfaces and classes for accessing file system attributes.

- java.nio.file.spi: Provides classes for creating a file system implementation.

These packages organize many types. `FileSystem`, `FileSystems`, and `FileSystemProvider` form the core of the improved file system interface.

File Systems and File System Providers

An operating system can host one or more file systems. For example, Unix/ Linux combines all mounted disks into one virtual file system. In contrast, Windows associates a separate file system with each active disk drive; for example, FAT16 for drive A: and NTFS for drive C:.

The `java.nio.file.FileSystem` class interfaces between Java code and a file system. Furthermore, `FileSystem` is a factory for obtaining many types of file system-related objects (such as file stores and paths) and services (such as watch services).

`FileSystem` cannot be instantiated because this class is abstract. Instead, the `java.nio.file.FileSystems` utility class is used to obtain `FileSystem`s via several factory methods. For example, the `FileSystem getDefault()` class method returns a `FileSystem` object for the default file system:

```
FileSystem fsDefault = FileSystems.getDefault();
```

`FileSystems` also declares a `FileSystem getFileSystem(URI uri)` class method for obtaining a `FileSystem` associated with the specified uniform resource identifier (URI) argument. Furthermore, `FileSystems` declares three `newFileSystem()` methods for creating new `FileSystem`s.

The abstract `java.nio.file.spi.FileSystemProvider` class is used by the `FileSystems` factory methods to obtain existing file systems or create new file systems. A concrete subclass of `FileSystemProvider` implements its various methods for copying, moving, and deleting files; for obtaining a path; for reading attributes and the targets of symbolic links; for creating directories, links, and symbolic links; and more.

Figure 12-1 shows how `FileSystem`, `FileSystems`, and `FileSystemProvider` are related.

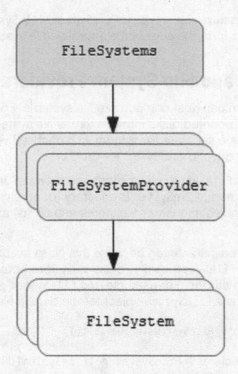

Figure 12-1. FileSystems methods instantiate FileSystemProviders to obtain FileSystems

A Java implementation provides concrete FileSystemProvider subclasses that describe different kinds of file system providers. If you're curious about the file system providers supported by your Java implementation, run the application whose source code appears in Listing 12-1.

Listing 12-1. Identifying Installed File System Providers

```
import java.nio.file.spi.FileSystemProvider;

import java.util.List;

public class ListProviders
{
   public static void main(String[] args)
   {
      List<FileSystemProvider> providers =
         FileSystemProvider.installedProviders();
      for (FileSystemProvider provider: providers)
         System.out.println(provider);
   }
}
```

Listing 12-1 invokes FileSystemProvider's List<FileSystemProvider> installedProviders() class method to obtain a list of the installed file system providers. It then iterates over this list, implicitly invoking each provider's toString() method and outputting the resulting string.

Compile Listing 12-1 as follows:

```
javac ListProviders.java
```

Run the resulting application as follows:

```
java ListProviders
```

When I run this application, I observe the following output:

```
sun.nio.fs.WindowsFileSystemProvider@4aa298b7
com.sun.nio.zipfs.ZipFileSystemProvider@7d4991ad
```

This output tells me two things: FileSystems that interface to the file systems that are native to my Windows 7 operating system are obtained from the WindowsFileSystemProvider subclass. Also, I can obtain FileSystems that are based on ZIP files.

With few exceptions, NIO.2's various types ultimately delegate to the foundational FileSystem, FileSystems, and FileSystemProvider types.

Locating Files with Paths

A file system stores files (definitely regular files and directories, and possibly symbolic links and hard links). Files are typically stored in hierarchies and are located by specifying *paths*, which are compact maps that navigate these hierarchies via separated name element sequences.

The java.nio.file.Path interface represents a hierarchical path to a file that may not exist. It optionally starts with a name element identifying a file system hierarchy and optionally continues with a sequence of directory elements separated by a separator character. The name element that is farthest from the *root* of the directory hierarchy is the name of a directory or other kind of file. The other name elements are directory names.

> **Note** Path declares FileSystem getFileSystem() to return a reference to the FileSystem that created the file described by the Path object.

A Path can represent a root, a root and a sequence of name elements, or one or more name elements. It signifies an *empty path* when it consists entirely of one name element that is empty. Accessing a file using an empty path is equivalent to accessing the file system's default directory.

> **Note**   Path declares File toFile() to return a File object representing its path. toFile() throws UnsupportedOperationException when the Path object isn't associated with the default provider. File declares Path toPath() to return a Path object representing the File object's abstract path. toPath() throws java.nio.file.InvalidPathException when a Path cannot be constructed from the abstract path. These methods let you mix Path and File in your source code so that you can slowly transition your legacy File-based code to code that uses the improved file system interface.

Getting a Path and Accessing Its Name Elements

FileSystem provides a Path getPath(String first, String... more) method for returning a Path object. The argument passed to first identifies the initial part of the path string. The variable arguments (varargs) list that's assigned to more identifies additional strings that are joined to first to form the complete path string.

> **Note**   When constructing a Path, its name elements are typically joined by using the name separator that's returned from FileSystem's String getSeparator() method. The resulting path string represents a system-dependent file path.

Consider the following example:

```
Path path = fsDefault.getPath("x", "y");
```

This example constructs a Path with y subordinate to x. You could also construct this Path as follows:

```
Path path = fsDefault.getPath("x\\y");
```

Unlike in the former example, I've included the backslash (\) name-separator character (escaped to satisfy the Java compiler) that Windows understands.

A Path must conform to the syntax that is parsed by the file system provider that created the FileSystem on which getPath() is called. Otherwise, this method will throw InvalidPathException.

> **Caution**   When constructing a Path, you should avoid hardcoding name-separator characters, such as the backslash on Windows. Although some separators are legal, such as backslash or forward slash (/) on Windows, other separators will probably result in InvalidPathException. For example, specifying :x:y (for some hypothetical file system) as a path on Windows will result in InvalidPathException.

NIO.2 provides a more convenient java.nio.file.Paths utility class with a pair of class methods for returning Path objects:

- Path get(String first, String... more)
- Path get(URI uri)

The first method is equivalent to calling getPath() on the default file system and returning the result:

```
return FileSystems.getDefault().getPath(first, more);
```

The second method is a bit more involved. It iterates over the installed file system providers to locate the provider that is identified by the given URI's scheme component. When this provider is found for the file scheme, this method executes the following code:

```
return FileSystems.getDefault().provider().getPath(uri);
```

After obtaining the default file system, FileSystem's FileSystemProvider provider() method is called to return the file system provider that created the FileSystem object. Then, FileSystemProvider's Path getPath(URI uri) method is called to convert the URI argument to a Path object.

For any other scheme, the installed providers list is searched for the first provider with a matching scheme. getPath(uri) is called on the provider.

get(String, String...) throws InvalidPathException when a path cannot be constructed because of bad syntax. get(URI) throws java.nio.file. FileSystemNotFoundException when no FileSystem matches the scheme and java.lang.IllegalArgumentException for a bad URI.

Path declares several methods for accessing its name elements:

- Path getFileName(): Return the name of the file denoted by this path as a Path object.

- Path getName(int index): Return the indexth name element in this path as a Path object. The index starts at 0, which represents the element closest to the root. The element farthest from the root is identified by one less than the name count.

- int getNameCount(): Return the number of name elements in the path.

- Path getParent(): Return the parent path or null when there is no parent.

- Path getRoot(): Return the root name element in this path as a Path object or null when there is no root.

- Path subpath(int beginIndex, int endIndex): Return a relative path that is a subsequence of the name elements in this path. The first name element (closest to the root) is located at beginIndex and the last name element (farthest from the root) is located at one less than endIndex.

Listing 12-2 presents the source code to an application that demonstrates path construction and these methods.

Listing 12-2. Constructing a Path and Accessing Its Name Elements

```
import java.nio.file.FileSystem;
import java.nio.file.FileSystems;
import java.nio.file.Path;

public class PathDemo
{
   public static void main(String[] args)
   {
      FileSystem fsDefault = FileSystems.getDefault();
      Path path = fsDefault.getPath("a", "b", "c");
      System.out.println(path);
      System.out.printf("File name: %s%n", path.getFileName());
      for (int i = 0; i < path.getNameCount(); i++)
         System.out.println(path.getName(i));
      System.out.printf("Parent: %s%n", path.getParent());
      System.out.printf("Root: %s%n", path.getRoot());
      System.out.printf("SubPath [0, 2): %s%n", path.subpath(0, 2));
   }
}
```

Compile Listing 12-2 as follows:

```
javac PathDemo.java
```

Run the resulting application as follows:

```
java PathDemo
```

I observe the following output:

```
a\b\c
File name: c
a
b
c
Parent: a\b
Root: null
SubPath [0, 2): a\b
```

Relative and Absolute Paths

The previous path examples demonstrate *relative paths*. You can prove this to yourself by invoking Path's boolean isAbsolute() method on a Path object. This method returns false to signify that the path isn't absolute. To create an *absolute path*, you need to pass a root as the first name element.

You obtain a file system's root(s) by calling FileSystem's Iterable<Path> getRootDirectories() method, which returns an iterator over Path instances that describe roots. Listing 12-3 presents the source code to an application that demonstrates this method and absolute path creation.

Listing 12-3. Demonstrating Root Directory Iteration and Absolute Path Creation

```
import java.nio.file.FileSystem;
import java.nio.file.FileSystems;
import java.nio.file.Path;

public class PathDemo
{
   public static void main(String[] args)
   {
      FileSystem fsDefault = FileSystems.getDefault();
      Path path = fsDefault.getPath("a", "b", "c");
      System.out.println(path);
      System.out.printf("Absolute: %b%n", path.isAbsolute());
      System.out.printf("Root: %s%n", path.getRoot());
```

```
        for (Path root: fsDefault.getRootDirectories())
        {
            path = fsDefault.getPath(root.toString(), "a", "b", "c");
            System.out.println(path);
            System.out.printf("Absolute: %b%n", path.isAbsolute());
            System.out.printf("Root: %s%n", path.getRoot());
        }
    }
}
```

Compile Listing 12-3 (javac PathDemo.java) and run the resulting application
(java PathDemo). I observe the following output:

```
a\b\c
Absolute: false
Root: null
C:\a\b\c
Absolute: true
Root: C:\
D:\a\b\c
Absolute: true
Root: D:\
E:\a\b\c
Absolute: true
Root: E:\
F:\a\b\c
Absolute: true
Root: F:\
```

If you have a relative path, you can convert it to an absolute path by calling
Path's Path toAbsolutePath() method, as demonstrated in Listing 12-4.

Listing 12-4. Converting a Relative Path to an Absolute Path

```
import java.nio.file.Path;
import java.nio.file.Paths;

public class PathDemo
{
    public static void main(String[] args)
    {
        Path path = Paths.get("a", "b", "c");
        System.out.printf("Path: %s%n", path.toString());
        System.out.printf("Absolute: %b%n", path.isAbsolute());
        path = path.toAbsolutePath();
        System.out.printf("Path: %s%n", path.toString());
        System.out.printf("Absolute: %b%n", path.isAbsolute());
    }
}
```

PathDemo calls Path's `String toString()` method to return a string representation of the path.

Compile Listing 12-4 (javac `PathDemo.java`) and run the resulting application (java `PathDemo`). I observe the following output:

```
Path: a\b\c
Absolute: false
Path: C:\prj\books\io\ch12\code\PathDemo\v3\a\b\c
Absolute: true
```

According to `toAbsolutePath()`'s JDK documentation, if the path is already absolute, this method returns the path. Otherwise, this method resolves the path in an implementation-dependent manner, typically by resolving the path against a file system default directory. Depending on the implementation, this method may throw an I/O error when the file system isn't accessible.

Normalization, Relativization, and Resolution

Path declares several methods to remove path redundancies, to create a relative path between two paths, and to resolve (join) two paths:

- `Path normalize()`
- `Path relativize(Path other)`
- `Path resolve(Path other)`
- `Path resolve(String other)`

`normalize()` is useful for removing redundancies from a path. For example, `reports/./2015/jan` includes the redundant "." (current directory) element. When normalized, this path becomes the shorter `reports/2015/jan`.

`relativize()` creates a relative path between two paths. For example, given current directory jan in the `reports/2015/jan` hierarchy, the relative path to navigate to `reports/2016/mar` is `../../2016/mar`.

`resolve()` is the inverse of `relativize()`. It lets you join a *partial path* (a path without a root element) to another path. For example, resolving apr against `reports/2015` results in `reports/2015/apr`.

Furthermore, Path declares the following methods to resolve a path string against the current path's parent path:

- `Path resolveSibling(Path other)`
- `Path resolveSibling(String other)`

I've created an application that demonstrates these methods. Listing 12-5 presents its source code.

Listing 12-5. Normalizing, Relativizing, and Resolving Paths

```java
import java.nio.file.FileSystems;
import java.nio.file.Path;
import java.nio.file.Paths;

public class PathDemo
{
   public static void main(String[] args)
   {
      Path path1 = Paths.get("reports", ".", "2015", "jan");
      System.out.println(path1);
      System.out.println(path1.normalize());
      path1 = Paths.get("reports", "2015", "..", "jan");
      System.out.println(path1.normalize());
      System.out.println();
      path1 = Paths.get("reports", "2015", "jan");
      System.out.println(path1);
      System.out.println(path1.relativize(Paths.get("reports", "2016",
                                                      "mar")));
      try
      {
         Path root = FileSystems.getDefault().getRootDirectories()
                               .iterator().next();
         if (root != null)
         {
            System.out.printf("Root: %s%n", root.toString());
            Path path = Paths.get(root.toString(), "reports", "2016",
                                  "mar");
            System.out.printf("Path: %s%n", path);
            System.out.println(path1.relativize(path));
         }
      }
      catch (IllegalArgumentException iae)
      {
         iae.printStackTrace();
      }
      System.out.println();
      path1 = Paths.get("reports", "2015");
      System.out.println(path1);
      System.out.println(path1.resolve("apr"));
      System.out.println();
      Path path2 = Paths.get("reports", "2015", "jan");
      System.out.println(path2);
      System.out.println(path2.getParent());
      System.out.println(path2.resolveSibling(Paths.get("mar")));
      System.out.println(path2.resolve(Paths.get("mar")));
   }
}
```

Compile Listing 12-5 (javac `PathDemo.java`) and run the resulting application (java `PathDemo`). I observe the following output:

```
reports\.\2015\jan
reports\2015\jan
reports\jan

reports\2015\jan
..\..\2016\mar
Root: C:\
Path: C:\reports\2016\mar
java.lang.IllegalArgumentException: 'other' is different type of Path
        at sun.nio.fs.WindowsPath.relativize(WindowsPath.java:388)
        at sun.nio.fs.WindowsPath.relativize(WindowsPath.java:44)
        at PathDemo.main(PathDemo.java:29)

reports\2015
reports\2015\apr

reports\2015\jan
reports\2015
reports\2015\mar
reports\2015\jan\mar
```

The output reveals `IllegalArgumentException`, which is thrown from `relativize()` when it cannot relativize its `Path` argument against the current `Path`. It cannot do so when one of the `Paths` has a root element.

The output also reveals the difference between `resolveSibling()` and `resolve()`. `resolveSibling()` resolves `mar` against `reports\2015` (the parent of `reports\2015\jan`); `resolve()` resolves `mar` against `reports\2015\jan`.

Additional Capabilities

Path declares additional methods for comparing paths, determining whether a path starts with or ends with another path, converting a path to a `java.net.URI` (Uniform Resource Identifier) object, and more. Listing 12-6 demonstrates most of these methods.

Listing 12-6. Demonstrating Additional Path Methods

```java
import java.io.IOException;

import java.nio.file.Path;
import java.nio.file.Paths;
```

```java
public class PathDemo
{
   public static void main(String[] args) throws IOException
   {
      Path path1 = Paths.get("a", "b", "c");
      Path path2 = Paths.get("a", "b", "c", "d");
      System.out.printf("path1: %s%n", path1.toString());
      System.out.printf("path2: %s%n", path2.toString());
      System.out.printf("path1.equals(path2): %b%n", path1.equals(path2));
      System.out.printf("path1.equals(path2.subpath(0, 3)): %b%n",
                        path1.equals(path2.subpath(0, 3)));
      System.out.printf("path1.compareTo(path2): %d%n",
                        path1.compareTo(path2));
      System.out.printf("path1.startsWith(\"x\"): %b%n",
                        path1.startsWith("x"));
      System.out.printf("path1.startsWith(Paths.get(\"a\"): %b%n",
                        path1.startsWith(Paths.get("a")));
      System.out.printf("path2.endsWith(\"d\"): %b%n",
                        path2.startsWith("d"));
      System.out.printf("path2.endsWith(Paths.get(\"c\", \"d\"): " +
                        "%b%n",
                        path2.endsWith(Paths.get("c", "d")));
      System.out.printf("path2.toUri(): %s%n", path2.toUri());
      Path path3 = Paths.get(".");
      System.out.printf("path3: %s%n", path3.toString());
      System.out.printf("path3.toRealPath(): %s%n", path3.toRealPath());
   }
}
```

Listing 12-6's main() method first obtains a reference to the current file system and uses this reference to create a pair of Path objects. After outputting each object's path, it demonstrates path equality by invoking the boolean equals(Object other) method.

You can also compare paths to determine whether they are equal or which path alphabetically precedes the other path. The main() method invokes Path's int compareTo(Path other) method for this purpose.

Next, main() calls Path's boolean startsWith(Path other), boolean startsWith(String other), boolean endsWith(Path other), and boolean endsWith(String other) methods to learn whether a path starts and ends with another path.

At this point, main() demonstrates Path's URI toUri() method to convert the current Path instance to a URI object. This method could throw java.io.IOError during the conversion.

Finally, main() demonstrates the Path toRealPath(LinkOption... options) method for returning the real path of the file represented by the Path object. This method generally derives, from this path, an absolute path that locates the same file as this path, but with name elements that represent the actual names of the directories and any nondirectory. It throws java.io.IOException when the file doesn't exist or an I/O error occurs.

You can pass a comma-delimited list of java.nio.file.LinkOption enum constants as arguments to this method. This enum defines the options for how symbolic links are handled. Currently, LinkOption declares only a NOFOLLOW_LINKS (don't follow symbolic links) constant.

Compile Listing 12-6 (javac PathDemo.java) and run the resulting application (java PathDemo). I observe the following output:

```
path1: a\b\c
path2: a\b\c\d
path1.equals(path2): false
path1.equals(path2.subpath(0, 3)): true
path1.compareTo(path2): -2
path1.startsWith("x"): false
path1.startsWith(Paths.get("a"): true
path2.endsWith("d"): false
path2.endsWith(Paths.get("c", "d"): true
path2.toUri(): file:///C:/prj/books/io/ch12/code/PathDemo/v5/a/b/c/d
path3: .
path3.toRealPath(): C:\prj\books\io\ch12\code\PathDemo\v5
```

Performing File System Tasks with Files

For the most part, you could work with FileSystem, FileSystems, and FileSystemProvider to perform various file system tasks, such as copy or move a file. However, there is an easier way to perform these tasks: invoke the java.nio.file.Files utility class's static methods.

> **Note** Files doesn't support path-matching and directory-watching tasks. However, Files exclusively supports walking the file tree and visiting its files.

Accessing File Stores

FileSystem relies on the java.nio.file.FileStore class to provide information about *file stores*, which are storage pools, devices, partitions, volumes, concrete file systems, or other implementation-specific means of file storage. A file store consists of a name, a type, space amounts (in bytes), and other information,

Files declares the FileStore getFileStore(Path path) method to return a FileStore representing the file store where the file identified by path is stored. Once you have the FileStore, you can call methods to obtain amounts of space, determine if the file store is read-only, and obtain the name and type of the file store:

- long getTotalSpace(): Return the size, in bytes, of the file store. This method throws IOException when an I/O error occurs.

- long getUnallocatedSpace(): Return the number of unallocated bytes in the file store. The returned number of unallocated bytes is a hint, but not a guarantee, that it's possible to use most or any of these bytes. The number of unallocated bytes is most likely to be accurate immediately after the space attributes are obtained. It's likely to be made inaccurate by any external I/O operations, including those made on the operating system outside of this JVM. This method throws IOException when an I/O error occurs.

- long getUsableSpace(): Return the number of bytes available to this JVM on the file store. The returned number of available bytes is a hint, but not a guarantee, that it's possible to use most or any of these bytes. The number of usable bytes is most likely to be accurate immediately after the space attributes are obtained. It's likely to be made inaccurate by any external I/O operations, including those made on the operating system outside of this JVM. This method throws IOException when an I/O error occurs.

- boolean isReadOnly(): Return true when this file store is read-only. A file store is read-only when it doesn't support write operations or other changes to files. Any attempt to create a file, open an existing file for writing, and so on, causes IOException to be thrown.

- String name(): Return the name of this file store. The format of the name is highly implementation-specific. It will typically be the name of the storage pool or volume. The returned string may differ from the string returned by the toString() method.

- String type(): Return the type of this file store. The format of the returned string is highly implementation-specific. It may indicate, for example, the format used or whether the file store is local or remote.

Listing 12-7 presents the source code to an application that obtains a file store corresponding to a path and outputs information about the file store.

Listing 12-7. Accessing a File Store and Outputting File Store Details

```
import java.io.IOException;

import java.nio.file.FileStore;
import java.nio.file.Files;
import java.nio.file.Paths;

public class FSDemo
{
   public static void main(String[] args) throws IOException
   {
      if (args.length != 1)
      {
         System.err.println("usage: java FSDemo path");
         return;
      }
      FileStore fs = Files.getFileStore(Paths.get(args[0]));
      System.out.printf("Total space: %d%n", fs.getTotalSpace());
      System.out.printf("Unallocated space: %d%n",
                        fs.getUnallocatedSpace());
      System.out.printf("Usable space: %d%n",
                        fs.getUsableSpace());
      System.out.printf("Read only: %b%n", fs.isReadOnly());
      System.out.printf("Name: %s%n", fs.name());
      System.out.printf("Type: %s%n%n", fs.type());
   }
}
```

Compile Listing 12-7 as follows:

```
javac FSDemo.java
```

Run the resulting application as follows:

```
java FSDemo FSDemo.java
```

In one run, I observed the following output:

```
Total space: 499808989184
Unallocated space: 108411215872
Usable space: 108411215872
Read only: false
Name:
Type: NTFS
```

The getFileStore() method focuses on a specific file store. If you want to iterate over all file stores for a given FileSystem object, you need to work with FileSystem's Iterable<FileStore> getFileStores() method, which lets you iterate over all of the file stores.

Listing 12-8 presents the source code to an application that iterates over all file stores for the default file system and outputs their names.

Listing 12-8. Iterating Over the Default File System's File Stores

```java
import java.io.IOException;

import java.nio.file.FileStore;
import java.nio.file.FileSystem;
import java.nio.file.FileSystems;

public class FSDemo
{
   public static void main(String[] args) throws IOException
   {
      FileSystem fsDefault = FileSystems.getDefault();
      for (FileStore fileStore: fsDefault.getFileStores())
         System.out.printf("Filestore: %s%n", fileStore);
   }
}
```

Compile Listing 12-8 (javac FSDemo.java) and run the resulting application (java FSDemo). I observe the following output:

```
Filestore: (C:)
Filestore: My Passport (E:)
Filestore: BACKUP (F:)
```

Managing Attributes

Files are associated with *attributes*, such as size, last modification time, hidden, permissions, and owner. NIO.2 supports attributes via the types in the java.nio.file.attribute package along with the attribute-oriented methods of the Files class and other types.

Attributes are grouped into *views*, where each view corresponds to a specific file system implementation. Some views let you read attributes in bulk by providing a readAttributes() method. Also, you can get and set attributes by calling Files's getAttribute() and setAttribute() methods.

Views are described by interfaces that descend from AttributeView, whose String name() method returns the view's name. This interface is subtyped by FileAttributeView, which is a view of attributes associated with files. FileAttributeView doesn't contribute any methods.

FileAttributeView is subtyped by the following interfaces:

- BasicFileAttributeView: Provides a view of a basic set of file attributes common to many file systems.

- FileOwnerAttributeView: Provides support for reading or updating a file owner.

- UserDefinedFileAttributeView: Provides a view of a file's user-defined attributes (also called *extended attributes*).

BasicFileAttributeView is subtyped by the following interfaces:

- DosFileAttributeView: Provides a view of the legacy MS-DOS/PC-DOS file attributes.

- PosixFileAttributeView: Provides a view of the file attributes commonly associated with files on file systems used by operating systems that implement the Portable Operating System Interface (POSIX) family of standards.

FileOwnerAttributeView is subtyped by the following interfaces:

- AclFileAttributeView: Provides support for reading or updating a file's ACL or file owner attributes.

- PosixFileAttributeView

As you can see, PosixFileAttributeView has two immediate parent interfaces; it's a specialized basic file attribute view and a specialized file owner attribute view. Figure 12-2 clarifies this relationship along with other relationships among the view hierarchy's interfaces.

Figure 12-2. *Relating view types; subtypes are indented to the right*

Determining View Support

Before working with any of these views, make sure that it's supported. One way to accomplish this task is to call FileSystem's Set<String> supportedFileAttributeViews() method, which returns a set of strings identifying views that are supported by the invoking FileSystem.

Listing 12-9 presents the source code to an application that outputs the names of views supported by the default `FileSystem`.

Listing 12-9. Outputting the Names of Default File System-Supported File Attribute Views

```java
import java.nio.file.FileSystem;
import java.nio.file.FileSystems;

public class FAVDemo
{
   public static void main(String[] args)
   {
      FileSystem fsDefault = FileSystems.getDefault();
      for (String view: fsDefault.supportedFileAttributeViews())
         System.out.println(view);
   }
}
```

Compile Listing 12-9 as follows:

```
javac FAVDemo.java
```

Run the resulting application as follows:

```
java FAVDemo
```

I observe the following output:

```
owner
dos
acl
basic
user
```

> **Note**   All `FileSystem`s support the basic file attribute view so you should see at least `basic` in the output.

You could also use `Files`'s `<V extends FileAttributeView> V getFileAttributeView(Path path, Class<V> type, LinkOption... options)` method, which returns an object created from an implementation of the view interface type or `null` when the view isn't supported, to accomplish this task. Listing 12-10 presents an application that uses this method in a utility method context to determine view support.

Listing 12-10. Determining Specific File Attribute View Support

```java
import java.nio.file.Files;
import java.nio.file.Paths;

import java.nio.file.attribute.AclFileAttributeView;
import java.nio.file.attribute.BasicFileAttributeView;
import java.nio.file.attribute.FileAttributeView;
import java.nio.file.attribute.PosixFileAttributeView;

public class FAVDemo
{
   public static void main(String[] args)
   {
      System.out.printf("Supports basic: %b%n",
                        isSupported(BasicFileAttributeView.class));
      System.out.printf("Supports posix: %b%n",
                        isSupported(PosixFileAttributeView.class));
      System.out.printf("Supports acl: %b%n",
                        isSupported(AclFileAttributeView.class));
   }

   static boolean isSupported(Class<? extends FileAttributeView> clazz)
   {
      return Files.getFileAttributeView(Paths.get("."), clazz) != null;
   }
}
```

Listing 12-10 declares an isSupported() utility method that takes a java.lang.Class object representing a FileAttributeView subinterface as an argument. It returns true when the view is supported or false when it isn't supported.

The Class argument and a Path object describing the current directory are passed to getFileAttributeView(), which returns either an object created from a class that implements the interface when the view is supported or null when it isn't supported.

Compile Listing 12-10 (javac FAVDemo.java) and run the resulting application (java FAVDemo). I observe the following output:

```
Supports basic: true
Supports posix: false
Supports acl: true
```

Ultimately, getFileAttributeView() provides a result for the FileSystem associated with the Path argument. Because Paths.get(".") returns a FileSystem for the default file system, isSupport() is relevant in a default file system context only.

Finally, a file store can support various file attribute views. Call either of FileStore's supportsFileAttributeView() methods to determine whether or not the file store supports the file attributes identified by the given file attribute view:

- boolean supportsFileAttributeView(Class<? extends FileAttributeView> type)

- boolean supportsFileAttributeView(String name)

One of these methods takes a Class object describing a subinterface of FileAttributeView as an argument:

```
System.out.printf("supports basic file attribute view: %b%n",
   fileStore.supportsFileAttributeView(BasicFileAttributeView.class));
```

The other method takes a string argument, which is one of the strings returned from FileSystem's supportedFileAttributeViews() method:

```
System.out.printf("supports basic file attribute view: %b%n",
   fileStore.supportsFileAttributeView("basic"));
```

Exploring the Basic View

The BasicFileAttributeView interface supports several basic attributes. The following list identifies each attribute in terms of its string name and type:

- creationTime (FileTime)

- fileKey (Object)

- isDirectory (Boolean)

- isOther (Boolean)

- isRegularFile (Boolean)

- isSymbolicLink (Boolean)

- lastAccessTime (FileTime)

- lastModifiedTime (FileTime)

- size (Long)

Each of creationTime, lastAccessTime, and lastModifiedTime has type java.nio.file.attribute.FileTime, an immutable class representing a file's timestamp. fileKey has type java.lang.Object. Each of isDirectory, isOther, isRegularFile, and isSymbolicLink has type java.lang.Boolean. size has type java.lang.Long.

BasicFileAttributeView declares the following methods:

- ▪ BasicFileAttributes readAttributes(): Read the basic file attributes as a bulk operation.

- ▪ void setTimes(FileTime lastModifiedTime, FileTime lastAccessTime, FileTime creationTime): Update any or all of the file's lastModifiedTime, lastAccessTime, and creationTime attributes.

These methods throw IOException when an I/O error occurs.

readAttributes() returns a java.nio.file.attribute.BasicFileAttributes object that offers type-safe methods for reading attribute values:

- ▪ FileTime creationTime()

- ▪ Object fileKey()

- ▪ boolean isDirectory()

- ▪ boolean isOther()

- ▪ boolean isRegularFile()

- ▪ boolean isSymbolicLink()

- ▪ FileTime lastAccessTime()

- ▪ FileTime lastModifiedTime()

- ▪ long size()

Note   On some file systems, it's possible to use an identifier or a combination of identifiers to uniquely identify a file. Such identifiers are known as *file keys*. File keys are important for operations such as file tree walks in file systems that support symbolic links, and for file systems that allow a file to be an entry in more than one directory. For example, on Unix-based file systems, the device ID and information node (inode) are commonly used for such purposes.

Reading Basic File Attribute Values in Bulk

Listing 12-11 presents the source code to an application that shows how to read a file's basic file attributes in bulk.

Listing 12-11. Reading Basic File Attributes in Bulk

```java
import java.io.IOException;

import java.nio.file.Files;
import java.nio.file.Path;
import java.nio.file.Paths;

import java.nio.file.attribute.BasicFileAttributes;

public class BFAVDemo
{
   public static void main(String[] args) throws IOException
   {
      if (args.length != 1)
      {
         System.err.println("usage: java BFAVDemo path");
         return;
      }
      Path path = Paths.get(args[0]);
      BasicFileAttributes bfa;
      bfa = Files.readAttributes(path, BasicFileAttributes.class);
      System.out.printf("Creation time: %s%n", bfa.creationTime());
      System.out.printf("File key: %s%n", bfa.fileKey());
      System.out.printf("Is directory: %b%n", bfa.isDirectory());
      System.out.printf("Is other: %b%n", bfa.isOther());
      System.out.printf("Is regular file: %b%n", bfa.isRegularFile());
      System.out.printf("Is symbolic link: %b%n", bfa.isSymbolicLink());
      System.out.printf("Last access time: %s%n", bfa.lastAccessTime());
      System.out.printf("Last modified time: %s%n", bfa.lastModifiedTime());
      System.out.printf("Size: %d%n", bfa.size());
   }
}
```

The attributes are read by calling Files's `<A extends BasicFileAttributes>`
`A readAttributes(Path path, Class<A> type, LinkOption... options)`
method. The argument passed to `path` is a `Path` object wrapping the single
command-line argument. `BasicFileAttributes.class` is passed to `type`
signifying that the basic file attributes corresponding to `path` are to be read.
Because nothing is passed to `options`, symbolic links are followed and the
attributes associated with the target of the link are read.

Compile Listing 12-11 as follows:

```
javac BFAVDemo.java
```

Run the resulting application as follows:

```
java BFAVDemo BFAVDemo.java
```

I observe the following output:

```
Creation time: 2015-09-14T21:39:43.655763Z
File key: null
Is directory: false
Is other: false
Is regular file: true
Is symbolic link: false
Last access time: 2015-09-14T21:39:43.655763Z
Last modified time: 2015-09-14T21:44:59.238814Z
Size: 1144
```

Getting and Setting Single Basic File Attribute Values

Files declares getAttribute() and setAttribute() methods that you can call to get or set single file attributes:

- Object getAttribute(Path path, String attribute, LinkOption... options)

- Path setAttribute(Path path, String attribute, Object value, LinkOption... options)

getAttribute() reads the value of a single file attribute. path identifies the file whose attribute value is to be read, attribute identifies the attribute's name, and options identifies how symbolic links are handled. Specify LinkOption.NOFOLLOW_LINKS when you want the value of the attribute for the symbolic link file. Omit this argument when you want the value of the attribute for the final target of the link.

The attribute parameter identifies the attribute to be read and adheres to the following syntax:

[view-name:]attribute-name

The square brackets delineate an optional component and the colon character (:) stands for itself. view-name is the name of a FileAttributeView that identifies a set of file attributes. If it's not specified, it defaults to basic, the name of the file attribute view that identifies the basic set of file attributes common to many file systems. attribute-name is the name of the attribute.

setAttribute() sets the value of a single file attribute. path identifies the file whose attribute value is to be set, attribute identifies the attribute's name and follows the previously specified syntax, value identifies the new value for the attribute, and options identifies how symbolic links are handled.

Listing 12-12 presents the source code to an application that shows how to get and set single basic file attribute values.

Listing 12-12. Getting and Setting Single Basic File Attribute Values

```
import java.io.IOException;

import java.nio.file.Files;
import java.nio.file.Path;
import java.nio.file.Paths;

import java.nio.file.attribute.FileTime;

import java.time.Instant;

public class BFAVDemo
{
   public static void main(String[] args) throws IOException
   {
      if (args.length < 1 || args.length > 2)
      {
         System.err.println("usage: java BFAVDemo path [set]");
         return;
      }
      Path path = Paths.get(args[0]);
      boolean setAttr = false;
      if (args.length == 2)
         setAttr = true;
      System.out.printf("Creation time: %s%n",
                        Files.getAttribute(path, "creationTime"));
      System.out.printf("File key: %s%n",
                        Files.getAttribute(path, "fileKey"));
      System.out.printf("Is directory: %b%n",
                        Files.getAttribute(path, "isDirectory"));
      System.out.printf("Is other: %b%n",
                        Files.getAttribute(path, "isOther"));
      System.out.printf("Is regular file: %b%n",
                        Files.getAttribute(path, "isRegularFile"));
      System.out.printf("Is symbolic link: %b%n",
                        Files.getAttribute(path, "isSymbolicLink"));
      System.out.printf("Last access time: %s%n",
                        Files.getAttribute(path, "lastAccessTime"));
      System.out.printf("Last modified time: %s%n",
                        Files.getAttribute(path, "lastModifiedTime"));
      System.out.printf("Size: %d%n", Files.getAttribute(path, "size"));
```

```
    if (setAttr)
    {
        Files.setAttribute(path, "lastModifiedTime",
                           FileTime.from(Instant.now().plusSeconds(60)));
        System.out.printf("Last modified time: %s%n",
                          Files.getAttribute(path, "lastModifiedTime"));
    }
  }
}
```

Listing 12-12 obtains each basic file attribute value and outputs the value. You must specify at least one command-line argument, which identifies the path to a file. If you specify a second argument, this object's lastModifiedTime attribute is set (with help from FileTime's FileTime from(Instant instant) method) to the current time plus one minute.

Compile Listing 12-12 (javac BFAVDemo.java) and run the application as follows:

```
java BFAVDemo BFAVDemo.java
```

You should observe output that's similar to the output presented here:

```
Creation time: 2015-09-15T02:58:36.036073Z
File key: null
Is directory: false
Is other: false
Is regular file: true
Is symbolic link: false
Last access time: 2015-09-15T02:58:36.036073Z
Last modified time: 2015-09-15T03:07:25.763372Z
Size: 1885
```

Now, run BFAVDemo as follows:

```
java BFAVDemo BFAVDemo.java set
```

This time, after outputting basic file attribute values, the last modified time will be set to the current time plus one minute.

> **Tip** Use BasicFileAttributeView's setTimes() method to set the creation time, last access time, and last modified time in one method call.

Files declares several convenience methods for accessing specific basic file attributes:

- FileTime getLastModifiedTime(Path path, LinkOption... options)

- boolean isRegularFile(Path path, LinkOption... options)

- boolean isSymbolicLink(Path path)

- Path setLastModifiedTime(Path path, FileTime time)

- long size(Path path)

Exploring the DOS View

The DosFileAttributeView interface extends BasicFileAttributeView and supports the following four MS-DOS/PC-DOS file attributes:

- archive (Boolean)

- hidden (Boolean)

- readonly (Boolean)

- system (Boolean)

DosFileAttributeView declares the following methods:

- DosFileAttributes readAttributes(): Read the DOS file attributes as a bulk operation.

- void setArchive(boolean value): Update the value of the archive attribute.

- void setHidden(boolean value): Update the value of the hidden attribute.

- void setReadOnly(boolean value): Update the value of the readonly attribute.

- void setSystem(boolean value): Update the value of the system attribute.

These methods throw IOException when an I/O error occurs.

readAttributes() returns a java.nio.file.attribute.DosFileAttributes object that offers type-safe methods for reading attribute values:

- boolean isArchive()

- boolean isHidden()

■ `boolean isReadOnly()`

■ `boolean isSystem()`

Reading DOS File Attribute Values in Bulk

Listing 12-13 presents the source code to an application that shows how to read a file's DOS file attributes in bulk.

Listing 12-13. Reading DOS File Attributes in Bulk

```java
import java.io.IOException;

import java.nio.file.Files;
import java.nio.file.Path;
import java.nio.file.Paths;

import java.nio.file.attribute.DosFileAttributes;

public class DFAVDemo
{
   public static void main(String[] args) throws IOException
   {
      if (args.length != 1)
      {
         System.err.println("usage: java DFAVDemo path");
         return;
      }
      Path path = Paths.get(args[0]);
      DosFileAttributes dfa;
      dfa = Files.readAttributes(path, DosFileAttributes.class);
      System.out.printf("Is archive: %b%n", dfa.isArchive());
      System.out.printf("Is hidden: %b%n", dfa.isHidden());
      System.out.printf("Is readonly: %b%n", dfa.isReadOnly());
      System.out.printf("Is system: %b%n", dfa.isSystem());
   }
}
```

Compile Listing 12-13 as follows:

```
javac DFAVDemo.java
```

Assuming that the DOS file attribute view is supported, run the resulting application as follows:

```
java DFAVDemo DFAVDemo.java
```

I observe the following output:

```
Is archive: true
Is hidden: false
Is readonly: false
Is system: false
```

Getting and Setting Single DOS File Attribute Values

Listing 12-14 presents the source code to an application that shows how to get and set single DOS file attribute values.

Listing 12-14. Getting and Setting Single DOS File Attribute Values

```java
import java.io.IOException;

import java.nio.file.Files;
import java.nio.file.Path;
import java.nio.file.Paths;

import java.nio.file.attribute.FileTime;

import java.time.Instant;

public class DFAVDemo
{
   public static void main(String[] args) throws IOException
   {
      if (args.length < 1 || args.length > 2)
      {
         System.err.println("usage: java DFAVDemo path [set]");
         return;
      }
      Path path = Paths.get(args[0]);
      boolean setAttr = false;
      if (args.length == 2)
         setAttr = true;
      System.out.printf("Is archive: %b%n",
                        Files.getAttribute(path, "dos:archive"));
      System.out.printf("Is hidden: %b%n",
                        Files.getAttribute(path, "dos:hidden"));
      System.out.printf("Is readonly: %b%n",
                        Files.getAttribute(path, "dos:readonly"));
      System.out.printf("Is system: %b%n",
                        Files.getAttribute(path, "dos:system"));
```

```
    if (setAttr)
    {
        Files.setAttribute(path, "dos:system", true);
        System.out.printf("Is system: %s%n",
                            Files.getAttribute(path, "dos:system"));
    }
  }
}
```

Unlike with basic file attributes, DOS file attribute names require a prefix, which happens to be dos:.

Compile Listing 12-14 (javac DFAVDemo.java) and run the application as follows:

```
java DFAVDemo DFAVDemo.java
```

Assuming that the DOS file attribute view is supported, you should observe the following output:

```
Is archive: true
Is hidden: false
Is readonly: false
Is system: false
```

Now, run DFAVDemo as follows:

```
java DFAVDemo DFAVDemo.java set
```

This time, after outputting DOS attribute values, the system attribute should be set.

Exploring the POSIX View

The PosixFileAttributeView interface extends BasicFileAttributeView and supports the POSIX group owner and nine access permissions attributes:

- group (GroupPrincipal)

- permissions (Set<PosixFilePermission>)

PosixFileAttributeView declares the following methods:

- PosixFileAttributes readAttributes(): Read the POSIX file attributes as a bulk operation.

- void setGroup(GroupPrincipal group): Update the file group-owner.

- void setPermissions(Set<PosixFilePermission> perms): Update the file permissions.

These methods throw IOException when an I/O error occurs. setPermissions() throws java.lang.ClassCastException when the java.util.Set object contains elements that are not of type java.nio.file.attribute.PosixFilePermission, which is an enum that declares GROUP_EXECUTE, GROUP_READ, GROUP_WRITE, OTHERS_EXECUTE, OTHERS_READ, OTHERS_WRITE, OWNER_EXECUTE, OWNER_READ, and OWNER_WRITE constants.

readAttributes() returns a java.nio.file.attribute.PosixFileAttributes object that offers type-safe methods for reading attribute values:

- GroupPrincipal group()

- UserPrincipal owner()

- Set<PosixFilePermission> permissions()

The empty java.nio.file.attribute.UserPrincipal interface represents an identity for determining access rights to objects in a file system and extends java.security.Principal. The empty java.nio.file.attribute. GroupPrincipal interface represents a group identity and extends UserPrincipal.

Reading POSIX File Attribute Values in Bulk

Listing 12-15 presents the source code to an application that shows how to read a file's POSIX file attributes in bulk.

Listing 12-15. Reading POSIX File Attributes in Bulk

```
import java.io.IOException;

import java.nio.file.Files;
import java.nio.file.Path;
import java.nio.file.Paths;

import java.nio.file.attribute.PosixFileAttributes;
import java.nio.file.attribute.PosixFilePermission;

public class PFAVDemo
{
   public static void main(String[] args) throws IOException
   {
      if (args.length != 1)
      {
         System.err.println("usage: java PFAVDemo path");
         return;
      }
```

```
        Path path = Paths.get(args[0]);
        PosixFileAttributes pfa;
        pfa = Files.readAttributes(path, PosixFileAttributes.class);
        System.out.printf("Group: %s%n", pfa.group());
        for (PosixFilePermission perm: pfa.permissions())
            System.out.printf("Permission: %s%n", perm);
    }
}
```

Compile Listing 12-15 as follows:

```
javac PFAVDemo.java
```

Assuming that the POSIX file attribute view is supported, run the resulting application as follows:

```
java PFAVDemo PFAVDemo.java
```

Because I'm running Windows 7, POSIX isn't supported and I observe a thrown UnsupportedOperationException message.

Getting and Setting Single POSIX File Attribute Values

Listing 12-16 presents the source code to an application that shows how to get and set single POSIX file attribute values.

Listing 12-16. Getting and Setting Single POSIX File Attribute Values

```
import java.io.IOException;

import java.nio.file.Files;
import java.nio.file.Path;
import java.nio.file.Paths;

import java.nio.file.attribute.GroupPrincipal;
import java.nio.file.attribute.PosixFilePermission;

import java.util.Set;

public class PFAVDemo
{
    public static void main(String[] args) throws IOException
    {
        if (args.length < 1 || args.length > 2)
        {
            System.err.println("usage: java PFAVDemo path [group]");
            return;
        }
```

```
Path path = Paths.get(args[0]);
boolean setAttr = false;
if (args.length == 2)
   setAttr = true;
System.out.printf("Group: %b%n",
                    Files.getAttribute(path, "posix:group"));
@SuppressWarnings("unchecked")
Set<PosixFilePermission> perms =
   (Set<PosixFilePermission>)
   Files.getAttribute(path, "posix: permissions");
for (PosixFilePermission perm: perms)
   System.out.printf("Permission: %s%n", perm);
if (setAttr)
{
   GroupPrincipal gp = path.getFileSystem().
                           getUserPrincipalLookupService().
                           lookupPrincipalByGroupName(args[1]);
   Files.setAttribute(path, "posix:group", gp);
   System.out.printf("Group: %b%n",
                       Files.getAttribute(path, "posix:group"));
}
}
}
```

Unlike with basic file attributes, POSIX file attribute names require a prefix, which happens to be posix:.

To change the group attribute, you need to obtain a new GroupPrincipal object that corresponds to the specified group name command-line argument. This task is accomplished by following these steps:

1. Calling Path's FileSystem getFileSystem() method to return the FileSystem that created the Path object.

2. Calling FileSystem's UserPrincipalLookupService getUserPrincipalLookupService() method to return the java.nio.file.attribute.UserPrincipalLookupService object for obtaining UserPrincipals and GroupPrincipals.

3. Calling UserPrincipalLookupService's GroupPrincipal lookupPrincipalByGroupName(String group) method to return the desired GroupPrincipal object.

Compile Listing 12-16 (javac PFAVDemo.java) and, assuming that the POSIX file attribute view is supported, run this application on an arbitrary file. I observe UnsupportedOperationException.

The Files class declares the following convenience methods for getting and setting the POSIX permissions attribute:

- Set<PosixFilePermission> getPosixFilePermissions
  (Path path, LinkOption... options)

- Path setPosixFilePermissions(Path path,
  Set<PosixFilePermission> perms)

For example, instead of specifying

```
Set<PosixFilePermission> perms =
        (Set<PosixFilePermission>)
        Files.getAttribute(path, "posix: permissions");
```

you could more conveniently specify

```
Set<PosixFilePermission> perms = Files.getPosixFilePermissions(path);
```

Exploring the File Owner View

Many file systems support the concept of file ownership. A *file owner* is the identity of the owner that created a file. NIO.2 supports file ownership by providing the FileOwnerAttributeView interface, which supports the following attribute:

- owner (UserPrincipal)

FileOwnerAttributeView declares the following methods to access this attribute:

- UserPrincipal getOwner(): Read the file owner.

- void setOwner(UserPrincipal owner): Update the file owner.

These methods show that a file owner is implemented as a user principal. They throw IOException when an I/O error occurs.

You should never need to work directly with these methods because Files declares the following more convenient methods:

- UserPrincipal getOwner(Path path, LinkOption... options)

- Path setOwner(Path path, UserPrincipal owner)

> **Note**   You can also access the file owner attribute via `Files.getAttribute()`
> or `Files.setAttribute()`. You will need to specify `owner:owner` for the
> view prefix and attribute name.

Listing 12-17 presents the source code to an application that demonstrates
getOwner() and setOwner().

Listing 12-17. Getting and Setting File Ownership

```java
import java.io.IOException;

import java.nio.file.Files;
import java.nio.file.Path;
import java.nio.file.Paths;

import java.nio.file.attribute.UserPrincipal;

public class FOAVDemo
{
   public static void main(String[] args) throws IOException
   {
      if (args.length != 1)
      {
         System.err.println("usage: java FOAVDemo path");
         return;
      }
      Path path = Paths.get(args[0]);
      System.out.printf("Owner: %s%n", Files.getOwner(path));
      UserPrincipal up = path.getFileSystem().
                            getUserPrincipalLookupService().
                            lookupPrincipalByName("jeff");
      System.out.println(up);
      Files.setOwner(path, up);
      System.out.printf("Owner: %s%n", Files.getOwner(path));
   }
}
```

FOAVDemo's main() method first validates the command line. It requires a
single command-line argument that identifies the path to a file.

main() subsequently obtains a Path object to the file. It invokes getOwner()
on this Path to obtain the current owner of the file and then outputs the owner.

Before the owner can be changed, a UserPrincipal named jeff is obtained
and output. (You must add this principal to your operating system before
you can run the application.)

setOwner() is called to change the file's ownership to jeff. Then, getOwner() is called and its value is output to verify that the owner has been changed.

Compile Listing 12-17 as follows:

```
javac FOAVDemo.java
```

Assuming that a file named test exists, run the resulting application as follows:

```
java FOAVDemo test
```

On my Windows 7 machine, I initially observed the following output:

```
Owner: Owner-PC\Owner (User)
Owner-PC\jeff (User)
Exception in thread "main" java.nio.file.FileSystemException: test: This
security ID may not be assigned as the owner of this object.

        at sun.nio.fs.WindowsException.translateToIOException(Windows
        Exception.java:86)
        at sun.nio.fs.WindowsException.rethrowAsIOException(Windows
        Exception.java:97)
        at sun.nio.fs.WindowsException.rethrowAsIOException(Windows
        Exception.java:102)
        at sun.nio.fs.WindowsAclFileAttributeView.setOwner(WindowsAclFile
        AttributeView.java:201)
        at sun.nio.fs.FileOwnerAttributeViewImpl.setOwner(FileOwnerAttribute
        ViewImpl.java:102)
        at java.nio.file.Files.setOwner(Files.java:2127)
        at FOAVDemo.main(FOAVDemo.java:24)
```

The exception is thrown by setOwner() for the following reason: *The owner of a new object must be one of the users or groups you have been given the right to assign as the owner. Typically, this is your user account and, if you are an administrator, the administrator's local group.*

The solution to this problem is to elevate the privilege of the java application by running cmd (the command interpreter) as an administrator. You can accomplish this task by completing the following steps:

1. Go to the Start menu.

2. In the Search Programs and Files text field, input **cmd**.

3. While holding down the Shift and Ctrl keys, press the Enter key.

4. The resulting User Account Control window asks if you want to make changes. Click the Yes button and you'll observe the Administrator command window.

This time, running java FOAVDemo test results in the following output:

```
Owner: BUILTIN\Administrators (Alias)
Owner-PC\jeff (User)
Owner: Owner-PC\jeff (User)
```

> **Note**   POSIXFileAttributeView extends FileOwnerAttributeView, inheriting the owner attribute. Files on a POSIX file system have a file owner in addition to a group owner and access permissions.

Exploring the ACL View

The AclFileAttributeView interface extends FileOwnerAttributeView and supports the following attribute:

- acl (List<AclEntry>)

AclFileAttributeView declares the following methods to access this attribute:

- List<AclEntry> getAcl(): Read the ACL into a java.util.List of java.nio.file.attribute.AclEntrys.

- void setAcl(List<AclEntry> acl): Update (replace) the ACL.

These methods throw IOException when an I/O error occurs.

The AclEntry class describes an entry in an ACL. It has four components:

- type determines if the entry grants or denies access. It's read by calling the AclEntryType type() method. The java.nio.file.attribute.AclEntryType enum defines ALARM (generate an alarm, in a system-dependent way, for the access specified in the permissions component of the ACL entry), ALLOW (explicitly grant access to a regular file or directory), AUDIT (log, in a system-dependent way, the access specified in the permissions component of the ACL entry), and DENY (explicitly deny access to a regular file or directory entry) type constants.

- principal, sometimes called the "who" component, is a UserPrincipal corresponding to the identity that the entry grants or denies access. It's read by calling the UserPrincipal principal() method.

- permissions is a set of permissions. It's read by calling the Set<AclEntryPermission> permissions() method. The java.nio.file.attribute.AclEntryPermission enum defines APPEND_DATA (permission to append data to a file), DELETE (permission to delete the file), DELETE_CHILD (permission to delete a file in a directory), EXECUTE (permission to execute a regular file), READ_ACL (permission to read the ACL attribute), READ_ATTRIBUTES (the ability to read nonACL file attributes), READ_DATA (permission to read the file's data), READ_NAMED_ATTRS (permission to read the file's named attributes), SYNCHRONIZE (permission to access the file locally at the server with synchronous reads and writes), WRITE_ACL (permission to write the ACL attribute), WRITE_ATTRIBUTES (the ability to write nonACL file attributes), WRITE_DATA (permission to modify the file's data), WRITE_NAMED_ATTRS (permission to write the file's named attributes), and WRITE_OWNER (permission to change the owner) permission constants.

- flags is a set of flags that indicate how entries are inherited and propagated. It's read by calling the Set<AclEntryFlag> flags() method. The java.nio.file.attribute.AclEntryFlag enum defines DIRECTORY_INHERIT (can be placed on a directory and indicates that the ACL entry should be added to each new directory created), FILE_INHERIT (can be placed on a directory and indicates that the ACL entry should be added to each new nondirectory file created), INHERIT_ONLY (can be placed on a directory but does not apply to the directory, only to newly-created files/directories as specified by the FILE_INHERIT and DIRECTORY_INHERIT flags), and NO_PROPAGATE_INHERIT (can be placed on a directory to indicate that the ACL entry should not be placed on the newly-created directory, which is inheritable by subdirectories of the created directory), flag constants.

Listing 12-18 presents the source code to an application that demonstrates reading the acl and inherited owner attributes.

Listing 12-18. Reading and Outputting a File's Owner and ACL Information

```java
import java.io.IOException;

import java.nio.file.Files;
import java.nio.file.Path;
import java.nio.file.Paths;

import java.util.List;

import java.nio.file.attribute.AclEntry;

public class ACLAVDemo
{
   public static void main(String[] args) throws IOException
   {
      if (args.length != 1)
      {
         System.err.println("usage: java ACLAVDemo path");
         return;
      }
      Path path = Paths.get(args[0]);
      System.out.printf("Owner: %s%n%n",
         Files.getAttribute(path, "acl:owner"));
      @SuppressWarnings("unchecked")
      List<AclEntry> aclentries =
         (List<AclEntry>) Files.getAttribute(path, "acl:acl");
      for (AclEntry aclentry: aclentries)
         System.out.printf("%s%n%n", aclentry);
   }
}
```

Unlike with basic file attributes, ACL file attribute names require a prefix, which happens to be acl:.

Compile Listing 12-18 as follows:

```
javac ACLAVDemo.java
```

Run the resulting application as follows:

```
java ACLAVDemo ACLAVDemo.java
```

I observe the following output:

```
Owner: Owner-PC\Owner (User)

NT AUTHORITY\Authenticated Users:READ_DATA/WRITE_DATA/APPEND_DATA/
READ_NAMED_ATTRS/WRITE_NAMED_ATTRS/EXECUTE/READ_ATTRIBUTES/WRITE_ATTRIBUTES/
DELETE/READ_ACL/SYNCHRONIZE:ALLOW

NT AUTHORITY\SYSTEM:READ_DATA/WRITE_DATA/APPEND_DATA/READ_NAMED_ATTRS/
WRITE_NAMED_ATTRS/EXECUTE/DELETE_CHILD/READ_ATTRIBUTES/WRITE_ATTRIBUTES/
DELETE/READ_ACL/WRITE_ACL/WRITE_OWNER/SYNCHRONIZE:ALLOW

BUILTIN\Administrators:READ_DATA/WRITE_DATA/APPEND_DATA/READ_NAMED_ATTRS/
WRITE_NAMED_ATTRS/EXECUTE/READ_ATTRIBUTES/WRITE_ATTRIBUTES/READ_ACL/
SYNCHRONIZE:ALLOW

BUILTIN\Users:READ_DATA/WRITE_DATA/APPEND_DATA/READ_NAMED_ATTRS/WRITE_NAMED_
ATTRS/EXECUTE/READ_ATTRIBUTES/WRITE_ATTRIBUTES/READ_ACL/SYNCHRONIZE:ALLOW
```

You can create an ACL entry by using the AclEntry.Builder class. The following example shows how to create a builder:

```
AclEntry.Builder builder = AclEntry.Builder.newBuilder();
```

You then invoke AclEntry.Builder methods such as AclEntry.Builder setType(AclEntryType type) to configure the builder. When you are finished, call AclEntry.Builder's AclEntry build() method to build the entry. Note that the type and principal must be set to build an AclEntry:

```
builder.build();
```

After building your ACL entries, add them to a List<AclEntry> object and pass this object to the value parameter in a Files.setAttribute() method call, to update the ACL.

Exploring the User-Defined View

In addition to the previous built-in file attributes, you can define your own. For example, you might want to provide a description attribute for the objects of your file system. You can define attributes by using the UserDefinedFileAttributeView interface. It declares the following methods:

- void delete(String name): Delete a user-defined attribute.

- List<String> list(): Return a list of user-defined attribute names.

- `int read(String name, ByteBuffer dst)`: Read the value of a user-defined attribute into a buffer.

- `int size(String name)`: Return the size of the value of a user-defined attribute.

- `int write(String name, ByteBuffer src)`: Write the value of a user-defined attribute from a buffer.

These methods throw IOException when an I/O error occurs. size() throws java.lang.ArithmeticException when the attribute size is larger than java.lang.Integer.MAX_VALUE. read() throws IllegalArgumentException for a read-only destination buffer.

Before you can define your own attributes, you need to determine if the file store supports the desired attributes. Accomplish this task by calling either of FileStore's supportsFileAttributeView() methods. The following code fragment demonstrates:

```
FileStore fs = Files.getFileStore(path);
if (!fs.supportsFileAttributeView(UserDefinedFileAttributeView.class))
   System.out.println("User-defined attributes are supported.");
else
   System.out.println("User-defined attributes are not supported.");
```

Listing 12-19 presents the source code to an application that demonstrates a user-defined file.description attribute for associating a description with a file.

Listing 12-19. Associating a Description with a File

```
import java.io.IOException;

import java.nio.ByteBuffer;

import java.nio.charset.Charset;

import java.nio.file.Files;
import java.nio.file.Path;
import java.nio.file.Paths;

import java.nio.file.attribute.UserDefinedFileAttributeView;
```

```
public class UDAVDemo
{
    public static void main(String[] args) throws IOException
    {
        if (args.length != 2)
        {
            System.err.println("usage: java UDAVDemo path w | l | r | d");
            return;
        }
        Path path = Paths.get(args[0]);
        UserDefinedFileAttributeView udfav =
            Files.getFileAttributeView(path,
                                       UserDefinedFileAttributeView.class);
        switch (args[1].charAt(0))
        {
            case 'W':
            case 'w': udfav.write("file.description",
                                  Charset.defaultCharset().encode("sample"));
                      break;

            case 'L':
            case 'l': for (String name: udfav.list())
                          System.out.println(name);
                      break;

            case 'R':
            case 'r': int size = udfav.size("file.description");
                      ByteBuffer buf = ByteBuffer.allocateDirect(size);
                      udfav.read("file.description", buf);
                      buf.flip();
                      System.out.println(Charset.defaultCharset().decode(buf));
                      break;

            case 'D':
            case 'd': udfav.delete("file.description");
        }
    }
}
```

UDAVDemo is called with two arguments: the path of a file and a letter that
identifies a user-defined attribute operation for the associated path:

- W: Write the file.description attribute with value
  sample.

- L: List all user-defined attributes.

- R: Read the value of the file.description attribute.

- D: Delete the file.description attribute.

After obtaining a `UserDefinedAttributeView` object for the specified path, `main()` executes the appropriate method to carry out the operation identified by the aforementioned letter.

Compile Listing 12-19 as follows:

```
javac UDAVDemo.java
```

Run the resulting application as follows:

```
java UDAVDemo UDAVDemo.java w
```

You should observe no output. Continue by executing the following command:

```
java UDAVDemo UDAVDemo.java l
```

You should observe the following output:

```
file.description
```

Now, execute the following command:

```
java UDAVDemo UDAVDemo.java r
```

You should observe the following output:

```
sample
```

Finally, execute the following command to delete `file.description`:

```
java UDAVDemo UDAVDemo.java d
```

You should observe no output.

Exploring the File Store View

`AttributeView` is also subtyped by `java.nio.file.attribute.FileStoreAttributeView`, which is a view of attributes associated with a file store. This interface declares no methods.

A file store has the `totalSpace`, `unallocatedSpace`, and `usableSpace` attributes. You can access the values of these attributes by calling `FileStore`'s `getAttribute()` method.

The getAttribute() method takes a single string argument that identifies an attribute according to the view-name:attribute-name syntax. For the WindowsFileStore subclass, I've found that a view name isn't required for the totalSpace, unallocatedSpace, and usableSpace names:

```
System.out.printf("total space: %d%n",
                  fileStore.getAttribute("totalSpace"));
System.out.printf("unallocated space: %d%n",
                  fileStore.getAttribute("unallocatedSpace"));
System.out.printf("usable space: %d%n",
                  fileStore.getAttribute("usableSpace"));
```

> **Note** Instead of accessing totalSpace, unallocatedSpace, and usableSpace via getAttribute(), it's better to use FileStore's type-safe getTotalSpace(), getUnallocatedSpace(), and getUsableSpace() methods, which I demonstrated earlier in this chapter.

In contrast, you need to specify volume as the view-name when accessing the Windows-specific vsn, isRemovable, and isCdrom attributes:

```
System.out.printf("volume serial number: %b%n",
                  fileStore.getAttribute("volume:vsn"));
System.out.printf("is removable: %b%n",
                  fileStore.getAttribute("volume:isRemovable"));
System.out.printf("is CD-ROM: %b%n",
                  fileStore.getAttribute("volume:isCdrom"));
```

The totalSpace, unallocatedSpace, and usableSpace attributes are standard attributes that are available to every file store. However, file stores can have nonstandard attributes, such as a compression indicator. You can access these nonstandard attributes by working with FileStoreAttributeView.

The empty FileStoreAttributeView interface can be extended by interfaces that identify groups of nonstandard custom file store attributes. However, the standard class library doesn't expose any subinterfaces. If you have access to a custom interface, you can call the following method:

```
<V extends FileStoreAttributeView> V getFileStoreAttributeView(Class<V> type)
```

This method is used where the file store attribute view declares type-safe methods to read or update the file store attributes. The type parameter specifies the type of the attribute view required and the method returns an instance of this type when supported.

Managing Files and Directories

Paths let you locate files. You will commonly use paths with assorted Files methods to manage regular files, directories, and more. Management tasks that you can perform range from checking a path to determine if the file it represents exists to deleting a file.

Checking Paths

The Files class declares a pair of methods for checking a path to learn whether or not the file that it represents exists:

- boolean exists(Path path, LinkOption... options): Check the file represented by path to determine if it exists. By default, symbolic links are followed, but if you pass LinkOption.NOFOLLOW_LINKS to options, symbolic links are not followed. Return true when the file exists; return false when the file doesn't exist or its existence cannot be determined.

- boolean notExists(Path path, LinkOption... options): Check the file represented by path to determine if it doesn't exist. By default, symbolic links are followed, but if you pass LinkOption.NOFOLLOW_LINKS to options, symbolic links are not followed. Return true when the file doesn't exist; return false when the file exists or its existence cannot be determined.

> **Note**   Expression !exists(path) isn't equivalent to notExists(path). This is probably because !exists() isn't *atomic* (executed as a single operation), whereas notExists() is atomic. Also, when exists() and notExists() return false, the existence of the file cannot be verified.

The Files class also declares several is-prefixed methods for checking a path for additional conditions:

- boolean isDirectory(Path path, LinkOption... options): Check that path represents a directory. It returns true for a directory and false for not a directory, when there is no file backing the path, or when it cannot be determined that path represents a directory. Specify LinkOption.NOFOLLOW_LINKS when you don't want this method to follow symbolic links.

- boolean isExecutable(Path path): Check that path represents an executable file. It returns true when the file exists and is executable and false when the file doesn't exist, when execute access would be denied because the JVM has insufficient privileges, or when access cannot be determined.

- boolean isHidden(Path path): Check whether the file represented by path is hidden. The exact definition of hidden is operating system-dependent. For example, Unix considers a file to be hidden when its name begins with a period character. On Windows, a file is considered hidden when it isn't a directory and the DOS hidden attribute is set. This method returns true when the file is considered hidden; otherwise, it returns false. It throws IOException when an I/O error occurs.

- boolean isReadable(Path path): Check that path represents a readable file. It returns true when the file exists and is readable and false when the file doesn't exist, when read access would be denied because the JVM has insufficient privileges, or when access cannot be determined.

- boolean isRegularFile(Path path, LinkOption... options): Check that path represents a regular file. It returns true for a regular file and false for not a regular file, when there is no file backing the path, or when it cannot be determined that path represents a regular file. Specify LinkOption.NOFOLLOW_LINKS when you don't want this method to follow symbolic links.

- boolean isSameFile(Path path1, Path path2): Check whether path1 and path2 locate the same file, returning true when this is the case. If the two Path objects are associated with different file system providers, this method returns false. It throws IOException when an I/O error occurs.

- boolean isWritable(Path path): Check that path represents a writable file. It returns true when the file exists and is writable and false when the file doesn't exist, when write access would be denied because the JVM has insufficient privileges, or when access cannot be determined.

Each of isExecutable(), isReadable(), and isWritable() checks that a file exists and that the JVM has appropriate privileges for executing the file, opening it for reading, or opening it for writing. Depending on the implementation, the method might need to read file permissions, ACLs, or other file attributes to check the effective access to the file. Consequently, the method might not be atomic with respect to other file system operations.

The return value from exists(), notExists(), isExecutable(), isReadable(), and isWritable() is immediately outdated. The file system may experience changes in the time between the method call and the use of its result. This race condition (https://en.wikipedia.org/wiki/Race_condition) is known as *time-of-check-to-time-of-use (TOCTTOU)*. Check out https://en.wikipedia.org/wiki/Time_of_check_to_time_of_use for more information.

Listing 12-20 presents the source code to an application that demonstrates these path-checking methods.

Listing 12-20. Checking Paths for Various Conditions

```
import java.io.IOException;

import java.nio.file.Files;
import java.nio.file.Path;
import java.nio.file.Paths;

public class CheckPath
{
   public static void main(String[] args) throws IOException
   {
      if (args.length < 1 || args.length > 2)
      {
         System.err.println("usage: java CheckPath path1 [path2]");
         return;
      }
      Path path1 = Paths.get(args[0]);
      System.out.printf("Path1: %s%n", path1);
      System.out.printf("Exists: %b%n", Files.exists(path1));
      System.out.printf("Not exists: %b%n", Files.notExists(path1));
      System.out.printf("Is directory: %b%n", Files.notExists(path1));
      System.out.printf("Is executable: %b%n", Files.isExecutable(path1));
      try
      {
         System.out.printf("Hidden: %b%n", Files.isHidden(path1));
      }
      catch (IOException ioe)
      {
         ioe.printStackTrace();
      }
```

```
System.out.printf("Is readable: %b%n", Files.isReadable(path1));
System.out.printf("Is regular file: %b%n",
                  Files.isRegularFile(path1));
System.out.printf("Is writable: %b%n",
                  Files.isWritable(path1));
if (args.length == 2)
{
    Path path2 = Paths.get(args[1]);
    System.out.printf("Path2: %s%n", path2);
    System.out.printf("Is same path: %b%n",
                      Files.isSameFile(path1, path2));
}
    }
}
```

Compile Listing 12-20 as follows:

```
javac CheckPath.java
```

Run the resulting application as follows:

```
java CheckPath CheckPath.java
```

You should observe the following output:

```
Path1: CheckPath.java
Exists: true
Not exists: false
Is directory: false
Is executable: true
Hidden: false
Is readable: true
Is regular file: true
Is writable: true
```

It might not always be obvious that two paths point to the same file. For example, one path might be absolute and the other path relative, as demonstrated here:

```
java CheckPath C:\prj\books\io\ch12\code\CheckPath\CheckPath.java ↵
.\CheckPath.java
```

This command line runs `CheckPath` on a Windows operating system with absolute and relative paths to the same `CheckPath.java` file. I observe the following output:

```
Path1: C:\prj\books\io\ch12\code\CheckPath\CheckPath.java
Exists: true
Not exists: false
Is directory: false
Is executable: true
Hidden: false
Is readable: true
Is regular file: true
Is writable: true
Path2: .\CheckPath.java
Is same path: true
```

Creating Files

You can create a new and empty regular file by calling the `Files` class's `Path createFile(Path path, FileAttribute<?>... attrs)` method. When creating a file, you must specify a `path` and optionally specify a varargs list of file attributes.

The `attrs` parameter specifies a list of file attribute objects whose classes implement the `java.nio.file.attribute.FileAttribute` interface. Each attribute is identified by its name. If more than one attribute of the same name is included in the list, all but the last occurrence are ignored.

`createFile()` returns the `Path` to the file on success. It throws `UnsupportedOperationException` when the list includes an attribute that cannot be set atomically when creating the file, `java.nio.file.FileAlreadyExistsException` when a file with the same name already exists, and `IOException` when an I/O error occurs or the parent directory doesn't exist.

Note `FileAlreadyExistsException` is an example of an *optional specific exception*. It's optional because it's thrown when the underlying operating system can detect the specific error leading to the exception. If the error cannot be detected, its `IOException` ancestor is thrown instead.

Listing 12-21 presents the source code to an application that demonstrates `createFile()` without file attributes.

Listing 12-21. Creating an Empty File

```java
import java.io.IOException;

import java.nio.file.Files;
import java.nio.file.Paths;

public class CFDemo
{
   public static void main(String[] args) throws IOException
   {
      if (args.length != 1)
      {
         System.err.println("usage: java CFDemo path");
         return;
      }
      Files.createFile(Paths.get(args[0]));
   }
}
```

Compile Listing 12-21 as follows:

```
javac CFDemo.java
```

Run the resulting application as follows:

```
java CFDemo x
```

You should observe no output as well as a zero-byte file named x in the current directory. If you run this application again, you should observe a `FileAlreadyExistsException` message on the standard error stream.

`FileAttribute` is the return type of the `PosixFilePermissions` class's `FileAttribute<Set<PosixFilePermission>> asFileAttribute(Set<PosixFilePermission> perms)` method, which creates a `FileAttribute` that encapsulates a copy of the given file permissions. When creating a regular file, you can use this method to assign a set of permissions on a POSIX file system, as follows:

```java
Set<PosixFilePermission> perms =
   PosixFilePermissions.fromString("rw-------");
FileAttribute<Set<PosixFilePermission>> fa =
   PosixFilePermissions.asFileAttribute(perms);
Files.createFile(Paths.get("report"), fa);
```

Creating and Deleting Temporary Files

Applications often need to create and work with temporary regular files. For example, temporary files would probably be used by a memory-intensive video-editing application. Also, an application that performs external sorting (https://en.wikipedia.org/wiki/External_sorting) would output intermediate sorted data to a temporary file.

You create a temporary file by working with either of the following methods:

- Path createTempFile(Path dir, String prefix, String suffix, FileAttribute<?>... attrs)

- Path createTempFile(String prefix, String suffix, FileAttribute<?>... attrs)

The first method creates this file in the directory identified by dir and the second method creates this file in the default temporary-file directory (identified by the Java property java.io.tmpdir). The name of the temporary file begins with the specified prefix, continues with a sequence of digits, and ends with the specified suffix. Either prefix or suffix may be null. When prefix is null, nothing appears before the digit sequence. When suffix is null, .tmp follows the digit sequence.

On success, each method returns the path to the newly-created file that didn't exist before this method was invoked. Otherwise, each method throws IOException when an I/O error occurs (or, for the first method, when the directory identified by dir doesn't exist), IllegalArgumentException when prefix or suffix cannot be used to create a candidate file name, or UnsupportedOperationException when the attrs list includes an attribute that cannot be set atomically when creating the file.

Listing 12-22 presents the source code to an application that demonstrates the first createTempFile() method (without file attributes).

Listing 12-22. Creating an Empty Temporary File

```
import java.io.IOException;

import java.nio.file.Files;
import java.nio.file.Paths;

public class CTFDemo
{
   public static void main(String[] args) throws IOException
   {
```

```
    if (args.length != 1)
    {
        System.err.println("usage: java CTFDemo path");
        return;
    }
    Files.createTempFile(Paths.get(args[0]), "video", null);
  }
}
```

Listing 12-22 describes an application that takes a single command-line argument, which is a path to a directory in which to store the temporary file. The temporary file is assigned the prefix video and (by virtue of suffix being assigned a null argument) the suffix .tmp.

Compile Listing 12-22 as follows:

```
javac CTFDemo.java
```

Run the resulting application as follows:

```
java CTFDemo .
```

The period character signifies the current directory. You should observe an empty file with a name similar to video5826353313510732011.tmp in this directory.

When CTFDemo ends, the temporary file remains behind, which isn't tidy and would consume disk space if I chose to write data to it. It's better to delete the temporary file before the application ends. There are three ways to accomplish this task:

- Add a *shutdown hook* (a runtime mechanism that lets you clean up resources or save data before the JVM shuts down) via the java.lang.Runtime class's void addShutdownHook(Thread hook) method.

- Convert the returned Path object to a File object (via Path's toFile() method) and invoke File's void deleteOnExit() method on the File object.

- Work with the Files class's newOutputStream() method and NIO.2's DELETE_ON_CLOSE constant. You'll learn about this method and constant later in this chapter.

Listing 12-23 expands on Listing 12-22 by using toFile() followed by deleteOnExit() to register the temporary file for deletion.

Listing 12-23. Registering a Temporary File for Deletion on Application Exit

```java
import java.io.IOException;

import java.nio.file.Files;
import java.nio.file.Path;
import java.nio.file.Paths;

public class CTFDemo
{
    public static void main(String[] args) throws IOException
    {
        if (args.length != 1)
        {
            System.err.println("usage: java CTFDemo path");
            return;
        }
        Path path = Files.createTempFile(Paths.get(args[0]), "video", null);
        path.toFile().deleteOnExit();
    }
}
```

Compile Listing 12-23 (javac CTFDemo.java) and run the resulting application
(java CTFDemo .). You should not observe the temporary file in the current
directory after the application terminates.

Reading Files

The Files class provides support for reading regular file content by declaring
the following methods for reading all bytes or all text lines into memory:

- byte[] readAllBytes(Path path)

- List<String> readAllLines(Path path)

- List<String> readAllLines(Path path, Charset cs)

readAllBytes(Path path) reads the contents of the file identified by path
into a byte array and returns this array. It ensures that the file is closed after
all bytes have been read. IOException is thrown when an I/O error occurs
while reading from the file, and java.lang.OutOfMemoryError is thrown when
an array of the required size cannot be allocated (perhaps the file exceeds 2
gigabytes in length). readAllBytes() is intended for simple cases where it's
convenient to read all bytes into a byte array. It's not intended for reading in
large files.

readAllLines(Path path) behaves as if you specified Files.
readAllLines(path, java.nio.charset.StandardCharsets.UTF_8);.

readAllLines(Path path, Charset cs) reads all lines from the file identified by path into a list of strings and returns this list. Bytes from the file are decoded into characters using charset cs. It currently recognizes carriage return (\u000D), line feed (\u000A), or carriage return followed by line feed as line terminators. Also, it ensures that the file is closed after all lines have been read. IOException is thrown when an I/O error occurs while reading from the file or a malformed or unmappable byte sequence is read. readAllLines() is intended for simple cases where it's convenient to read all lines in a single operation. It's not intended for reading in large files.

Listing 12-24 describes an application that uses readAllLines(Path path) to read all lines from a text file. These lines are subsequently output.

Listing 12-24. Dumping a Text File to the Standard Output Stream

```
import java.io.IOException;

import java.nio.file.Files;
import java.nio.file.Paths;

import java.util.List;

public class DumpText
{
   public static void main(String[] args) throws IOException
   {
      if (args.length != 1)
      {
         System.err.println("usage: java DumpText textfilepath");
         return;
      }
      List<String> lines = Files.readAllLines(Paths.get(args[0]));
      for (String line: lines)
         System.out.println(line);
   }
}
```

Compile Listing 12-24 as follows:

```
javac DumpText.java
```

Run the resulting application as follows:

```
java DumpText DumpText.java
```

You should observe a duplicate of Listing 12-24 on the standard output stream. If you try to dump a binary file, you will probably discover a java.nio.charset.MalformedInputException message instead.

The former methods are limited to reading smaller files into memory. For very large files, `Files` offers the following methods:

- `BufferedReader newBufferedReader(Path path)`

- `BufferedReader newBufferedReader(Path path, Charset cs)`

- `InputStream newInputStream(Path path, OpenOption... options)`

`newBufferedReader(Path path)` behaves as if you specified `Files.new BufferedReader(path, StandardCharsets.UTF_8);`.

`newBufferedReader(Path path, Charset cs)` opens the file identified by path and returns a `java.io.BufferedReader` (with the default buffer size) that may be used to read text from the file in an efficient manner. Bytes from the file are decoded into characters using charset cs. Reading starts at the beginning of the file. `IOException` is thrown when an I/O error occurs. This exception is also thrown when one of `BufferedReader`'s `read()` methods reads a malformed or unmappable byte sequence.

`newInputStream(Path path, OpenOption... options)` opens the file identified by path, returning a `java.io.InputStream` to read from the file. The stream will not be buffered, and it's not required to support the `mark()` or `reset()` methods. The stream will be safe for access by multiple concurrent threads. Reading commences at the beginning of the file.

A varargs list of `java.nio.file.OpenOptions` may be passed. These options configure how to open or create the file. The `java.nio.file.StandardOpenOption` enum implements this interface and provides the following constants:

- APPEND: If the file is opened for WRITE access, write bytes to the end of the file rather than to the beginning.

- CREATE: Create a new file when it doesn't exist.

- CREATE_NEW: Create a new file, failing when the file already exists.

- DELETE_ON_CLOSE: Make a best effort to delete the file when the file is closed.

- DSYNC: Require that every update to the file's content be written synchronously to the underlying storage device.

- READ: Open the file for read access.

■ SPARSE: Open a sparse file (https://en.wikipedia.org/
wiki/Sparse_file). When used with the CREATE_NEW
option, SPARSE provides a hint that the new file will be
sparse. The option is ignored when the file system
doesn't support the creation of sparse files.

■ SYNC: Require that every update to the file's content or
metadata be written synchronously to the underlying
storage device.

■ TRUNCATE_EXISTING: Truncate the length of an existing
file that's opened for WRITE access to 0.

■ WRITE: Open the file for write access.

Not all of these constants apply to newInputStream(); some of them apply to
the newOutputStream() method, which I'll discuss later in this chapter.

When no options are present, this method opens the file with the READ option.

IOException is thrown when an I/O error occurs. IllegalArgumentException
is thrown when an invalid combination of options is specified.
UnsupportedOperationException is thrown when an unsupported option
(such as WRITE) is specified.

Listing 12-25 describes an application that demonstrates
newBufferedReader(Path path).

Listing 12-25. Dumping a Text File to the Standard Output Stream, Revisited

```
import java.io.BufferedReader;
import java.io.IOException;

import java.nio.file.Files;
import java.nio.file.Paths;

public class DumpText
{
   public static void main(String[] args) throws IOException
   {
      if (args.length != 1)
      {
         System.err.println("usage: java DumpText textfilepath");
         return;
      }
      BufferedReader br = Files.newBufferedReader(Paths.get(args[0]));
      String line;
      while ((line = br.readLine()) != null)
         System.out.println(line);
   }
}
```

Compile Listing 12-25 (javac DumpText.java) and run the resulting application (java DumpText DumpText.java). You should observe the same output as previously shown.

Writing Files

The Files class provides support for writing regular file content by declaring the following methods for writing all bytes or all text lines to a file:

- Path write(Path path, byte[] bytes, OpenOption... options)

- Path write(Path path, Iterable<? extends CharSequence> lines, Charset cs, OpenOption... options)

- Path write(Path path, Iterable<? extends CharSequence> lines, OpenOption... options)

write(Path path, byte[] bytes, OpenOption... options) writes bytes to the file identified by path. The options parameter specifies how the file is created or opened. When no options are present, this method operates as if the CREATE, TRUNCATE_EXISTING, and WRITE options are present. All bytes in the byte array are written to the file. The file is then closed, even when an exception is thrown. This method throws UnsupportedOperationException when an unsupported open option (such as READ) is specified. It throws IOException when an I/O error occurs.

write(Path path, Iterable<? extends CharSequence> lines, Charset cs, OpenOption... options) writes lines of text to the file identified by path. Each line is a char sequence that's written to the file in sequence with each line terminated by the operating system's line separator, as defined by the Java property line.separator. Characters are encoded into bytes using charset cs. The options parameter specifies how the file is created or opened. When no options are present, this method operates as if the CREATE, TRUNCATE_EXISTING, and WRITE options are present. All lines are written to the file. The file is then closed, even when an exception is thrown. This method throws UnsupportedOperationException when an unsupported open option is specified. It throws IOException when an I/O error occurs or when the text cannot be encoded using the specified charset.

write(Path path, Iterable<? extends CharSequence> lines, OpenOption... options) behaves as if you specified Files.write(path, lines, StandardCharsets.UTF_8, options);.

Listing 12-26 describes an application that reads a web page and saves its HTML text to a file named page.html.

Listing 12-26. Saving Web Page HTML to a Text File

```java
import java.io.BufferedReader;
import java.io.InputStreamReader;
import java.io.IOException;

import java.net.URL;

import java.nio.file.Files;
import java.nio.file.Paths;

import java.util.ArrayList;
import java.util.List;

public class SavePage
{
   public static void main(String[] args) throws IOException
   {
      if (args.length != 1)
      {
         System.err.println("usage: java SavePage url");
         return;
      }
      URL url = new URL(args[0]);
      InputStreamReader isr = new InputStreamReader(url.openStream());
      BufferedReader br = new BufferedReader(isr);
      List<String> lines = new ArrayList<>();
      String line;
      while ((line = br.readLine()) != null)
         lines.add(line);
      Files.write(Paths.get("page.html"), lines);
   }
}
```

Listing 12-26 uses an input stream reader to connect a buffered reader to the java.net.URL object's input stream. Each line is read by calling BufferedReader's readLine() method and is stored in a list of strings. This list is subsequently written to page.html via write(Path path, Iterable<? extends CharSequence> lines, OpenOption... options).

Compile Listing 12-26 as follows:

```
javac SavePage.java
```

Run the resulting application as follows:

```
java SavePage http://apress.com
```

You should observe a page.html file containing the HTML content of Apress's main web page.

The former methods are limited to writing smaller amounts of content to files. For very large amounts of content, Files offers the following methods:

- BufferedWriter newBufferedWriter(Path path, Charset cs, OpenOption... options)

- BufferedWriter newBufferedWriter(Path path, OpenOption... options)

- OutputStream newOutputStream(Path path, OpenOption... options)

newBufferedWriter(Path path, Charset cs, OpenOption... options) opens or creates the file identified by path for writing and returns a java.io.BufferedWriter (with the default buffer size) that may be used to efficiently write text. Characters are encoded into bytes using charset cs. The options parameter specifies how the file is created or opened. When no options are present, this method works as if the CREATE, TRUNCATE_EXISTING, and WRITE options are present. It throws UnsupportedOperationException when an unsupported option (such as READ) is specified. It throws IOException when an I/O error occurs.

newBufferedWriter(Path path, OpenOption... options) behaves as if you specified Files.newBufferedWriter(path, StandardCharsets.UTF_8, options);.

newOutputStream(Path path, OpenOption... options) opens the file identified by path, returning a java.io.OutputStream to write to the file. The stream will not be buffered and will be safe for access by multiple concurrent threads. The options parameter specifies how the file is created or opened. When no options are specified, this method works as if the CREATE, TRUNCATE_EXISTING, and WRITE options are present. It throws UnsupportedOperationException when an unsupported option (such as READ) is specified. It throws IOException when an I/O error occurs.

Listing 12-27 describes an application that demonstrates newBufferedWriter(Path path, OpenOption... options).

Listing 12-27. Saving Web Page HTML to a Text File, Revisited

```
import java.io.BufferedReader;
import java.io.BufferedWriter;
import java.io.InputStreamReader;
import java.io.IOException;

import java.net.URL;
```

```java
import java.nio.file.Files;
import java.nio.file.Paths;

public class SavePage
{
   public static void main(String[] args) throws IOException
   {
      if (args.length != 1)
      {
         System.err.println("usage: java SavePage url");
         return;
      }
      URL url = new URL(args[0]);
      InputStreamReader isr = new InputStreamReader(url.openStream());
      BufferedReader br = new BufferedReader(isr);
      BufferedWriter bw = Files.newBufferedWriter(Paths.get("page.html"));
      String line;
      while ((line = br.readLine()) != null)
      {
         bw.write(line, 0, line.length()); bw.newLine();
      }
      bw.close(); // You must close the file to write data to storage.
   }
}
```

Compile Listing 12-27 (javac SavePage.java) and run the resulting application (java SavePage http://apress.com). You should observe the same result as you observed for the previous version of this application.

Randomly Accessing Files

Chapter 3 introduced the java.io.RandomAccessFile class for creating and/ or opening regular files for random access. NIO.2 provides an equivalent java.nio.channels.SeekableByteChannel interface.

SeekableByteChannel extends the java.nio.channels.ByteChannel interface and describes a byte channel that maintains a current position and allows the position to be changed. Table 12-1 presents its methods.

Table 12-1. The Methods That Define a Seekable Byte Channel

Method	Description
`long position()`	Return this channel's position, which is a non-negative count of bytes from the beginning of the seekable entity to the current position. This method throws `java.nio.channels.ClosedChannelException` when this channel is closed and `IOException` when some other I/O error occurs.
`SeekableByteChannel position(long newPosition)`	Set this channel's position to `newPosition`, a non-negative count of bytes from the beginning of the entity. Setting the position to a value greater than the current size is legal but doesn't change the size of the entity. A later attempt to read bytes at such a position immediately returns an end-of-file indication. A later attempt to write bytes at the position causes the entity to grow to accommodate the new bytes; the values of any bytes between the previous end-of-file and the newly-written bytes are unspecified. Setting the channel's position isn't recommended when connected to an entity that's opened with the `APPEND` option. When opened for append, the position is advanced to the end before writing. This method throws `ClosedChannelException` when this channel is closed, `IllegalArgumentException` when the new position is negative, and `IOException` when some other I/O error occurs.
`int read(ByteBuffer dst)`	Read a sequence of bytes from this channel into the given buffer. Bytes are read starting at this channel's current position, and then the position is updated with the number of bytes actually read. The number of bytes read is returned. When end-of-stream is reached, `-1` is returned. This method throws `ClosedChannelException` when this channel is closed; `java.nio.channels.AsynchronousCloseException` when another thread closes this channel while a read operation is in progress; `java.nio.channels.ClosedByInterruptException` when another thread interrupts the current thread while the read operation is in progress, thereby closing the channel and setting the current thread's interrupt status; and `IOException` when some other I/O error occurs.

(continued)

Table 12-1. (*continued*)

Method	Description
`long size()`	Return the current size (in bytes) of the entity to which this channel is connected. This method throws `ClosedChannelException` when this channel is closed and `IOException` when some other I/O error occurs.
`SeekableByteChannel truncate(long size)`	Truncate the entity to which this channel is connected to size. If `size` is less than the current size, the entity is truncated, discarding any bytes beyond the new end. If `size` is greater than or equal to the current size, the entity isn't modified. In either case, when the current position is greater than `size` the position is set to `size`. This method throws `java.nio.channels.NonWritableChannelException` when this channel wasn't opened for writing, `ClosedChannelException` when this channel is closed, `IllegalArgumentException` when `size` is negative, and `IOException` when some other I/O error occurs.
`int write(ByteBuffer src)`	Write a sequence of bytes to this channel from the given buffer. Bytes are written starting at this channel's current position, unless the channel is connected to an entity that's opened with the `APPEND` option, in which case the position is first advanced to the end. The entity to which the channel is connected is grown, when necessary, to accommodate the written bytes, and then the position is updated with the number of bytes actually written. This method returns a count of the bytes written to the channel. It throws `ClosedChannelException` when this channel is closed; `AsynchronousCloseException` when another thread closes this channel while the write operation is in progress; `ClosedByInterruptException` when another thread interrupts the current thread while the write operation is in progress, thereby closing the channel and setting the current thread's interrupt status; and `IOException` when some other I/O error occurs.

JDK 7 refactored the `java.nio.channels.FileChannel` class to implement `SeekableByteChannel`. In Chapter 7, I covered `SeekableByteChannel`'s methods in a `FileChannel` context. I specified `FileChannel position(long newPosition)` and `FileChannel truncate(long size)` instead of specifying `SeekableByteChannel position(long newPosition)` and `SeekableByteChannel truncate(long size)` because `SeekableByteChannel`'s documentation recommends that the method return types be specialized by classes that implement SeekableByteChannel so that method invocations on the implementation classes can be chained together.

The Files class lets you obtain a SeekableByteChannel by providing the following methods:

- SeekableByteChannel newByteChannel(Path path, OpenOption... options)

- SeekableByteChannel newByteChannel(Path path, Set<? extends OpenOption> options, FileAttribute<?>... attrs)

Each method opens or creates a regular file, returning a seekable byte channel to access the file. It throws IllegalArgumentException when an invalid combination of open options is specified, UnsupportedOperationException when an unsupported open option is specified, and IOException when an I/O error occurs.

I've created an application that demonstrates SeekableByteChannel in a FileChannel context and also in a more generic context. Listing 12-28 presents the application's source code.

Listing 12-28. Demonstrating SeekableByteChannel

```java
import java.io.IOException;

import java.nio.ByteBuffer;

import java.nio.channels.FileChannel;
import java.nio.channels.SeekableByteChannel;

import java.nio.file.Files;
import java.nio.file.Path;
import java.nio.file.Paths;

import java.util.EnumSet;

import static java.nio.file.StandardOpenOption.*;

public class SBCDemo
{
    final static int RECLEN = 50;

    public static void main(String[] args) throws IOException
    {
        Path path = Paths.get("emp");
        FileChannel fc;
        fc = FileChannel.open(path, CREATE, WRITE, SYNC).position(RECLEN * 2);
```

```
        ByteBuffer buffer = ByteBuffer.wrap("John Doe".getBytes());
        fc.write(buffer);
        fc.close();
        buffer.clear();
        SeekableByteChannel sbc;
        sbc = Files.newByteChannel(path, EnumSet.of(READ)).
                position(RECLEN * 2);
        sbc.read(buffer);
        sbc.close();
        System.out.println(new String(buffer.array()));
    }
}
```

Listing 12-28's main() method first obtains a path to an emp (employee) file. It then invokes FileChannel's FileChannel open(Path path, OpenOption... options) method to open or create and then return a channel to this file.

> **Note** NIO.2 added FileChannel open(Path path, OpenOption... options) and FileChannel open(Path path, Set<? extends OpenOption> options, FileAttribute<?>... attrs) methods to the FileChannel class so that you would no longer have to rely on a classic I/O type (such as RandomAccessFile) to obtain a file channel.

The open() method is called with the CREATE (create a new file when it doesn't exist), WRITE (open the file for write access), and SYNC (require that every update to the file's content or metadata be written synchronously to the underlying storage device) options.

After successfully obtaining a seekable file channel, main() invokes position() on the channel to set the read/write position to twice the length of a record. (Assume that emp is a flat file database divided into records, with each record having a length of RECLEN bytes.) Because position() returns a FileChannel, this method call is chained to the result of the open() method.

At this point, a byte buffer is created by invoking java.nio.ByteBuffer's ByteBuffer wrap(byte[] array) method to wrap the byte array returned from "John Doe".getBytes() into a buffer. The byte buffer is then written to the file channel, which is subsequently closed. The emp file should contain the John Doe byte sequence starting at position 100.

main() now opens emp and reads the recently written contents, which are output. It approaches these tasks generically via newByteChannel() and SeekableByteChannel. Rather than hardcode FileChannel in the source code, it can be advantageous to work with SeekableByteChannel instead, for the same reason that you would declare a list collection variable using the List interface as opposed to the java.util.ArrayList list-implementation class: you want to minimize source code changes should you change list-implementation classes. Although FileChannel is currently the only implementation of SeekableByteChannel, that could change in the future and you might want to minimize source code changes.

After closing the seekable byte channel, I chose to invoke ByteBuffer's byte[] array() method to return the array that backs the byte buffer, for convenience. I pass this array to a java.lang.String constructor to convert the byte array to a string, which I then print. Although array() throws UnsupportedOperationException when the buffer isn't backed by an accessible array, this isn't the case in this example.

Compile Listing 12-28 as follows:

```
javac SBCDemo.java
```

Run the resulting application as follows:

```
java SBCDemo
```

You should observe the following output (along with an emp file in the current directory):

```
John Doe
```

Creating Directories

You can create a new directory by calling the Files class's Path createDirectory(Path dir, FileAttribute<?>... attrs) method. When creating a directory, you must specify a path and optionally specify a varargs list of file attributes.

The attrs parameter specifies a list of file attribute objects whose classes implement the FileAttribute interface. Each attribute is identified by its name. If more than one attribute of the same name is included in the list, all but the last occurrence are ignored.

createDirectory() returns the Path to the directory on success. It throws UnsupportedOperationException when the list includes an attribute that cannot be set atomically when creating the file, FileAlreadyExistsException when a file with the same name already exists, and IOException when an I/O error occurs or the parent directory doesn't exist.

Listing 12-29 presents the source code to an application that demonstrates createDirectory() without file attributes.

Listing 12-29. Creating an Empty Directory

```java
import java.io.IOException;

import java.nio.file.Files;
import java.nio.file.Paths;

public class CDDemo
{
   public static void main(String[] args) throws IOException
   {
      if (args.length != 1)
      {
         System.err.println("usage: java CDDemo path");
         return;
      }
      Files.createDirectory(Paths.get(args[0]));
   }
}
```

Compile Listing 12-29 as follows:

```
javac CDDemo.java
```

Run the resulting application as follows:

```
java CDDemo x
```

You should observe no output as well as an empty directory named x in the current directory. If you run this application again, you should observe a FileAlreadyExistsException message on the standard error stream.

Now, run the resulting application as follows:

```
java CDDemo a/b
```

If directory a doesn't exist before executing this command, you'll receive a message stating that java.nio.file.NoSuchFileException has been thrown. When creating a directory, all specified ancestor directories must exist or this exception is thrown. You can ensure that they exist by working with the Files class's Path createDirectories(Path dir, FileAttribute<?>... attrs) method, which creates a directory after creating all nonexistent ancestor directories. Unlike with createDirectory(), an exception isn't thrown when the directory couldn't be created because it already exists.

FileAttribute is the return type of the PosixFilePermissions class's File Attribute<Set<PosixFilePermission>> asFileAttribute(Set<PosixFile Permission> perms) method, which creates a FileAttribute that encapsulates a copy of the given file permissions. You can use this method when creating a directory to assign a set of permissions on a POSIX file system, as follows:

```
Set<PosixFilePermission> perms =
    PosixFilePermissions.fromString("rw-------");
FileAttribute<Set<PosixFilePermission>> fa =
    PosixFilePermissions.asFileAttribute(perms);
Files.createDirectory(Paths.get("images"), fa);
```

Creating and Deleting Temporary Directories

Applications often need to create and work with temporary directories in which to store temporary files. You create a temporary directory by working with either of the following methods:

- Path createTempDirectory(Path dir, String prefix, FileAttribute<?>... attrs)

- Path createTempDirectory(String prefix, FileAttribute<?>... attrs)

The first method creates this directory in the directory identified by dir and the second method creates this directory in the default temporary-file directory (identified by the Java property java.io.tmpdir). The name of the temporary directory begins with the specified prefix and continues with a sequence of digits. You can pass null to prefix. When prefix is null, nothing appears before the digit sequence.

On success, each method returns the path to the newly-created directory that didn't exist before this method was invoked. Otherwise, each method throws IOException when an I/O error occurs or the directory dir/temporary directory doesn't exist, IllegalArgumentException when prefix cannot be used to create a candidate directory name, or UnsupportedOperationException when the attrs list includes an attribute that cannot be set atomically when creating the directory.

Listing 12-30 presents the source code to an application that demonstrates the first createTempDirectory() method (without file attributes).

Listing 12-30. Creating an Empty Temporary Directory

```
import java.io.IOException;

import java.nio.file.Files;
import java.nio.file.Paths;
```

```
public class CTDDemo
{
   public static void main(String[] args) throws IOException
   {
      if (args.length != 1)
      {
         System.err.println("usage: java CTDDemo path");
         return;
      }
      Files.createTempDirectory(Paths.get(args[0]), "images");
   }
}
```

Listing 12-30 describes an application that takes a single command-line argument, which is a path to a directory in which to store the temporary directory. The temporary directory is assigned the prefix images.

Compile Listing 12-30 as follows:

```
javac CTDDemo.java
```

Run the resulting application as follows:

```
java CTDDemo .
```

The period character signifies the current directory. You should observe an empty directory with a name similar to images403981294881023944 in this directory.

When CTDDemo ends, the temporary directory remains behind, which isn't tidy and consumes disk space. It's better to delete the temporary directory before the application ends. There are two ways to accomplish this task:

- Add a shutdown hook via the Runtime class's void addShutdownHook(Thread hook) method.

- Convert the returned Path object to a File object (via Path's toFile() method) and invoke File's void deleteOnExit() method on the File object.

Listing 12-31 expands on Listing 12-30 by using a shutdown hook to remove a temporary directory before the JVM shuts down.

Listing 12-31. Using a Shutdown Hook to Remove a Temporary Directory on JVM Exit

```
import java.io.IOException;

import java.nio.file.Files;
import java.nio.file.Path;
import java.nio.file.Paths;
```

```
public class CTDDemo
{
    public static void main(String[] args) throws IOException
    {
        if (args.length != 1)
        {
            System.err.println("usage: java CTDDemo path");
            return;
        }
        Path path = Files.createTempDirectory(Paths.get(args[0]), "images");
        Runtime.getRuntime().addShutdownHook(new Thread()
                                             {
                                                 @Override
                                                 public void run()
                                                 {
                                                     try
                                                     {
                                                         Files.delete(path);
                                                     }
                                                     catch (IOException ioe)
                                                     {
                                                         ioe.printStackTrace();
                                                     }
                                                 }
                                             });
    }
}
```

Listing 12-31 creates a shutdown hook that registers a java.lang.Thread subclass object whose overriding run() method will execute before the JVM ends. Specifically, it will execute Files.delete(path); to delete the temporary directory. I'll discuss this method later in this chapter.

Compile Listing 12-31 (javac CTDDemo.java) and run the resulting application (java CTDDemo .). You should not observe the temporary directory in the current directory after the application terminates.

Listing Directory Content

It's often necessary to obtain a list of a directory's entries. NIO.2 provides the java.nio.file.DirectoryStream<T> interface to assist with this task. DirectoryStream subtypes java.lang.Iterable<T>, which makes a directory stream a target for the convenient enhanced for loop statement.

DirectoryStream also subtypes java.io.Closeable, which subtypes java.lang.AutoCloseable. This arrangement makes it possible to use DirectoryStream with the try-with-resources statement to automatically close the directory stream.

> **Note**   When not using try-with-resources, invoke the directory stream's
> close() method after iteration is completed to free any resources held for the
> open directory. A stream is automatically closed when the application ends.

DirectoryStream inherits Iterable's Iterator<T> iterator() method,
which makes directory streams the targets of enhanced for loops. Also,
DirectoryStream declares a nested Filter<T> interface that's implemented
by classes to decide if a directory entry should be accepted or filtered.

You can obtain a DirectoryStream by calling one of the Files class's
newDirectoryStream() methods:

- DirectoryStream<Path> newDirectoryStream(Path dir)

- DirectoryStream<Path> newDirectoryStream(Path dir,
  DirectoryStream.Filter<? super Path> filter)

- DirectoryStream<Path> newDirectoryStream(Path dir,
  String glob)

newDirectoryStream(Path dir) opens a directory, returning a DirectoryStream
to iterate over all entries in the directory. The elements returned by the
directory stream's iterator are of type Path; each Path object represents an
entry in the directory. The Path objects are obtained as if by resolving the
name of the directory entry against dir. This method throws IOException
when an I/O error occurs and java.nio.file.NotDirectoryException when
the path couldn't be opened because it's not a directory.

Listing 12-32 presents an application that obtains and outputs all entries in
the specified directory.

Listing 12-32. Obtaining and Outputting All Entries in a Directory

```java
import java.io.IOException;

import java.nio.file.DirectoryStream;
import java.nio.file.Files;
import java.nio.file.Path;
import java.nio.file.Paths;

public class DSDemo
{
   public static void main(String[] args) throws IOException
   {
```

```
    if (args.length != 1)
    {
        System.err.println("usage: java DSDemo dirpath");
        return;
    }
    Path path = Paths.get(args[0]);
    DirectoryStream<Path> ds = Files.newDirectoryStream(path);
    for (Path p: ds)
        System.out.println(p);
    }
}
```

In Listing 12-32, I didn't bother to use try-with-resources, for convenience. (After all, this is just a small throw-away application.) Also, I didn't bother to call close() because the directory stream is closed automatically when the application terminates.

Compile Listing 12-32 as follows:

```
javac DSDemo.java
```

Run the resulting application as follows:

```
java DSDemo .
```

I obtained the following output:

```
.\DSDemo.class
.\DSDemo.java
```

newDirectoryStream(Path dir, DirectoryStream.Filter<? super Path> filter) opens a directory, returning a DirectoryStream to iterate over the entries in the directory. The elements returned by the directory stream's iterator are of type Path; each Path object represents an entry in the directory. The Path objects are obtained as if by resolving the name of the directory entry against dir. The entries returned by the iterator are filtered by the given filter. This method throws IOException when an I/O error occurs and NotDirectoryException when the path couldn't be opened because it's not a directory.

To create a filter, you need to subclass DirectoryStream.Filter<T> and override its boolean accept(T path) method, making sure to pass Path to T.

This method must return true when path is accepted (included in the directory stream); otherwise, it must return false. The following example demonstrates a filter:

```
DirectoryStream.Filter<Path> filter;
filter = new DirectoryStream.Filter<Path>()
        {
           @Override
           public boolean accept(Path path) throws IOException
           {
              return path.toString().endsWith(".java");
           }
        };
```

This filter accepts only those entries having the .java file extension.

Listing 12-33 presents an application that obtains and outputs all entries in the specified directory that match a specific file extension.

Listing 12-33. Obtaining and Outputting All Directory Entries That Match an Extension

```
import java.io.IOException;

import java.nio.file.DirectoryStream;
import java.nio.file.Files;
import java.nio.file.Path;
import java.nio.file.Paths;

public class DSDemo
{
    public static void main(String[] args)
    {
        if (args.length != 2)
        {
            System.err.println("usage: java DSDemo dirpath ext");
            return;
        }
        DirectoryStream.Filter<Path> filter;
        filter = new DirectoryStream.Filter<Path>()
                {
                    @Override
                    public boolean accept(Path path) throws IOException
                    {
                        return path.toString().endsWith(args[1]);
                    }
                };
```

```
        Path path = Paths.get(args[0]);
        try (DirectoryStream<Path> ds =
                Files.newDirectoryStream(path, filter))
        {
            for (Path p: ds)
                System.out.println(p);
        }
        catch (IOException ioe)
        {
            ioe.printStackTrace();
        }
    }
}
```

Compile Listing 12-33 (javac DSDemo.java) and run the resulting application. For example, I specified the following command line:

```
java DSDemo \temp .java
```

I then observed several files in my \temp directory whose extension is .java.

newDirectoryStream(Path dir, String glob) is similar to the previous method but uses a *globbing pattern* (a simple regular expression-type pattern) to filter files. Also, it throws java.util.regex.PatternSyntaxException when the pattern is invalid.

Listing 12-34 presents a variation of Listing 12-33 that uses newDirectory Stream(Path dir, String glob).

Listing 12-34. Obtaining and Outputting All Directory Entries That Match an Extension, Revisited

```
import java.io.IOException;

import java.nio.file.DirectoryStream;
import java.nio.file.Files;
import java.nio.file.Path;
import java.nio.file.Paths;

public class DSDemo
{
    public static void main(String[] args)
    {
        if (args.length != 2)
        {
            System.err.println("usage: java DSDemo dirpath ext");
            return;
        }
```

```
    Path path = Paths.get(args[0]);
    try (DirectoryStream<Path> ds =
            Files.newDirectoryStream(path, args[1]))
    {
       for (Path p: ds)
          System.out.println(p);
    }
    catch (IOException ioe)
    {
       ioe.printStackTrace();
    }
  }
}
```

Compile Listing 12-34 (javac DSDemo.java) and run the resulting application. For example, I specified the following command line with *.java as the globbing pattern (the double quotes surrounding "*.java" prevent problems related to wildcard expansion on Windows 7):

```
java DSDemo \temp "*.java"
```

I then observed a list of files that have the .java file extension.

Copying Files

A sore spot for many developers regarding the File class is its lack of a copy() method for copying files to other files. The Files class addresses this shortcoming by providing three copy() methods:

- long copy(InputStream in, Path target, CopyOption... options): Copy from a classic I/O input stream to a path.

- long copy(Path source, OutputStream out): Copy from a path to a classic I/O output stream.

- Path copy(Path source, Path target, CopyOption... options): Copy from one path to another.

copy(InputStream in, Path target, CopyOption... options) copies all bytes from input stream in to the target path. On return, the input stream will be at end-of-stream.

A varargs list of java.nio.file.CopyOptions may be passed. These options configure the copy operation. The java.nio.file.StandardCopyOption enum implements this interface and provides the following constants:

- ATOMIC_MOVE: Perform the move as an atomic file system operation. This constant isn't used by the copy() methods because it's meaningless in a copy context.

- COPY_ATTRIBUTES: Copy attributes as well as content.

- REPLACE_EXISTING: Replace an existing target.

CopyOption is also implemented by the LinkOption enum, which provides a NOFOLLOW_LINKS constant (don't follow symbolic links), and which I presented earlier in this chapter.

By default, the copy operation fails when the target already exists or is a symbolic link. If REPLACE_EXISTING is specified and the target already exists, the target is replaced (unless it's a nonempty directory). If the target exists and is a symbolic link, the symbolic link is replaced.

This method returns the number of bytes read or written. It throws IOException for an I/O error, FileAlreadyExistsException when the target exists but cannot be replaced because REPLACE_EXISTING wasn't specified, DirectoryNotEmptyException when REPLACE_EXISTING is specified and the target is a nonempty directory, and UnsupportedOperationException when options includes an unsupported copy option (such as ATOMIC_MOVE).

> **Caution** If an I/O error occurs while reading from the input stream or writing to the target path, it may do so after the target has been created and after some bytes have been read or written. Consequently, the input stream may not be at end-of-stream and may be in an inconsistent state. It's strongly recommended that the input stream be closed immediately when an I/O error occurs.

Listing 12-35 refactors Listing 12-27's SavePage application to use copy(InputStream in, Path target, CopyOption... options) to copy a web page to a file.

Listing 12-35. Saving Web Page HTML via copy(InputStream, Path, CopyOption...)

```
import java.io.IOException;

import java.net.URL;

import java.nio.file.Files;
import java.nio.file.Paths;
```

```
public class SavePage
{
   public static void main(String[] args) throws IOException
   {
      if (args.length != 1)
      {
         System.err.println("usage: java SavePage url");
         return;
      }
      URL url = new URL(args[0]);
      Files.copy(url.openStream(), Paths.get("page.html"));
   }
}
```

Listing 12-35's use of copy() to copy from the URL's input stream to the
Path's page.html file results in a much shorter listing than its Listing 12-27
counterpart.

Compile Listing 12-35 (javac SavePage.java) and run the application (java
SavePage http://apress.com). You should observe a page.html file with
similar content to that generated by the earlier SavePage application.

copy(Path source, OutputStream out) copies all bytes from the source
path to output stream out. If the given output stream is flushable, its flush()
method may need to be invoked after this method finishes so as to flush any
buffered output. This method returns the number of bytes read or written. It
throws IOException when an I/O error occurs while reading or writing.

Caution   If an I/O error occurs while reading from the source path or writing
to the output stream, it may do so after some bytes have been read or written.
Therefore, the output stream may be in an inconsistent state. It's strongly
recommended that the output stream be closed immediately after the I/O error.

Listing 12-36 presents the source code to an application that copies all
bytes from a source path to a file output stream.

Listing 12-36. Copying from a Source Path to a File Output Stream

```
import java.io.FileOutputStream;
import java.io.IOException;

import java.nio.file.Files;
import java.nio.file.Paths;
```

```
public class Copy
{
    public static void main(String[] args) throws IOException
    {
        if (args.length != 2)
        {
            System.err.println("usage: java Copy src dst");
            return;
        }
        Files.copy(Paths.get(args[0]), new FileOutputStream(args[1]));
    }
}
```

Compile Listing 12-36 as follows:

```
javac Copy.java
```

Run the resulting application as follows:

```
java Copy Copy.java Copy.bak
```

You should observe, in the current directory, a Copy.bak file containing the same content as Copy.java.

copy(Path source, Path target, CopyOption... options) copies a source path to a target path adhering to the specified copy options. By default, the copy operation fails when the target exists or is a symbolic link. However, when the source and target are the same, the method will complete without performing a copy.

There are a few additional items to note:

- Attributes will not necessarily be copied to the target.

- When symbolic links are supported and the source is a symbolic link, the final target of the link is copied.

- When the source is a directory, copy() creates an empty directory in the target location (directory entries are not copied).

You may specify the following copy options:

- COPY_ATTRIBUTES: Attempt to copy the attributes associated with this path to the target. The exact attributes that are copied are file system-dependent and therefore unspecified. Minimally, lastModifiedTime is copied to the target when supported by both the source and target file stores. Note that copying timestamps may result in precision loss.

- NOFOLLOW_LINKS: Symbolic links are not followed. When the path is a symbolic link, the symbolic link itself and not the target of the link is copied. It's implementation-specific as to whether attributes can be copied to the new link. In other words, COPY_ATTRIBUTES may be ignored when copying a symbolic link.

- REPLACE_EXISTING: When the target exists, the target is replaced unless it's a nonempty directory. When the target exists and is a symbolic link, the symbolic link itself and not the target of the link is replaced.

This method returns the target Path object. It throws UnsupportedOperationException when options includes an unsupported copy option, IOException when an I/O error occurs, FileAlreadyExistsException when the target exists but cannot be replaced because the REPLACE_EXISTING option was not specified, and DirectoryNotEmptyException when REPLACE_EXISTING was specified but the path cannot be replaced because it's a nonempty directory.

Listing 12-37 presents the source code to an application that copies all bytes from a source path to a target path.

Listing 12-37. Copying from a Source Path to a Target Path

```java
import java.io.IOException;

import java.nio.file.DirectoryNotEmptyException;
import java.nio.file.Files;
import java.nio.file.FileAlreadyExistsException;
import java.nio.file.Path;
import java.nio.file.Paths;
import java.nio.file.StandardCopyOption;

public class Copy
{
    public static void main(String[] args)
    {
        if (args.length != 2)
        {
            System.err.println("usage: java Copy source target");
            return;
        }
        Path source = Paths.get(args[0]);
        Path target = Paths.get(args[1]);
        try
        {
            Files.copy(source, target, StandardCopyOption.REPLACE_EXISTING);
        }
```

```
   catch (FileAlreadyExistsException faee)
   {
      System.err.printf("%s: file already exists%n", target);
   }
   catch (DirectoryNotEmptyException dnee)
   {
      System.err.printf("%s: not empty%n", target);
   }
   catch (IOException ioe)
   {
      System.err.printf("I/O error: %s%n", ioe.getMessage());
   }
}
}
```

After obtaining the source and target paths, `main()` invokes `copy()` with the `REPLACE_EXISTING` option to replace the target when it exists. Without this option, `FileAlreadyExistsException` would be thrown.

Compile Listing 12-37 (`javac Copy.java`) and run the resulting application as follows:

```
java Copy Copy.java Copy.bak
```

You should observe a `Copy.bak` file with identical content to `Copy.java`.

In the same directory as `Copy.java`, create a directory named x. Then copy any file into this directory. Finally, execute the following command line:

```
java Copy Copy.java x
```

You should receive a message about x not being empty as a result of `DirectoryNotEmptyException` being thrown.

Moving Files

`File`'s lack of a proper file-move capability has also bothered many developers. The `Files` class addresses this problem by providing the `Path move(Path source, Path target, CopyOption... options)` method.

`move(Path source, Path target, CopyOption... options)` moves the source path to target. It fails when target exists except when source and target are the same, in which case this method has no effect. If source is a symbolic link, the link (and not its target) is moved.

The following copy options are supported:

- ATOMIC_MOVE: The move is performed as an atomic file system operation and all other options are ignored. When the target exists, either the existing target is replaced or this method fails by throwing IOException. If the move cannot be performed as an atomic file system operation, java.nio.file. AtomicMoveNotSupportedException is thrown.

- REPLACE_EXISTING: When the target exists, the target is replaced unless it's a nonempty directory. When the target exists and is a symbolic link, the symbolic link itself and not the target of the link is replaced.

Moving a path will copy the lastModifiedTime attribute to the target when supported by the source and target file stores. Copying timestamps may result in precision loss. A move() implementation may also attempt to copy other attributes. It's not required to fail when they cannot be copied.

This method returns the target Path object. It throws UnsupportedOperationException when options includes an unsupported copy option, FileAlreadyExistsException when target exists but cannot be replaced because REPLACE_EXISTING isn't specified, DirectoryNotEmptyException when REPLACE_EXISTING is specified but the file cannot be replaced because it's a nonempty directory, AtomicMoveNotSupportedException when options includes ATOMIC_MOVE but the file cannot be moved as an atomic file system operation, and IOException when an I/O error occurs.

Note   move() may be used to move an empty directory. When invoked to move a nonempty directory, the directory is moved when it doesn't require moving the directory's entries. For example, renaming a directory on the same file store will usually not require moving the directory entries. When moving a directory requires that its entries be moved, this method fails (by throwing IOException).

Listing 12-38 presents the source code to an application that copies all bytes from a source path to a target path.

Listing 12-38. Moving a Source Path to a Target Path

```java
import java.io.IOException;

import java.nio.file.DirectoryNotEmptyException;
import java.nio.file.Files;
import java.nio.file.FileAlreadyExistsException;
import java.nio.file.Path;
import java.nio.file.Paths;

public class Move
{
   public static void main(String[] args)
   {
      if (args.length != 2)
      {
         System.err.println("usage: java Move source target");
         return;
      }
      Path source = Paths.get(args[0]);
      Path target = Paths.get(args[1]);
      try
      {
         Files.move(source, target);
      }
      catch (FileAlreadyExistsException faee)
      {
         System.err.printf("%s: file already exists%n", target);
      }
      catch (DirectoryNotEmptyException dnee)
      {
         System.err.printf("%s: not empty%n", target);
      }
      catch (IOException ioe)
      {
         System.err.printf("I/O error: %s%n", ioe.getMessage());
      }
   }
}
```

Compile Listing 12-38 as follows:

```
javac Move.java
```

Run the resulting application as follows:

```
java Move report.txt report.bak
```

This example assumes the existence of a report.txt file. When Move finishes, you should discover a report.bak file instead of report.txt.

Deleting Files

The Files class includes a pair of methods for deleting a file:

- void delete(Path path)
- boolean deleteIfExists(Path path)

delete(Path path) deletes the file identified by path. If path identifies a directory, the directory must be empty. If path identifies a symbolic link, the symbolic link (and not the final target of the link) is deleted. NoSuchFileException is thrown when the file doesn't exist, DirectoryNotEmptyException is thrown when path identifies a directory that couldn't be deleted, and IOException is thrown when an I/O error occurs.

I previously demonstrated delete(Path path) in the context of using a shutdown hook to delete a temporary directory.

deleteIfExists(Path path) deletes the file identified by path when it exists. If path identifies a symbolic link, the symbolic link (and not the final target of the link) is deleted. This method returns true when the file is deleted; otherwise, it returns false. DirectoryNotEmptyException is thrown when path identifies a directory that couldn't be deleted, and IOException is thrown when an I/O error occurs.

Listing 12-39 presents the source code to an application that demonstrates deleteIfExists().

Listing 12-39. Deleting a File When It Exists

```
import java.io.IOException;

import java.nio.file.Files;
import java.nio.file.Paths;

public class Delete
{
   public static void main(String[] args) throws IOException
   {
      if (args.length != 1)
      {
         System.err.println("usage: java Delete path");
         return;
      }
```

```
    if (!Files.deleteIfExists(Paths.get(args[0])))
        System.err.printf("%s does not exist%n", args[0]);
    }
}
```

Compile Listing 12-39 as follows:

```
javac Delete.java
```

Run the resulting application as follows:

```
java Delete x
```

When there is no directory x in the current directory, you should observe the following message:

```
x does not exist
```

Otherwise, you should observe no message.

Managing Symbolic and Hard Links

File systems store regular files, directories, and *links*, which are files that point to real files, directories, or other links. Links are classified as symbolic (also known as soft) or hard. Along with providing methods that take symbolic links into account (such as the copy() and move() methods), the Files class provides several methods for managing symbolic links. It also provides a method for creating hard links.

Managing Symbolic Links

A *symbolic link* (*soft link* or *symlink*) is a special file that references another file. Symbolic links are typically invisible to applications; operations on symbolic links are automatically redirected to the link's *target* (the file or directory being pointed to), except for when a symbolic link is deleted or renamed, in which case it's the link that's deleted or renamed and not the target. Figure 12-3 illustrates a symbolic link.

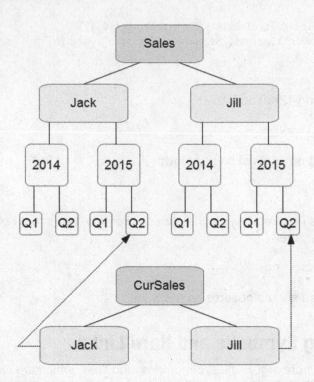

Figure 12-3. *Jack and Jill's symbolic links point to the most current quarterly sales directories (for brevity, Q3 and Q4 are ignored)*

In Figure 12-3, the Jack and Jill files under CurSales are actually symbolic links to Sales\Jack\2015\Q2 and Sales\Jill\2015\Q2, respectively. The Q2 directories are the actual targets of these links. Each link is *resolved* by substituting the actual location in the file system for the symbolic link.

Many file systems use symbolic links extensively. Now and then, a symbolic link may be created that produces a *circular reference* (where the target of a link points back to the original link). For example, directory X could point to directory Y, which contains a subdirectory that points back to X. A circular reference can be problematic when recursively walking a file tree, which is a task that I'll discuss later in this chapter. However, NIO.2's file tree-walking feature takes this possibility into account.

The Files class provides the Path createSymbolicLink(Path link, Path target, FileAttribute<?>... attrs) method for creating a symbolic link to a target. The link parameter identifies the symbolic link path and the target parameter identifies the target path, which may be absolute or relative and may not exist. When the target is a relative path, file system operations on the resulting link are relative to the link path. The attrs parameter identifies optional attributes to set atomically when creating the link. Each attribute is identified by its name. When more than one attribute of the same name is included, all but the last occurrence is ignored. This method returns the link Path object. It throws UnsupportedOperationException when the implementation doesn't support symbolic links or attrs includes an attribute that cannot be set atomically when creating the symbolic link, FileAlreadyExistsException when the link name already exists, and IOException when an I/O error (such as the file store not supporting symbolic links) occurs.

Listing 12-40 presents the source code to an application that demonstrates symbolic link creation.

Listing 12-40. Creating a Symbolic Link

```
import java.io.IOException;

import java.nio.file.Files;
import java.nio.file.Paths;

public class CSLDemo
{
    public static void main(String[] args) throws IOException
    {
        if (args.length != 2)
        {
            System.err.println("usage: java CSLDemo linkpath targetpath");
            return;
        }
        Files.createSymbolicLink(Paths.get(args[0]), Paths.get(args[1]));
    }
}
```

Compile Listing 12-40 as follows:

```
javac CSLDemo.java
```

Assuming the existence of target, a subdirectory of the current directory, run the application as follows:

```
java CSLDemo link target
```

If you run this command line on Windows 7, you might encounter the following error message:

```
Exception in thread "main" java.nio.file.FileSystemException: link:
A required privilege is not held by the client.

        at sun.nio.fs.WindowsException.translateToIOException(Windows
        Exception.java:86)
        at sun.nio.fs.WindowsException.rethrowAsIOException(Windows
        Exception.java:97)
        at sun.nio.fs.WindowsException.rethrowAsIOException(Windows
        Exception.java:102)
        at sun.nio.fs.WindowsFileSystemProvider.createSymbolicLink(Windows
        FileSystemProvider.java:585)
        at java.nio.file.Files.createSymbolicLink(Files.java:1043)
        at CSLDemo.main(CSLDemo.java:15)
```

The solution to this problem is to elevate the privilege of the java application by running cmd (the command interpreter) as an administrator. I showed how to perform this task earlier in this chapter (in order to change the file owner).

Run the application again. This time, you should observe no output. Instead, you should observe a <SYMLINKD> link [target] entry in the current directory.

You might want to determine if an arbitrary path represents a symbolic link. You can accomplish this task by calling the Files class's boolean isSymbolicLink(Path path) method, which returns true when path is a symbolic link; and returns false when path identifies a nonexistent file, is not a symbolic link, or it cannot be determined if the file is a symbolic link.

Listing 12-41 presents the source code to an application that demonstrates symbolic link determination.

Listing 12-41. Determining if a Path is a Symbolic Link

```
import java.nio.file.Files;
import java.nio.file.Paths;

public class ISLDemo
{
   public static void main(String[] args)
   {
      if (args.length != 1)
      {
         System.err.println("usage: java ISLDemo path");
         return;
      }
```

```
      if (Files.isSymbolicLink(Paths.get(args[0])))
        System.out.println("is symbolic link");
      else
        System.out.println("is not symbolic link");
   }
}
```

Compile Listing 12-41 as follows:

```
javac ISLDemo.java
```

Assuming the existence of the previous target directory and link symbolic link, run the application as follows:

```
java ISLDemo link
```

You should observe the following output:

```
is symbolic link
```

Now, run the application as follows:

```
java ISLDemo target
```

You should observe the following output:

```
is not symbolic link
```

Finally, you might want to be able to read the target of a symbolic link so that you can interact with the target directly. You can accomplish this task by invoking the Files class's Path readSymbolicLink(Path link) method.

readSymbolicLink(Path link) reads the target of the symbolic link identified by link. On success, this method returns the target's Path object, which will be associated with the same file system as link. If the file system doesn't support symbolic links, this method throws UnsupportedOperationException. Also, it throws IOException when an I/O error occurs and java.nio.file. NotLinkException when the target could not be read because path is not a symbolic link.

Listing 12-42 presents the source code to an application that shows you how to read a symbolic link to obtain the target.

Listing 12-42. Reading a Symbolic Link

```java
import java.io.IOException;

import java.nio.file.Files;
import java.nio.file.Path;
import java.nio.file.Paths;

public class RSLDemo
{
   public static void main(String[] args) throws IOException
   {
      if (args.length != 1)
      {
         System.err.println("usage: java ISLDemo linkpath");
         return;
      }
      if (!Files.isSymbolicLink(Paths.get(args[0])))
         System.out.println("is not symbolic link");
      else
      {
         Path targetpath = Files.readSymbolicLink(Paths.get(args[0]));
         System.out.println(targetpath);
      }
   }
}
```

Compile Listing 12-42 as follows:

```
javac RSLDemo.java
```

Assuming the existence of the previous target directory and link symbolic link, run the application as follows:

```
java RSLDemo link
```

You should observe the following output:

```
target
```

Now, run the application as follows:

```
java RSLDemo target
```

You should observe the following output:

```
is not symbolic link
```

Managing Hard Links

A *hard link* is a directory entry that associates a name with a file on a file system. It's basically the same entity as the original file. All attributes are identical: they have the same file permissions, timestamps, and so on. Figure 12-4 differentiates between a soft link and a hard link.

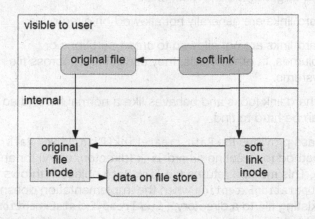

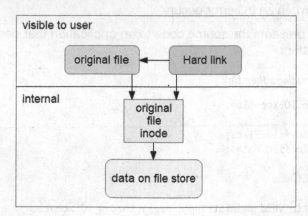

Figure 12-4. A soft link (top) versus a hard link (bottom) in an inode context

Figure 12-4 shows how soft links (symbolic links) and hard links work in a Linux context. The upper half of each diagram shows the user perception of a soft link or a hard link as an alias for some file. However, the bottom part shows what is really happening.

For a soft link, the file points to an inode and the soft link points to another inode. The soft link inode references the file inode, which points to the data on the file store. For a hard link, both the file and the hard link point to the file inode, which points to the data on the file store.

Hard links are more restrictive than soft links:

- The target of the link must exist.

- Hard links are generally not allowed on directories.

- Hard links are not allowed to cross partitions or volumes. In other words, they cannot exist across file systems.

- A hard link looks and behaves like a normal file and so can be hard to find.

The Files class provides the Path createLink(Path link, Path existing) method for creating a hard link (directory entry) for an existing file. This method returns the link Path object. It throws UnsupportedOperationException when the implementation doesn't support adding an existing file to a directory, FileAlreadyExistsException when the entry couldn't be created because the link name already exists, and IOException when an I/O error occurs.

Listing 12-43 presents the source code to an application that demonstrates hard link creation.

Listing 12-43. Creating a Hard Link

```
import java.io.IOException;

import java.nio.file.Files;
import java.nio.file.Paths;

public class CLDemo
{
   public static void main(String[] args) throws IOException
   {
      if (args.length != 2)
      {
         System.err.println("usage: java CLDemo linkpath existfilepath");
         return;
      }
      Files.createLink(Paths.get(args[0]), Paths.get(args[1]));
   }
}
```

Compile Listing 12-43 as follows:

```
javac CLDemo.java
```

Assuming the existence of a `report.txt` file, run the resulting application as follows:

```
java CLDemo myrep report.txt
```

You should observe no output. Instead, you should observe a `myrep` entry in the directory. This entry identifies the same content and attributes as `report.txt`. If you change either `myrep` or `report.txt`, the changes can be observed in the other.

Walking the File Tree

The `Files` class's `copy()`, `move()`, and `delete()` methods copy, move, and delete a single file instead of multiple objects. When combined with NIO.2's File Tree-Walking API, you can use these methods to copy, move, and delete hierarchies of files.

Exploring the File Tree-Walking API

The File Tree-Walking API provides the ability to walk a file tree and visit all of its files (regular files, directories, and links). As well as providing a private implementation that performs the walk, this API provides a public interface for an application to use.

The public interface is centered about the `java.nio.file.FileVisitor<T>` interface type, which describes a *visitor*. At various points during a walk, the File Tree-Walking implementation calls this interface's methods to notify the visitor that a file has been encountered and to provide other notifications:

- `FileVisitResult postVisitDirectory(T dir, IOException ioe)`

- `FileVisitResult preVisitDirectory(T dir, BasicFileAttributes attrs)`

- `FileVisitResult visitFile(T file, BasicFileAttributes attrs)`

- `FileVisitResult visitFileFailed(T file, IOException ioe)`

Each method is called with various arguments that the application code can interrogate. When the method is finished, it returns one of the following constants that are declared in the java.nio.file.FileVisitResult enum type:

- CONTINUE: Continue the walk. When returned from the preVisitDirectory() method, it indicates that the entries in the directory should also be visited.

- SKIP_SIBLINGS: Continue without visiting the siblings of this file. If returned from the preVisitDirectory() method, the entries in the directory are also skipped and the postVisitDirectory() method is not invoked.

- SKIP_SUBTREE: Continue without visiting the entries in this directory. This result is only meaningful when returned from the preVisitDirectory() method; otherwise, this result type is the same as CONTINUE.

- TERMINATE: Terminate the walk.

FileVisitResult postVisitDirectory(T dir, IOException ioe) is invoked for a directory dir after the entries in the directory and all of their descendants have been visited. It's also invoked when iteration of the directory completes prematurely (by visitFile() returning SKIP_SIBLINGS, or by an I/O error when iterating over the directory). The value passed to ioe is null when the iteration of the directory completes without an error; otherwise, the value is the I/O exception that caused the iteration of the directory to complete prematurely.

FileVisitResult preVisitDirectory(T dir, BasicFileAttributes attrs) is invoked for a directory dir before entries in the directory are visited. If this method returns CONTINUE, entries in the directory are visited. If this method returns SKIP_SUBTREE or SKIP_SIBLINGS, entries in the directory (and any descendants) will not be visited. For SKIP_SIBLINGS, postVisitDirectory() will not be called. The value passed to attrs identifies the directory's basic attributes.

FileVisitResult visitFile(T file, BasicFileAttributes attrs) is invoked for a nondirectory file in a directory. The value passed to attrs identifies the file's basic attributes.

FileVisitResult visitFileFailed(T file, IOException ioe) is invoked for a file that could not be visited because its attributes could not be read, the file is a directory that could not be opened, or for another reason. The value passed to ioe identifies the I/O exception that prevented the file from being visited.

Each method throws IOException when an I/O error occurs.

The java.nio.file.SimpleFileVisitor<T> class implements all four methods, offering the default behavior of visiting all files and rethrowing I/O errors. Each method except for visitFileFailed() returns CONTINUE; visitFileFailed() rethrows the I/O exception that prevented the file from being visited.

SimpleFileVisitor declares a protected constructor, which means that you cannot instantiate this class directly. Instead, you must subclass SimpleFileVisitor, which is demonstrated here:

```
class DoNothingVisitor extends SimpleFileVisitor<Path>
{
}
```

After declaring and implementing a visitor class, you can pass an instance of this class along with a Path object that identifies the start of the walk to the following method in the Files class:

```
Path walkFileTree(Path start, FileVisitor<? super Path> visitor)
```

This method initiates a depth-first walk of the entire file tree rooted in start. It invokes the various methods in visitor as necessary. If one of these methods throws IOException, walkFileTree() also throws IOException. The following example demonstrates a walk that starts in the current directory:

```
Files.walkFileTree(Paths.get("."), new DoNothingVisitor());
```

Don't expect to see any output. Instead, you will need to codify the visitor methods to generate output. This task is demonstrated in Listing 12-44.

Listing 12-44. Visiting a File Tree and Reporting Last Modified Times and Sizes

```
import java.io.IOException;

import java.nio.file.Files;
import java.nio.file.FileVisitResult;
import java.nio.file.Path;
import java.nio.file.Paths;
import java.nio.file.SimpleFileVisitor;

import java.nio.file.attribute.BasicFileAttributes;
```

```java
public class FTWDemo
{
    public static void main(String[] args) throws IOException
    {
        if (args.length != 1)
        {
            System.err.println("usage: java FTWDemo path");
            return;
        }
        class DoNothingVisitor extends SimpleFileVisitor<Path>
        {
            @Override
            public FileVisitResult postVisitDirectory(Path dir,
                                                      IOException ioe)
                throws IOException
            {
                System.out.printf("postVisitDirectory: %s %s%n%n", dir, ioe);
                return super.postVisitDirectory(dir, ioe);
            }

            @Override
            public FileVisitResult preVisitDirectory(Path dir,
                                                     BasicFileAttributes attrs)
                throws IOException
            {
                System.out.printf("preVisitDirectory: %s%n", dir);
                System.out.printf("   lastModifiedTime: %s%n",
                                  attrs.lastModifiedTime());
                System.out.printf("   size: %d%n%n", attrs.size());
                return super.preVisitDirectory(dir, attrs);
            }

            @Override
            public FileVisitResult visitFile(Path file,
                                             BasicFileAttributes attrs)
                throws IOException
            {
                System.out.printf("visitFile: %s%n%n", file);
                System.out.printf("   lastModifiedTime: %s%n",
                                  attrs.lastModifiedTime());
                System.out.printf("   size: %d%n%n", attrs.size());
                return super.visitFile(file, attrs);
            }

            @Override
            public FileVisitResult visitFileFailed(Path file,
                                                   IOException ioe)
                throws IOException
```

```
      {
         System.out.printf("visitFileFailed: %s %s%n%n", file, ioe);
         return super.visitFileFailed(file, ioe);
      }
   }
   Files.walkFileTree(Paths.get(args[0]), new DoNothingVisitor());
   }
}
```

Listing 12-44 expands the DoNothingVisitor local class by overriding SimpleFileVisitor's methods. The overriding methods output argument values and then defer to the superclass methods.

Compile Listing 12-44 as follows:

`javac FTWDemo.java`

Run the resulting application as follows:

`java FTWDemo .`

This command line causes the current directory's file tree to be walked. In my case, this directory contains FTWDemo$1DoNothingVisitor.class, FTWDemo.class, and FTWDemo.java. I observe the following output:

```
preVisitDirectory: .
   lastModifiedTime: 2015-09-24T19:31:17.841828Z
   size: 4096

visitFile: .\FTWDemo$1DoNothingVisitor.class

   lastModifiedTime: 2015-09-24T19:25:00.93227Z
   size: 2226

visitFile: .\FTWDemo.class

   lastModifiedTime: 2015-09-24T19:25:00.93727Z
   size: 878

visitFile: .\FTWDemo.java

   lastModifiedTime: 2015-09-24T19:24:53.190827Z
   size: 2324

visitFile: .\out

   lastModifiedTime: 2015-09-24T19:31:17.841828Z
   size: 0

postVisitDirectory: . null
```

To observe output from visitFileFailed(), I executed the following command line:

```
java FTWDemo D:
```

This command line attempts to walk the file tree of a disc inserted into my DVD drive (D:). Because there was no disc in this drive when I ran the application, I observe the following output instead:

```
visitFileFailed: D: java.nio.file.FileSystemException: D:: The device is
not ready.
Exception in thread "main" java.nio.file.FileSystemException: D:: The device
is not ready.

        at sun.nio.fs.WindowsException.translateToIOException(Windows
        Exception.java:86)
        at sun.nio.fs.WindowsException.rethrowAsIOException(Windows
        Exception.java:97)
        at sun.nio.fs.WindowsException.rethrowAsIOException(Windows
        Exception.java:102)
        at sun.nio.fs.WindowsFileAttributeViews$Basic.readAttributes(Windows
        FileAttributeViews.java:53)
        at sun.nio.fs.WindowsFileAttributeViews$Basic.readAttributes(Windows
        FileAttributeViews.java:38)
        at sun.nio.fs.WindowsFileSystemProvider.readAttributes(WindowsFile
        SystemProvider.java:193)
        at java.nio.file.Files.readAttributes(Files.java:1737)
        at java.nio.file.FileTreeWalker.getAttributes(FileTreeWalker.
        java:219)
        at java.nio.file.FileTreeWalker.visit(FileTreeWalker.java:276)
        at java.nio.file.FileTreeWalker.walk(FileTreeWalker.java:322)
        at java.nio.file.Files.walkFileTree(Files.java:2662)
        at java.nio.file.Files.walkFileTree(Files.java:2742)
        at FTWDemo.main(FTWDemo.java:64)
```

The Path walkFileTree(Path start, FileVisitor<? super Path> visitor) method is a shortcut for executing the following method:

```
Path walkFileTree(Path start, Set<FileVisitOption> options, int maxDepth,
                  FileVisitor<? super Path> visitor)
```

As well as requiring a path and a visitor, this method also requires a set of java.nio.file.FileVisitOptions and integer arguments. FileVisitOption is an enum that declares file visit option constants. The only currently supported option is FOLLOW_LINKS (follow symbolic links). The integer identifies the maximum number of directory levels to walk. A value of Integer.MAX_VALUE indicates that all levels should be walked.

If the options parameter includes the FOLLOW_LINKS option, this method keeps track of directories visited so that cycles can be detected. A *cycle* arises when a directory entry is an ancestor of the directory. Cycle detection is performed by recording directory file keys, or, when file keys are not available, by invoking the isSameFile() method to test if a directory is the same file as an ancestor. When a cycle is detected, it's treated as an I/O error and visitFileFailed() is invoked with a java.nio.file.FileSystemLoopException object argument.

The former walkFileTree() method invokes this walkFileTree() method as follows (it doesn't follow symbolic links and visits all levels of the file tree):

```
walkFileTree(start, EnumSet.noneOf(FileVisitOption.class),
             Integer.MAX_VALUE, visitor)
```

Copying a File Tree

The File Tree-Walking API can be used to copy a file tree. Listing 12-45 presents the source code to an application that accomplishes this task.

Listing 12-45. Copying a File Tree

```
import java.io.IOException;

import java.nio.file.Files;
import java.nio.file.FileVisitOption;
import java.nio.file.FileVisitResult;
import java.nio.file.Path;
import java.nio.file.Paths;
import java.nio.file.SimpleFileVisitor;
import java.nio.file.StandardCopyOption;

import java.nio.file.attribute.BasicFileAttributes;

import java.util.EnumSet;

public class Copy
{
    public static class CopyVisitor extends SimpleFileVisitor<Path>
    {
        private Path fromPath;
        private Path toPath;

        private StandardCopyOption copyOption =
            StandardCopyOption.REPLACE_EXISTING;
```

```java
CopyVisitor(Path fromPath, Path toPath)
{
    this.fromPath = fromPath;
    this.toPath = toPath;
}

@Override
public FileVisitResult preVisitDirectory(Path dir,
                                          BasicFileAttributes attrs)
    throws IOException
{
    System.out.println("dir = " + dir);
    System.out.println("fromPath = " + fromPath);
    System.out.println("toPath = " + toPath);
    System.out.println("fromPath.relativize(dir) = " +
                        fromPath.relativize(dir));
    System.out.println("toPath.resolve(fromPath.relativize(dir)) = " +
                        toPath.resolve(fromPath.relativize(dir)));

    Path targetPath = toPath.resolve(fromPath.relativize(dir));
    if (!Files.exists(targetPath))
        Files.createDirectory(targetPath);
    return FileVisitResult.CONTINUE;
}

@Override
public FileVisitResult visitFile(Path file, BasicFileAttributes attrs)
    throws IOException
{
    System.out.println("file = " + file);
    System.out.println("fromPath = " + fromPath);
    System.out.println("toPath = " + toPath);
    System.out.println("fromPath.relativize(file) = " +
                        fromPath.relativize(file));
    System.out.println("toPath.resolve(fromPath.relativize(file)) = " +
                        toPath.resolve(fromPath.relativize(file)));

    Files.copy(file, toPath.resolve(fromPath.relativize(file)),
                copyOption);
    return FileVisitResult.CONTINUE;
}

@Override
public FileVisitResult visitFileFailed(Path file, IOException ioe)
{
    System.err.println(ioe);
    return FileVisitResult.CONTINUE;
}
}
```

```
public static void main(String[] args) throws IOException
{
    if (args.length != 2)
    {
        System.err.println("usage: java Copy source target");
        return;
    }

    Path source = Paths.get(args[0]);
    Path target = Paths.get(args[1]);

    if (!Files.exists(source))
    {
        System.err.printf("%s source path doesn't exist%n", source);
        return;
    }

    if (!Files.isDirectory(source)) // Is source a nondirectory?
    {
        if (Files.exists(target))
            if (Files.isDirectory(target)) // Is target a directory?
                target = target.resolve(source.getFileName());

        try
        {
            Files.copy(source, target, StandardCopyOption.REPLACE_EXISTING);
        }
        catch (IOException ioe)
        {
            System.err.printf("I/O error: %s%n", ioe.getMessage());
        }
        return;
    }

    if (Files.exists(target) && !Files.isDirectory(target)) // Is target
                                                            // an
    {                                                       // existing
                                                            // file?
        System.err.printf("%s is not a directory%n", target);
        return;
    }

    EnumSet<FileVisitOption> options
        = EnumSet.of(FileVisitOption.FOLLOW_LINKS);
    CopyVisitor copier = new CopyVisitor(source, target);
    Files.walkFileTree(source, options, Integer.MAX_VALUE, copier);
}
}
```

Listing 12-45 presents a Copy class with a CopyVisitor nested class (discussed later) and a main() method as its members.

main() first verifies that exactly two command-line arguments, which identify the source and target paths of the copy operation, have been specified and then obtains their Path objects. Next, main() invokes the Files class's exists() method on the source path (there is no point in attempting to copy a nonexistent file). If this method returns false, the source path doesn't exist, an error message is output, and the application terminates.

main() now determines which file-copy operation (nondirectory to nondirectory, nondirectory to directory, or directory hierarchy to directory hierarchy) to perform. It tests the source path, via Files.isDirectory(source), to find out if it describes a nondirectory file or a directory.

If the source path describes a nondirectory file, the compound statement following if (!Files.isDirectory(source)) is executed. This statement first determines whether the target path exists, and, if so, whether or not it describes a directory. If the target path describes an existing directory, the file name is extracted from the source path and resolved against the target path so that the source file will be copied into the directory (and not replace the directory). For example, if the source path is foo (a regular file) and the target path is bak (a directory), the target path following resolution is bak\foo (on Windows). If the target path doesn't exist, it will be assumed to be a nondirectory. In any case, the copy operation is performed. If the target exists, it's replaced.

At this point, the source path must describe a directory (directly or via a symbolic link). Because the only other permitted file-copy operation is directory hierarchy to directory hierarchy, main() verifies that the target path describes an existing directory (via Files.exists(target) && !Files. isDirectory(target)), outputting an error message and terminating the application when this isn't the case.

Finally, main() prepares NIO.2's file tree-walking mechanism to walk through all nondirectory files and directories in the source hierarchy and copy them to the target; and then initiates the walk.

main() creates an enumerated set of FileVisitOptions (the only option presented by this interface is FOLLOW_LINKS—follow symbolic links so that the target of a link instead of the link itself will be copied) and then instantiates CopyVisitor, which I'll describe shortly, passing the source and target paths to its constructor. main() initiates the walk by invoking walkFileTree() with the source path, the options list, Integer.MAX_VALUE (walk all directory levels), and the CopyVisitor object as arguments.

walkFileTree() performs a depth-first walk of the file tree rooted at the source path. During this walk, it invokes the various methods provided by CopyVisitor.

Before visiting a directory, walkFileTree() invokes preVisitDirectory() with a path to the directory and the directory's basic attributes as arguments.

After outputting certain information (which is useful for learning more about this aspect of the walk, and which helps you become comfortable with relativization and resolution), preVisitDirectory() executes Path targetPath = toPath.resolve(fromPath.relativize(dir)); for the following reason: Each incoming directory path is relative to the source path (known in CopyVisitor as fromPath) and it must be made relative to the target path (known in CopyVisitor as toPath). For example, suppose the source path is s, s contains directory d, and the target path is t. When the method is called, dir contains s\d. Relativization produces d; resolution produces t\d.

Variable targetPath is assigned the resolved result (for example, t\d). preVisitDirectory() determines if this directory exists and creates the directory (via the Files class's Path createDirectory(Path dir, FileAttribute<?>... attrs) method) when it doesn't exist. Assuming that createDirectory() doesn't throw IOException, preVisitDirectory() returns FileVisitResult.CONTINUE to continue the walk.

visitFile() is much simpler. It performs the copy operation (after relativizing and resolving the file from the source to the target) and then returns CONTINUE to continue the walk.

Finally, visitFileFailed() is called for a file that could not be visited; for example, the file's attributes could not be read or the file is a directory that could not be opened. It outputs the exception and continues the walk, by returning CONTINUE.

Compile Listing 12-45 as follows:

```
javac Copy.java
```

Before running the resulting application, create, in the current directory, a directory structure consisting of directory s with subdirectory d and, in d, file foo. Then, run the application as follows:

```
java Copy s t
```

You should observe the following messages along with an identical directory hierarchy rooted in t:

```
dir = s
fromPath = s
toPath = t
fromPath.relativize(dir) =
toPath.resolve(fromPath.relativize(dir)) = t
dir = s\d
fromPath = s
toPath = t
fromPath.relativize(dir) = d
toPath.resolve(fromPath.relativize(dir)) = t\d
file = s\d\foo
fromPath = s
toPath = t
fromPath.relativize(file) = d\foo
toPath.resolve(fromPath.relativize(file)) = t\d\foo
```

You might want to preserve source directory attributes (such as lastModifiedTime) in the equivalent target directory when performing the copy. You would accomplish this task by executing the appropriate code in the postVisitDirectory() method (after the files have been copied). For example, add the following method to Listing 12-45 to preserve lastModifiedTime:

```
@Override
public FileVisitResult postVisitDirectory(Path dir, IOException ioe)
{
    if (ioe == null)
    {
        Path newdir = toPath.resolve(fromPath.relativize(dir));
        try
        {
            FileTime time = Files.getLastModifiedTime(dir);
            Files.setLastModifiedTime(newdir, time);
        }
        catch (IOException ioe2)
        {
            System.err.printf("cannot change lastModifiedTime: %s%n",
                              newdir);
        }
    }
    else
        System.err.println(ioe); // should probably throw the exception
                                 // to terminate the walk

    return FileVisitResult.CONTINUE;
}
```

Before leaving this discussion, we should also consider how Copy behaves when a cycle is detected. To find out, we need to create a cycle. I've chosen to use Windows 7's mklink program (for making symbolic or hard links) for this task. Because C:\prj\books\io\ch12\code\Copy\v4 is the current directory, I execute the following command (with elevated privilege) to create a symbolic link named link that points to v4's parent directory:

```
mklink /D link ..\v4
```

/D is specified to create a directory symbolic link. This program generates the following output:

```
symbolic link created for link <<===>> ..\v4
```

I now execute the following command line:

```
java Copy link link2
```

I observe the following prefix of the output:

```
java.nio.file.FileSystemLoopException: link\link
dir = link
fromPath = link
toPath = link2
fromPath.relativize(dir) =
toPath.resolve(fromPath.relativize(dir)) = link2
file = link\Copy$CopyVisitor.class
fromPath = link
toPath = link2
fromPath.relativize(file) = Copy$CopyVisitor.class
toPath.resolve(fromPath.relativize(file)) = link2\Copy$CopyVisitor.class
file = link\Copy.class
fromPath = link
toPath = link2
fromPath.relativize(file) = Copy.class
toPath.resolve(fromPath.relativize(file)) = link2\Copy.class
file = link\Copy.java
fromPath = link
toPath = link2
fromPath.relativize(file) = Copy.java
toPath.resolve(fromPath.relativize(file)) = link2\Copy.java
dir = link\link2
fromPath = link
toPath = link2
fromPath.relativize(dir) = link2
toPath.resolve(fromPath.relativize(dir)) = link2\link2
```

```
file = link\link2\Copy$CopyVisitor.class
fromPath = link
toPath = link2
fromPath.relativize(file) = link2\Copy$CopyVisitor.class
toPath.resolve(fromPath.relativize(file)) = link2\link2\Copy$CopyVisitor.
class
file = link\link2\Copy.class
fromPath = link
toPath = link2
fromPath.relativize(file) = link2\Copy.class
toPath.resolve(fromPath.relativize(file)) = link2\link2\Copy.class
file = link\link2\Copy.java
fromPath = link
toPath = link2
fromPath.relativize(file) = link2\Copy.java
toPath.resolve(fromPath.relativize(file)) = link2\link2\Copy.java
dir = link\link2\link2
fromPath = link
toPath = link2
fromPath.relativize(dir) = link2\link2
toPath.resolve(fromPath.relativize(dir)) = link2\link2\link2
file = link\link2\link2\Copy$CopyVisitor.class
fromPath = link
toPath = link2
fromPath.relativize(file) = link2\link2\Copy$CopyVisitor.class
toPath.resolve(fromPath.relativize(file)) = link2\link2\link2\
Copy$CopyVisitor.class
file = link\link2\link2\Copy.class
fromPath = link
toPath = link2
fromPath.relativize(file) = link2\link2\Copy.class
toPath.resolve(fromPath.relativize(file)) = link2\link2\link2\Copy.class
file = link\link2\link2\Copy.java
fromPath = link
toPath = link2
fromPath.relativize(file) = link2\link2\Copy.java
toPath.resolve(fromPath.relativize(file)) = link2\link2\link2\Copy.java
dir = link\link2\link2\link2
fromPath = link
toPath = link2
fromPath.relativize(dir) = link2\link2\link2
toPath.resolve(fromPath.relativize(dir)) = link2\link2\link2\link2
```

This output continues indefinitely because of the cycle. copy() creates a
link2 directory; copies Copy.java, Copy.class, and Copy$CopyVisitor.class
into this directory; creates a link2 subdirectory; copies these files into this
subdirectory; creates a link2 subdirectory of this subdirectory; copies these

files into this newest subdirectory; and so on. Although `visitFileFailed()` reported the cycle, it's foolish for this method to return CONTINUE. It would be much better to throw the exception and avoid having to subsequently delete huge file hierarchies.

Deleting a File Tree

The File Tree-Walking API can be used to delete a file tree. Listing 12-46 presents the source code to an application that accomplishes this task.

Listing 12-46. Deleting a File Tree

```java
import java.io.IOException;

import java.nio.file.Files;
import java.nio.file.FileVisitResult;
import java.nio.file.Path;
import java.nio.file.Paths;
import java.nio.file.SimpleFileVisitor;

import java.nio.file.attribute.BasicFileAttributes;

public class Delete
{
   public static void main(String[] args) throws IOException
   {
      if (args.length != 1)
      {
         System.err.println("usage: java Delete path");
         return;
      }

      class DeleteVisitor extends SimpleFileVisitor<Path>
      {
         @Override
         public FileVisitResult postVisitDirectory(Path dir,
                                                    IOException ioe)
            throws IOException
         {
            if (ioe == null)
               if (Files.deleteIfExists(dir))
                  System.out.printf("deleted directory %s%n", dir);
               else
                  System.out.printf("couldn't delete directory %s%n", dir);
            else
               throw ioe;
            return FileVisitResult.CONTINUE;
         }
```

```
        @Override
        public FileVisitResult visitFile(Path file,
                                          BasicFileAttributes attr)
            throws IOException
        {
            if (Files.deleteIfExists(file))
                System.out.printf("deleted regular file %s%n", file);
            else
                System.out.printf("couldn't delete regular file %s%n", file);
            return FileVisitResult.CONTINUE;
        }
    }

    Files.walkFileTree(Paths.get(args[0]), new DeleteVisitor());
   }
}
```

Listing 12-46's main() method accomplishes the delete. It first verifies that exactly one command-line argument (identifying the file tree to be deleted) has been specified. It then obtains the argument's Path object and instantiates the DeleteVisitor local class. Both objects are passed to walkFileTree(), which walks the file tree rooted in this path. Symbolic links are not followed.

> **Note**   Delete is designed to delete symbolic links and not their targets. A symbolic link might point to a file that exists outside of the file tree and that shouldn't be deleted.

DeleteVisitor deletes a nondirectory file in its visitFile() method. This method performs the deletion by calling deleteIfExists(). If this method returns true, a message about the file being deleted is output. Otherwise, a message about not being able to delete the file is output. (The file could be deleted by an external process between the time it was discovered during the walk and the time that deleteIfExists() is called.)

Because a directory cannot be deleted until its regular file and other entries have been deleted, DeleteVisitor deletes a directory in its postVisitDirectory() method. When this method is called, all of the entries in the directory will have been deleted. deleteIfExists() is called to perform the deletion.

postVisitDirectory() will only attempt to delete the directory when an exception did not occur while visiting the nondirectory files. If an exception occurs, the exception is re-thrown.

Compile Listing 12-46 as follows:

```
javac Delete.java
```

Assume the following file tree in the current directory:

```
sales
   joe
      2015
         q1
            sales.txt
```

Run the resulting application as follows:

```
java Delete sales
```

You should observe the following output:

```
deleted regular file sales\joe\2015\q1\sales.txt
deleted directory sales\joe\2015\q1
deleted directory sales\joe\2015
deleted directory sales\joe
deleted directory sales
```

Moving a File Tree

The File Tree-Walking API can be used to move a file tree. Listing 12-47 presents the source code to an application that accomplishes this task.

Listing 12-47. Moving a File Tree

```java
import java.io.IOException;

import java.nio.file.Files;
import java.nio.file.FileVisitResult;
import java.nio.file.Path;
import java.nio.file.Paths;
import java.nio.file.SimpleFileVisitor;
import java.nio.file.StandardCopyOption;

import java.nio.file.attribute.BasicFileAttributes;

public class Move
{
    public static void main(String[] args) throws IOException
    {
```

```java
if (args.length != 2)
{
   System.err.println("usage: java Move srcpath destpath");
   return;
}

class MoveVisitor extends SimpleFileVisitor<Path>
{
   private Path srcPath, dstPath;

   MoveVisitor(Path srcPath, Path dstPath)
   {
      this.srcPath = srcPath;
      this.dstPath = dstPath;
   }

   @Override
   public FileVisitResult postVisitDirectory(Path dir,
                                                IOException ioe)
      throws IOException
   {
      if (ioe == null)
         Files.delete(dir);
      else
         throw ioe;
      return FileVisitResult.CONTINUE;
   }

   @Override
   public FileVisitResult preVisitDirectory(Path dir,
                                                BasicFileAttributes attrs)
      throws IOException
   {
      Path targetPath = dstPath.resolve(srcPath.relativize(dir));
      Files.copy(dir, targetPath, StandardCopyOption.REPLACE_EXISTING,
               StandardCopyOption.COPY_ATTRIBUTES);
      return FileVisitResult.CONTINUE;
   }

   @Override
   public FileVisitResult visitFile(Path file,
                                       BasicFileAttributes attr)
      throws IOException
   {
      Path targetPath = dstPath.resolve(srcPath.relativize(file));
      Files.move(file, targetPath,
               StandardCopyOption.REPLACE_EXISTING,
               StandardCopyOption.ATOMIC_MOVE);
```

```
            return FileVisitResult.CONTINUE;
        }
    }

    Path src = Paths.get(args[0]);
    Path dst = Paths.get(args[1]);
    Files.walkFileTree(src, new MoveVisitor(src, dst));
    }
}
```

Listing 12-47's main() method accomplishes the move. It first verifies that exactly two command-line arguments (identifying the file tree to be moved and its new location) have been specified. It then obtains each argument's Path object and instantiates the MoveVisitor local class, passing the source and destination Path objects to MoveVisitor's constructor. Lastly, main() calls walkFileTree() to walk the file tree rooted in the source path. Symbolic links are not followed.

Before a directory's entries can be moved, the directory must be moved. MoveVisitor's preVisitDirectory() method accomplishes this task. You might think that you could use the move() method instead. However, when move() is invoked to move a nonempty directory, the directory is moved only when it doesn't require moving the directory's entries. When the entries must be moved, this method fails (by throwing IOException). The solution is to use the copy() method, which does the following: when the file is a directory, copy() creates an empty directory in the target location (entries in the directory are not copied).

copy() is called with the REPLACE_EXISTING and COPY_ATTRIBUTES options. REPLACE_EXISTING configures the copy as follows: when the target exists, the target is replaced when it's not a nonempty directory. When the target exists and is a symbolic link, the symbolic link itself and not the target of the link is replaced. COPY_ATTRIBUTES attempts to copy the attributes associated with the directory to the target. The exact file attributes that are copied are file system-dependent and therefore unspecified. Minimally, lastModifiedTime is copied to the target when supported by both the source and target file stores. The copying of timestamps may result in precision loss.

Nondirectory files are moved in the visitFile() method by calling move() with REPLACE_EXISTING and ATOMIC_MOVE options. ATOMIC_MOVE configures the move as follows: the move is performed as an atomic file system operation and all other options are ignored (I also specified REPLACE_EXISTING anyway). When the target exists, it's implementation-specific if the existing file is replaced or if this method fails by throwing IOException. If the move cannot be performed as an atomic file system operation, AtomicMoveNotSupportedException is thrown. This can arise, for example, when the target location is on a different file store and would require that the file be copied.

Finally, the directory that was copied in preVisitDirectory() is deleted in postVisitDirectory(), which completes the directory "move".

Compile Listing 12-47 as follows:

```
javac Move.java
```

Assume the following file tree in the current directory:

```
sales
   joe
      2015
         q1
            sales.txt
```

Run the resulting application as follows:

```
java Move sales salesbak
```

You should observe no output. Instead, you should observe a salesbak directory with an identical hierarchy to the sales hierarchy. The sales directory should not be present.

Working with Additional Capabilities

You've explored nearly all of the methods in the Files class, but there is still one group of methods to explore. These methods are designed for use with Java 8's Streams API and *lambda expressions* (anonymous functions that are passed to constructors or methods for subsequent execution):

- Stream<Path> find(Path start, int maxDepth, BiPredicate<Path,BasicFileAttributes> matcher, FileVisitOption... options)

- Stream<String> lines(Path path)

- Stream<String> lines(Path path, Charset cs)

- Stream<Path> list(Path dir)

- Stream<Path> walk(Path start, FileVisitOption... options)

- Stream<Path> walk(Path start, int maxDepth, FileVisitOption... options)

> **Note**   As I mentioned in the book's introduction, I assume that you're familiar
> with the Streams API and lambdas, and won't discuss them in this book. If
> you're unfamiliar with streams, check out my article called "Java SE 8's New
> Streams API" (www.informit.com/articles/article.aspx?p=2198914).

The find() method returns a java.util.stream.Stream<Path> object that is
lazily populated with the Paths of those files that are accepted by a
java.util.function.BiPredicate object. Listing 12-48 presents the source
code to an application that demonstrates find() and BiPredicate.

Listing 12-48. Streaming and Outputting the Paths of All Files That Match a File Extension

```java
import java.io.IOException;

import java.nio.file.Files;
import java.nio.file.Path;
import java.nio.file.Paths;

import java.nio.file.attribute.BasicFileAttributes;

import java.util.List;

import java.util.function.BiPredicate;

import java.util.stream.Collectors;
import java.util.stream.Stream;

public class StreamsDemo
{
   public static void main(String[] args)
   {
      if (args.length != 2)
      {
         System.err.println("usage: java StreamsDemo dirpath ext");
         return;
      }
      BiPredicate<Path, BasicFileAttributes> predicate = (path, attrs) ->
         attrs.isRegularFile() &&
         path.getFileName().toString().endsWith(args[1]);
      try (Stream<Path> stream = Files.find(Paths.get(args[0]), 1,
           predicate))
      {
         List<Path> entries = stream.collect(Collectors.toList());
         for (Path entry: entries)
            System.out.println(entry);
      }
```

```
      catch (IOException ioe)
      {
         ioe.printStackTrace();
      }
   }
}
```

After verifying that two command-line arguments (a directory path and a file extension) have been passed, main() uses a lambda to create a two-argument *predicate* (Boolean-valued function). This predicate returns true when the path identifies a regular file and its file name ends with the specified file extension. Otherwise, it returns false.

Because Stream inherits from AutoCloseable (streams are closed when they're no longer needed), I invoke find() and obtain the Stream in the context of a try-with-resources statement. I then obtain a list of those entries that match the predicate and iterate over the entries, outputting each entry to the standard output stream.

Compile Listing 12-48 as follows:

```
javac StreamsDemo.java
```

I chose to run the resulting application against my C:\windows directory and exe files as follows:

```
java StreamsDemo C:\windows exe
```

I then observed the following output:

```
C:\windows\bfsvc.exe
C:\windows\explorer.exe
C:\windows\fveupdate.exe
C:\windows\HelpPane.exe
C:\windows\hh.exe
C:\windows\IsUninst.exe
C:\windows\kindlegen.exe
C:\windows\notepad.exe
C:\windows\regedit.exe
C:\windows\splwow64.exe
C:\windows\twunk_16.exe
C:\windows\twunk_32.exe
C:\windows\unins000.exe
C:\windows\winhlp32.exe
C:\windows\write.exe
```

The lines() methods return Stream<String> objects that are lazily populated with lines of text. lines(Path path) decodes bytes into characters via the UTF-8 charset. In contrast, lines(Path path, Charset cs) performs this decoding via charset cs. Listing 12-49 presents the source code to an application that demonstrates lines(Path path).

Listing 12-49. Streaming and Outputting All Lines from a Text File

```java
import java.io.IOException;

import java.nio.file.Files;
import java.nio.file.Paths;

public class StreamsDemo
{
   public static void main(String[] args) throws IOException
   {
      if (args.length != 1)
      {
         System.err.println("usage: java StreamsDemo textfilepath");
         return;
      }
      Files.lines(Paths.get(args[0])).forEach(System.out::println);
   }
}
```

In this application, main() first verifies that exactly one command-line argument (identifying a text file path) has been specified. It then invokes lines() on this path and forEach() on the resulting stream to iterate over the strings. I pass a System.out::println *method reference* (a compact representation of a lambda) argument to forEach(), which it executes to output the string. The stream is closed when the application ends.

Compile Listing 12-49 (javac StreamsDemo.java) and run the resulting application (java StreamsDemo StreamsDemo.java). You should observe the contents of the text file on the standard output stream.

For brevity, I'm ignoring the remaining methods. If you need help using them, check out "Java 8 Friday Goodies: The New New I/O APIs" at http://blog.jooq.org/2014/01/24/java-8-friday-goodies-the-new-new-io-apis/.

Using Path Matchers and Watch Services

The Files class provides utility methods for most of the file system tasks that you'll encounter while working with I/O. However, it doesn't provide methods to handle path-matching and watch services. For these tasks, you need to work directly with FileSystem.

Matching Paths

We commonly take advantage of pattern matching to filter out those entries of interest when obtaining a directory listing. For example, we might specify ls -l *.html (Unix/Linux) or dir *.html to obtain a list of those files whose extension is .html.

NIO.2 provides java.nio.file.PathMatcher to support the pattern matching of paths. This interface declares a single method:

```
boolean matches(Path path)
```

matches() compares its path argument with the PathMatcher's current pattern. It returns true when there is a match; otherwise, it returns false.

FileSystem's PathMatcher getPathMatcher(String syntaxAndPattern) method returns a PathMatcher object for matching paths against the pattern described by syntaxAndPattern, which identifies a pattern language (syntax) and a pattern (pattern) via this syntax:

```
syntax:pattern
```

Two pattern languages are supported: regex and glob. When you specify regex for syntax, you can specify any regular expression for pattern. For example, you might specify regex:([^\s]+(\.(?i)(png|jpg))$) to match all files with .png and .jpg extensions. (Chapter 9 covers regular expressions.)

Alternatively, you can specify glob for syntax. The glob pattern language is more limited than regex; it resembles regular expressions with a simpler syntax. The JDK documentation offers several examples of glob expressions, which I repeat here:

- *.java: Match a path that represents a file name ending in .java.

- *.*: Match file names containing a period character.

- *.{java,class}: Match file names ending with .java or .class.

- foo.?: Match file names starting with foo. and a single character extension.

- /home/*/*: Match Unix-like paths such as /home/gus/data.

- /home/**: Match Unix-like paths such as /home/gus and /home/gus/data.

- C:*: Match Windows-like paths such as C:\foo and C:\bar. (The backslash is escaped. As a Java string literal, the pattern would be "C:*".)

The JDK documentation also identifies several rules for interpreting glob patterns. I repeat these rules here:

- The * character matches zero or more characters of a name element without crossing directory boundaries.

- The ** characters match zero or more characters crossing directory boundaries.

- The ? character matches exactly one character of a name element.

- The backslash character (\) is used to escape characters that would otherwise be interpreted as special characters. For example, the expression \\ matches a single backslash and the expression \{ matches a left brace.

- The [and] characters delimit a bracket expression that matches a single character of a name element out of a set of characters. For example, [abc] matches a, b, or c. The hyphen (-) may be used to specify a range, so [a-z] specifies a range that matches from a to z (inclusive). These forms can be mixed, so [abce-g] matches a, b, c, e, f, or g. If the character after the [is a !, the ! is used for negation, so [!a-c] matches any character except for a, b, or c.

- Within a bracket expression, the *, ?, and \ characters match themselves. The hyphen matches itself when it's the first character in the brackets, or when it's the first character after the ! when negating.

- The { and } characters identify a group of subpatterns, where the group matches when any subpattern in the group matches. The comma is used to separate the subpatterns. Groups cannot be nested.

- Leading period/dot characters in file names are treated as regular characters in match operations. For example, the * glob pattern matches file name .login.

- All other characters match themselves in an implementation-dependent manner. This includes characters representing any name separators.

- The matching of root elements is highly implementation-dependent and is not specified.

Listing 12-50 shows you how to obtain a `PathMatcher` object and use this object to match paths.

Listing 12-50. Demonstrating Path-Matching

```java
import java.nio.file.FileSystem;
import java.nio.file.FileSystems;
import java.nio.file.Path;
import java.nio.file.PathMatcher;

public class PathMatcherDemo
{
   public static void main(String[] args)
   {
      if (args.length != 2)
      {
         System.err.println("usage: java PatchMatcherDemo " +
                            "syntax:pattern path");
         return;
      }
      FileSystem fsDefault = FileSystems.getDefault();
      PathMatcher pm = fsDefault.getPathMatcher(args[0]);
      if (pm.matches(fsDefault.getPath(args[1])))
         System.out.printf("%s matches pattern%n", args[1]);
      else
         System.out.printf("%s doesn't match pattern%n", args[1]);
   }
}
```

Compile Listing 12-50 as follows:

```
javac PathMatcherDemo.java
```

Run the resulting application as follows:

```
java PathMatcherDemo glob:*.java PathMatcherDemo.java
```

You should observe the following output:

```
PathMatcherDemo.java matches pattern
```

Now, run the application as follows:

```
java PathMatcherDemo glob:*.java PathMatcherDemo.txt
```

This time, you should observe the following output:

```
PathMatcherDemo.txt doesn't match pattern
```

While you're trying out this application, execute the following command line:

```
java PathMatcherDemo "regex:([^\s]+(\.(?i)(png|jpg))$)" figure1.jpg
```

The double quotes surrounding regex:([^\s]+(\.(?i)(png|jpg))$) are necessary on Windows. You should observe the following output:

```
figure1.jpg matches pattern
```

You would observe similar output for a second argument of figure1.png. However, you would observe that figure1.gif doesn't match the pattern.

Watching Directories

The improved file system interface includes a Watch Service API that's used to watch registered directories for changes and events. For example, a file manager can use a *watch service* to monitor a directory for changes so that it can update its list-of-files display when files are created or deleted.

The Watch Service API consists of the following types in the java.nio.file package:

- Watchable: An interface that describes any object that may be registered with a watch service so that it can be watched for changes and events. Because Path extends Watchable, all entries in directories represented as Paths can be watched.

- WatchEvent<T>: An interface describing any event or repeated event for an object that's registered with a watch service.

- WatchEvent<T>.Kind: A nested interface that identifies an event kind (such as directory entry creation).

- WatchEvent<T>.Modifier: A nested interface qualifying how a watchable is registered with a watch service. This interface isn't used at this time.

- WatchKey: An interface describing a token representing the registration of a watchable with a watch service.

- WatchService: An interface describing any object that watches registered objects for changes and events.

- StandardWatchEventKinds: A class describing four event kind constants (directory entry creation, deletion, or modification; and overflow, which indicates that events may have been lost because the file system is generating them too quickly).

- ClosedWatchServiceException: A class describing an unchecked exception that's thrown when an attempt is made to invoke an operation on a watch service that's closed.

You would typically perform the following steps to interact with the Watch Service API:

1. Create a WatchService object to watch one or more directories with the current or some other file system. This object is known as a *watcher*.

2. Register each directory to be monitored with the watcher. When registering a directory, specify the kinds of events (described by the StandardWatchEventKinds class) of which you want to receive notification. For each registration, you will receive a WatchKey instance that serves as a registration token.

3. Implement an infinite loop to wait for incoming events. When an event occurs, the key is signaled and placed into the watcher's queue.

4. Retrieve the key from the watcher's queue. You can obtain the file name from the key.

5. Retrieve each pending event for the key (there might be multiple events) and process as needed.

6. Reset the key and resume waiting for events.

7. Close the watch service. The watch service exits when the thread exits or when it's explicitly closed (by invoking its close() method).

You create a WatchService object by invoking FileSystem's WatchService newWatchService() method:

```
WatchService watcher = FileSystems.getDefault().newWatchService();
```

You register a Path object with the watch service by invoking either of its registration methods, which identify the watch service and event kinds:

- WatchKey register(WatchService ws, WatchEvent. Kind<?>... events)

- WatchKey register(WatchService ws, WatchEvent. Kind<?>[] events, WatchEvent.Modifier... modifiers)

An invocation of the former register() method behaves as if you specified watchable.register(watcher, events, new WatchEvent.Modifier[0]);.

Each register() method returns a WatchKey object representing the registration of this object with the given watch service.

Within a loop, you will typically invoke WatchService's WatchKey take() method to retrieve and remove the next watch key. This method blocks until a watch key is available. Alternatively, you can call one of WatchService's poll() methods to avoid blocking or to set an upper limit on the block time.

> **Note** A watch key has state. It's in the *ready state* when initially created and in the *signaled state* when an event is detected (the watch key is then queued for retrieval by poll() or take()). Events detected while the key is in the signaled state are queued but don't cause the key to be requeued for retrieval.

After extracting the watch key, you would call its List<WatchEvent<?>> pollEvents() method to retrieve and remove all pending events. You would then iterate over the returned list of WatchEvents, identifying the kind of event and taking the appropriate action.

Finally, you reset the key by calling WatchKey's boolean reset() method. Calling reset() immediately requeues the watch key to the watch service when there are pending events. If there are no pending events, the watch key is put into the ready state and will remain in this state until an event is detected or the watch key is canceled. This method returns true when the watch key is valid and has been reset. When it returns false, the watch key couldn't be reset because it's no longer valid. You can use this condition to exit the infinite loop.

I've created an application that demonstrates how to interact with a watch service. The application doesn't call close() because the watch service is closed automatically when the application ends (although it's unlikely that the loop will ever terminate). Listing 12-51 presents the source code.

Listing 12-51. Watching a Directory for Creations, Deletions, and Modifications

```java
import java.io.IOException;

import java.nio.file.FileSystem;
import java.nio.file.FileSystems;
import java.nio.file.Path;

import java.nio.file.WatchEvent;
import java.nio.file.WatchKey;
import java.nio.file.WatchService;

import static java.nio.file.StandardWatchEventKinds.*;

public class WatchServiceDemo
{
   public static void main(String[] args) throws IOException
   {
      if (args.length != 1)
      {
         System.err.println("usage: java WatchServiceDemo directory");
         return;
      }
      FileSystem fsDefault = FileSystems.getDefault();
      WatchService ws = fsDefault.newWatchService();
      Path dir = fsDefault.getPath(args[0]);
      dir.register(ws, ENTRY_CREATE, ENTRY_DELETE, ENTRY_MODIFY);
      for (;;)
      {
         WatchKey key;
         try
         {
            key = ws.take();
         }
         catch (InterruptedException ie)
         {
            return;
         }
         for (WatchEvent event: key.pollEvents())
         {
            WatchEvent.Kind kind = event.kind();
            if (kind == OVERFLOW)
            {
               System.out.println("overflow");
               continue;
            }
            WatchEvent ev = (WatchEvent) event;
            Path filename = (Path) ev.context();
            System.out.printf("%s: %s%n", ev.kind(), filename);
         }
```

```
        boolean valid = key.reset();
        if (!valid)
            break;
    }
  }
}
```

WatchServiceDemo's main() method first validates that a single command-line argument identifying a directory to watch has been specified. It then creates a watch service, converts the command-line argument to a Path object, and registers the Path object with the watch service. Events are to be triggered when any entries are created, deleted, or modified in the directory identified by the Path object.

At this point, an infinite loop is entered to take the next watch key and poll its events. For each event, the kind is determined by calling WatchEvent's WatchEvent.Kind<T> kind() method. If the kind is OVERFLOW, a message stating this fact is output. Otherwise, WatchEvent's T context() method is called to return the event context, which is subsequently output. For ENTRY_CREATE, ENTRY_DELETE, and ENTRY_MODIFY events, the context is a Path identifying the relative path between the directory registered with the watch service and the entry that's created, deleted, or modified.

Lastly, the loop attempts to reset the key. If reset fails because the key is no longer valid (perhaps because the watch service has been closed), the loop is broken and the application ends. *Resetting the key is very important. If you fail to invoke reset(), this key will not receive any further events.*

Compile Listing 12-51 as follows:

```
javac WatchServiceDemo.java
```

Run the resulting application with a suitable directory argument. For example, I specified the following:

```
java WatchServiceDemo \temp
```

Within the \temp directory, I executed the following commands:

```
md foo
rd foo
copy con test
abc
```

I then pressed the F6 function key.

In the command window where WatchServiceDemo is running, I observed the following output:

```
ENTRY_CREATE: foo
ENTRY_DELETE: foo
ENTRY_CREATE: test
ENTRY_MODIFY: test
ENTRY_MODIFY: test
```

The extra ENTRY_MODFIY: test line probably has to do with writing out the file metadata when the file is closed.

Note   If you attempt to run this application with a nondirectory argument, you will probably observe NotDirectoryException.

EXERCISES

The following exercises are designed to test your understanding of Chapter 12's content:

1. Define file system and file.

2. The File-based file system interface is problematic. For example, File's delete() method returns false when it cannot delete a file. Why is this behavior a problem?

3. Identify the packages that implement the improved file system interface.

4. Identify the types that form the core of the improved file system interface.

5. How do you obtain a reference to the default file system?

6. How would you create a new file system?

7. Define path.

8. True or false: The Path interface represents a hierarchical path to a file that must exist.

9. Describe the element layout of a Path object.

10. What methods do Path and File provide for converting from Path to File and from File to Path?

11. Identify the FileSystem method that returns a Path object.

12. What happens when you attempt to create a `Path` object using syntax that doesn't conform to the syntax that is parsed by the file system provider that created the `FileSystem` responsible for creating the `Path` object?

13. Which methods does the `Paths` class provide for more conveniently returning `Path` objects?

14. Identify `Path`'s methods for returning its name elements.

15. True or false: `Path`'s `boolean isRelative()` method returns `false` to signify an absolute path.

16. How do you obtain a file system's root(s)?

17. How do you convert a relative path to an absolute path?

18. Identify `Path`'s method for removing path redundancies, creating a relative path between two paths, and resolving (joining) two paths.

19. How do you resolve a path string against the current path's parent path?

20. How do you convert the current `Path` instance to a URI object?

21. What does the `Path toRealPath(LinkOption... options)` method accomplish?

22. True or false: The `Files` class provides `static` methods for performing path-matching and directory-watching tasks.

23. Define file store.

24. What method does the `Files` class provide for obtaining a file store?

25. What information can you obtain about a file store?

26. How can you access all available file stores for a given file system?

27. What support does NIO.2 offer for working with attributes?

28. How are attributes organized?

29. Describe the attribute type hierarchy.

30. How can you identify all supported attribute views for a given file system?

31. What are basic attributes? Identify the view for managing basic attributes and name the basic attributes.

32. True or false: You can read basic attributes in bulk by calling `BasicFileAttributeView`'s `BasicFileAttributes readAttributes()` method.

33. Define file key.

34. When you call the Files class's getAttribute() or setAttribute() method to get or set a basic or other kind of attribute value, what syntax must you follow for identifying the attribute?

35. What do the UserPrincipal and GroupPrincipal interfaces represent?

36. When would FileOwnerAttributeView's setOwner() method throw FileSystemException on a Windows operating system?

37. The AclEntry class describes an entry in an ACL. Identify its components.

38. True or false: You can define your own file attributes.

39. Identity the attributes supported by FileStoreAttributeView.

40. True or false: !exists(path) is equivalent to notExists(path).

41. What is the isDirectory() method's default policy on symbolic links?

42. Why should you be careful when using the return values from exists(), notExists(),isExecutable(), isReadable(), and isWritable()?

43. What does the createFile() method do when called to create a file that already exists?

44. Define optional specific exception.

45. How would you set POSIX file permissions when creating a file?

46. In which directory does Path createTempFile(String prefix, String suffix, FileAttribute<?>... attrs) create a temporary file?

47. Identify three ways to delete a temporary file before an application exits.

48. Identify NIO.2's three methods for reading all bytes or lines of text from a regular file into memory.

49. The methods in the previous exercise are great for reading the contents of small regular files into memory. What methods would you use to read very large files (whose contents probably don't fit into memory)?

50. The newInputStream() method supports a varargs list of open options. Identify and describe the open options supported by the StandardOpenOption enum. (Not all of these options apply to newInputStream().)

51. Identify NIO.2's three methods for writing all bytes or lines of text from memory to a regular file.

52. The methods in the previous exercise are great for writing the contents of memory to small regular files. What methods would you use to write very large amounts of content (which probably doesn't fit into memory) to regular files?

53. True or false: When no options are specified, `newOutputStream()` works as if the `CREATE`, `TRUNCATE_EXISTING`, and `WRITE` options are present.

54. What is the purpose of the `SeekableByteChannel` interface?

55. The `FileChannel` class implements `SeekableByteChannel`. Why does it specify `FileChannel position(long newPosition)` and `FileChannel truncate(long size)` instead of specifying `SeekableByteChannel position(long newPosition)` and `SeekableByteChannel truncate(long size)`?

56. How do you obtain a `SeekableByteChannel` object?

57. What did NIO.2 add to the `FileChannel` class so that you would no longer have to rely on a classic I/O type (such as `RandomAccessFile`) to obtain a file channel?

58. What method does the `Files` class provide for creating a directory?

59. True or false: The `Files` class's directory-creation method automatically creates nonexistent ancestor directories of the directory being created.

60. Identify the `Files` class's methods for creating temporary directories.

61. What does NIO.2 provide for obtaining a list of a directory's entries?

62. How do you filter a list of directory entries so that only desired entries are returned?

63. What methods does `Files` provide to copy a file to another file?

64. Two of the `copy()` methods support a varargs list of copy options. Identify and describe the copy options supported by the `StandardCopyOption` enum.

65. What other copy option can be passed to these `copy()` methods?

66. What method does `Files` provide to move a file to another file?

67. What copy options are supported by this file-movement method?

68. Identify the `Files` methods for deleting files.

69. Define symbolic link and circular reference.

70.   Identify the `Files` method for creating a symbolic link to a target.

71.   How do you determine if an arbitrary path represents a symbolic link?

72.   How do you read the target of a symbolic link?

73.   Define hard link.

74.   In what ways are hard links more restrictive than soft links?

75.   Identify the `Files` method for creating a hard link for an existing file.

76.   Describe the File Tree-Walking API.

77.   Identify the types that comprise the public portion of the File Tree-Walking API.

78.   True or false: `SKIP_SUBTREE` is only meaningful when returned from the `preVisitDirectory()` method; otherwise, this result type is the same as `CONTINUE`.

79.   What methods does the `Files` class provide for walking the file tree?

80.   What does the `Stream<Path> find(Path start, int maxDepth, BiPredicate<Path,BasicFileAttributes> matcher, FileVisitOption... options)` method accomplish?

81.   How does NIO.2 support path-matching?

82.   What is the purpose of the Watch Service API?

83.   Identify and describe the types that comprise the Watch Service API.

84.   Exercise 22 in Chapter 2 asked you to create a Touch application. Rewrite this application to use NIO.2 types.

Summary

NIO.2 improves the file system interface that was previously limited to the File class. The improved file system interface features methods throwing exceptions, support for symbolic links, broad and efficient support for file attributes, directory streams, support for alternative file systems via custom file system providers, support for file copying and file moving, support for walking the file tree/visiting files and watching directories, and more.

The improved file system interface is implemented mainly by the various types in the java.nio.file, java.nio.file.attribute, and java.nio.file.spi packages. FileSystem, FileSystems, and FileSystemProvider form the core of the improved file system interface.

Chapter 13 presents NIO.2's support for asynchronous I/O.

Asynchronous I/O

NIO provides *multiplexed I/O* (a combination of nonblocking I/O, discussed in Chapter 7, and readiness selection, discussed in Chapter 8) to facilitate the creation of highly scalable servers. Client code registers a socket channel with a selector to be notified when the channel is ready to start I/O.

NIO.2 provides *asynchronous I/O*, which lets client code initiate an I/O operation and subsequently notifies the client when the operation is complete. Like multiplexed I/O, asynchronous I/O is also commonly used to facilitate the creation of highly scalable servers.

> **Note** Multiplexed I/O is often used with operating systems that offer highly scalable and performant polling interfaces—Linux and Solaris are examples. Asynchronous I/O is often used with operating systems that provide highly scalable and performant asynchronous I/O facilities—newer Windows operating systems come to mind.

This chapter first presents an overview of asynchronous I/O. It then explores asynchronous file channels, socket channels, and channel groups.

Asynchronous I/O Overview

The `java.nio.channels.AsynchronousChannel` interface describes an *asynchronous channel*, which is a channel that supports asynchronous I/O operations (reads, writes, and so on). An I/O operation is initiated by calling a method that returns a future or requires a completion handler argument:

- `Future<V> operation(...)`: Call operation and return a `java.util.concurrent.Future<V>` interface object, where V is operation's result type. Future methods may be called to check if the I/O operation has completed, to wait for its completion, and to retrieve the result.

- `void operation(... A attachment, CompletionHandler<V,? super A> handler)`: Call operation with attachment (an object attached to the I/O operation to provide context when consuming the result) and handler, which is an instance of the `java.nio.channels.CompletionHandler<V, A>` interface, as arguments. A is the type of the attachment. V is the result type of the I/O operation. The `attachment` is important for cases where a stateless `CompletionHandler` object is used to consume the result of many I/O operations. The handler is invoked to consume the result of the I/O operation when it completes or fails.

`CompletionHandler` declares the following methods to consume the result of an operation when it completes successfully, and to learn why the operation failed and take appropriate action:

- `void completed(V result, A attachment)`: Called when the operation completes successfully. The operation's result is identified by `result` and the object attached to the operation when it was initiated is identified by `attachment`.

- `void failed(Throwable t, A attachment)`: Called when the operation fails. The reason why the operation failed is identified by t and the object attached to the operation when it was initiated is identified by `attachment`.

After being called, the method returns immediately. You then call `Future` methods or provide code in the `CompletionHandler` implementation to learn more about the I/O operation status and/or process the I/O operation's results.

CANCELLATION

Future declares the boolean cancel(boolean mayInterruptIfRunning) method to cancel execution. This method causes all threads waiting on the result of the I/O operation to throw java.util.concurrent.CancellationException. Whether the underlying I/O operation can be cancelled is highly implementation-specific and is therefore not specified. If cancellation leaves the channel or the entity to which it's connected in an inconsistent state, the channel is put into an implementation-specific error state that prevents further attempts to initiate I/O operations that are similar to the cancelled operation. For example, if an operation is cancelled, but the implementation cannot guarantee that bytes have not been read from the channel, it puts the channel into an error state. Further attempts to initiate an operation cause an unspecified runtime exception to be thrown. Similarly, if an operation is cancelled, but the implementation cannot guarantee that bytes have not been written to the channel, subsequent attempts to initiate an operation will fail with an unspecified runtime exception.

If cancel() is invoked with mayInterruptIfRunning set to true, the I/O operation may be interrupted by closing the channel. In this case, all threads waiting on the I/O operation result throw CancellationException and any other I/O operations outstanding on the channel complete by throwing java.nio.channels.AsynchronousCloseException.

When cancel() is invoked to cancel reads or writes, it's recommended that all buffers used in the I/O operations be discarded, or that care be taken to ensure that the buffers are not accessed while the channel remains open.

AsynchronousChannel extends the java.nio.channels.Channel interface (see Chapter 7 for a discussion of Channel), inheriting its isOpen() and close() methods. The close() method is subject to the following additional stipulation: Any outstanding asynchronous operations on this channel will complete with thrown AsynchronousCloseException objects. After a channel is closed, further attempts to initiate asynchronous I/O operations complete immediately with cause java.nio.channels.ClosedChannelException.

> **Note** Asynchronous channels are safe for use by multiple concurrent threads. Some channel implementations may support concurrent reading and writing, but may not allow more than one read and one write to be outstanding at any given time.

The `java.nio.channels.AsynchronousByteChannel` interface extends `AsynchronousChannel`. It offers the following four methods:

- `Future<Integer> read(ByteBuffer dst)`: Read a sequence of bytes from this channel into the byte buffer. Return a `Future` to access the bytes when available.

- `<A> void read(ByteBuffer dst, A attachment, CompletionHandler<Integer,? super A> handler)`: Read a sequence of bytes from this channel into the byte buffer. Access the bytes in the `CompletionHandler`.

- `Future<Integer> write(ByteBuffer src)`: Write a sequence of bytes to this channel from the byte buffer. Return a `Future` to access the write count when available.

- `<A> void write(ByteBuffer src, A attachment, CompletionHandler<Integer,? super A> handler)`: Write a sequence of bytes to this channel from the byte buffer. Access the write count in the `CompletionHandler`.

The `read()` methods throw `java.nio.channels.ReadPendingException` when the channel doesn't allow more than one read to be outstanding and a previous read has not completed. The `write()` methods throw `java.nio.channels.WritePendingException` when the channel doesn't allow more than one write to be outstanding and a previous write has not completed.

Caution   A `java.nio.ByteBuffer` object isn't safe for use by multiple concurrent threads. When a read or write is initiated, care must be taken to ensure that the buffer isn't accessed until the operation completes.

Asynchronous File Channels

The abstract `java.nio.channels.AsynchronousFileChannel` class describes an asynchronous channel for reading, writing, and manipulating a file. This channel is created when a file is opened by invoking one of `AsynchronousFileChannel`'s `open()` methods, as follows:

```
AsynchronousFileChannel ch;
ch = AsynchronousFileChannel.open(Paths.get("somefile"));
```

The file contains a variable-length sequence of bytes that can be read and written, and whose current size can be queried. The size of the file increases when bytes are written beyond its current size; the size decreases when the file is truncated.

Files are read and written by calling AsynchronousFileChannel's read() and write() methods. One pair returns a Future and the other pair receives a CompletionHandler as an argument.

> **Caution** AsynchronousFileChannel implements AsynchronousChannel instead of AsynchronousByteChannel because this class's read() and write() methods take position arguments and AsynchronousByteChannel's read() and write() methods don't support the concept of position.

An asynchronous file channel doesn't have a current position within the file. Instead, the file position is passed as an argument to each read() and write() method that initiates asynchronous operations.

> **Note** The read() and write() methods must provide an absolute position (relative to zero) in the file from which to read and write. There is no point for a file to have an associated position and for reads/writes to occur relative to this position because reads/writes can be initiated before previous operations have completed and the order in which they occur isn't guaranteed. For the same reason, there are no methods in the AsynchronousFileChannel class (as there are in java.nio.channels.FileChannel) for setting and querying the position.

In addition to supporting reads and writes, AsynchronousFileChannel defines the following operations:

- Updates made to a file may be forced out to the underlying storage device, ensuring that data isn't lost in case of a system crash. Call void force(boolean metaData) to accomplish this task.

- A region of a file may be locked against access by other programs. Call the various lock() and tryLock() methods to accomplish this task. Two of the lock() methods return a Future and take a CompletionHandler as an argument.

I've created an AFCDemo application that uses AsynchronousFileChannel to open a file and read up to the first 1024 bytes in a Future context. Listing 13-1 presents the source code.

Listing 13-1. Reading Bytes from a File and Polling the Returned Future for Completion

```java
import java.io.IOException;

import java.nio.ByteBuffer;

import java.nio.channels.AsynchronousFileChannel;

import java.nio.file.Path;
import java.nio.file.Paths;

import java.util.concurrent.Future;

public class AFCDemo
{
    public static void main(String[] args) throws Exception
    {
        if (args.length != 1)
        {
            System.err.println("usage: java AFCDemo path");
            return;
        }
        Path path = Paths.get(args[0]);
        AsynchronousFileChannel ch = AsynchronousFileChannel.open(path);
        ByteBuffer buf = ByteBuffer.allocate(1024);
        Future<Integer> result = ch.read(buf, 0);
        while (!result.isDone())
        {
            System.out.println("Sleeping...");
            Thread.sleep(500);
        }
        System.out.println("Finished = " + result.isDone());
        System.out.println("Bytes read = " + result.get());
        ch.close();
    }
}
```

After verifying that a single command-line argument identifying a file path has been specified, the main() method obtains a java.nio.file.Path object that wraps this argument and passes it to AsynchronousFileChannel's AsynchronousFileChannel open(Path file, OpenOption... options) method. This method is called to open an existing file for reading.

> **Note** The AsynchronousFileChannel open(Path file, OpenOption... options) method attempts to open or create a file for reading and/or writing, returning an asynchronous file channel to access the file. A variable number of options described by the java.nio.file.OpenOption interface and implemented by the java.nio.file.StandardOpenOption enum may be passed as arguments. When no options are specified, open() attempts to open an existing file for reading.

Assuming that an existing file is opened successfully, a byte buffer is allocated and a read operation starting at position 0 is initiated. The returned Future<Integer> object is repeatedly interrogated by calling its isDone() method, which returns true when the operation completes. Until this method returns true, the while loop alternately outputs a sleeping message and sleeps for 500 milliseconds. Lastly, the done status and number of bytes read are output, and the channel is closed.

Compile Listing 13-1 as follows:

```
javac AFCDemo.java
```

Run the resulting application as follows:

```
java AFCDemo AFCDemo.java
```

You should observe output similar to the following:

```
Sleeping...
Finished = true
Bytes read = 907
```

I've also created a second AFCDemo application that uses AsynchronousFileChannel to open a file and read up to the first 1024 bytes in a CompletionHandler context. Listing 13-2 presents the source code.

Listing 13-2. Reading Bytes from a File and Displaying the Results in a Completion Handler

```
import java.io.IOException;

import java.nio.ByteBuffer;

import java.nio.channels.AsynchronousFileChannel;
import java.nio.channels.CompletionHandler;
```

```java
import java.nio.file.Path;
import java.nio.file.Paths;

public class AFCDemo
{
   public static void main(String[] args) throws Exception
   {
      if (args.length != 1)
      {
         System.err.println("usage: java AFCDemo path");
         return;
      }
      Path path = Paths.get(args[0]);
      AsynchronousFileChannel ch = AsynchronousFileChannel.open(path);
      ByteBuffer buf = ByteBuffer.allocate(1024);
      Thread mainThd = Thread.currentThread();
      ch.read(buf, 0, null,
              new CompletionHandler<Integer, Void>()
              {
                 @Override
                 public void completed(Integer result, Void v)
                 {
                    System.out.println("Bytes read = " + result);
                    mainThd.interrupt();
                 }
                 @Override
                 public void failed(Throwable t, Void v)
                 {
                    System.out.println("Failure: " + t.toString());
                    mainThd.interrupt();
                 }
              });
      System.out.println("Waiting for completion");
      try
      {
         mainThd.join();
      }
      catch (InterruptedException ie)
      {
         System.out.println("Terminating");
      }
      ch.close();
   }
}
```

The main() method verifies that a single command-line argument identifying
a file path has been specified, and then obtains a Path object that wraps this
argument and attempts to open this path. If successful, main() allocates a
byte buffer, obtains the main thread reference, and calls read().

The read() call doesn't require an attachment, but does require a completion handler. This handler's completed() method is called when successful and outputs the number of bytes read. The handler's failed() method is called on failure and outputs a suitable failure message.

Whether the operation succeeds or fails, each method invokes interrupt() on the main thread reference. The methods do so because, after outputting a message, the main thread calls the join() method on its java.lang. Thread reference, which causes the main thread to block indefinitely. The thread can be woken up only by throwing java.lang.InterruptedException, and this happens only when the interrupt() method is called after the I/O operation completes. Lastly, main() closes the channel.

Compile Listing 13-2 as follows:

```
javac AFCDemo.java
```

A JDK 7 compiler would report an error about mainThd not being declared final, as in final Thread mainThd = Thread.currentThread();. JDK 8 doesn't require mainThd to be declared final as long as this variable is *effectively final* (a variable that isn't modified after being initialized).

Run the resulting application as follows:

```
java AFCDemo AFCDemo.java
```

You should observe the following output:

```
Waiting for completion
Bytes read = 1024
Terminating
```

Asynchronous Socket Channels

The abstract java.nio.channels.AsynchronousServerSocketChannel class describes an asynchronous channel for stream-oriented listening sockets. Its counterpart channel for stream-oriented connecting sockets is described by the abstract java.nio.channels.AsynchronousSocketChannel class.

> **Note** AsynchronousServerSocketChannel implements
> AsynchronousChannel instead of AsynchronousByteChannel because it
> doesn't declare read()/write() methods. AsynchronousSocketChannel
> implements AsynchronousByteChannel.

AsynchronousServerSocketChannel

To obtain an AsynchronousServerSocketChannel object, invoke this class's AsynchronousServerSocketChannel open() class method, as follows:

```
AsynchronousServerSocketChannel ch;
ch = AsynchronousServerSocketChannel.open();
```

According to AsynchronousServerSocketChannel's documentation, this method returns an asynchronous server socket channel that's bound to the default group. The alternative AsynchronousServerSocketChannel open(AsynchronousChannelGroup group) method returns an asynchronous server socket channel that's bound to the specified group. I'll discuss asynchronous channel groups later in this chapter.

You can configure an asynchronous server socket channel by invoking the <T> AsynchronousServerSocketChannel setOption(SocketOption<T> name, T value) generic method. The only documented options that are supported are SO_RCVBUF and SO_REUSEADDR.

A newly-created and possibly configured asynchronous server socket channel is open but not yet bound to a local address. It can be bound to a local address and configured to listen for connections by invoking one of AsynchronousServerSocketChannel's bind() methods. Once bound, either of its accept() methods (one method returns a Future and the other method takes a CompletionHandler argument) is used to initiate the accepting of connections to the channel's socket. Attempting to invoke accept() on an unbound channel results in java.nio.channels.NotYetBoundException.

> **Note** Asynchronous server socket channels are safe for use by multiple concurrent threads, although at most one accept operation can be outstanding at any time. If a thread initiates an accept operation before a previous accept operation ends, java.nio.channels.AcceptPendingException is thrown.

To demonstrate AsynchronousServerSocketChannel, I've created a Server application consisting of Server, Attachment, ConnectionHandler, and ReadWriteHandler classes. Listing 13-3 presents Server's source code.

Listing 13-3. Launching a Server That Handles Connections and Reads/Writes Asynchronously

```java
import java.io.IOException;

import java.net.InetSocketAddress;

import java.nio.channels.AsynchronousServerSocketChannel;

public class Server
{
    private final static int PORT = 9090;

    private final static String HOST = "localhost";

    public static void main(String[] args)
    {
        AsynchronousServerSocketChannel channelServer;
        try
        {
            channelServer = AsynchronousServerSocketChannel.open();
            channelServer.bind(new InetSocketAddress(HOST, PORT));
            System.out.printf("Server listening at %s%n",
                              channelServer.getLocalAddress());
        }
        catch (IOException ioe)
        {
            System.err.println("Unable to open or bind server socket channel");
            return;
        }

        Attachment att = new Attachment();
        att.channelServer = channelServer;
        channelServer.accept(att, new ConnectionHandler());

        try
        {
            Thread.currentThread().join();
        }
        catch (InterruptedException ie)
        {
            System.out.println("Server terminating");
        }
    }
}
```

Listing 13-3's main() method first attempts to open an asynchronous server socket channel and then bind it to a local address, which happens to be port 9090 on the localhost. It then calls AsynchronousServerSocketChannel's

SocketAddress getLocalAddress() method to return the socket address to which this channel's socket (the local socket) is bound. Finally, it outputs a message stating that the server is listening at this address.

If an exception is thrown, the server outputs a message and terminates. Otherwise, it creates an Attachment object and initializes the object's channelServer field to the newly-opened asynchronous server socket channel. (For convenience, I directly access public fields instead of calling getter and setter methods.) This field will be accessed by the ConnectionHandler object that is subsequently created, and which is passed with the Attachment object to the <A> void accept(A attachment, Compl etionHandler<AsynchronousSocketChannel,? super A> handler) generic method. accept() listens for incoming connections and processes them accordingly via the ConnectionHandler object.

At this point, main()'s thread of execution blocks by calling Thread.join(). The only way to unblock this thread and return from main() is to interrupt the thread from another thread. However, I have not implemented this feature.

The server can interact with multiple clients simultaneously via a single ConnectionHandler object and multiple ReadWriteHandler objects (one object per client). The Attachment class lets the connection and read/write handlers conveniently access the server socket channel. Also, it records client-specific details. Listing 13-4 presents Attachment's source code.

Listing 13-4. Bundling Fields That the Server and Clients Use to Communicate

```
import java.net.SocketAddress;

import java.nio.ByteBuffer;

import java.nio.channels.AsynchronousServerSocketChannel;
import java.nio.channels.AsynchronousSocketChannel;

public class Attachment
{
    public AsynchronousServerSocketChannel channelServer;
    public AsynchronousSocketChannel channelClient;
    public boolean isReadMode;
    public ByteBuffer buffer;
    public SocketAddress clientAddr;
}
```

The channelServer field stores the reference to the server socket channel that was created in the Server class's main() method. It's used by the connection handler to call AsynchronousServerSocketChannel's accept() method.

The channelClient field stores the reference to the socket channel that is passed to ConnectionHandler's completed() method in response to accept() successfully accepting a client connection. It's also used in this method to perform an initial read() call, and to perform read()/write() calls in the ReadWriteHandler object.

The isReadMode field indicates that a read (true) or write (false) operation was performed before the ReadWriteHandler object's completed() method was called. For a read, completed() obtains and outputs the read data. The completed() method ends by performing the opposite operation.

The buffer field identifies the byte buffer that's created in the connection handler and that's used to communicate bytes between the server and a client. Each client has its own byte buffer.

Finally, the clientAddr field stores the java.net.SocketAddress of the remote client. It stores the client's socket address and is output as part of various client-specific messages.

Listing 13-5 presents ConnectionHandler's source code.

Listing 13-5. Managing Connections from Clients

```java
import java.io.IOException;

import java.net.SocketAddress;

import java.nio.ByteBuffer;

import java.nio.channels.AsynchronousSocketChannel;
import java.nio.channels.CompletionHandler;

public class ConnectionHandler
    implements CompletionHandler<AsynchronousSocketChannel, Attachment>
{
    @Override
    public void completed(AsynchronousSocketChannel channelClient,
                          Attachment att)
    {
        try
        {
            SocketAddress clientAddr = channelClient.getRemoteAddress();
            System.out.printf("Accepted connection from %s%n", clientAddr);

            att.channelServer.accept(att, this);

            Attachment newAtt = new Attachment();
            newAtt.channelServer = att.channelServer;
            newAtt.channelClient = channelClient;
```

```
            newAtt.isReadMode = true;
            newAtt.buffer = ByteBuffer.allocate(2048);
            newAtt.clientAddr = clientAddr;
            ReadWriteHandler rwh = new ReadWriteHandler();
            channelClient.read(newAtt.buffer, newAtt, rwh);
        }
        catch (IOException ioe)
        {
            ioe.printStackTrace();
        }
    }

    @Override
    public void failed(Throwable t, Attachment att)
    {
        System.out.println("Failed to accept connection");
    }
}
```

ConnectionHandler is a CompletionHandler that responds to incoming connections. Its completed() method is called when a connection is successful; otherwise, its failed() method is called.

The completed() method's first task is to obtain and output the client's socket address for identification. I specified channelClient.getRemoteAddress() instead of channelClient.getLocalAddress() to return the client's socket address because the socket corresponding to channelClient was created on the server side and it communicates with the client-side socket. Calling getLocalAddress() on channelClient returns the server-side socket address. Calling getRemoteAddress() on channelClient returns the client-side socket address.

Next, completed() calls accept() on the server socket channel with the passed Attachment object and a reference to the current completion handler as arguments. This call allows the server to respond to the next incoming connection.

The accept() method is called on the server socket channel referenced from the Attachment object passed to completed(). This same object is passed as the first argument to accept(). None of the other fields in the Attachment object have been initialized because they aren't required. This Attachment object is only needed to identify the server socket channel.

After calling accept(), a second Attachment object is created and initialized in preparation for reading from the client. Also, a ReadWriteHandler object is created to respond to the read operation. The new Attachment object's byte buffer, the new Attachment object, and the ReadWriteHandler object are passed as arguments to the client socket channel's read() method.

Listing 13-6 presents ReadWriteHandler's source code.

Listing 13-6. Managing Reads and Writes with the Client

```java
import java.io.IOException;

import java.nio.channels.CompletionHandler;

import java.nio.charset.Charset;

public class ReadWriteHandler
    implements CompletionHandler<Integer, Attachment>
{
    private final static Charset CSUTF8 = Charset.forName("UTF-8");

    @Override
    public void completed(Integer result, Attachment att)
    {
        if (result == -1)
        {
            try
            {
                att.channelClient.close();
                System.out.printf("Stopped listening to client %s%n",
                                  att.clientAddr);
            }
            catch (IOException ioe)
            {
                ioe.printStackTrace();
            }
            return;
        }

        if (att.isReadMode)
        {
            att.buffer.flip();
            int limit = att.buffer.limit();
            byte bytes[] = new byte[limit];
            att.buffer.get(bytes, 0, limit);
            System.out.printf("Client at %s sends message: %s%n",
                              att.clientAddr,
                              new String(bytes, CSUTF8));

            att.isReadMode = false;

            att.buffer.rewind();
            att.channelClient.write(att.buffer, att, this);
        }
        else
```

```
    {
        att.isReadMode = true;

        att.buffer.clear();
        att.channelClient.read(att.buffer, att, this);
    }
}

    @Override
    public void failed(Throwable t, Attachment att)
    {
        System.out.println("Connection with client broken");
    }
}
```

ReadWriteHandler is a CompletionHandler that responds to read() or write() method completions. Its completed() method is called to respond to a successful read() or write(), which includes issuing a counterpart write() or read(). Its failed() method is called when the client breaks off its connection with the server.

The completed() method's first task is to respond to a read() call that returns -1, which indicates that no bytes could be read because end-of-stream has been reached. (The client may have terminated before writing data.) It closes the client socket channel, outputs a message to indicate that the server is no longer listening to the client, and returns.

Assuming that the read/write handler is operating in read mode (true), the buffer contents are flipped and extracted to a bytes array, which is subsequently converted to a string that is output.

The read/write handler is then configured for write mode by assigning false to isReadMode, the buffer is rewound in preparation for being written, and the buffer along with the attachment and current completion handler are passed to the client socket channel's write() method so that the buffer contents can be sent to the client.

After a successful write operation, the read/write handler's completed() method is called. Because isReadMode is no longer true, the else part of the if-else statement executes. It toggles isReadMode to true, clears the buffer, and initiates a read operation to read from the client. This pattern continues until the client presents nothing more to read and the completion handler can terminate. (This latter scenario will probably never happen.)

Compile Listings 13-3 through 13-6 as follows:

```
javac Server.java
```

Run the resulting application as follows:

```
java Server
```

You should observe the following initial output:

```
Server listening at /127.0.0.1:9090
```

AsynchronousSocketChannel

You can obtain an AsynchronousSocketChannel object by invoking this class's AsynchronousSocketChannel open() class method, as follows:

```
AsynchronousSocketChannel ch = AsynchronousSocketChannel.open();
```

According to AsynchronousSocketChannel's documentation, this method returns an asynchronous socket channel that's bound to the default group. The alternative AsynchronousSocketChannel open(AsynchronousChannelGroup group) method returns an asynchronous socket channel that's bound to the specified group. Again, I'll discuss asynchronous channel groups later in this chapter.

You can configure an asynchronous socket channel by invoking the <T> AsynchronousSocketChannel setOption(SocketOption<T> name, T value) generic method. The only documented options that are supported are SO_RCVBUF, SO_SNDBUF, SO_KEEPALIVE, SO_REUSEADDR, and TCP_NODELAY.

A newly-created and possibly configured asynchronous socket channel is open but not yet connected. A connected asynchronous socket channel is created when a connection is made to the socket of an asynchronous server socket channel. It's not possible to create an asynchronous socket channel for an arbitrary, preexisting socket.

A newly-created socket channel is connected by invoking either of its connect() methods; one connect() method returns a Future and the other connect() method requires a CompletionHandler argument.

Once connected, a socket channel remains connected until closed. Whether or not a socket channel is connected may be determined by invoking its SocketAddress getRemoteAddress() method, which returns the socket address of the remote socket (or null when there is no connection). An attempt to invoke an I/O operation on an unconnected channel results in NotYetConnectedException.

> **Note**   Asynchronous socket channels are safe for use by multiple concurrent
> threads. They support concurrent reads and writes, although at most one read
> and one write can be outstanding at any time. If a thread initiates a read before
> a previous read has completed, ReadPendingException will be thrown.
> Similarly, an attempt to initiate a write before a previous write has completed
> will throw WritePendingException.

To demonstrate AsynchronousSocketChannel, I've created a Client
application consisting of the Client, Attachment, and ReadWriteHandler
classes. Listing 13-7 presents Client's source code.

Listing 13-7. Launching a Client That Handles Reads/Writes Asynchronously

```java
import java.io.IOException;

import java.net.InetSocketAddress;

import java.nio.ByteBuffer;

import java.nio.channels.AsynchronousSocketChannel;

import java.nio.charset.Charset;

import java.util.concurrent.ExecutionException;

public class Client
{
    private final static Charset CSUTF8 = Charset.forName("UTF-8");

    private final static int PORT = 9090;

    private final static String HOST = "localhost";

    public static void main(String[] args)
    {
        AsynchronousSocketChannel channel;
        try
        {
            channel = AsynchronousSocketChannel.open();
        }
        catch (IOException ioe)
        {
            System.err.println("Unable to open client socket channel");
            return;
        }
```

```
try
{
    channel.connect(new InetSocketAddress(HOST, PORT)).get();
    System.out.printf("Client at %s connected%n",
                      channel.getLocalAddress());
}
catch (ExecutionException | InterruptedException eie)
{
    System.err.println("Server not responding");
    return;
}
catch (IOException ioe)
{
    System.err.println("Unable to obtain client socket channel's " +
                       "local address");
    return;
}

Attachment att = new Attachment();
att.channel = channel;
att.isReadMode = false;
att.buffer = ByteBuffer.allocate(2048);
att.mainThd = Thread.currentThread();

byte[] data = "Hello".getBytes(CSUTF8);
att.buffer.put(data);
att.buffer.flip();
channel.write(att.buffer, att, new ReadWriteHandler());

try
{
    att.mainThd.join();
}
catch (InterruptedException ie)
{
    System.out.println("Client terminating");
}
}
}
```

Listing 13-7's main() method first attempts to open an asynchronous
socket channel and connect it to the server at port 9090 on the localhost. It
then calls AsynchronousSocketChannel's SocketAddress getLocalAddress()
method to return the socket address to which this channel's socket (the
local socket) is bound, and it then outputs a message stating that the client
is connected at this address.

If an exception is thrown, the server outputs a message and terminates. Otherwise, it creates an `Attachment` object and initializes its fields in preparation for a `write()` method call.

An initial message is created and stored in a buffer, which is then written to the socket channel. The `Attachment` object and a newly-created `ReadWriteHandler` object (which responds to the `write()` call and performs additional `write()`s and `read()`s are passed to `write()`.

At this point, `main()`'s thread of execution blocks itself by calling `Thread.join()`. The only way to unblock this thread and return from `main()` is to interrupt the thread from another thread. `ReadWriteHandler` takes care of this task, as you will see later.

Listing 13-8 presents `Attachment`'s source code.

Listing 13-8. Binding Fields for Subsequent Communication

```
import java.nio.ByteBuffer;

import java.nio.channels.AsynchronousSocketChannel;

public class Attachment
{
    public AsynchronousSocketChannel channel;
    public boolean isReadMode;
    public ByteBuffer buffer;
    public Thread mainThd;
}
```

The channel field identifies the asynchronous socket channel. It's subsequently accessed by `ReadWriteHandler`'s `completed()` method to perform reads and writes.

The `isReadMode` field is a toggle that lets `completed()` know if it needs to perform a read or a write.

The `buffer` field identifies the byte buffer that's created in `Client`'s `main()` method, and that's used to communicate bytes between the server and a client. Each client has its own byte buffer.

Finally, the `mainThd` field references a `Thread` object that identifies `main()`'s thread. The `completed()` method invokes `interrupt()` on this reference to interrupt the client so that this application can exit.

Listing 13-9 presents ReadWriteHandler's source code.

Listing 13-9. Managing Reads and Writes with the Server

```
import java.io.BufferedReader;
import java.io.InputStreamReader;
import java.io.IOException;

import java.nio.channels.CompletionHandler;

import java.nio.charset.Charset;

public class ReadWriteHandler implements CompletionHandler<Integer,
Attachment>
{
   private final static Charset CSUTF8 = Charset.forName("UTF-8");

   private BufferedReader conReader =
      new BufferedReader(new InputStreamReader(System.in));

   @Override
   public void completed(Integer result, Attachment att)
   {
      if (att.isReadMode)
      {
         att.buffer.flip();
         int limit = att.buffer.limit();
         byte[] bytes = new byte[limit];
         att.buffer.get(bytes, 0, limit);
         String msg = new String(bytes, CSUTF8);
         System.out.printf("Server responded: %s%n", msg);

         try
         {
            msg = "";
            while (msg.length() == 0)
            {
               System.out.print("Enter message (\"end\" to quit): ");
               msg = conReader.readLine();
            }
            if (msg.equalsIgnoreCase("end"))
            {
               att.mainThd.interrupt();
               return;
            }
         }
      }
```

```
        catch (IOException ioe)
        {
            System.err.println("Unable to read from console");
        }

        att.isReadMode = false;
        att.buffer.clear();
        byte[] data = msg.getBytes(CSUTF8);
        att.buffer.put(data);
        att.buffer.flip();
        att.channel.write(att.buffer, att, this);
    }
    else
    {
        att.isReadMode = true;

        att.buffer.clear();
        att.channel.read(att.buffer, att, this);
    }
}

@Override
public void failed(Throwable t, Attachment att)
{
    System.err.println("Server not responding");
    System.exit(1);
}
}
```

ReadWriteHandler is a CompletionHandler that responds to read() or
write() completions. Its completed() method is called to respond to a
successful read() or write(), which includes issuing a counterpart write()
or read(). Its failed() method is called when the client breaks off its
connection with the server.

The completed() method's first task is to determine if a read() has been
performed and respond accordingly. If so, it extracts the buffer's bytes into
an array, which is converted to a string that is subsequently output.

Next, completed() gives the user the opportunity to enter a message
that will be sent to the server. If the user specifies end, the client thread is
interrupted and the client terminates. Any other message's bytes are
extracted from the string and stored in the buffer, which is subsequently
written to the socket channel.

If a read() call had not occurred, completed() would execute the else part
of the if-else statement. After setting isReadMode to true, it empties the
buffer and calls read().

To put this into perspective, here is what happens when the client starts running.

1. Client's main() method sets isReadMode to false, stores a Hello message in the buffer, and write()s the message to the channel, which results in the message being sent to and displayed by the server.

2. The server's read/write handler write()s this message back to the client.

3. Because isReadMode is false, Client's read/write handler's completed() method executes the else part of the if-else statement, setting isReadMode to true and calling read(), which stores in the buffer the Hello bytes written by the server.

4. Client's read/write handler's completed() method is called. It notes that isReadMode is true, extracts the bytes from the buffer, and outputs the equivalent string as part of a Server responded message.

5. The client will now obtain a message from the user and act accordingly.

Compile Listings 13-7 through 13-9 as follows:

```
javac Client.java
```

Run the resulting application as follows:

```
java Client
```

Assuming that the server is running as shown previously, you should observe output that's similar to the following initial output:

```
Client at /0:0:0:0:0:0:0:0:55359 connected
Server responded: Hello
Enter message ("end" to quit):
```

Continuing, you should observe output that's similar to the following output on the server side:

```
Accepted connection from /127.0.0.1:55359
Client at /127.0.0.1:55359 sends message: Hello
```

As you enter messages via the client, you'll see them echoed on the server starting with "Client at /127.0.0.1:xxxxx sends message:" (xxxxx indicates the port number) and on the client starting with "Server responded:". When you terminate the client, it displays Client terminating; the server displays Connection with client broken.

Asynchronous Channel Groups

The abstract java.nio.channels.AsynchronousChannelGroup class describes a grouping of asynchronous channels for the purpose of resource sharing. A *group* has an associated *thread pool* to which tasks are submitted, to handle I/O events and to dispatch to completion handlers that consume the results of asynchronous operations performed on the group's channels.

> **Note**   The associated thread pool is *owned* by the group; termination of the group results in the associated thread pool being shut down.

AsynchronousServerSocketChannels and AsynchronousSocketChannels belong to groups. When you create an AsynchronousServerSocketChannel or an AsynchronousSocketChannel via the noargument open() method, the channel is bound to the *default group*, which is the system-wide channel group that's automatically constructed and maintained by the Java virtual machine (JVM). The default group has an associated thread pool that creates new threads as needed. You can configure the default group by initializing the following system properties at JVM startup:

- java.nio.channels.DefaultThreadPool.threadFactory: The value of this property is the fully-qualified name of a concrete java.util.concurrent.ThreadFactory class. The class is loaded using the system classloader and instantiated. The factory's newThread(Runnable r) method is invoked to create each thread for the default group's thread pool. If the process to load and instantiate the value of the property fails, an unspecified error is thrown during the construction of the default group. (If the ThreadFactory for the default group is not configured, the pooled threads of the default group are *daemon threads*.)

- `java.nio.channels.DefaultThreadPool.initialSize`: The value of `initialSize` specifies the initialize size of the default group's thread pool. If the string-based value cannot be parsed as an integer, it causes an unspecified error to be thrown during the construction of the default group.

You might prefer to define your own channel group because it gives you more control over the threads that are used to service the I/O operations. Furthermore, it provides the mechanisms to shut down threads and to await termination. You would create your own asynchronous channel group by calling one of the following class methods:

- `AsynchronousChannelGroupwithCachedThreadPool (ExecutorService executor, int initialSize)`: Create an asynchronous channel group with a given thread pool (specified as a `java.util.concurrent.ExecutorService` object) that creates new threads as needed.

- `AsynchronousChannelGroup withFixedThreadPool(int nThreads, ThreadFactory threadFactory)`: Create an asynchronous channel group with a fixed thread pool.

- `AsynchronousChannelGroup withThreadPool (ExecutorService executor)`: Create an asynchronous channel group with a given thread pool (specified as an ExecutorService object).

The following example creates a new channel group that has a fixed pool of 20 threads. Each thread is constructed with the default thread factory from the `java.util.concurrent.Executors` class:

```
AsynchronousChannelGroup group;
group = AsynchronousChannelGroup.
            withFixedThreadPool(20,
                                Executors.defaultThreadFactory());
```

After creating a group, you can bind an asynchronous server socket channel and an asynchronous socket channel to the group by calling the following class methods in their respective classes:

- `AsynchronousServerSocketChannel open(AsynchronousChannelGroup group)`

- `AsynchronousSocketChannel open(AsynchronousChannelGroup group)`

The following example creates an asynchronous server socket channel and an asynchronous socket channel that are bound to the previously-created group:

```
AsynchronousServerSocketChannel chServer;
chServer = AsynchronousServerSocketChannel.open(group);
AsynchronousSocketChannel chClient = AsynchronousSocketChannel.open(group);
```

> **Note**   When writing a completion handler, it's important to avoid operations that may block the thread. The entire application could block when all threads are blocked. For a custom or cached thread pool, the queue could grow very large and ultimately result in an out-of-memory situation.

You'll primarily instantiate AsynchronousChannelGroup and bind your socket channels to this group for shutdown and termination. The void shutdown() method initiates an orderly shutdown of a group. An orderly shutdown marks the group as shutdown; attempting to construct a channel that binds to the group results in java.nio.channels.ShutdownChannelGroupException. Whether or not a group is shut down can be tested by calling the boolean isShutdown() method.

Once shut down, the group terminates when all asynchronous channels that are bound to the group are closed, all actively executing completion handlers have run to completion, and resources used by the group are released. No attempt is made to stop or interrupt threads that are executing completion handlers. The boolean isTerminated() method is used to test if the group has terminated, and the boolean awaitTermination(long timeout, TimeUnit unit) method is used to block until the group has terminated.

The void shutdownNow() method is used to initiate a forceful shutdown of the group. In addition to the actions performed by an orderly shutdown, shutdownNow() closes all open channels in the group as if by invoking each channel's close() method.

The following example demonstrates the aforementioned methods:

```
// Initiate an I/O operation that isn't satisfied.

channel.accept(null, completionHandler);

// After the operation has begun, the channel group is used to control
// the shutdown.
```

```
if (!group.isShutdown())
{
    // After the group is shut down, no more channels can be bound to it.

    group.shutdown();
}

if (!group.isTerminated())
{
    // Forcibly shut down the group. The channel is closed and the
    // accept operation aborts.

    group.shutdownNow();
}

// The group should be able to terminate; wait for 10 seconds maximum.

group.awaitTermination(10, TimeUnit.SECONDS);
```

What About AsynchronousFileChannel?

AsynchronousFileChannels don't belong to groups. However, they are associated with a thread pool to which tasks are submitted, to handle I/O events and to dispatch to completion handlers that consume the results of I/O operations on the channel.

The completion handler for an I/O operation initiated on a channel is guaranteed to be invoked by one of the threads in the thread pool, which ensures that the completion handler is run by a thread with the expected identity. If an I/O operation completes immediately and the initiating thread is itself a thread in the thread pool, the completion handler may be invoked directly by the initiating thread.

When an asynchronous file channel is created without specifying a thread pool, the channel is associated with a system-dependent default thread pool that may be shared with other channels. The default thread pool is configured by the system properties defined by AsynchronousChannelGroup.

An asynchronous file channel created by AsynchronousFileChannel's AsynchronousFileChannel open(Path file, OpenOption... options) class method is associated with the default thread pool. You can associate a file channel with another thread pool by calling the AsynchronousFileChannel open(Path file, Set<? extends OpenOption> options, ExecutorService executor, FileAttribute<?>... attrs) class method. Here, executor identifies the desired thread pool.

EXERCISES

The following exercises are designed to test your understanding of Chapter 13's content:

1. Define asynchronous channel.

2. Identify the two ways to initiate an I/O operation with an asynchronous channel.

3. True or false: After a channel is closed, further attempts to initiate asynchronous I/O operations complete immediately with cause `AsynchronousCloseException`.

4. Identify the methods declared by the `AsynchronousByteChannel` interface.

5. True or false: The `ByteBuffer` object is safe for use by multiple concurrent threads.

6. Identify the class for reading, writing, and manipulating a file asynchronously.

7. True or false: An asynchronous file channel doesn't have a current position within a file.

8. If you pass no options to `AsynchronousFileChannel`'s `AsynchronousFileChannel open(Path file, OpenOption...options)` method, what is this method's default behavior?

9. How do you obtain an `AsynchronousServerSocketChannel` object or an `AsynchronousSocketChannel` object?

10. Identify `AsynchronousServerSocketChannel`'s documented socket options.

11. After obtaining an `AsynchronousServerSocketChannel` object, what must you do before you can call either of its `accept()` methods?

12. After obtaining an `AsynchronousSocketChannel` object, what must you do before you can perform reads and writes?

13. How do you determine if an asynchronous socket channel is connected to an asynchronous server socket channel?

14. True or false: Asynchronous socket channels are safe for use by multiple concurrent threads.

15. What is the purpose of the `AsynchronousChannelGroup` class?

16. What does a group use for task submission?

17. Identify the system properties for configuring the default group.

18.   Describe AsynchronousChannelGroup's shutDownNow() method.

19.   True or false: AsynchronousFileChannels belong to groups.

20.   Write a Copy application that uses AsynchronousFileChannel to copy a source file to a destination file asynchronously.

Summary

Asynchronous I/O lets client code initiate an I/O operation and subsequently notifies the client when the operation is complete. The AsynchronousChannel interface describes an asynchronous channel that supports asynchronous I/O operations (reads, writes, and so on). An I/O operation is initiated by calling a method that returns a Future or requires a CompletionHandler argument.

CompletionHandler declares a completed() method to consume the result of an operation when it completes successfully. It also declares a failed() method to report operation failure (in terms of an exception) and allow an application to take appropriate action.

The AsynchronousByteChannel interface extends AsynchronousChannel and declares a pair of read() methods and a pair of write() methods. Each pair consists of a method that returns a Future and a method that requires a CompletionHandler argument.

The abstract AsynchronousFileChannel class describes an asynchronous channel for reading, writing, and manipulating a file. The abstract AsynchronousServerSocketChannel class describes an asynchronous channel for stream-oriented listening sockets. Its counterpart channel for stream-oriented connecting sockets is described by the abstract AsynchronousSocketChannel class.

The abstract AsynchronousChannelGroup class describes a grouping of asynchronous channels for the purpose of resource sharing. A group has an associated thread pool to which tasks are submitted, to handle I/O events and to dispatch to completion handlers that consume the results of asynchronous operations performed on the group's channels.

AsynchronousServerSocketChannels and AsynchronousSocketChannels created via their noargument open() methods are bound to the default group. They can be bound to groups created from AsynchronousChannelGroup's class methods by passing these group objects to their open(AsynchronousChannelGroup) methods.

AsynchronousFileChannels don't belong to groups. However, they are associated with a default thread pool, which can be configured or replaced.

Chapter 14 presents NIO.2's completion of socket channel functionality.

Completion of Socket Channel Functionality

Completion of socket channel functionality is JDK 7's final contribution to NIO.2. The java.nio.channels package's DatagramChannel, ServerSocketChannel, and SocketChannel classes have been extended to support binding and option configuration. Also, channel-based multicasting is supported. This chapter wraps up the book by introducing you to these capabilities.

Binding and Option Configuration

NIO's DatagramChannel, ServerSocketChannel, and SocketChannel classes don't completely abstract a network socket. To bind into the channel's socket, or to get/set socket options, you have to first retrieve the peer socket by invoking each class's socket() method.

This counterintuitive mix of socket channel and socket APIs exists because there wasn't enough time to define a full socket channel API for the JDK 1.4 release. JDK 7 overcame this problem by introducing the java.nio.channels.NetworkChannel interface.

NetworkChannel represents a channel to a network socket. This interface is implemented by DatagramChannel, ServerSocketChannel, SocketChannel, java.nio.channels.AsynchronousServerSocketChannel (see Chapter 13), and java.nio.channels.AsynchronousSocketChannel (see Chapter 13).

Table 14-1 presents NetworkChannel's methods.

Table 14-1. *The Methods that Define a Network Channel*

Method	Description
NetworkChannel bind(SocketAddress local)	Bind this channel's socket to a local address. Once an association is established, the socket remains bound until this channel is closed. If you pass null to local, the socket will be bound to an address that is assigned automatically. bind() returns this channel on success. Otherwise, it throws java.nio.channels. AlreadyBoundException when the socket is already bound, java.nio.channels.UnsupportedAddressTypeException when the type of the given address is not supported, java.nio.channels.ClosedChannelException when this channel is closed, and java.io.IOException when some other I/O error occurs.
SocketAddress getLocalAddress()	Return the socket address to which this channel's socket is bound. When this channel is bound to an Internet Protocol (IP) socket address, the return value from this method is of type java.net.InetSocketAddress. getLocalAddress() throws ClosedChannelException when this channel is closed and IOException when an I/O error occurs.
<T> T getOption (SocketOption<T> name)	Return the value of the socket option identified by name. A return value of null might be valid for some socket options. getOption() throws java.lang. UnsupportedOperationException when this channel doesn't support this socket option, ClosedChannelException when this channel is closed, and IOException when an I/O error occurs.
<T> NetworkChannel setOption (SocketOption<T> name, T value)	Set the value of the socket option identified by name to value. Passing null to value might be valid for some socket options. setOption() returns this channel. It throws UnsupportedOperationException when this channel doesn't support this socket option, java.lang.IllegalArgumentException when the value passed to value isn't valid for this socket option, ClosedChannelException when this channel is closed, and IOException when an I/O error occurs.
Set<SocketOption<?>> supportedOptions()	Return a set of the socket options supported by this channel. This method will continue to return the set of options even after this channel is closed.

The arguments passed to getOption()'s and setOption()'s name parameters must be of the java.net.SocketOption interface type. JDK 7 also added the java.net.StandardSocketOptions class, which implements this interface and enumerates various SocketOption constants, such as SO_RCVBUF (size of socket receive buffer) and TCP_NODELAY (disable the Nagle algorithm).

The classes that implement NetworkChannel don't support all of the socket options identified by StandardSocketOptions constants. For example, ServerSocketChannel supports only SO_RCVBUF and SO_REUSEADDR. Each class's Java documentation identifies its supported constants. When in doubt, call supportedOptions() to find out what options are supported.

As well as providing NetworkChannel, JDK 7 upgraded DatagramChannel, ServerSocketChannel, and SocketChannel with several useful methods:

- DatagramChannel received a SocketAddress getRemoteAddress() method that returns the remote address to which this channel's socket is connected.

- ServerSocketChannel received a ServerSocketChannel bind(SocketAddress local, int backlog) method that also lets you specify the maximum number of pending connections.

- SocketChannel received SocketChannel shutdownInput() and SocketChannel shutdownOutput() methods that shut down the connection for reading or writing, respectively, without closing this channel. Also, it received a SocketAddress getRemoteAddress() method that returns the remote address to which this channel's socket is connected.

Listing 7-7's ChannelServer application had to invoke socket() when binding the channel's socket to a local address, obtaining the local address, and obtaining the remote address. Listing 14-1 simplifies this code by making it NetworkChannel-compliant and using getRemoteAddress().

Listing 14-1. Demonstrating the Improved ServerSocketChannel

```
import java.io.IOException;

import java.net.InetSocketAddress;

import java.nio.ByteBuffer;

import java.nio.channels.ServerSocketChannel;
import java.nio.channels.SocketChannel;
```

```java
public class ChannelServer
{
    public static void main(String[] args) throws IOException
    {
        System.out.println("Starting server…");
        ServerSocketChannel ssc = ServerSocketChannel.open();
        ssc.bind(new InetSocketAddress(9999));
        ssc.configureBlocking(false);
        String msg = "Local address: " + ssc.getLocalAddress();
        ByteBuffer buffer = ByteBuffer.wrap(msg.getBytes());
        while (true)
        {
            System.out.print(".");
            SocketChannel sc = ssc.accept();
            if (sc != null)
            {
                System.out.println();
                System.out.println("Received connection from " +
                                   sc.getRemoteAddress());
                buffer.rewind();
                sc.write(buffer);
                sc.close();
            }
            else
                try
                {
                    Thread.sleep(100);
                }
                catch (InterruptedException ie)
                {
                    assert false; // shouldn't happen
                }
        }
    }
}
```

Listing 14-1 replaces ssc.socket().bind(new InetSocketAddress(9999));
with ssc.bind(new InetSocketAddress(9999));, ssc.socket().
getLocalSocketAddress(); with ssc.getLocalAddress();, and sc.socket().
getRemoteSocketAddress() with sc.getRemoteAddress().

Listing 14-2 expands on Listing 7-8's ChannelClient application by invoking
supportedOptions() to obtain a set of supported options, which are
subsequently output, and by invoking getOption() to obtain the value of the
SO_RCVBUF option, which is also output.

Listing 14-2. Obtaining Supported Options and the Receive Buffer Size

```java
import java.io.IOException;

import java.net.InetSocketAddress;
import java.net.SocketOption;
import java.net.StandardSocketOptions;

import java.nio.ByteBuffer;

import java.nio.channels.SocketChannel;

import java.util.Set;

public class ChannelClient
{
   public static void main(String[] args)
   {
      try
      {
         SocketChannel sc = SocketChannel.open();
         Set<SocketOption<?>> options = sc.supportedOptions();
         for (SocketOption<?> option: options)
            System.out.println(option);
         System.out.println(sc.getOption(StandardSocketOptions.SO_RCVBUF));
         sc.configureBlocking(false);
         InetSocketAddress addr = new InetSocketAddress("localhost", 9999);
         sc.connect(addr);

         while (!sc.finishConnect())
            System.out.println("waiting to finish connection");

         ByteBuffer buffer = ByteBuffer.allocate(200);
         while (sc.read(buffer) >= 0)
         {
            buffer.flip();
            while (buffer.hasRemaining())
               System.out.print((char) buffer.get());
            buffer.clear();
         }
         sc.close();
      }
      catch (IOException ioe)
      {
         System.err.println("I/O error: " + ioe.getMessage());
      }
   }
}
```

Compile Listings 14-1 and 14-2 and run the resulting applications as demonstrated in Chapter 7. I observe the following `ChannelClient` output:

```
SO_KEEPALIVE
TCP_NODELAY
IP_TOS
SO_LINGER
SO_SNDBUF
SO_RCVBUF
SO_REUSEADDR
SO_OOBINLINE
8192
Local address: /0:0:0:0:0:0:0:0:9999
```

Channel-Based Multicasting

JDK 7 introduced support for channel-based *IP multicasting*, which is the transmission of IP datagrams to members of a *group* (zero or more hosts identified by a single destination address). Multicasting is the Internet version of broadcasting in which a television or radio signal is broadcast from a *source*, and is available to everyone in the signal area with a suitable and active receiving device.

A group is identified by a *class D IP address*, which is a multicast group IPv4 address that ranges from 224.0.0.1 through 239.255.255.255. A new *receiver* (client) joins a multicast group by connecting to the group via the group's IP address. The receiver then listens for incoming datagrams.

JDK 7 introduced the `java.nio.channels.MulticastChannel` interface to support multicasting. `MulticastChannel` extends `NetworkChannel` and is implemented by the `DatagramChannel` class. It declares a pair of `join()` methods for joining a group and a `close()` method for closing the channel.

A receiver calls the `MembershipKey join(InetAddress group, NetworkInterface ni)` method to join a multicast group to begin receiving all datagrams sent to the group. It's called with the group's IP address and the network interface on which to join the group as its arguments. When this method succeeds, it returns a `java.nio.channels.MembershipKey` instance that serves as a token representing membership in the group.

> **Note** A network interface is described by an instance of the `java.net.NetworkInterface` class. To obtain a `NetworkInterface` instance, call various `NetworkInterface` class methods, such as `NetworkInterface getByInetAddress(InetAddress addr)`.

Alternatively, a receiver can call the MembershipKey join(InetAddress group, NetworkInterface ni, InetAddress source) method to join a multicast group and receive datagrams from a specific source address. Because membership is cumulative, this method can be reinvoked with the same group and network interface to allow reception of datagrams sent by other source addresses to the group.

> **Note** The first join() method is analogous to a cable television provider that requires you to subscribe to packages of channels, including those channels that are not of interest. The second join() method is analogous to a cable television provider that lets you subscribe to specific channels of interest.

The second join() method demonstrates *source filtering* in which you can filter datagrams based on their sources. You would call this method to receive datagrams from specific IP sources. This form of source filtering is known as *include-mode filtering*.

MembershipKey declares several methods:

- MembershipKey block(InetAddress source): Block multicast datagrams from the given source address when this membership key is not source-specific and the operating system supports source filtering.

- MulticastChannel channel(): Return the channel for which this membership key was created.

- void drop(): Drop membership.

- InetAddress group(): Return the multicast group for which this membership key was created.

- boolean isValid(): Return whether this membership is valid (true) or not (false).

- NetworkInterface networkInterface(): Return the network interface for which this membership key was created.

- InetAddress sourceAddress(): Return the source address when this membership key is source-specific; return null when this membership is not source-specific.

- MembershipKey unblock(InetAddress source): Unblock multicast datagrams from the given source address that was previously blocked via block().

You can use `MembershipKey`'s `block()` method to perform a second form of source filtering in which a group is joined to receive all multicast datagrams except those from specific IP source addresses. This form of source filtering, which is known as *exclude-mode filtering*, is demonstrated here:

```
MembershipKey key = dc.join(group, nif).block(source1).block(source2);
```

Once a channel has joined a group, it receives multicast datagrams in the same manner as unicast datagrams. When finished with the group, it drops its membership by calling `MembershipKey`'s `drop()` method. It calls `MulticastChannel`'s `close()` method after dropping all group memberships.

To create a multicast server or multicast client, there are three important items to keep in mind:

- When creating the datagram channel, specify the protocol family that corresponds to the address type of the multicast groups that the channel will join. There is no guarantee that a channel to a socket in one protocol family can join and receive multicast datagrams when the address of the multicast group corresponds to another protocol family. For example, it's implementation-specific if a channel to an IPv6 socket can join an IPv4 multicast group and receive multicast datagrams sent to the group.

- You create a datagram channel by calling `DatagramChannel`'s `DatagramChannel open(ProtocolFamily family)` class method. This method requires an argument whose class implements the `java.net.ProtocolFamily` interface. Because `ProtocolFamily` is implemented by the `java.net.StandardProtocolFamily` enum, you would pass one of this enum's `INET` (for IPv4) or `INET6` (for IPv6) constants to `family`.

- The channel's socket should be bound to the wildcard address. If the socket is bound to a specific address, rather than the wildcard address, it's implementation-specific if multicast datagrams are received by the socket.

- The `InetSocketAddress` class declares an `InetSocketAddress(int port)` constructor that creates a socket address where the IP address is the wildcard address and the port number is the specified port value.

- The `SO_REUSEADDR` option should be enabled prior to binding the socket. This is required to allow multiple members of the group to bind to the same address.

I've created multicast server and client applications that demonstrate channel-based multicasting. Listing 14-3 presents the server.

Listing 14-3. Demonstrating a Channel-Based Multicast Server

```java
import java.io.IOException;

import java.net.InetAddress;
import java.net.InetSocketAddress;
import java.net.NetworkInterface;
import java.net.StandardProtocolFamily;
import java.net.StandardSocketOptions;

import java.nio.ByteBuffer;

import java.nio.channels.DatagramChannel;
import java.nio.channels.MembershipKey;

public class ChannelServer
{
    final static int PORT = 9999;

    public static void main(String[] args) throws IOException
    {
        NetworkInterface ni;
        ni = NetworkInterface.getByInetAddress(InetAddress.getLocalHost());
        DatagramChannel dc;
        dc = DatagramChannel.open(StandardProtocolFamily.INET)
                            .setOption(StandardSocketOptions.SO_REUSEADDR,
                                       true)
                            .bind(new InetSocketAddress(PORT))
                            .setOption(StandardSocketOptions.IP_MULTICAST_IF,
                                       ni);
        InetAddress group = InetAddress.getByName("239.255.0.1");

        int i = 0;
        while (true)
        {
            ByteBuffer bb = ByteBuffer.wrap(("line " + i).getBytes());
            dc.send(bb, new InetSocketAddress(group, PORT));
            i++;
        }
    }
}
```

`ChannelServer`'s `main()` method first obtains a network interface and then opens and configures a datagram channel. Next, it obtains the group IP address and enters an infinite loop that sends byte buffers of string-based messages to the group.

Listing 14-4 presents the companion client application.

Listing 14-4. Demonstrating a Channel-Based Multicast Client

```java
import java.io.IOException;

import java.net.InetAddress;
import java.net.InetSocketAddress;
import java.net.NetworkInterface;
import java.net.StandardProtocolFamily;
import java.net.StandardSocketOptions;

import java.nio.ByteBuffer;

import java.nio.channels.DatagramChannel;
import java.nio.channels.MembershipKey;

public class ChannelClient
{
   final static int PORT = 9999;

   public static void main(String[] args) throws IOException
   {
      NetworkInterface ni;
      ni = NetworkInterface.getByInetAddress(InetAddress.getLocalHost());
      DatagramChannel dc;
      dc = DatagramChannel.open(StandardProtocolFamily.INET)
                          .setOption(StandardSocketOptions.SO_REUSEADDR,
                                     true)
                          .bind(new InetSocketAddress(PORT))
                          .setOption(StandardSocketOptions.IP_MULTICAST_IF,
                                     ni);
      InetAddress group = InetAddress.getByName("239.255.0.1");
      MembershipKey key = dc.join(group, ni);

      ByteBuffer response = ByteBuffer.allocate(50);
      while (true)
      {
         dc.receive(response);
         response.flip();
         while (response.hasRemaining())
            System.out.print((char) response.get());
         System.out.println();
         response.clear();
      }
   }
}
```

ChannelClient's main() method is identical to ChannelServer's equivalent until the join() call to join the group at the specified group IP address. A byte buffer is then allocated to store datagrams. After receiving a datagram, the buffer is flipped, its content is output, and the buffer is cleared.

Compile these listings and run the resulting applications in separate windows. Here is a portion of ChannelClient's output.

```
line 156573
line 156574
line 156575
line 156576
line 156577
line 156578
line 156579
line 156580
line 156581
line 156582
```

Run a second ChannelClient application in another window. You should observe similar output in that window.

EXERCISES

The following exercises are designed to test your understanding of Chapter 14's content:

1. What capabilities does NIO.2 provide for completing socket channel functionality?

2. How did JDK 7 overcome the counterintuitive mix of socket channel and socket APIs?

3. Identify the exceptions that are thrown by SocketChannel's shutdownInput() and shutdownOutput() methods.

4. How does JDK 7 support multicasting?

5. True or false: The MembershipKey join(InetAddress group, NetworkInterface ni, InetAddress source) method performs exclude-mode filtering.

6. Write an EnumNI application that enumerates your machine's network interfaces, outputting their names.

7. Modify Listing 14-4's `ChannelClient` application to also demonstrate dropping membership from the group and closing the channel before quitting the application.

8. Create a `StockServer` application that repeatedly broadcasts the open, low, high, and close share prices for a stock as floating-point values. Each broadcast should randomly adjust the low, high, and close values, subject to the following constraints: the low share price must not exceed the high share price, the close share price must not be lower than the low share price, and the close share price must not be higher than the high share price. Create a `StockClient` application that joins a group to repeatedly receive these prices, which it outputs.

Summary

JDK 7 completed socket channel functionality by extending the `DatagramChannel`, `ServerSocketChannel`, and `SocketChannel` classes to support binding and option configuration. These capabilities are declared in the `NetworkChannel` interface, which these and other classes implement.

JDK 7 also completed socket channel functionality by introducing support for channel-based multicasting. This support consists of `MulticastChannel` (an interface that extends `NetworkChannel`), the `MembershipKey` class, and an `open(ProtocolFamily)` method in the `DatagramChannel` class.

Appendix A presents the answers to each chapter's exercises.

Part **V**

Appendices

Appendix A

Answers to Exercises

Each of Chapters 1 through 14 closes with an "Exercises" section that tests your understanding of the chapter's material. The answers to those exercises are presented in this appendix.

Chapter 1: I/O Basics and APIs

1. The API categories that comprise classic I/O are File, RandomAccessFile, the stream classes, and the writer/reader classes.

2. The benefit of the try-with-resources statement is a reduction in verbosity. You can use this statement to automatically close open files and other resources instead of having to provide this resource-closing code.

3. The API categories that comprise NIO are buffers, channels, selectors, regular expressions, charsets, and a printf-style formatting facility based mainly on the Formatter class.

4. The Selector class (and related types) let Java programs leverage readiness selection.

5. The API categories that comprise NIO.2 are an improved file system interface, asynchronous I/O, and the completion of socket channel functionality.

6. NIO.2 completes the socket channel functionality by adding binding support and option configuration to the `DatagramChannel`, `ServerSocketChannel`, and `SocketChannel` classes. It also introduces a `MulticastChannel` interface.

Chapter 2: File

1. The purpose of the `File` class is to offer access to the underlying operating system's available file system(s).

2. Instances of the `File` class contain the paths of files and directories that might not exist in their file systems.

3. A path is a compact map that locates and identifies a file system object (also known as a file).

4. The difference between an absolute path and a relative path is as follows: an absolute path starts with the root directory symbol; no other information is required to locate the file/directory that it denotes. In contrast, a relative path doesn't start with the root directory symbol; it's interpreted via information taken from another path.

5. You obtain the current user directory (also known as the working directory) by specifying `System.getProperty("user.dir")`.

6. A parent path consists of all path components except for the last name.

7. Normalize means to replace separator characters with the default name-separator character so that the path is compliant with the underlying file system.

8. You obtain the default name-separator character by accessing `File`'s `separator` and `separatorChar` class fields. The first field stores the character as a `char` and the second field stores it as a `String`.

9. A canonical path is a path that's absolute and unique and is formatted the same way every time.

10. The difference between File's getParent() and getName() methods is that getParent() returns the parent path and getName() returns the last name in the path's name sequence.

11. The answer is false: File's exists() method determines whether a file or directory exists.

12. A normal file (also known as a regular file) is not a directory and satisfies other operating system-dependent criteria: it's not a symbolic link or named pipe, for example. Any nondirectory file created by a Java application is guaranteed to be a normal file.

13. File's lastModified() method returns the time that the file denoted by this File object's path was last modified or 0 when the file doesn't exist or an I/O error occurred during this method call. The returned value is measured in milliseconds since the Unix epoch (00:00:00 GMT, January 1, 1970).

14. File's listRoots() method returns an array of File objects denoting the root directories (roots) of available file systems.

15. The answer is true: File's list() method returns an array of Strings where each entry is a file name rather than a complete path.

16. The difference between the FilenameFilter and FileFilter interfaces is as follows: FilenameFilter declares a single boolean accept(File dir, String name) method, whereas FileFilter declares a single boolean accept(String path) method. Either method accomplishes the same task of accepting (by returning true) or rejecting (by returning false) the inclusion of the file or directory identified by the argument(s) in a directory listing.

17. The answer is false: File's createNewFile() method checks for file existence and creates the file when it doesn't exist in a single operation that's atomic with respect to all other file system activities that might affect the file.

18. The default temporary directory where File's
     createTempFile(String, String) method creates
     temporary files can be located by reading the
     java.io.tmpdir system property.

19. You ensure that a temporary file is removed when the
     Java virtual machine (JVM) ends normally (it doesn't
     crash and the power isn't lost) by registering the
     temporary file for deletion through a call to File's
     deleteOnExit() method.

20. The boolean canExecute() method was introduced
     by Java 6. It returns true when the file or directory
     object identified by the abstract path exists and is
     executable.

21. You would accurately compare two File objects by
     first calling File's getCanonicalFile() method on
     each File object and then comparing the returned
     File objects.

22. Listing A-1 presents the Touch application that was
     called for in Chapter 2.

Listing A-1. Setting a File or Directory's Timestamp to the Current Time

```java
import java.io.File;

import java.util.Date;

public class Touch
{
   public static void main(String[] args)
   {
      if (args.length != 1)
      {
         System.err.println("usage: java Touch path");
         return;
      }
      new File(args[0]).setLastModified(new Date().getTime());
   }
}
```

Chapter 3: RandomAccessFile

1. The purpose of the RandomAccessFile class is to create and/or open files for random access in which a mixture of write and read operations at various locations can occur until the file is closed.

2. A file's metadata is data about the file and not the actual file contents. Examples of metadata include the file's length and the time the file was last modified.

3. The purpose of the "rwd" and "rws" mode arguments is to ensure than any writes to a file located on a local storage device are written to the device, which guarantees that critical data isn't lost when the system crashes. No guarantee is made when the file doesn't reside on a local device.

4. A file pointer is a cursor that identifies the location of the next byte to write or read. When an existing file is opened, the file pointer is set to its first byte at offset 0. The file pointer is also set to 0 when the file is created.

5. When you write past the end of the file, the file is extended.

6. The answer is false: when you call RandomAccessFile's seek(long) method to set the file pointer's value, and when this value is greater than the length of the file, the file's length doesn't change. The file length will only change by writing after the offset has been set beyond the end of the file.

7. Method void write(int b) writes the lower eight bits of b to the file at the current file pointer position.

8. FileDescriptor's sync() method tells the underlying operating system to empty the contents of the open file's output buffers to their associated local disk device. sync() returns after all modified data and attributes have been written to the relevant device.

9. A flat file database is a single file organized into records and fields. A record stores a single entry (such as a part in a parts database) and a field stores a single attribute of the entry (such as a part number).

10. Listing A-2 presents the RAFDemo application that was called for in Chapter 3.

Listing A-2. Demonstrating RandomAccessFile

```java
import java.io.IOException;
import java.io.RandomAccessFile;

public class RAFDemo
{
   final static String MSG = "Test";

   public static void main(String[] args)
   {
      try (RandomAccessFile raf = new RandomAccessFile("data", "rw"))
      {
         raf.writeInt(127);
         raf.writeChars(MSG);
         raf.seek(0);
         System.out.println(raf.readInt());
         for (int i = 0; i < MSG.length(); i++)
            System.out.print(raf.readChar());
         System.out.println();
      }
      catch (IOException ioe)
      {
         ioe.printStackTrace();
      }
   }
}
```

Chapter 4: Streams

1. A stream is an ordered sequence of bytes of arbitrary length. Bytes flow over an output stream from an application to a destination and flow over an input stream from a source to an application.

2. The purpose of OutputStream's flush() method is to write any buffered output bytes to the destination. If the intended destination of this output stream is an abstraction provided by the underlying operating system (such as a file), flushing the stream only guarantees that bytes previously written to the stream are passed to the underlying operating system for writing; it doesn't guarantee that they're actually written to a physical device such as a disk drive.

3. The answer is true: OutputStream's close() method automatically flushes the output stream. If an application ends before close() is called, the output stream is automatically closed and its data is flushed.

4. The purpose of InputStream's mark(int) and reset() methods is to re-read a portion of a stream. mark(int) marks the current position in this input stream. A subsequent call to reset() repositions this stream to the last marked position so that subsequent read operations re-read the same bytes. Don't forget to call markSupported() to find out if the subclass supports mark() and reset().

5. You would access a copy of a ByteArrayOutputStream instance's internal byte array by calling ByteArrayOutputStream's toByteArray() method.

6. The answer is false: FileOutputStream and FileInputStream don't provide internal buffers to improve the performance of write and read operations.

7. You would use PipedOutputStream and PipedInputStream to communicate data between a pair of executing threads.

8. A filter stream is a stream that buffers, compresses/uncompresses, encrypts/decrypts, or otherwise manipulates an input stream's byte sequence before it reaches its destination.

9. Two streams are chained together when a stream instance is passed to another stream class's constructor.

10. You improve the performance of a file output stream by chaining a `BufferedOutputStream` instance to a `FileOutputStream` instance and calling the `BufferedOutputStream` instance's `write()` methods so that data is buffered before flowing to the file output stream. You improve the performance of a file input stream by chaining a `BufferedInputStream` instance to a `FileInputStream` instance so that data flowing from a file input stream is buffered before being returned from the `BufferedInputStream` instance by calling this instance's `read()` methods.

11. `DataOutputStream` and `DataInputStream` support `FileOutputStream` and `FileInputStream` by providing methods to write and read primitive-type values and strings in an operating system-independent way. In contrast, `FileOutputStream` and `FileInputStream` provide methods for writing/reading bytes and arrays of bytes only.

12. Object serialization is a JVM mechanism for serializing object state into a stream of bytes. Its deserialization counterpart is a JVM mechanism for deserializing this state from a byte stream.

13. The three forms of serialization and deserialization that Java supports are default serialization and deserialization, custom serialization and deserialization, and externalization.

14. The purpose of the `Serializable` interface is to tell the JVM that it's okay to serialize objects of the implementing class.

15. When the serialization mechanism encounters an object whose class doesn't implement `Serializable`, it throws an instance of the `NotSerializableException` class.

16. The three stated reasons for Java not supporting unlimited serialization are as follows: security, performance, and objects not amenable to serialization.

17. You initiate serialization by creating an `ObjectOutputStream` instance and calling its `writeObject()` method. You initiate deserialization by creating an `ObjectInputStream` instance and calling its `readObject()` method.

18. The answer is false: class fields are not automatically serialized.

19. The purpose of the `transient` reserved word is to mark instance fields that don't participate in default serialization and default deserialization.

20. The deserialization mechanism causes `readObject()` to throw an instance of the `InvalidClassException` class when it attempts to deserialize an object whose class has changed.

21. The deserialization mechanism detects that a serialized object's class has changed as follows: Every serialized object has an identifier. The deserialization mechanism compares the identifier of the object being deserialized with the serialized identifier of its class (all serializable classes are automatically given unique identifiers unless they explicitly specify their own identifiers) and causes `InvalidClassException` to be thrown when it detects a mismatch.

22. You can add an instance field to a class and avoid trouble when deserializing an object that was serialized before the instance field was added by introducing a `long serialVersionUID = long integer value;` declaration into the class. The `long integer` value must be unique and is known as a stream unique identifier (SUID). You can use the JDK's `serialver` tool to help with this task.

23. You customize the default serialization and deserialization mechanisms without using externalization by declaring private void `writeObject(ObjectOutputStream)` and void `readObject(ObjectInputStream)` methods in the class.

24. You tell the serialization and deserialization mechanisms to serialize or deserialize the object's normal state before serializing or deserializing additional data items by first calling `ObjectOutputStream`'s `defaultWriteObject()` method in `writeObject(ObjectOutputStream)` or by first calling `ObjectInputStream`'s `defaultReadObject()` method in `readObject(ObjectInputStream)`.

25. Externalization differs from default and custom serialization and deserialization in that it offers complete control over the serialization and deserialization tasks.

26. A class indicates that it supports externalization by implementing the `Externalizable` interface instead of `Serializable` and by declaring void `writeExternal(ObjectOutput)` and void `readExternal(ObjectInput in)` methods instead of void `writeObject(ObjectOutputStream)` and void `readObject(ObjectInputStream)` methods.

27. The answer is true: during externalization, the deserialization mechanism throws `InvalidClassException` with a "no valid constructor" message when it doesn't detect a public noargument constructor.

28. The difference between `PrintStream`'s `print()` and `println()` methods is that the `print()` methods don't append a line terminator to their output, whereas the `println()` methods append a line terminator.

29. PrintStream's noargument void `println()` method outputs the `line.separator` system property's value to ensure that lines are terminated in a portable manner (such as a carriage return followed by a newline/line feed on Windows, or only a newline/line feed on Unix/Linux).

30. You redirect the standard input, standard output, and standard error streams by creating new stream source and destination objects and passing them as arguments to System's `setIn(InputStream)`, `setOut(PrintStream)`, and `setErr(PrintStream)` methods.

31. Listing A-3 presents the Copy application that was called for in Chapter 4.

Listing A-3. Copying a Source File to a Destination File with Buffered I/O

```java
import java.io.BufferedInputStream;
import java.io.BufferedOutputStream;
import java.io.FileInputStream;
import java.io.FileNotFoundException;
import java.io.FileOutputStream;
import java.io.IOException;

public class Copy
{
   public static void main(String[] args)
   {
      if (args.length != 2)
      {
         System.err.println("usage: java Copy srcfile dstfile");
         return;
      }
      BufferedInputStream bis = null;
      BufferedOutputStream bos = null;
      try
      {
         FileInputStream fis = new FileInputStream(args[0]);
         bis = new BufferedInputStream(fis);
         FileOutputStream fos = new FileOutputStream(args[1]);
         bos = new BufferedOutputStream(fos);
         int b; // I chose b instead of byte because byte is a reserved
                // word.
         while ((b = bis.read()) != -1)
            bos.write(b);
      }
```

```
      catch (FileNotFoundException fnfe)
      {
         System.err.println(args[0] + " could not be opened for input, or "
                           + args[1] + " could not be created for output");
      }
      catch (IOException ioe)
      {
         System.err.println("I/O error: " + ioe.getMessage());
      }
      finally
      {
         if (bis != null)
            try
            {
               bis.close();
            }
            catch (IOException ioe)
            {
               assert false; // shouldn't happen in this context
            }

         if (bos != null)
            try
            {
               bos.close();
            }
            catch (IOException ioe)
            {
               assert false; // shouldn't happen in this context
            }
      }
   }
}
```

32. Listing A-4 presents the Split application that was called for in Chapter 4.

Listing A-4. Splitting a Large File into Numerous Smaller Part Files

```
import java.io.BufferedInputStream;
import java.io.BufferedOutputStream;
import java.io.File;
import java.io.FileInputStream;
import java.io.FileOutputStream;
import java.io.IOException;
```

```java
public class Split
{
    static final int FILESIZE = 1400000;
    static byte[] buffer = new byte[FILESIZE];

    public static void main(String[] args)
    {
        if (args.length != 1)
        {
            System.err.println("usage: java Split path");
            return;
        }
        File file = new File(args[0]);
        long length = file.length();
        int nWholeParts = (int) (length / FILESIZE);
        int remainder = (int) (length % FILESIZE);
        System.out.printf("Splitting %s into %d parts%n", args[0],
                        (remainder == 0) ? nWholeParts : nWholeParts + 1);
        BufferedInputStream bis = null;
        BufferedOutputStream bos = null;
        try
        {
            FileInputStream fis = new FileInputStream(args[0]);
            bis = new BufferedInputStream(fis);
            for (int i = 0; i < nWholeParts; i++)
            {
                bis.read(buffer);
                System.out.println("Writing part " + i);
                FileOutputStream fos = new FileOutputStream("part" + i);
                bos = new BufferedOutputStream(fos);
                bos.write(buffer);
                bos.close();
                bos = null;
            }
            if (remainder != 0)
            {
                int br = bis.read(buffer);
                if (br != remainder)
                {
                    System.err.println("Last part mismatch: expected " +
                                    remainder + " bytes");
                    System.exit(0);
                }
                System.out.println("Writing part " + nWholeParts);
                FileOutputStream fos = new FileOutputStream("part" +
                                    nWholeParts);
                bos = new BufferedOutputStream(fos);
                bos.write(buffer, 0, remainder);
            }
        }
    }
}
```

```
catch (IOException ioe)
{
   ioe.printStackTrace();
}
finally
{
   if (bis != null)
      try
      {
         bis.close();
      }
      catch (IOException ioe)
      {
         assert false; // shouldn't happen in this context
      }
   if (bos != null)
      try
      {
         bos.close();
      }
      catch (IOException ioe)
      {
         assert false; // shouldn't happen in this context
      }
   }
  }
}
```

Chapter 5: Writers and Readers

1. Java's stream classes are not good at streaming characters because those classes have no knowledge of character encodings.

2. Java provides writer and reader classes as the preferred alternative to stream classes when it comes to character I/O.

3. The answer is false: Reader doesn't declare an available() method.

4. The purpose of the OutputStreamWriter class is to serve as a bridge between an incoming sequence of characters and an outgoing stream of bytes. Characters written to this writer are encoded into

bytes according to the default or specified character encoding. The purpose of the InputStreamReader class is to serve as a bridge between an incoming stream of bytes and an outgoing sequence of characters. Characters read from this reader are decoded from bytes according to the default or specified character encoding.

5. You identify the default character encoding by reading the value of the file.encoding system property.

6. The purpose of the FileWriter class is to conveniently connect to the underlying file output stream using the default character encoding. The purpose of the FileReader class is to conveniently connect to the underlying file input stream using the default character encoding.

7. BufferedWriter provides the newLine() method for writing a line separator.

8. Listing A-5 presents the CircleInfo application that was called for in Chapter 5.

Listing A-5. Reading Lines of Text from Standard Input That Represent Circle Radii and Outputting Circumference and Area Based on the Current Radius

```java
import java.io.BufferedReader;
import java.io.InputStreamReader;
import java.io.IOException;

public class CircleInfo
{
   public static void main(String[] args) throws IOException
   {
      InputStreamReader isr = new InputStreamReader(System.in);
      BufferedReader br = new BufferedReader(isr);
      while (true)
      {
         System.out.print("Enter circle's radius: ");
         String str = br.readLine();
         double radius;
```

```
        try
        {
            radius = Double.valueOf(str).doubleValue();
            if (radius <= 0)
                System.err.println("radius must not be 0 or negative");
            else
            {
                System.out.println("Circumference: " + Math.PI * 2.0 *
                                    radius);
                System.out.println("Area: " + Math.PI * radius * radius);
                System.out.println();
            }
        }
        catch (NumberFormatException nfe)
        {
            System.err.println("not a number: " + nfe.getMessage());
        }
    }
  }
}
```

Chapter 6: Buffers

1. A buffer is an object that stores a fixed amount of data to be sent to or received from an I/O service (an operating system component for performing input/output). It sits between an application and a channel that writes the buffered data to the service or reads the data from the service and deposits it into the buffer.

2. A buffer's four properties are capacity, limit, position, and mark.

3. When you invoke Buffer's array() method on a buffer backed by a read-only array, this method throws ReadOnlyBufferException.

4. When you invoke Buffer's flip() method on a buffer, the limit is set to the current position and then the position is set to zero. When the mark is defined, it's discarded. The buffer is now ready to be drained.

5. When you invoke Buffer's reset() method on a buffer where a mark has not been set, this method throws InvalidMarkException.

6. The answer is false: buffers are not thread-safe.

7. The abstract classes that extend the abstract Buffer class are ByteBuffer, CharBuffer, DoubleBuffer, FloatBuffer, IntBuffer, LongBuffer, and ShortBuffer. Furthermore, ByteBuffer is subclassed by the abstract MappedByteBuffer class.

8. You create a byte buffer by invoking one of its allocate(), allocateDirect(), or wrap() class methods.

9. A view buffer is a buffer that manages another buffer's data.

10. A view buffer is created by calling a Buffer subclass's duplicate() method.

11. You create a read-only view buffer by calling a Buffer subclass method such as ByteBuffer asReadOnlyBuffer() or CharBuffer asReadOnlyBuffer().

12. ByteBuffer's methods for storing a single byte in a byte buffer are ByteBuffer put(int index, byte b) and ByteBuffer put(byte b). ByteBuffer's methods for fetching a single byte from a byte buffer are byte get(int index) and byte get().

13. Attempting to use the relative put() method or the relative get() method when the current position is greater than or equal to the limit causes BufferOverflowException or BufferUnderflowException to occur.

14. The equivalent of executing buffer.flip(); is to execute buffer.limit(buffer.position()).position(0);.

15. The answer is false: calling flip() twice doesn't return you to the original state. Instead, the buffer has a zero size.

16. The difference between Buffer's clear() and reset() methods is as follows: the clear() method marks a buffer as empty, whereas reset() changes the buffer's current position to the previously set mark or throws InvalidMarkException when there's no previously set mark.

17. ByteBuffer's compact() method compacts a buffer by copying all bytes between the current position and the limit to the beginning of the buffer. The byte at index p = position() is copied to index 0, the byte at index p + 1 is copied to index 1, and so on until the byte at index limit() - 1 is copied to index n = limit() - 1 - p. The buffer's current position is then set to n + 1 and its limit is set to its capacity. The mark, when defined, is discarded.

18. The purpose of the ByteOrder class is to help you deal with byte-order issues when writing/reading multibyte values to/from a multibyte buffer.

19. A direct byte buffer is a byte buffer that interacts with channels and native code to perform I/O. The direct byte buffer attempts to store byte elements in a memory area that a channel uses to perform direct (raw) access via native code that tells the operating system to drain or fill the memory area directly.

20. You obtain a direct byte buffer by invoking ByteBuffer's allocateDirect() method.

21. It can be expensive to create a direct byte buffer because memory extraneous to the JVM's heap will need to be allocated by the operating system, and setting up/tearing down this memory might take longer than when the buffer was located within the heap.

22. Listing A-6 presents the ViewBufferDemo application that was called for in Chapter 6.

Listing A-6. Viewing a Byte Sequence as a Character Sequence

```
import java.nio.ByteBuffer;
import java.nio.CharBuffer;

public class ViewBufferDemo
{
   public static void main(String[] args)
   {
      ByteBuffer bb = ByteBuffer.allocate(6);
      byte zero = 0;
      bb.put(zero).put((byte) 0x6e).put(zero).put((byte) 0x69)
        .put(zero).put((byte) 0x6f);
      bb.rewind();
      CharBuffer cb = bb.asCharBuffer();
      for (int i = 0; i < cb.limit(); i++)
         System.out.print(cb.get());
   }
}
```

Chapter 7: Channels

1. A channel is an object that represents an open connection to a hardware device, a file, a network socket, an application component, or another entity that's capable of performing write, read, and other I/O operations. Channels efficiently transfer data between byte buffers and operating system-based I/O service sources or destinations.

2. The capabilities that the Channel interface provides are closing a channel (via the close() method) and determining whether or not a channel is open (via the isOpen() method).

3. The three interfaces that directly extend Channel are WritableByteChannel, ReadableByteChannel, and InterruptibleChannel.

4. The answer is true: a channel that implements InterruptibleChannel is asynchronously closeable.

5. The two ways to obtain a channel are to invoke a Channels class method, such as WritableByteChannel newChannel(OutputStream outputStream), and to invoke a channel method on a classic I/O class, such as RandomAccessFile's FileChannel getChannel() method.

6.   Scatter/gather I/O is the ability to perform a single I/O operation across multiple buffers.

7.   The `ScatteringByteChannel` and `GatheringByteChannel` interfaces are provided for achieving scatter/gather I/O.

8.   A file channel is a channel to an underlying file.

9.   The answer is false: file channels support scatter/gather I/O.

10.   An exclusive lock gives a single writer process access to a file region; it prohibits additional file locks from being applied simultaneously to the region. A shared lock gives one of multiple reader processes access to the same file region; it does not prohibit other shared locks but does prohibit an exclusive lock from being applied simultaneously to the region.

11.   The fundamental difference between `FileChannel`'s `lock()` and `tryLock()` methods is that the `lock()` methods can block and the `tryLock()` methods never block.

12.   The `FileLock` `lock()` method throws `OverlappingFileLockException` when either a lock is already held that overlaps this lock request or another thread is waiting to acquire a lock that will overlap with this request.

13.   The pattern that you should adopt to ensure that an acquired file lock is always released appears here:

```
FileLock lock = fileChannel.lock(); // Assume fileChannel exists.
try
{
    // interact with the file channel
}
catch (IOException ioe)
{
    // handle the exception
}
finally
{
    lock.release();
}
```

14. `FileChannel` provides the `MappedByteBuffer map(FileChannel.MapMode mode, long position, long size)` method for mapping a region of a file into memory.

15. The three file-mapping modes are read-only, read-write, and private. They're described by the `READ_ONLY`, `READ_WRITE`, and `PRIVATE` constants declared by the `FileChannel.MapMode` enumerated type.

16. The private file-mapping mode corresponds to copy-on-write. Changes made to the resulting buffer will not be propagated to the file and will not be visible to other programs that have mapped the same file. Instead, changes will cause private copies of the modified portions of the buffer to be created. These changes are lost when the buffer is garbage collected.

17. The `FileChannel` methods that optimize the common practice of performing bulk transfers are `transferFrom()` and `transferTo()`.

18. The answer is true: socket channels are selectable and can function in nonblocking mode.

19. The three classes that describe socket channels are `ServerSocketChannel`, `SocketChannel`, and `DatagramChannel`.

20. The answer is false: datagram channels are thread-safe.

21. Socket channels support nonblocking mode because the blocking nature of sockets created from Java's socket classes is a serious limitation to a network-oriented Java application's scalability.

22. You would obtain a socket channel's associated socket by invoking its `socket()` method.

23. You obtain a server socket channel by invoking `ServerSocketChannel`'s `open()` class method.

24. Listing A-7 presents the `Copy` application that was called for in Chapter 7.

Listing A-7. Copying a File via a Byte Buffer and a File Channel

```java
import java.io.FileInputStream;
import java.io.FileNotFoundException;
import java.io.FileOutputStream;
import java.io.IOException;

import java.nio.ByteBuffer;

import java.nio.channels.FileChannel;

public class Copy
{
   public static void main(String[] args)
   {
      if (args.length != 2)
      {
         System.err.println("usage: java Copy srcfile dstfile");
         return;
      }
      try (FileInputStream fis = new FileInputStream(args[0]);
           FileChannel fcSrc = fis.getChannel();
           FileOutputStream fos = new FileOutputStream(args[1]);
           FileChannel fcDest = fos.getChannel())
      {
         ByteBuffer buffer = ByteBuffer.allocateDirect(2048);
         while ((fcSrc.read(buffer)) != -1)
         {
            buffer.flip();
            while (buffer.hasRemaining())
               fcDest.write(buffer);
            buffer.clear();
         }
      }
      catch (FileNotFoundException fnfe)
      {
         System.err.println(args[0] +
                            " could not be opened for input, or " +
                            args[1] +
                            " could not be created for output");
      }
      catch (IOException ioe)
      {
         System.err.println("I/O error: " + ioe.getMessage());
      }
   }
}
```

Chapter 8: Selectors

1. A selector is an object created from a subclass of the abstract `Selector` class. It maintains a set of channels that it examines to determine which of them are ready for reading, writing, completing a connection sequence, accepting another connection, or some combination of these tasks. The actual work is delegated to the operating system via a POSIX `select()` or similar system call.

2. The three main types that support selectors are `SelectableChannel`, `SelectionKey`, and `Selector`.

3. The answer is false: file channels cannot be used with selectors. Only channels that implement `SelectableChannel` can be used with selectors. `FileChannel` doesn't implement `SelectableChannel`.

4. `SelectionKey` provides the boolean `isReadable()` method as a convenient alternative to the expression `key.readyOps() & OP_READ != 0`.

Chapter 9: Regular Expressions

1. A regular expression (also known as a regex or regexp) is a string-based pattern that represents the set of strings that match this pattern.

2. Instances of the `Pattern` class represent patterns via compiled regexes. Regexes are compiled for performance reasons; pattern matching via compiled regexes is much faster than if the regexes were not compiled.

3. `Pattern`'s `compile()` methods throw `PatternSyntaxException` when they discover illegal syntax in their regular expression arguments.

4. Instances of the `Matcher` class attempt to match compiled regexes against input text.

5. The difference between Matcher's matches() and lookingAt() methods is that, unlike matches(), lookingAt() doesn't require the entire region to be matched.

6. A character class is a set of characters appearing between [and].

7. There are six kinds of character classes: simple, negation, range, union, intersection, and subtraction.

8. The answer is false: a subtraction character class consists of multiple &&-separated nested character classes, where at least one nested character class is a negation character class, and it matches all characters except for those indicated by the negation character class/classes.

9. A capturing group saves a match's characters for later recall during pattern matching.

10. A zero-length match is a match of zero length in which the start and end indexes are equal.

11. A quantifier is a numeric value implicitly or explicitly bound to a pattern. Quantifiers are categorized as greedy, reluctant, or possessive.

12. The difference between greedy and reluctant quantifiers is that a greedy quantifier attempts to find the longest match, whereas a reluctant quantifier attempts to find the shortest match.

13. Possessive and greedy quantifiers differ in that a possessive quantifier only makes one attempt to find the longest match, whereas a greedy quantifier can make multiple attempts.

14. Listing A-8 presents the ReplaceText application that was called for in Chapter 9.

Listing A-8. Replacing All Matches of the Pattern with Replacement Text

```
import java.util.regex.Matcher;
import java.util.regex.Pattern;
import java.util.regex.PatternSyntaxException;

public class ReplaceText
{
   public static void main(String[] args)
   {
      if (args.length != 3)
      {
         System.err.println("usage: java ReplaceText text oldText newText");
         return;
      }
      try
      {
         Pattern p = Pattern.compile(args[1]);
         Matcher m = p.matcher(args[0]);
         String result = m.replaceAll(args[2]);
         System.out.println(result);
      }
      catch (PatternSyntaxException pse)
      {
         System.err.println(pse);
      }
   }
}
```

Chapter 10: Charsets

1. A charset is a coded character set combined with a character-encoding scheme.

2. The purpose of the Charset class is to translate between byte sequences and the characters that are encoded into these sequences.

3. The standard charsets supported by the JVM are US-ASCII, ISO-8859-1, UTF-8, UTF-16BE, UTF-16LE, and UTF-16.

4. The purpose of the byte order mark is to tell a decoder how a UTF-16-encoded byte sequence was encoded.

5. You obtain the default charset by invoking Charset's
    Charset defaultCharset() factory method.

6. Charset's Charset forName(String charsetName)
    factory method throws UnsupportedCharsetException
    when the desired charset isn't supported by the JVM.

7. You would typically encode a string via a Charset
    instance by invoking Charset's ByteBuffer
    encode(String s) method, which returns a new
    ByteBuffer object containing the bytes that encode
    the characters from s. You could also invoke
    Charset's ByteBuffer encode(CharBuffer cb)
    method.

8. The Charset methods that perform the actual
    encoding and decoding tasks are CharsetEncoder
    newEncoder() and CharsetDecoder newDecoder().

9. String's byte[] getBytes() method returns a new
    byte array containing the characters of this string
    encoded using the operating system's default
    charset.

10. Listing A-9 presents the AvailCharsets application
    that was called for in Chapter 10.

Listing A-9. Obtaining and Outputting a Map of Available Charsets

```
import java.nio.charset.Charset;

import java.util.SortedMap;

public class AvailCharsets
{
    public static void main(String[] args)
    {
        SortedMap<String, Charset> acs = Charset.availableCharsets();
        System.out.println(acs);
    }
}
```

Chapter 11: Formatter

1. The three nonexception types that contribute to NIO's `printf`-style formatting facility are `Formatter`, `Formattable`, and `FormattableFlags`.

2. You reference an argument from within a format specifier string by specifying the argument's 1-based index followed by the dollar sign character. For example, 1$ references the first argument and 2$ references the second argument.

3. The %n format specifier outputs an operating system-specific line separator.

4. Listing A-10 presents the `FormatterDemo` application that was called for in Chapter 11.

Listing A-10. Formatting Output to an External `StringBuilder` Object

```java
import java.util.Formatter;

public class FormatterDemo
{
   public static void main(String[] args)
   {
      StringBuilder output = new StringBuilder();
      Formatter formatter = new Formatter(output);
      formatter.format("%d", 123);
      System.out.println(formatter.toString());
      output.setLength(0);
      formatter.format("%x", 123);
      System.out.println(formatter.toString());
      output.setLength(0);
      formatter.format("%c", 'X');
      System.out.println(formatter.toString());
      output.setLength(0);
      formatter.format("%f", 0.1);
      System.out.println(formatter.toString());
      output.setLength(0);
      formatter.format("%s%n", "Hello, World");
      System.out.println(formatter.toString());
      output.setLength(0);
      formatter.format("%10.2f", 98.375);
      System.out.println(formatter.toString());
      output.setLength(0);
      formatter.format("%05d", 123);
```

```
System.out.println(formatter.toString());
output.setLength(0);
formatter.format("%1$d %1$d", 123);
System.out.println(formatter.toString());
output.setLength(0);
formatter.format("%d %d", 123);
System.out.println(formatter.toString());
output.setLength(0);
formatter.close();
    }
}
```

Chapter 12: Improved File System Interface

1. A file system is an operating system component that manages file-based data storage. A file is a regular file, a directory, a symbolic link, or a hard link.

2. Having File's delete() method return false when something goes wrong is a problem because you don't know why the file could not be deleted (it may not exist or the user may not have the appropriate permission). Throwing a specific exception is more helpful.

3. The packages that implement the improved file system interface are java.nio.file, java.nio.file.attribute, and java.nio.file.spi.

4. The types that form the core of the improved file system interface are FileSystem, FileSystems, and FileSystemProvider.

5. You obtain a reference to the default file system by calling the FileSystems class's FileSystem getDefault() class method.

6. You create a new file system by calling the FileSystems class's newFileSystem() methods with the appropriate arguments.

7. A path is a compact map that navigates a hierarchy of files via a separated name element sequence.

8. The answer is false: the Path interface represents a hierarchical path to a file that may not exist.

9. A `Path` object's stored path optionally starts with a name element identifying a file system hierarchy and optionally continues with a sequence of directory elements separated by a separator character. The name element that is farthest from the root of the directory hierarchy is the name of a directory or other kind of file. The other name elements are directory names.

10. `Path` declares `File toFile()` to return a `File` object representing its path. `File` declares `Path toPath()` to return a `Path` object representing the `File` object's abstract path.

11. `FileSystem` provides a `Path getPath(String first, String... more)` method for returning a `Path` object.

12. When you attempt to create a `Path` object using syntax that doesn't conform to the syntax that is parsed by the file system provider that created the `FileSystem` responsible for creating the `Path` object, `InvalidPathException` is thrown.

13. The methods that the `Paths` class provides for more conveniently returning `Path` objects are `Path get(String first, String... more)` and `Path get(URI uri)`.

14. `Path`'s methods for returning its name elements are `Path getFileName()`, `Path getName(int index)`, `int getNameCount()`, `Path getParent()`, `Path getRoot()`, and `Path subpath(int beginIndex, int endIndex)`.

15. The answer is false: `Path`'s boolean `isAbsolute()` method returns `true` to signify an absolute path. There is no `isRelative()` method.

16. You obtain a file system's root(s) by calling `FileSystem`'s `Iterable<Path> getRootDirectories()` method, which returns an iterator over `Path` instances that describe roots.

17. You convert a relative path to an absolute path by calling `Path`'s `Path toAbsolutePath()` method.

18.   Path's method for removing path redundancies, creating a relative path between two paths, and resolving (joining) two paths are Path normalize(), Path relativize(Path other), Path resolve(Path other), and Path resolve(String other), respectively.

19.   You resolve a path string against the current path's parent path by calling Path's Path resolveSibling(Path other) or Path resolveSibling(String other) method.

20.   You convert the current Path instance to a URI object by calling Path's URI toURI() method.

21.   The Path toRealPath(LinkOption... options) method returns the real path of the file represented by the Path object. This method generally derives, from this path, an absolute path that locates the same file as this path, but with name elements that represent the actual names of the directories and any nondirectory. You can pass a comma-delimited list of LinkOption enum constants as arguments. This enum defines the options for how symbolic links are handled. Currently, LinkOption declares only a NOFOLLOW_LINKS (don't follow symbolic links) constant.

22.   The answer is false: the Files class doesn't provide static methods for performing path-matching and directory-watching tasks. You need to call FileSystem methods to obtain path-matchers and watch services.

23.   A file store is a storage pool, device, partition, volume, concrete file system, or other implementation-specific means of file storage. A file store consists of a name, a type, space amounts (in bytes), and other information. A file store is represented by the FileStore class.

24.   The Files class provides the FileStore getFileStore(Path path) method to return a FileStore representing the file store where the file identified by path is stored.

25. You can obtain amounts of space (total, unallocated, and usable), an indication if the file store is read-only, and the name and type of the file store.

26. You can obtain all file stores for a given file system by calling FileSystem's Iterable<FileStore> getFileStores() method, which lets you iterate over all of the file stores.

27. The support offered by NIO.2 for working with attributes are the types stored in the java.nio.file. attribute package along with the attribute-oriented methods of the Files class and other types.

28. Attributes are organized into views where each view corresponds to a specific file system implementation.

29. The attribute type hierarchy is rooted in AttributeView. This interface is subtyped by FileAttributeView. FileAttributeView is subtyped by BasicFileAttributeView, FileOwnerAttributeView, and UserDefinedFileAttributeView. BasicFileAttributeView is subtyped by DosFileAttributeView and PosixFileAttributeView. FileOwnerAttributeView is subtyped by AclFileAttributeView and PosixFileAttributeView. AttributeView is also subtyped by FileStoreAttributeView.

30. You can identify all supported attribute views for a given file system by calling FileSystem's Set<String> supportedFileAttributeViews() method, which returns a set of strings identifying views that are supported by the invoking FileSystem.

31. Basic attributes are those attributes that are common to many file systems. The view for managing basic attributes is BasicFileAttributeView. The basic attributes are creationTime, fileKey, isDirectory, isOther, isRegularFile, isSymbolicLink, lastAccessTime, lastModifiedTime, and size.

32. The answer is true: you can read basic attributes in bulk by calling `BasicFileAttributeView`'s `BasicFileAttributes readAttributes()` method. You would accomplish this task indirectly by calling the `Files` class's `<A extends BasicFileAttributes>` `A readAttributes(Path path, Class<A> type, LinkOption... options)` method, passing `BasicFileAttributes.class` to `type`.

33. A file key is an identifier or a combination of identifiers that uniquely identifies a file.

34. When you call the `Files` class's `getAttribute()` or `setAttribute()` method to get or set a basic or other kind of attribute value, the syntax that you must follow for identifying the attribute is `[view-name:]` `attribute-name`. You don't have to specify the `view-name` for basic attributes because `basic` is the default `view-name`.

35. `UserPrincipal` represents an identity for determining access rights to objects in a file system and extends `Principal`. `GroupPrincipal` represents a group identity and extends `UserPrincipal`.

36. `FileOwnerAttributeView`'s `setOwner()` method throws `FileSystemException` on a Windows operating system when a security ID cannot be assigned as the owner, which must be one of the users or groups that you have been given the right to assign as the owner. The solution is to elevate the privilege of the Java application.

37. An `AclEntry`'s components are `type`, `principal`, `permissions`, and `flags`. The components are described by the `AclEntryType`, `UserPrincipal`, `AclEntryPermission`, and `AclEntryFlag` types.

38. The answer is true: you can define your own file attributes. Use the `UserDefinedFileAttributeView` type for this task.

39. The attributes supported by `FileStoreAttributeView` are `totalSpace`, `unallocatedSpace`, and `usableSpace`. You can access the values of these attributes by passing these names to `FileStore`'s `getAttribute()` method, although it's preferred to access them via `FileStore`'s type-safe `getTotalSpace()`, `getUnallocatedSpace()`, and `getUsableSpace()` methods.

40. The answer is false: `!exists(path)` is not equivalent to `notExists(path)`.

41. The `isDirectory()` method's default policy on symbolic links is to follow them. If you don't want to follow symbolic links, pass `LinkOption.NOFOLLOW_LINKS` to this method.

42. You should be careful when using the return values from `exists()`, `notExists()`, `isExecutable()`, `isReadable()`, and `isWritable()` because the return values are immediately outdated. The file system may experience changes in the time between the method call and the use of its result.

43. The `createFile()` method throws `FileAlreadyExistsException` when called to create a file that already exists.

44. An optional specific exception is an exception that's thrown when the underlying operating system can detect the specific error leading to the exception. If the error cannot be detected, its `IOException` ancestor is thrown instead.

45. You would set POSIX file permissions when creating a file by calling the `PosixFilePermissions` class's `FileAttribute<Set<PosixFilePermission>>` `asFileAttribute(Set<PosixFilePermission> perms)` method to create a `FileAttribute` that encapsulates a copy of the given file permissions, and then passing `asFileAttribute()`'s return value as the second argument to `createFile()`.

46. The Path createTempFile(String prefix, String suffix, FileAttribute<?>... attrs) method creates the temporary file in the default temporary-file directory (identified by the Java property java.io.tmpdir).

47. Three ways to delete a temporary file before an application exits are as follows:

- Add a shutdown hook via the Runtime class's void addShutdownHook(Thread hook) method and delete the file in the shutdown hook.

- Convert the returned Path object to a File object (via Path's toFile() method) and invoke File's void deleteOnExit() method on the File object.

- Work with the Files class's newOutputStream() method and NIO.2's DELETE_ON_CLOSE constant.

48. NIO.2's three methods for reading all bytes or lines of text from a regular file into memory are byte[] readAllBytes(Path path), List<String> readAllLines(Path path), and List<String> readAllLines(Path path, Charset cs).

49. The methods you would use to read very large files (whose contents probably don't fit into memory) are BufferedReader newBufferedReader(Path path), BufferedReader newBufferedReader(Path path, Charset cs), and InputStream newInputStream(Path path, OpenOption... options).

50. The open options supported by the StandardOpenOption enum are as follows:

- APPEND: If the file is opened for WRITE access, write bytes to the end of the file rather than to the beginning.

- CREATE: Create a new file when it doesn't exist.

- CREATE_NEW: Create a new file, failing when the file already exists.

- DELETE_ON_CLOSE: Make a best effort to delete the file when the file is closed.

- DSYNC: Require that every update to the file's content be written synchronously to the underlying storage device.

- READ: Open the file for read access.

- SPARSE: Open a sparse file. When used with the CREATE_NEW option, SPARSE provides a hint that the new file will be sparse. The option is ignored when the file system doesn't support the creation of sparse files.

- SYNC: Require that every update to the file's content or metadata be written synchronously to the underlying storage device.

- TRUNCATE_EXISTING: Truncate the length of an existing file that's opened for WRITE access to 0.

- WRITE: Open the file for write access.

51. NIO.2's three methods for writing all bytes or lines of text from memory to a regular file are Path write(Path path, byte[] bytes, OpenOption... options), Path write(Path path, Iterable<? extends CharSequence> lines, Charset cs, OpenOption... options), and Path write(Path path, Iterable<? extends CharSequence> lines, OpenOption... options).

52. The methods you use to write very large files (whose contents probably don't fit into memory) are BufferedWriter newBufferedWriter(Path path, Charset cs, OpenOption... options), BufferedWriter newBufferedWriter(Path path, OpenOption... options), and OutputStream newOutputStream(Path path, OpenOption... options).

53. The answer is true: when no options are specified, newOutputStream() works as if the CREATE, TRUNCATE_EXISTING, and WRITE options are present.

54. The purpose of the SeekableByteChannel interface is to describe byte channels that can be randomly accessed. It provides the ability to obtain the current position and to change the current position to a new position.

55. The FileChannel class specifies FileChannel position(long newPosition) and FileChannel truncate(long size) instead of specifying SeekableByteChannel position(long newPosition) and SeekableByteChannel truncate(long size) for the following reason: SeekableByteChannel's documentation recommends that the method return types be specialized by classes that implement SeekableByteChannel so that method invocations on the implementation classes can be chained together.

56. You obtain a SeekableByteChannel object by calling the Files class's SeekableByteChannel newByteChannel(Path path, OpenOption... options) method or its SeekableByteChannel newByteChannel(Path path, Set<? extends OpenOption> options, FileAttribute<?>... attrs) method.

57. NIO.2 added FileChannel open(Path path, OpenOption... options) and FileChannel open(Path path, Set<? extends OpenOption> options, FileAttribute<?>... attrs) methods to the FileChannel class so that you would no longer have to rely on a classic I/O type (such as RandomAccessFile) to obtain a file channel.

58. The Files class provides the Path createDirectory(Path dir, FileAttribute<?>... attrs) method for creating a directory.

59. The answer is false: the Files class's directory-creation method doesn't automatically create nonexistent ancestor directories of the directory being created. You need to use the createDirectories() method for that task.

60. The Files class's methods for creating temporary directories are Path createTempDirectory(Path dir, String prefix, FileAttribute<?>... attrs) and Path createTempDirectory(String prefix, FileAttribute<?>... attrs).

61. NIO.2 provides the DirectoryStream<T> interface along with the DirectoryStream<Path> newDirectoryStream(Path dir), DirectoryStream<Path> newDirectoryStream(Path dir, DirectoryStream.Filter<? super Path> filter), and DirectoryStream<Path> newDirectoryStream(Path dir, String glob) methods in the Files class for obtaining a list of a directory's entries.

62. You filter a list of directory entries so that only desired entries are returned by subclassing DirectoryStream.Filter<T> and overriding its boolean accept(T path) method, making sure to pass Path to T. This method must return true when path is accepted (included in the directory stream); otherwise, false must be returned.

63. Files provides long copy(InputStream in, Path target, CopyOption... options), long copy(Path source, OutputStream out), and Path copy(Path source, Path target, CopyOption... options) methods to copy a file to another file.

64. The copy options supported by the StandardCopyOption enum are as follows:

    ■ ATOMIC_MOVE: Perform the move as an atomic file system operation. This constant isn't used by the copy() methods because it's meaningless in a copy context.

    ■ COPY_ATTRIBUTES: Copy attributes as well as content.

    ■ REPLACE_EXISTING: Replace an existing target.

65. The other copy option that can be passed to these copy() methods is NOFOLLOW_LINKS (symbolic links are not followed). This copy option is provided by the LinkOption enum, which (along with StandardCopyOption) implements the CopyOption interface. Ultimately, all copy options are CopyOption instances.

66. Files provides the Path move(Path source, Path target, CopyOption... options) method to move a file to another file.

67. The copy options supported by this file-movement method are ATOMIC_MOVE and REPLACE_EXISTING.

68. The Files methods for deleting files are void delete(Path path) and boolean deleteIfExists(Path path).

69. A symbolic link (soft link or symlink) is a special file that references another file. A circular reference is the target of a link pointing back to the original link.

70. The Files class provides the Path createSymbolicLink(Path link, Path target, FileAttribute<?>... attrs) method for creating a symbolic link to a target.

71. You determine if an arbitrary path represents a symbolic link by calling the Files class's boolean isSymbolicLink(Path path) method. It returns true when path is a symbolic link and returns false when path identifies a nonexistent file, is not a symbolic link, or it cannot be determined if the file is a symbolic link.

72. You read the target of a symbolic link by calling the Files class's Path readSymbolicLink(Path link) method.

73. A hard link is a directory entry that associates a name with a file on a file system. It's basically the same entity as the original file. All attributes are identical: they have the same file permissions, timestamps, and so on.

74. Hard links are more restrictive than soft links in the following ways:

    ■ The target of the link must exist.

    ■ Hard links are generally not allowed on directories.

    ■ Hard links are not allowed to cross partitions or volumes. In other words, they cannot exist across file systems.

    ■ A hard link looks and behaves like a normal file and therefore can be hard to find.

75. The Files class provides the Path createLink(Path link, Path existing) method for creating a hard link (directory entry) for an existing file.

76. The File Tree-Walking API provides the ability to walk a file tree and visit all of its files (regular files, directories, and links). As well as providing a private implementation that performs the walk, this API provides a public interface for an application to use.

77. The types that comprise the public portion of the File Tree-Walking API are FileVisitor<T>, FileVisitResult, SimpleFileVisitor<T>, FileVisitOption, and FileSystemLoopException.

78. The answer is true: SKIP_SUBTREE is only meaningful when returned from the preVisitDirectory() method; otherwise this result type is the same as CONTINUE.

79. The Files class provides Path walkFileTree(Path start, FileVisitor<? super Path> visitor) and Path walkFileTree(Path start, Set<FileVisitOption> options, int maxDepth, FileVisitor<? super Path> visitor) for walking the file tree.

80. The Stream<Path> find(Path start, int maxDepth, BiPredicate<Path,BasicFileAttributes> matcher, FileVisitOption... options) method returns a Stream<Path> object that is lazily populated with the Paths of those files that are accepted by a BiPredicate object.

81. NIO.2 supports path-matching as follows: FileSystem's PathMatcher getPathMatcher(String syntaxAndPattern) method returns a PathMatcher object for matching paths against the pattern described by syntaxAndPattern, which identifies a pattern language (syntax) and a pattern (pattern) via this syntax. The PathMatcher interface declares a boolean matches(Path path) method that compares its path argument with the PathMatcher's current pattern. It returns true when there is a match; otherwise, it returns false.

82. The purpose of the Watch Service API is to watch registered directories for changes and events. For example, a file manager can use a watch service to monitor a directory for changes so that it can update its list-of-files display when files are created or deleted.

83. The following types comprise the Watch Service API:

    ■ Watchable: An interface that describes any object that may be registered with a watch service so that it can be watched for changes and events. Because Path extends Watchable, all entries in directories represented as Paths can be watched.

    ■ WatchEvent<T>: An interface describing any event or repeated event for an object that's registered with a watch service.

    ■ WatchEvent<T>.Kind: A nested interface that identifies an event kind (such as directory entry creation).

    ■ WatchEvent<T>.Modifier: A nested interface qualifying how a watchable is registered with a watch service. This interface isn't used at this time.

    ■ WatchKey: An interface describing a token representing the registration of a watchable with a watch service.

    ■ WatchService: An interface describing any object that watches registered objects for changes and events.

    ■ StandardWatchEventKinds: A class describing four event kind constants (directory entry creation, deletion, or modification; and overflow, which indicates that events may have been lost because the file system is generating them too quickly).

    ■ ClosedWatchServiceException: A class describing an unchecked exception that's thrown when an attempt is made to invoke an operation on a watch service that's closed.

84. Listing A-11 presents the Touch application that was called for in Chapter 12.

Listing A-11. Setting a File or Directory's Timestamp to the Current Time via NIO.2

```java
import java.io.IOException;

import java.nio.file.Files;
import java.nio.file.Paths;

import java.nio.file.attribute.FileTime;

import java.time.Instant;

public class Touch
{
   public static void main(String[] args) throws IOException
   {
      if (args.length != 1)
      {
         System.err.println("usage: java Touch path");
         return;
      }
      Files.setLastModifiedTime(Paths.get(args[0]),
                                FileTime.from(Instant.now()));
   }
}
```

Chapter 13: Asynchronous I/O

1. An asynchronous channel supports asynchronous I/O operations (reads, writes, and so on).

2. The two ways to initiate an I/O operation with an asynchronous channel are as follows: call a method that returns a Future and call a method that takes a CompletionHandler argument.

3. The answer is false: after a channel is closed, further attempts to initiate asynchronous I/O operations complete immediately with cause ClosedChannelException.

4. The methods declared by the AsynchronousByteChannel interface are Future<Integer> read(ByteBuffer dst), <A> void read(ByteBuffer dst, A attachment, CompletionHandler<Integer,? super A> handler), Future<Integer> write(ByteBuffer src), and <A> void write(ByteBuffer src, A attachment, CompletionHandler<Integer,? super A> handler).

5. The answer is false: the ByteBuffer object isn't safe for use by multiple concurrent threads.

6. The class for reading, writing, and manipulating a file asynchronously is AsynchronousFileChannel.

7. The answer is true: an asynchronous file channel doesn't have a current position within a file.

8. If you pass no options to AsynchronousFileChannel's AsynchronousFileChannel open(Path file, OpenOption... options) method, this method attempts to open an existing file.

9. You obtain an AsynchronousServerSocketChannel object or an AsynchronousSocketChannel object by calling either of each abstract class's two open() methods.

10. AsynchronousServerSocketChannel's documented socket options are SO_RCVBUF and SO_REUSEADDR.

11. After obtaining an AsynchronousServerSocketChannel object, you must bind this channel to a local address and configure it to listen for connections by invoking one of AsynchronousServerSocketChannel's bind() methods before you can call either of its accept() methods.

12. After obtaining an AsynchronousSocketChannel object, you must connect it to the socket of an asynchronous server socket channel by invoking one of AsynchronousSocketChannel's connect() methods before you can perform reads and writes.

13. You determine if an asynchronous socket channel is connected to an asynchronous server socket channel by calling AsynchronousSocketChannel's getRemoteAddress() method, which returns null when the channel's socket isn't connected.

14. The answer is true: asynchronous socket channels are safe for use by multiple concurrent threads.

15. The purpose of the AsynchronousChannelGroup class is to describe a grouping of asynchronous channels for the purpose of resource sharing.

16.   A group uses a thread pool for task submission.

17.   The system properties for configuring the default
       group are java.nio.channels.DefaultThreadPool.
       threadFactory and java.nio.channels.
       DefaultThreadPool.initialSize.

18.   The void shutdownNow() method is used to initiate
       a forceful shutdown of the group. In addition to the
       actions performed by an orderly shutdown,
       shutdownNow() closes all open channels in the group
       as if by invoking each channel's close() method.

19.   The answer is false: AsynchronousFileChannels don't
       belong to groups. However, they are associated with
       a thread pool to which tasks are submitted, to handle
       I/O events and to dispatch to completion handlers
       that consume the results of I/O operations on the
       channel.

20.   Listing A-12 presents the Copy application that was
       called for in Chapter 13.

Listing A-12. Copying a Source File to a Destination File Asynchronously

```java
import java.io.IOException;

import java.nio.ByteBuffer;

import java.nio.channels.AsynchronousFileChannel;
import java.nio.channels.CompletionHandler;

import java.nio.file.Paths;

import static java.nio.file.StandardOpenOption.*;

public class Copy
{
   final static Thread THDMAIN = Thread.currentThread();

   public static void main(String[] args) throws IOException
   {
      if (args.length != 2)
      {
         System.err.println("usage: java Copy src dest");
         return;
      }
```

```java
        copy(AsynchronousFileChannel.open(Paths.get(args[0])),
            AsynchronousFileChannel.open(Paths.get(args[1]), WRITE,
                                        TRUNCATE_EXISTING, CREATE));

      try
      {
         THDMAIN.join();
      }
      catch (InterruptedException ie)
      {
         System.out.println("done");
      }
   }

   public static void copy(AsynchronousFileChannel chSrc,
                           AsynchronousFileChannel chDest)
   {
      ByteBuffer buffer = ByteBuffer.allocate(8192);

      class ReadCompletionHandler implements CompletionHandler<Integer,
                                                               Integer>
      {
         @Override
         public void completed(Integer result, Integer pos)
         {
            if (result == -1)
            {
               THDMAIN.interrupt();
               return;
            }

            buffer.flip();
            chDest.write(buffer, pos, pos + result,
                        new CompletionHandler<Integer, Integer>()
                        {
                           @Override
                           public void completed(Integer result,
                                                 Integer newPos)
                           {
                              buffer.compact();
                              chSrc.read(buffer, newPos, newPos,
                                         ReadCompletionHandler.this);
                           }
```

```
                        @Override
                        public void failed(Throwable t, Integer pos)
                        {
                            System.out.println("write failure");
                            THDMAIN.interrupt();
                        }
                    });
        }

        @Override
        public void failed(Throwable t, Integer pos)
        {
            System.out.println("read failure");
            THDMAIN.interrupt();
        }
    }

    chSrc.read(buffer, 0, 0, new ReadCompletionHandler());
    }
}
```

Chapter 14: Completion of Socket Channel Functionality

1. The capabilities that NIO.2 provides for completing socket channel functionality are support for binding and option configuration in the DatagramChannel, ServerSocketChannel, and SocketChannel classes and support for channel-based multicasting.

2. JDK 7 overcame the counterintuitive mix of socket channel and socket APIs by introducing the NetworkChannel interface, which is implemented by the DatagramChannel, ServerSocketChannel, SocketChannel, AsynchronousServerSocketChannel, and AsynchronousSocketChannel classes.

3. The exceptions that are thrown by SocketChannel's shutdownInput() and shutdownOutput() methods are NotYetConnectedException, ClosedChannelException, and IOException.

4.   JDK 7 supports multicasting by introducing a
     `MulticastChannel` interface that extends
     `NetworkChannel`, by introducing a `MembershipKey`
     class, and by adding an `open(ProtocolFamily)`
     method to the `DatagramChannel` class.

5.   The answer is false: The `MembershipKey`
     `join(InetAddress group, NetworkInterface ni,`
     `InetAddress source)` method performs include-mode
     filtering.

6.   Listing A-13 presents the `EnumNI` application that was
     called for in Chapter 14.

Listing A-13. Enumerating Network Interfaces and Outputting Their Names

```
import java.net.NetworkInterface;

import java.util.Enumeration;

public class EnumNI
{
   public static void main(String[] args) throws Exception
   {
      Enumeration<NetworkInterface> e;
      e = NetworkInterface.getNetworkInterfaces();
      while (e.hasMoreElements())
         System.out.println(e.nextElement());
   }
}
```

7.   Listing A-14 presents the `ChannelClient` application
     that was called for in Chapter 15.

Listing A-14. Dropping Group Membership and Closing the Channel

```
import java.io.IOException;

import java.net.InetAddress;
import java.net.InetSocketAddress;
import java.net.NetworkInterface;
import java.net.StandardProtocolFamily;
import java.net.StandardSocketOptions;

import java.nio.ByteBuffer;

import java.nio.channels.DatagramChannel;
import java.nio.channels.MembershipKey;
```

```
public class ChannelClient
{
    final static int PORT = 9999;

    public static void main(String[] args) throws IOException
    {
        NetworkInterface ni;
        ni = NetworkInterface.getByInetAddress(InetAddress.getLocalHost());
        DatagramChannel dc;
        dc = DatagramChannel.open(StandardProtocolFamily.INET)
                            .setOption(StandardSocketOptions.SO_REUSEADDR,
                                       true)
                            .bind(new InetSocketAddress(PORT))
                            .setOption(StandardSocketOptions.IP_MULTICAST_IF,
                                       ni);
        InetAddress group = InetAddress.getByName("239.255.0.1");
        MembershipKey key = dc.join(group, ni);

        ByteBuffer response = ByteBuffer.allocate(50);
        for (int i = 0; i < 10; i++)
        {
            dc.receive(response);
            response.flip();
            while (response.hasRemaining())
                System.out.print((char) response.get());
            System.out.println();
            response.clear();
        }
        key.drop();
        dc.close();
    }
}
```

8. Listing A-15 presents the StockServer application
    that was called for in Chapter 14.

Listing A-15. Broadcasting a Stock's Fluctuating Share Prices

```
import java.io.IOException;

import java.net.InetAddress;
import java.net.InetSocketAddress;
import java.net.NetworkInterface;
import java.net.StandardProtocolFamily;
import java.net.StandardSocketOptions;

import java.nio.ByteBuffer;
```

```java
import java.nio.channels.DatagramChannel;
import java.nio.channels.MembershipKey;

public class StockServer
{
    final static int PORT = 9999;

    public static void main(String[] args) throws IOException
    {
        NetworkInterface ni;
        ni = NetworkInterface.getByInetAddress(InetAddress.getLocalHost());
        DatagramChannel dc;
        dc = DatagramChannel.open(StandardProtocolFamily.INET)
                            .setOption(StandardSocketOptions.SO_REUSEADDR,
                                       true)
                            .bind(new InetSocketAddress(PORT))
                            .setOption(StandardSocketOptions.IP_MULTICAST_IF,
                                       ni);
        InetAddress group = InetAddress.getByName("239.255.0.1");
        InetSocketAddress isa = new InetSocketAddress(group, PORT);

        float openPrice = 37.4f;
        float lowPrice = 37.22f;
        float highPrice = 37.48f;
        float closePrice = 37.41f;
        ByteBuffer payload = ByteBuffer.allocate(16);
        while (true)
        {
            // fluctuate by a factor of -0.5 to almost +0.5
            float fluctuation = (float) (Math.random() - 0.5);

            lowPrice += fluctuation;
            lowPrice = Math.max(lowPrice, -lowPrice);
            highPrice += fluctuation;
            highPrice = Math.max(highPrice, -lowPrice);
            closePrice += fluctuation;
            closePrice = Math.max(closePrice, -lowPrice);

            payload.putFloat(openPrice);
            payload.putFloat(lowPrice);
            payload.putFloat(highPrice);
            payload.putFloat(closePrice);
            payload.flip();
            dc.send(payload, isa);
            payload.clear();

            openPrice = closePrice;
        }
    }
}
```

Listing A-16 presents the StockClient application that was called for in Chapter 14.

Listing A-16. Receiving a Stock's Fluctuating Share Prices

```java
import java.io.IOException;

import java.net.InetAddress;
import java.net.InetSocketAddress;
import java.net.NetworkInterface;
import java.net.StandardProtocolFamily;
import java.net.StandardSocketOptions;

import java.nio.ByteBuffer;

import java.nio.channels.DatagramChannel;
import java.nio.channels.MembershipKey;

public class StockClient
{
   final static int PORT = 9999;

   public static void main(String[] args) throws IOException
   {
      NetworkInterface ni;
      ni = NetworkInterface.getByInetAddress(InetAddress.getLocalHost());
      DatagramChannel dc;
      dc = DatagramChannel.open(StandardProtocolFamily.INET)
                          .setOption(StandardSocketOptions.SO_REUSEADDR,
                                     true)
                          .bind(new InetSocketAddress(PORT))
                          .setOption(StandardSocketOptions.IP_MULTICAST_IF,
                                     ni);
      InetAddress group = InetAddress.getByName("239.255.0.1");
      MembershipKey key = dc.join(group, ni);

      ByteBuffer response = ByteBuffer.allocate(16);
      while (true)
      {
         dc.receive(response);
         response.flip();
         System.out.println("Open price: " + response.getFloat());
         System.out.println("Low price: " + response.getFloat());
         System.out.println("High price: " + response.getFloat());
         System.out.println("Close price: " + response.getFloat());
         response.clear();
      }
   }
}
```

Sockets and Network Interfaces

Chapter 7 introduced the concept of a *peer socket*, which is a socket that is associated with a channel. Chapter 14 introduced the concept of a network interface. This appendix introduces sockets, network interfaces, and the APIs for interacting with these networking features.

Note A *network* is a group of interconnected *nodes* (computing devices such as tablets, and peripherals such as scanners or laser printers) that can be shared among the network's users. Networks often use *TCP/IP* (http://en.wikipedia.org/wiki/TCP/IP_model) to communicate between nodes. TCP/IP includes *Transmission Control Protocol (TCP)*, which is a connection-oriented protocol; *User Datagram Protocol (UDP)*, which is a connectionless protocol; and *Internet Protocol (IP)*, which is the basic protocol over which TCP and UDP perform their tasks.

The java.net package provides types that support TCP/IP between *processes* (executing applications) running on *hosts* (computer-based TCP/IP nodes).

Sockets

Two processes communicate by way of *sockets*, which are endpoints in a communications link between these processes. Each endpoint is identified by an *IP address* that identifies the host and by a *port number* that identifies the process running on that host.

IP ADDRESSES AND PORT NUMBERS

An *IP address* is a 32-bit or 128-bit unsigned integer that uniquely identifies a network host or some other network node (a router, for example).

It is common to specify a 32-bit IP address as four 8-bit integer components in a period-separated decimal notation, where each component is a decimal integer ranging from 0 through 255 and is separated from the next component via a period (such as 127.0.0.1). A 32-bit IP address is often referred to as an *Internet Protocol Version 4 (IPv4) address* (see http://en.wikipedia.org/wiki/IPv4).

It's common to specify a 128-bit IP address as eight 16-bit integer components in colon-separated hexadecimal notation, where each component is a hexadecimal integer ranging from 0 through FFFF and is separated from the next component via a colon (such as 1080:0:0:0:8:800:200C:417A). A 128-bit IP address is often referred to as an *Internet Protocol Version 6 (IPv6) address* (see http://en.wikipedia.org/wiki/IPv6).

A *port number* is a 16-bit integer that uniquely identifies a process, which is the ultimate source or recipient of a message. Port numbers that are less than 1024 are reserved for standard processes. For example, port number 25 has traditionally identified the Simple Mail Transfer Protocol (SMTP) process for sending email, although port number 587 has largely obsoleted this older port number (see http://en.wikipedia.org/wiki/Smtp).

One process writes a *message* (a sequence of bytes) to its socket. The network management software portion of the underlying platform breaks the message into a sequence of *packets* (addressable message chunks that are often referred to as *IP datagrams*) and forwards them to the other process's socket, where they are recombined into the original message for processing.

Figure B-1 shows how two sockets communicate in a TCP/IP context.

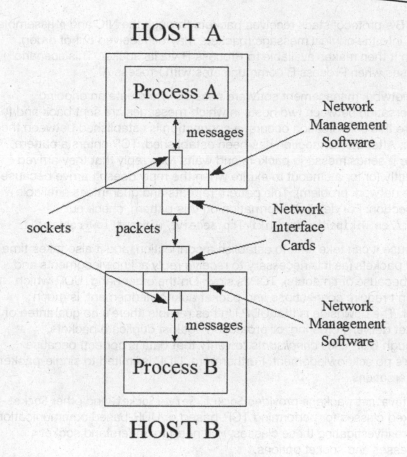

Figure B-1. *Two processes communicate via a pair of sockets*

In the context of Figure B-1, suppose that Process A wants to send a message to Process B. Process A sends that message to its socket with the destination socket address of Process B. Host A's network management software (often referred to as a *protocol stack*) obtains this message and reduces it to a sequence of packets, with each packet including the destination host's IP address and port number. The network management software then sends these packets through Host A's Network Interface Card (NIC) to Host B.

Note The NIC's various *network interfaces* are connections between a computer and a network.

Host B's protocol stack receives packets through the NIC and reassembles them into the original message (packets may be received out of order), which it then makes available to Process B via its socket. This scenario reverses when Process B communicates with Process A.

The network management software uses TCP to create an ongoing conversation between two hosts in which messages are sent back and forth. Before this conversation occurs, a connection is established between these hosts. After the connection has been established, TCP enters a pattern where it sends message packets and waits for a reply that they arrived correctly (or for a timeout to expire when the reply doesn't arrive because of some network problem). This pattern repeats and guarantees a reliable connection. For detailed information on this pattern, check out http://en.wikipedia.org/wiki/Tcp_receive_window#Flow_control.

Because it can take time to establish a connection, and it also takes time to send packets (as it is necessary to receive reply acknowledgments and also because of timeouts), TCP is slow. On the other hand, UDP, which doesn't require connections and packet acknowledgement, is much faster. The downside is that UDP isn't as reliable (there's no guarantee of packet delivery, ordering, or protection against duplicate packets, although UDP uses *checksums* to verify that data is correct) because there's no acknowledgment. Furthermore, UDP is limited to single-packet conversations.

The java.net package provides Socket, ServerSocket, and other Socket-suffixed classes for performing TCP-based or UDP-based communications. Before investigating these classes, you need to understand socket addresses and socket options.

Socket Addresses

An instance of a Socket-suffixed class is associated with a *socket address* comprised of an IP address and a port number. These classes often rely on the InetAddress class to represent the IPv4 or IPv6 address portion of the socket address; the port number is represented separately.

> **Note** InetAddress relies on its Inet4Address subclass to represent an IPv4 address and on its Inet6Address subclass to represent an IPv6 address.

InetAddress declares several class methods for obtaining an InetAddress instance. These methods include the following:

- InetAddress[] getAllByName(String host) returns an array of InetAddresses that store the IP addresses associated with host. You can pass either a domain name (such as "tutortutor.ca") or an IP address (such as "70.33.247.10") argument to this parameter. (To learn about domain names, check out Wikipedia's "Domain name" entry [http://en.wikipedia.org/wiki/Domain_name].) Pass null to obtain an InetAddress instance that stores the IP address of the *loopback interface* (a software-based network interface where outgoing data loops back as incoming data). This method throws UnknownHostException when no IP address for the specified host can be found, or when a scope identifier is specified for a global IPv6 address.

- InetAddress getByAddress(byte[] addr) returns an InetAddress object for the given raw IP address. The argument passed to addr is in *network byte order* (most significant byte comes first) where the highest order byte is stored in addr[0]. The addr array's length must be 4 bytes for an IPv4 address and 16 bytes for an IPv6 address. This method throws UnknownHostException when the array has another length.

- InetAddress getByAddress(String hostName, byte[] ipAddress) returns an InetAddress instance based on the hostname and IP address arguments. This method throws UnknownHostException when the array's length is neither 4 nor 16.

- InetAddress getByName(String host) returns an InetAddress instance based on the host argument, which can be a machine name (such as "tutortutor. ca") or a textual representation of its IP address. Passing null to host results in an InetAddress instance representing an address of the loopback interface being returned.

- InetAddress getLocalHost() returns the address of the *local host* (the current host), which is represented by hostname localhost or by an IP address that's commonly expressed as 127.0.0.1 (IPv4) or ::1 (IPv6). This method throws UnknownHostException when the local host couldn't be resolved into an address.

After you obtain an InetAddress object, you can interrogate it by invoking instance methods such as byte[] getAddress(), which returns the raw IP address (in network byte order) of this InetAddress object, and boolean isLoopbackAddress(), which determines whether or not this InetAddress object represents a loopback address.

Java 1.4 introduced the abstract SocketAddress class to represent a socket address "with no protocol attachment." (This class's creator might have anticipated that Java would eventually support low-level communication protocols other than the widely popular Internet Protocol.)

SocketAddress is subclassed by the concrete InetSocketAddress class, which represents a socket address as an IP address and a port number. It can also represent a hostname and a port number and will make an attempt to resolve the hostname.

InetSocketAddress instances are created by invoking InetSocketAddress(InetAddress addr, int port) and other constructors. After an instance has been created, you can call methods such as InetAddress getAddress() and int getPort() to return socket address components.

Socket Options

An instance of a Socket-suffixed class shares the concept of *socket options*, which are parameters for configuring socket behavior. Socket options are described by constants that are declared in the SocketOptions interface:

- IP_MULTICAST_IF: Specify the outgoing network interface for multicast packets (on *multihomed* [multiple NIC] hosts).

- IP_MULTICAST_IF2: Specify the outgoing network interface for multicast packets using an interface index.

- IP_MULTICAST_LOOP: Enable or disable local loopback of multicast datagrams.

- IP_TOS: Set the type-of-service (IPv4) or traffic class (IPv6) field in the IP header for a TCP or UDP socket.

- SO_BINDADDR: Fetch the socket's local address binding.

- SO_BROADCAST: Enable a socket to send broadcast messages.

- SO_KEEPALIVE: Turn on the socket's keepalive setting.

- SO_LINGER: Specify the number of seconds to wait when closing a socket when there is still some buffered data to be sent.

- SO_OOBINLINE: Enable inline reception of TCP urgent data.

- SO_RCVBUF: Set or get the maximum socket receive buffer size (in bytes).

- SO_REUSEADDR: Enable a socket's reuse address.

- SO_SNDBUF: Set or get the maximum socket send buffer size (in bytes).

- SO_TIMEOUT: Specify a timeout (in milliseconds) on blocking accept or read/receive (but not write/send) socket operations. (Don't block forever!)

- TCP_NODELAY: Disable Nagle's algorithm (http://en.wikipedia.org/wiki/Nagle's_algorithm). Written data to the network is not buffered, pending acknowledgement of previously written data.

SocketOptions also declares the following methods for setting and getting these options:

- void setOption(int optID, Object value)

- Object getOption(int optID)

optID is one of the aforementioned constants and value is an object of a suitable class (such as java.lang.Boolean).

SocketOptions is implemented by the abstract SocketImpl and DatagramSocketImpl classes. Concrete instances of these classes are wrapped by the various Socket-suffixed classes. As a result, you cannot invoke these methods. Instead, you work with the type-safe setter and getter methods provided by the Socket-suffixed classes for setting and getting these options.

For example, Socket declares void setKeepAlive(boolean keepAlive) for setting the SO_KEEPALIVE option, and ServerSocket declares void setSoTimeout(int timeout) for setting the SO_TIMEOUT option. Check the documentation on the Socket-suffixed classes to learn about these and other socket option methods.

> **Note** Socket option methods that apply to DatagramSocket also apply to its MulticastSocket subclass.

Socket and ServerSocket

The Socket and ServerSocket classes support TCP-based communications between client processes (such as an application running on a tablet) and server processes (such as an application running on one of your Internet Service Provider's computers that provides access to the World Wide Web). Because Socket is associated with the java.io.InputStream and java.io.OutputStream classes, sockets based on the Socket class are commonly referred to as *stream sockets*.

Socket supports the creation of client-side sockets. It declares several constructors for this purpose, including the following pair:

- Socket(InetAddress dstAddress, int dstPort) creates a stream socket and connects it to the specified port number (described by dstPort) at the specified IP address (described by dstAddress). This constructor throws java.io.IOException when an I/O error occurs while creating the socket, java.lang.IllegalArgumentException when the argument passed to dstPort is outside the valid range of port values, which is 0 through 65535, and java.lang.NullPointerException when dstAddress is null.

- Socket(String dstName, int dstPort) creates a stream socket and connects it to the port identified by dstPort on the host identified by dstName. When dstName is null, this constructor is equivalent to invoking Socket(InetAddress.getByName(null), port). It throws the same IOException and IllegalArgumentException instances as the previous constructor. However, instead of throwing NullPointerException, it throws UnknownHostException when the host's IP address cannot be determined.

After a Socket instance is created via these constructors, it's bound to an arbitrary local host socket address before a connection is made to the remote host socket address. *Binding* makes a client socket address available to a server socket so that a server process can communicate with the client process via the server socket.

Socket offers additional constructors. For example, Socket() and Socket(Proxy proxy) create unbound and unconnected sockets. Before using these sockets, they must be bound to local socket addresses, by calling void bind(SocketAddress localAddr), and then connections must be made, by calling Socket's connect() methods (void connect(SocketAddress remoteAddr), for example).

> **Note** A *proxy* is a host that sits between an intranet and the Internet for security purposes. Proxy settings are represented via instances of the Proxy class and help sockets communicate through proxies.

Another constructor is Socket(InetAddress dstAddress, int dstPort, InetAddress localAddr, int localPort), which lets you specify your own local host socket address via localAddr and localPort. This constructor automatically binds to the local socket address and then attempts a connection to the remote dstPort on dstAddress.

After creating a Socket instance, and possibly invoking bind() and connect() on that instance, an application invokes Socket's InputStream getInputStream() and OutputStream getOutputStream() methods to acquire an input stream for reading bytes from the socket and an output stream for writing bytes to the socket. Also, the application often calls Socket's void close() method to close the socket when it's no longer needed for I/O.

The following example demonstrates how to create a socket that's bound to port number 9999 on the local host and then access its input and output streams—exceptions are ignored for brevity:

```
Socket socket = new Socket("localhost", 9999);
InputStream is = socket.getInputStream();
OutputStream os = socket.getOutputStream();
// Do some work with the socket.
socket.close();
```

ServerSocket supports the creation of server-side sockets. It declares the following four constructors for this purpose:

- ServerSocket() creates an unbound server socket. You can bind this socket to a specific socket address (to which client sockets communicate) by invoking either of ServerSocket's two bind() methods. *Binding* makes the server socket address available to a client socket so that a client process can communicate with the server process via the client socket. This constructor throws IOException when an I/O error occurs while attempting to open the socket.

- ServerSocket(int port) creates a server socket bound to the specified port value and an IP address associated with one of the host's NICs. When you pass 0 to port, an arbitrary port number is chosen. The port number can be retrieved by calling int getLocalPort(). The maximum queue length for incoming connection requests from clients is set to 50. If a connection request arrives when the queue is full, the connection is refused. This constructor throws IOException when an I/O error occurs while attempting to open the socket and IllegalArgumentException when port's value lies outside the specified range of valid port values, which is between 0 and 65535, inclusive.

- ServerSocket(int port, int backlog) is equivalent to the previous constructor, but it also lets you specify the maximum queue length for incoming connections by passing a positive integer to backlog.

- ServerSocket(int port, int backlog, InetAddress localAddress) is equivalent to the previous constructor, but it also lets you specify a different IP address to which the server socket binds. (Any address is chosen when null is passed.) This constructor is useful for machines that have multiple NICs and you want to listen for connection requests on a specific NIC.

After a server socket is created via these constructors, a server application enters a loop that first invokes ServerSocket's Socket accept() method to listen for a connection request and return a Socket instance that lets it communicate with the associated client socket. It then communicates with the client socket to perform some kind of processing. When processing finishes, the server socket calls the client socket's close() method to terminate its connection with the client.

> **Note**   ServerSocket declares a void close() method for closing a server socket before terminating the server application. An unclosed socket is automatically closed when an application terminates.

The following example demonstrates how to create a server socket that's bound to port 9999 on the current host, listen for incoming connection requests, return their sockets, perform work on those sockets, and close the sockets; exceptions are ignored for brevity:

```
ServerSocket ss = new ServerSocket(9999);
while (true)
{
    Socket socket = ss.accept();
    // obtain socket input/output streams and communicate with socket
    socket.close();
}
```

The accept() method call blocks until a connection request is available and then returns a Socket object so that the server application can communicate with its associated client. The socket is closed after this communication takes place. The server socket is automatically closed when the application exits.

This example assumes that socket communication takes place on the server application's main thread, which is a problem when processing takes time to perform because server response time to incoming connection requests decreases.

To speed up response time, it's often necessary to communicate with the socket on a worker thread, as demonstrated in the following example:

```
ServerSocket ss = new ServerSocket(9999);
while (true)
{
    final Socket s = ss.accept();
    new Thread(new Runnable()
                {
                    @Override
                    public void run()
                    {
                        // obtain socket input/output streams and
                        // communicate with socket
                        try { s.close(); } catch (IOException ioe) {}
                    }
                }).start();
}
```

Each time a connection request arrives, accept() returns a Socket instance, and then a java.lang.Thread object is created whose *runnable* accesses that socket for communicating with the socket on a worker thread.

I've created EchoClient and EchoServer applications that demonstrate Socket and ServerSocket. Listing B-1 presents EchoClient's source code.

Listing B-1. Echoing Data to and Receiving It Back from a Server

```
import java.io.BufferedReader;
import java.io.InputStream;
import java.io.InputStreamReader;
import java.io.IOException;
import java.io.OutputStream;
import java.io.OutputStreamWriter;
import java.io.PrintWriter;
```

```java
import java.net.Socket;
import java.net.UnknownHostException;

public class EchoClient
{
   public static void main(String[] args)
   {
      if (args.length != 1)
      {
         System.err.println("usage  : java EchoClient message");
         System.err.println("example: java EchoClient \"This is a test.\"");
         return;
      }
      try
      {
         Socket socket = new Socket("localhost", 9999);
         OutputStream os = socket.getOutputStream();
         OutputStreamWriter osw = new OutputStreamWriter(os);
         PrintWriter pw = new PrintWriter(osw);
         pw.println(args[0]);
         pw.flush();
         InputStream is = socket.getInputStream();
         InputStreamReader isr = new InputStreamReader(is);
         BufferedReader br = new BufferedReader(isr);
         System.out.println(br.readLine());
      }
      catch (UnknownHostException uhe)
      {
         System.err.println("unknown host: " + uhe.getMessage());
      }
      catch (IOException ioe)
      {
         System.err.println("I/O error: " + ioe.getMessage());
      }
   }
}
```

EchoClient first verifies that it has received a single command-line argument and then creates a socket that will connect to a process running on port 9999 of the local host.

After creating the socket, EchoClient obtains an output stream for writing a string to the socket. Because the output stream can only handle a sequence of bytes, the java.io.OutputStreamWriter and java.io.PrintWriter classes are used to connect the writer that outputs characters to the byte-oriented output stream.

After instantiating `PrintWriter`, `EchoClient` invokes its `void println(String str)` method to write the string followed by a newline character. The `void flush()` method is subsequently called to ensure that all pending data is written to the server.

`EchoClient` now obtains an input stream for reading the string as a sequence of bytes. It then connects the reader (that inputs characters) to the byte-oriented input stream by instantiating `java.io.InputStreamReader` and `java.io.BufferedReader`.

Finally, `EchoClient` invokes `BufferedReader`'s `String readLine()` method to read the characters followed by a newline from the socket. (`readLine()` doesn't include the newline character in the returned string.) These characters followed by a newline are then written to standard output.

> **Note** In a long-running application, you would explicitly close the `socket` instance by invoking its `void close()` method when the socket is no longer needed. For brevity, I've chosen not to do so in this and most of the remaining Socket-suffixed class examples.

Listing B-2 presents `EchoServer`'s source code.

Listing B-2. Receiving Data from and Echoing It Back to a Client

```java
import java.io.BufferedReader;
import java.io.InputStream;
import java.io.InputStreamReader;
import java.io.IOException;
import java.io.OutputStream;
import java.io.OutputStreamWriter;
import java.io.PrintWriter;

import java.net.ServerSocket;
import java.net.Socket;

public class EchoServer
{
    public static void main(String[] args) throws IOException
    {
        System.out.println("Starting echo server...");
        ServerSocket ss = new ServerSocket(9999);
        while (true)
        {
            Socket s = ss.accept();
            try
```

```
        {
            InputStream is = s.getInputStream();
            InputStreamReader isr = new InputStreamReader(is);
            BufferedReader br = new BufferedReader(isr);
            String msg = br.readLine();
            System.out.println(msg);
            OutputStream os = s.getOutputStream();
            OutputStreamWriter osw = new OutputStreamWriter(os);
            PrintWriter pw = new PrintWriter(osw);
            pw.println(msg);
            pw.flush();
        }
        catch (IOException ioe)
        {
            System.err.println("I/O error: " + ioe.getMessage());
        }
        finally
        {
            try
            {
                s.close();
            }
            catch (IOException ioe)
            {
                assert false; // shouldn't happen in this context
            }
        }
    }
  }
}
```

EchoServer first outputs an introductory message to standard output and then creates a server socket that listens for connections on port 9999. It then enters an infinite loop, where each iteration invokes ServerSocket's Socket accept() method to block until a connection is received and then return a Socket object representing this connection.

After obtaining the socket, EchoServer obtains an input stream for reading from the socket. Because the input stream can only handle a sequence of bytes, the InputStreamReader and BufferedReader classes are used to connect the reader that inputs characters to the byte-oriented input stream.

EchoServer now obtains an output stream for writing the string as a sequence of bytes. It then connects the writer that outputs characters to the byte-oriented output stream by instantiating OutputStreamWriter and PrintWriter.

After outputting the message to standard output, EchoServer calls flush() to flush the output to the client. The client socket is then closed.

To experiment with these applications, first copy `EchoClient.java` and `EchoServer.java` to the same directory and open two console windows with this directory being current.

Compile these source files as follows:

```
javac *.java
```

Run EchoServer in one window as follows:

```
java EchoServer
```

You should observe the following output:

```
Starting echo server...
```

> **Note**   If you have an enabled *firewall* (http://en.wikipedia.org/wiki/
> Firewall_(computing)), you might need to enable port 9999.

Having started the server, run EchoClient in the other window as follows:

```
java EchoClient "This is a test."
```

You should observe "This is a test." in both windows.

DatagramSocket and MulticastSocket

The `DatagramSocket` and `MulticastSocket` classes let you perform UDP-based communications between a pair of hosts (DatagramSocket) or between many hosts (MulticastSocket). With either class, you communicate one-way messages via *datagram packets*, which are arrays of bytes associated with instances of the DatagramPacket class.

> **Note**   Although you might think that Socket and ServerSocket are all that you need, DatagramSocket and its MulticastSocket subclass have their uses. For example, consider a scenario in which a group of machines need to occasionally tell a server that they're alive. It shouldn't matter when the occasional message is lost or even when the message doesn't arrive on time. Another example is a low-priority stock ticker that periodically broadcasts stock prices. When a packet doesn't arrive, odds are that the next packet will arrive and you'll then receive notification of the latest prices. Timely rather than reliable or orderly delivery is more important in realtime applications.

DatagramPacket declares several constructors, with DatagramPacket(byte[] buf, int length) being the simplest. This constructor requires you to pass byte array and integer arguments to buf and length, where buf is a data buffer that stores data to be sent or received, and length (which must be less than or equal to buf.length) specifies the number of bytes (starting at buf[0]) to send/receive.

The following example demonstrates this constructor:

```
byte[] buffer = new byte[100];
DatagramPacket dgp = new DatagramPacket(buffer, buffer.length);
```

> **Note**   Additional constructors let you specify an offset into buf that identifies the storage location of the first outgoing or incoming byte, and/or let you specify a destination socket address.

DatagramSocket describes a socket for the client or server side of the UDP-communication link. Although this class declares several constructors, I find it convenient in this appendix to use the DatagramSocket() constructor for the client side and the DatagramSocket(int port) constructor for the server side. Either constructor throws SocketException when it cannot create the datagram socket or bind the datagram socket to a local port.

After an application instantiates DatagramSocket, it calls void send(DatagramPacket dgp) and void receive(DatagramPacket dgp) to send and receive datagram packets.

Listing B-3 demonstrates DatagramPacket and DatagramSocket in a server context.

Listing B-3. Receiving Datagram Packets from and Echoing Them Back to Clients

```java
import java.io.IOException;

import java.net.DatagramPacket;
import java.net.DatagramSocket;
import java.net.SocketException;

public class DGServer
{
   final static int PORT = 10000;

   public static void main(String[] args) throws SocketException
   {
      System.out.println("Server is starting");
```

```
        DatagramSocket dgs = new DatagramSocket(PORT);
        try
        {
            System.out.println("Send buffer size = " +
                               dgs.getSendBufferSize());
            System.out.println("Receive buffer size = " +
                               dgs.getReceiveBufferSize());
            byte[] data = new byte[100];
            DatagramPacket dgp = new DatagramPacket(data, data.length);
            while (true)
            {
                dgs.receive(dgp);
                System.out.println(new String(data));
                dgs.send(dgp);
            }
        }
        catch (IOException ioe)
        {
            System.err.println("I/O error: " + ioe.getMessage());
        }
    }
}
```

Listing B-3's main() method first creates a DatagramSocket object and binds the socket to port 10000 on the local host. It then invokes DatagramSocket's int getSendBufferSize() and int getReceiveBufferSize() methods to get the values of the SO_SNDBUF and SO_RCVBUF socket options, which are then output.

> **Note**   Sockets are associated with underlying platform send and receive buffers, and their sizes are accessed by calling getSendBufferSize() and getReceiveBufferSize(). Similarly, their sizes can be set by calling DatagramSocket's void setReceiveBufferSize(int size) and void setSendBufferSize(int size) methods. Although you can adjust these buffer sizes to improve performance, there's a practical limit with regard to UDP. The maximum size of a UDP packet that can be sent or received is 65,507 bytes under IPv4—it's derived from subtracting the 8-byte UDP header and 20-byte IP header values from 65,535. Although you can specify a send/receive buffer with a greater value, doing so is wasteful because the largest packet is restricted to 65,507 bytes. Also, attempting to send or receive a packet with a buffer length that exceeds 65,507 bytes results in IOException.

main() next instantiates DatagramPacket in preparation for receiving a datagram packet from a client and then echoing the packet back to the client. It assumes that packets will be 100 bytes or less in size.

Finally, main() enters an infinite loop that receives a packet, outputs packet content, and sends the packet back to the client. The client's addressing information is stored in DatagramPacket.

Compile Listing B-3 as follows:

```
javac DGServer.java
```

Run the resulting application as follows:

```
java DGServer
```

You should observe output that's the same as or similar to that shown here:

```
Server is starting
Send buffer size = 8192
Receive buffer size = 8192
```

Listing B-4 demonstrates DatagramPacket and DatagramSocket in a client context.

Listing B-4. Sending a Datagram Packet to and Receiving It Back from a Server

```
import java.io.IOException;

import java.net.DatagramPacket;
import java.net.DatagramSocket;
import java.net.InetAddress;
import java.net.SocketException;

public class DGClient
{
   final static int PORT = 10000;
   final static String ADDR = "localhost";

   public static void main(String[] args) throws SocketException
   {
      System.out.println("client is starting");
      DatagramSocket dgs = new DatagramSocket();
      try
      {
         byte[] buffer;
         buffer = "Send me a datagram".getBytes();
         InetAddress ia = InetAddress.getByName(ADDR);
```

```
          DatagramPacket dgp = new DatagramPacket(buffer, buffer.length,
                                                  ia, PORT);
          dgs.send(dgp);
          byte[] buffer2 = new byte[100];
          dgp = new DatagramPacket(buffer2, buffer.length, ia, PORT);
          dgs.receive(dgp);
          System.out.println(new String(dgp.getData()));
       }
       catch (IOException ioe)
       {
          System.err.println("I/O error: " + ioe.getMessage());
       }
   }
}
```

Listing B-4 is similar to Listing B-3, but there's one big difference. I use the DatagramPacket(byte[] buf, int length, InetAddress address, int port) constructor to specify the server's destination, which happens to be port 10000 on the local host, in the datagram packet. The send() method call routes the packet to this destination.

Compile Listing B-4 as follows:

javac DGClient.java

Run the resulting application as follows:

java DGClient

Assuming that DGServer is also running, you should observe the following output in DGClient's command window (and the last line of this output in DGServer's command window):

client is starting
Send me a datagram

MulticastSocket describes a socket for the client or server side of a UDP-based multicasting session. Two commonly used constructors are MulticastSocket() (create a multicast socket not bound to a port) and MulticastSocket(int port) (create a multicast socket bound to the specified port). Either constructor throws IOException when an I/O error occurs.

WHAT IS MULTICASTING?

Previous examples have demonstrated *unicasting*, which occurs when a server sends a message to a single client. However, it's also possible to broadcast the same message to multiple clients (such as transmit a "school closed due to bad weather" announcement to all members of a group of parents who have registered with an online program to receive this announcement); this activity is known as *multicasting*.

A server multicasts by sending a sequence of datagram packets to a special IP address, which is known as a *multicast group address*, and a specific port (as specified by a port number). Clients wanting to receive these datagram packets create a multicast socket that uses this port number. They request to join the group through a *join group operation* that specifies the special IP address. At this point, the client can receive datagram packets sent to the group and can even send datagram packets to other group members. After the client has read all datagram packets that it wants to read, it removes itself from the group by applying a *leave group operation* that specifies the special IP address.

IPv4 addresses 224.0.0.1 to 239.255.255.255 (inclusive) are reserved for use as multicast group addresses.

Listing B-5 presents a multicasting server.

Listing B-5. Multicasting Datagram Packets

```
import java.io.IOException;

import java.net.DatagramPacket;
import java.net.InetAddress;
import java.net.MulticastSocket;

public class MCServer
{
   final static int PORT = 10000;

   public static void main(String[] args)
   {
      try
      {
         MulticastSocket mcs = new MulticastSocket();
         InetAddress group = InetAddress.getByName("231.0.0.1");
         byte[] dummy = new byte[0];
         DatagramPacket dgp = new DatagramPacket(dummy, 0, group, PORT);
         int i = 0;
```

```
            while (true)
            {
                byte[] buffer = ("line " + i).getBytes();
                dgp.setData(buffer);
                dgp.setLength(buffer.length);
                mcs.send(dgp);
                i++;
            }
        }
        catch (IOException ioe)
        {
            System.err.println("I/O error: " + ioe.getMessage());
        }
    }
}
```

Listing B-5's main() method first creates a MulticastSocket instance via the MulticastSocket() constructor. The multicast socket doesn't need to bind to a port number because the port number is specified along with the multicast group's IP address (231.0.0.1) as part of the DatagramPacket instance that's subsequently created. (The dummy array is present to prevent a NullPointerException object from being thrown from the DatagramPacket constructor—this array isn't used to store data to be broadcasted.)

At this point, main() enters an infinite loop that first creates an array of bytes from a java.lang.String object, and it uses the platform's default character encoding to convert from Unicode characters to bytes. (Although extraneous java.lang.StringBuilder and String objects are created via expression "line " + i in each loop iteration, I'm not worried about their impact on garbage collection in this short throwaway application.)

This data buffer is subsequently assigned to the DatagramPacket object by calling its void setData(byte[] buf) method, and then the datagram packet is broadcast to all members of the group associated with port 10000 and multicast IP address 231.0.0.1.

Compile Listing B-5 as follows:

javac MCServer.java

Run the resulting application as follows:

java MCServer

You shouldn't observe any output.

Listing B-6 presents a multicasting client.

Listing B-6. Receiving Multicasted Datagram Packets

```
import java.io.IOException;

import java.net.DatagramPacket;
import java.net.InetAddress;
import java.net.MulticastSocket;

public class MCClient
{
   final static int PORT = 10000;

   public static void main(String[] args)
   {
      try
      {
         MulticastSocket mcs = new MulticastSocket(PORT);
         InetAddress group = InetAddress.getByName("231.0.0.1");
         mcs.joinGroup(group);
         for (int i = 0; i < 10; i++)
         {
            byte[] buffer = new byte[256];
            DatagramPacket dgp = new DatagramPacket(buffer, buffer.length);
            mcs.receive(dgp);
            byte[] buffer2 = new byte[dgp.getLength()];
            System.arraycopy(dgp.getData(), 0, buffer2, 0, dgp.getLength());
            System.out.println(new String(buffer2));
         }
         mcs.leaveGroup(group);
      }
      catch (IOException ioe)
      {
         System.err.println("I/O error: " + ioe.getMessage());
      }
   }
}
```

Listing B-6's main() method first creates a MulticastSocket instance bound to port 10000 via the MulticastSocket(int port) constructor. It then obtains an InetAddress object that contains multicast group IP address 231.0.0.1 and uses this object to join the group at this address by calling MulticastSocket's void joinGroup(InetAddress mcastaddr) method.

main() next receives 10 datagram packets, prints their contents, and leaves the group by calling MulticastSocket's void leaveGroup(InetAddress mcastaddr) method with the same multicast IP address as its argument.

> **Note** joinGroup() and leaveGroup() throw IOException when an I/O error occurs while attempting to join or leave the group or when the IP address is not a multicast IP address.

Because the client doesn't know exactly how long the arrays of bytes will be, it assumes 256 bytes to ensure that the data buffer will hold the entire array. If it tried to print out the returned array, you would see a lot of empty space after the actual data had been printed.

To eliminate this space, the client invokes DatagramPacket's int getLength() method to obtain the actual length of the array, creates a second byte array (buffer2) with this length, and uses System.arraycopy() to copy this many bytes to buffer2. After converting this byte array to a String object (via the String(byte[] bytes) constructor, which uses the platform's default character set), it prints the resulting characters to the standard output stream.

Compile Listing B-6 as follows:

```
javac MCClient.java
```

Run the resulting application as follows:

```
java MCClient
```

You should observe output similar to the following:

```
line 462615
line 462616
line 462617
line 462618
line 462619
line 462620
line 462621
line 462622
line 462623
line 462624
```

Network Interfaces

The NetworkInterface class represents a network interface in terms of a name (such as le0) and a list of IP addresses assigned to this interface. Although a network interface is often implemented on a physical NIC, it also can be implemented in software; for example, the *loopback interface* (which is useful for testing a client).

> **Note**   A *network interface* is the point of interconnection between a computer
> and a private or public network. It's generally a network interface card (NIC),
> but doesn't need a physical form. Instead, it can be implemented in software.
> For example, the loopback interface (127.0.0.1 for IPv4 and ::1 for IPv6) isn't
> a physical device but a piece of software simulating a network interface. The
> loopback interface is commonly used in test environments.

Table B-1 presents NetworkInterface's methods.

Table B-1. `NetworkInterface Methods`

Method	Description
`boolean equals(Object obj)`	Compare this NetworkInterface object with obj. The result is true if and only if obj isn't null and represents the same network interface as this object. (Two NetworkInterface objects represent the same network interface when their names and addresses are the same.)
`static NetworkInterface getByInetAddress(InetAddress address)`	Return the NetworkInterface corresponding to the given address or null when no interface has this address. This method throws SocketException when an I/O error occurs and NullPointerException when address is null.
`static NetworkInterface getByName(String interfaceName)`	Return the NetworkInterface with the specified name, or return null when there's no such network interface. This method throws SocketException on an I/O error and NullPointerException when interfaceName is null.
`String getDisplayName()`	Return this network interface's *display name* (a human-readable string describing the network device).
`byte[] getHardwareAddress()`	Return an array of bytes containing this network interface's hardware address, which is often referred to as the *media access control (MAC)* address. When the interface doesn't have a MAC address, or when the address cannot be accessed (perhaps the user doesn't have sufficient privileges), the method returns null. This method throws SocketException when an I/O error occurs.

(continued)

Table B-1. (*continued*)

Method	Description
Enumeration<InetAddress> getInetAddresses()	Return an *enumeration* (the results of an iteration) with all or a subset of the addresses bound to this network interface.
List<InterfaceAddress> getInterfaceAddresses()	Return a java.util.List containing this network interface's InterfaceAddresses.
int getMTU()	Return this network interface's *maximum transmission unit (MTU)*. This method throws SocketException when an I/O error occurs.
String getName()	Return this network interface's name (such as eth0 or lo).
static Enumeration<NetworkInterface> getNetworkInterfaces()	Return all of the network interfaces on this machine, or return null when no network interfaces could be found. This method throws SocketException when an I/O error occurs.
NetworkInterface getParent()	Return this network interface's parent NetworkInterface when this network interface is a subinterface. When this network interface has no parent, or when it's a physical (nonvirtual) interface, this method returns null. (A physical network interface can be logically divided into multiple *virtual subinterfaces*, which are commonly used in routing and switching. These subinterfaces can be organized into a hierarchy where the physical network interface serves as the root.)
Enumeration<NetworkInterface> getSubInterfaces()	Return an enumeration containing the virtual subinterfaces that are attached to this network interface. For example, eth0:1 is a subinterface of eth0.
int hashCode()	This method is overridden because equals() is overridden.
boolean isLoopback()	Return true when this network interface reflects outgoing data back to itself as incoming data. This method throws SocketException when an I/O error occurs.
boolean isPointToPoint()	Return true when this network interface is point-to-point (such as a PPP connection through a modem). This method throws SocketException when an I/O error occurs.

(*continued*)

Table B-1. (*continued*)

Method	Description
`boolean isUp()`	Return `true` when this network interface is *up* (routing entries have been established) and *running* (platform resources have been allocated). This method throws `SocketException` when an I/O error occurs.
`boolean isVirtual()`	Return `true` when this network interface is a virtual subinterface. On some platforms, virtual subinterfaces are network interfaces created as children of a physical network interface and given different settings (such as address or MTU). Usually, the name of the interface will be the name of the parent followed by a colon (:) and a number identifying the child because there can be several virtual subinterfaces attached to a single physical network interface.
`boolean supportsMulticast()`	Return `true` when this network interface supports *multicasting*. This method throws `SocketException` when an I/O error occurs.
`String toString()`	Return a string representation of this network interface.

You can use these methods to gather useful information about your platform's network interfaces. For example, Listing B-7 presents an application that iterates over all network interfaces, invoking the methods listed in Table B-1 that:

- Obtain the network interface's name and display name
- Determine if the network interface is a loopback interface
- Determine if the network interface is up and running
- Obtain the MTU
- Determine if the network interface supports multicasting
- Enumerate all of the network interface's virtual subinterfaces

Listing B-7. Enumerating All Network Interfaces

```java
import java.net.NetworkInterface;
import java.net.SocketException;

import java.util.Collections;
import java.util.Enumeration;

public class NetInfo
{
    public static void main(String[] args) throws SocketException
    {
        Enumeration<NetworkInterface> eni;
        eni = NetworkInterface.getNetworkInterfaces();
        for (NetworkInterface ni: Collections.list(eni))
        {
            System.out.println("Name = " + ni.getName());
            System.out.println("Display Name = " + ni.getDisplayName());
            System.out.println("Loopback = " + ni.isLoopback());
            System.out.println("Up and running = " + ni.isUp());
            System.out.println("MTU = " + ni.getMTU());
            System.out.println("Supports multicast = " +
                                    ni.supportsMulticast());
            System.out.println("Sub-interfaces");
            Enumeration<NetworkInterface> eni2;
            eni2 = ni.getSubInterfaces();
            for (NetworkInterface ni2: Collections.list(eni2))
                System.out.println("   " + ni2);
            System.out.println();
        }
    }
}
```

> **Tip** The `java.util.Collections` class's `ArrayList<T>`
> `list(Enumeration<T> enumeration)` method is useful for converting a
> legacy enumeration to a modern array list.

Compile Listing B-7 as follows:

```
javac NetInfo.java
```

Run the resulting application as follows:

```
java NetInfo
```

When I run `NetInfo` on my Windows 7 platform, I observe information that begins with the following output:

```
Name = lo
Display Name = Software Loopback Interface 1
Loopback = true
Up and running = true
MTU = -1
Supports multicast = true
Sub-interfaces

Name = net0
Display Name = WAN Miniport (SSTP)
Loopback = false
Up and running = false
MTU = -1
Supports multicast = true
Sub-interfaces
```

The complete output reveals a different MTU size for a few network interfaces. Each size represents the maximum length of a message that can fit into an *IP datagram* without needing to fragment the message into multiple IP datagrams. This fragmentation has performance implications, especially in the context of networked games. For this reason alone, the getMTU() method is a valuable member of `NetworkInterface`.

The getInterfaceAddresses() method returns a list of `InterfaceAddress` objects, with each object containing a network interface's IP address along with broadcast address and subnet mask (IPv4) or network prefix length (IPv6).

Table B-2 presents `InterfaceAddress`'s methods.

Table B-2. InterfaceAddress Methods

Method	Description
`boolean equals(Object obj)`	Compare this `InterfaceAddress` object with `obj`. Return `true` when `obj` is also an `InterfaceAddress`, and when both objects contain the same `InetAddress`, the same subnet masks/network prefix lengths (depending on IPv4 or IPv6), and the same broadcast addresses.
`InetAddress getAddress()`	Return this `InterfaceAddress`'s IP address, as an `InetAddress` object.
`InetAddress getBroadcast()`	Return this `InterfaceAddress`'s broadcast address (IPv4) or `null` (IPv6); IPv6 doesn't support broadcast addresses.
`short getNetworkPrefixLength()`	Return this `InterfaceAddress`'s network prefix length (IPv6) or subnet mask (IPv4). Oracle's Java documentation shows 128 (::1/128) and 10 (fe80::203:baff:fe27:1243/10) as typical IPv6 values. Typical IPv4 values are 8 (255.0.0.0), 16 (255.255.0.0), and 24 (255.255.255.0).
`int hashCode()`	Return this `InterfaceAddress`'s hash code. The hash code is a combination of the `InetAddress`'s hash code, the broadcast address (when present) hash code, and the network prefix length.
`String toString()`	Return a string representation of this `InterfaceAddress`. This representation has the form `InetAddress / network prefix length [broadcast address]`.

Listing B-8, which extends Listing B-7 (with a few lines removed), enumerates all network interfaces, outputting their display names, and enumerates each network interface's interface addresses, outputting interface address information.

Listing B-8. Enumerating All Network Interfaces and Interface Addresses

```java
import java.net.InterfaceAddress;
import java.net.NetworkInterface;
import java.net.SocketException;

import java.util.Collections;
import java.util.Enumeration;
import java.util.Iterator;
import java.util.List;
```

```java
public class NetInfo
{
   public static void main(String[] args) throws SocketException
   {
      Enumeration<NetworkInterface> eni;
      eni = NetworkInterface.getNetworkInterfaces();
      for (NetworkInterface ni: Collections.list(eni))
      {
         System.out.println("Name = " + ni.getName());
         List<InterfaceAddress> ias = ni.getInterfaceAddresses();
         Iterator<InterfaceAddress> iter = ias.iterator();
         while (iter.hasNext())
            System.out.println(iter.next());
         System.out.println();
      }
   }
}
```

Compile Listing B-8 (javac NetInfo.java) and execute this application
(java NetInfo). When I run NetInfo on my Windows 7 platform, I observe
the following information:

```
Name = lo
/127.0.0.1/8 [/127.255.255.255]
/0:0:0:0:0:0:0:1/128 [null]

Name = net0

Name = net1

Name = net2

Name = ppp0

Name = eth0

Name = eth1

Name = eth2

Name = ppp1

Name = net3

Name = eth3
/x.x.x.x/24 [/x.x.x.x]
/x:x:x:x:x:x:x:x%eth3/64 [null]
```

```
Name = net4
/x:x:x:x:x:x:x:x%net4/64 [null]

Name = eth4

Name = eth5
/x.x.x.x/24 [/x.x.x.x]
/x:x:x:x:x:x:x:x%eth5/64 [null]

Name = net5
/x:x:x:x:x:x:x:x%net5/128 [null]

Name = net6
/x:x:x:x:x:x:x:x%net6/128 [null]

Name = net7

Name = eth6

Name = eth7

Name = eth8

Name = eth9

Name = eth10

Name = eth11

Name = eth12

Name = eth13

Name = eth14
```

Using Network Interfaces with Sockets

NetworkInterface is useful for a *multihomed* system, which is a system
with multiple NICs. Using NetworkInterface, you can specify the NIC to use
for a specific network activity. For example, assume your machine has two
configured NICs and you want to send data to a server. You create a socket
as follows:

```
Socket socket = new Socket();
socket.connect(new InetSocketAddress(address, port));
```

Before sending the data, the operating system (OS) determines which interface is to be used. However, if you have a preference or otherwise need to specify the NIC to use, you can query the OS for the appropriate interfaces and find an address on the interface you want to use. When you create the socket and bind it to that address, the OS uses the associated interface. Consider the following example:

```
NetworkInterface nif = NetworkInterface.getByName("bge0");
Enumeration<InetAddress> nifAddresses = nif.getInetAddresses();
Socket socket = new Socket();
socket.bind(new InetSocketAddress(nifAddresses.nextElement(), 0));
socket.connect(new InetSocketAddress(address, port));
```

You can also use NetworkInterface to identify the local interface on which a multicast group is to be joined. Consider the following example:

```
NetworkInterface nif = NetworkInterface.getByName("bge0");
MulticastSocket ms = new MulticastSocket();
ms.joinGroup(new InetSocketAddress(hostname, port), nif);
```

These are just two of the many ways to use NetworkInterface with the various Socket classes.

Index

A

accept() method, 182–183, 211
Access control lists (ACLs), 260
allocateDirect() method, 447
allocate() method, 447
American Standard Code
    for Information
    Interchange (ASCII), 113
append() method, 53, 116
array() method, 446
AsynchronousByteChannel
    interface, 415
AsynchronousChannel, 389
AsynchronousChannelGroup
    AsynchronousChannelGroupwith
      CachedThreadPool, 411
    AsynchronousChannelGroup
      withFixedThreadPool, 411
    AsynchronousChannelGroup
      withThreadPool, 411
    class methods, 411
    default group, 410
    java.nio.channels.
      DefaultThreadPool.
      initialSize, 411
    java.nio.channels.
      DefaultThreadPool.
      threadFactory, 410
    java.util.concurrent.
      Executors class, 411
    shutdown() method, 412
    shutdownNow() method, 412
    thread pool, 410

AsynchronousFileChannel
    completed() method, 395
    completion handler, 413
    failed() method, 395
    interrupt() method, 395
    isDone() method, 393
    lock() and tryLock() methods, 391
    main() method, 392, 394
    open() method, 390, 393
    read() and write() methods, 391
    reading bytes in
      CompletionHandler
      context, 393
    reading bytes in
      Future context, 392
    thread pool, 413
    void force, 391
Asynchronous I/O, 471
    asynchronous
      channel, 388–389, 395
    asynchronous channel groups
      (see Asynchronous
      ChannelGroup)
    asynchronous file channels (see
      AsynchronousFileChannel)
    asynchronous server
      socket channel
      (see AsynchronousServer
      SocketChannel)
    AsynchronousSocketChannel
      (see Asynchronous
      SocketChannel)
    cancellation method, 389
    CompletionHandler, 388, 415

G

H

Get the eBook for only $5!

Why limit yourself?

Now you can take the weightless companion with you wherever you go and access your content on your PC, phone, tablet, or reader.

Since you've purchased this print book, we're happy to offer you the eBook in all 3 formats for just $5.

Convenient and fully searchable, the PDF version enables you to easily find and copy code—or perform examples by quickly toggling between instructions and applications. The MOBI format is ideal for your Kindle, while the ePUB can be utilized on a variety of mobile devices.

To learn more, go to www.apress.com/companion or contact support@apress.com.

Printed in the United States
By Bookmasters